S0-BOL-470

HAMPTON-BROWN
HIGH POINT
SUCCESS IN LANGUAGE • LITERATURE • CONTENT

ALFREDO SCHIFINI
DEBORAH SHORT
JOSEFINA VILLAMIL TINAJERO

HAMPTON-BROWN

Curriculum Reviewers

Tedi Armet
ESL Coordinator
Fort Bend Independent School District
Sugar Land, Texas

Maggie Brookshire
ELD Teacher, Grade 6
Emerald Middle School
Cajon Valley Unified School District
El Cajon, California

Lily Dam
Administrator
Dallas Independent School District
Dallas, Texas

Judy Doss
ELD Teacher and Coordinator
Burbank High School
Burbank Unified School District
Burbank, California

Rossana Font-Carrasco
ESOL Teacher
Paul W. Bell Middle School
Miami-Dade County School District 5
Miami, Florida

Jillian Friedman
ESOL Teacher
Howard Middle School
Orange County Public Schools
Orlando, Florida

Vivian Kahn
ESL Teacher/Site Coordinator
Halsey Intermediate School 296
Community School District 32
New York, New York

Suzanne Lee
Principal
Josiah Quincy School
Boston, Massachusetts

Carolyn McGavock
ESL Teacher
Rafael Cordero Bilingual Academy
Junior High School 45
Community School District 4
New York, New York

Juan Carlos Méndez
ESL/Bilingual Staff Developer
Community School District 9
Bronx, New York

Cynthia Nelson-Mosca
Language Minority Services Director
Cicero School District 99
Cicero, Illinois

Kim-Anh Nguyen
Title 7 Coordinator
Franklin McKinley School District
San Jose, California

Ellie Paiewonsky
Director of Bilingual/ESL
Technical Assistance Center of Nassau
Board of Cooperative Educational Services
Massapequa Park, New York

Jeanne Perrin
ESL Specialist
Boston Public Schools
Boston, Massachusetts

Rebecca Peurifoy
Instructional Specialist
Rockwall Independent School District
Rockwall, Texas

Marjorie Rosenberg
ESOL/Bilingual Instructional Specialist
Montgomery County Public Schools
Rockville, Maryland

Harriet Rudnit
Language Arts Reading Teacher
Grades 6–8
Lincoln Hall Middle School
Lincolnwood, Illinois

Olga Ryzhikov
ESOL Teacher
Forest Oak Middle School
Montgomery County, Maryland

Dr. Wageh Saad, Ed.D.
Coordinator of Bilingual and
Compensatory Education
Dearborn Public Schools
Dearborn, Michigan

Gilbert Socas
ESOL Teacher
West Miami Middle School
Miami-Dade County Public Schools
Miami, Florida

Acknowledgments

Every effort has been made to secure permission, but if any omissions have been made, please let us know. We gratefully acknowledge the following permissions:

Susan Bergholz Literary Services: From *The House on Mango Street* by Sandra Cisneros. Copyright © 1984 by Sandra Cisneros. Published by Vintage Books, a division of Random House, Inc., and in hardcover by Alfred A. Knopf, 1994. **Acknowledgments continue on page 495.**

Hampton-Brown
P.O. Box 223220
Carmel, California 93922
1–800–333–3510

Printed in the United States of America
ISBN 0-7362-0933-6

02 03 04 05 06 07 08 09 10 9 8 7 6 5

Get the Message!

A Sense of Place

FOLLOW YOUR DREAMS

UNIT 5 Overcoming Obstacles

Joy

A happy heart.

 words

⊔ mouth

人 two legs

The mouth and legs together represent an older person. Wise words from a respected person bring good fortune and joy to the heart.

Joy, Ed Young, mixed media. Copyright © 1997.

Get the Message!

Look at the symbols this artist uses to portray a joyful heart. With a partner, create your own set of symbols that portray a feeling. Have other students guess what feeling you are trying to express through your art. What did you learn about how messages can be communicated? Can communication occur without words?

9

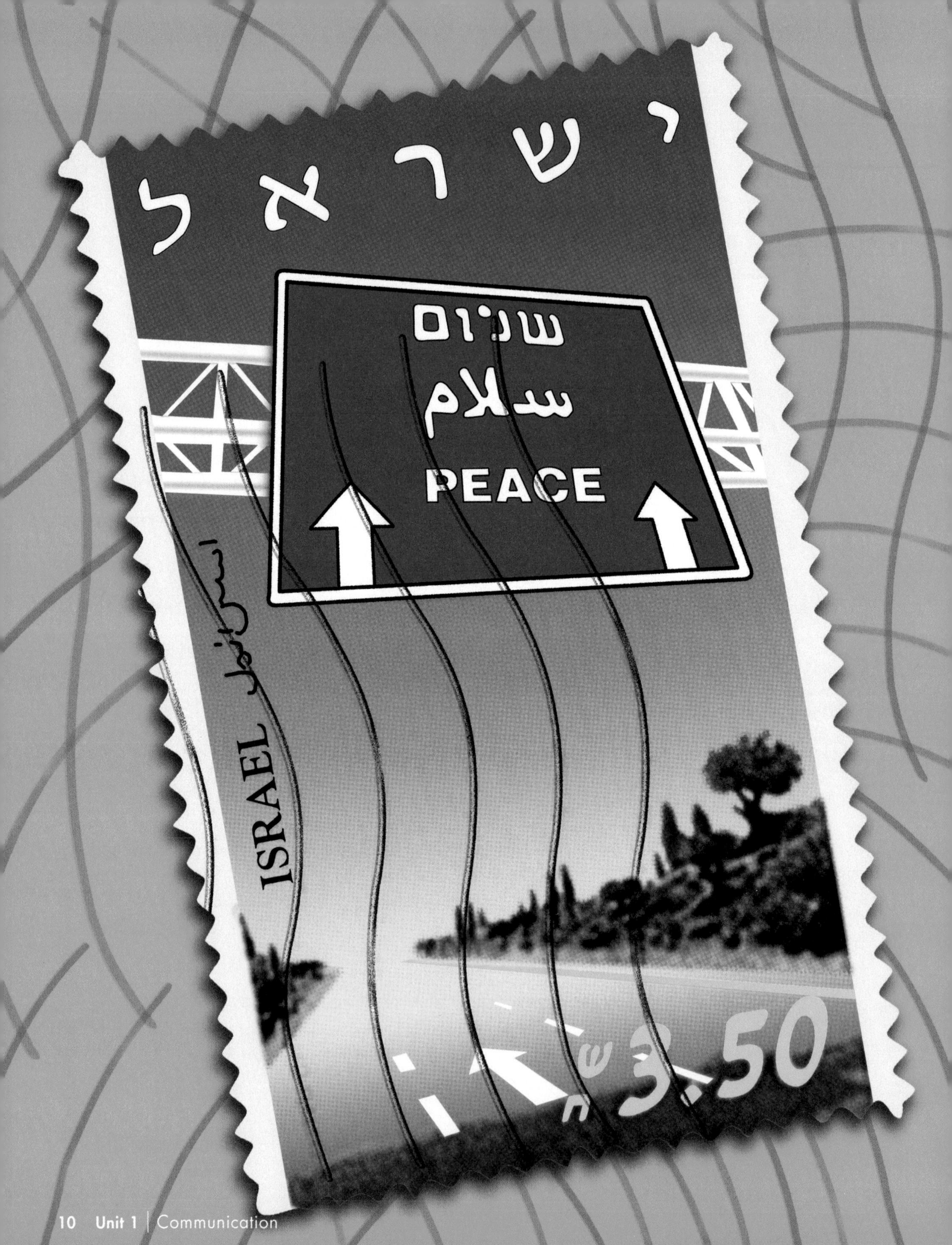
ישראל
שלום
سلام
PEACE
ISRAEL
3.50

Messages That Matter

- Why do people send messages?

- How do people add to—or take away from—the meaning of other people's thoughts?

- Why do some messages affect us more deeply than others?

THEME-RELATED BOOKS

Zora Hurston and the Chinaberry Tree
by William Miller

Zora's mother teaches her that dreams, like each branch of the chinaberry tree, are always within reach.

The Unbreakable Code
by Sara Hoagland Hunter

John, a Navajo boy, learns from his grandfather how a code based on the Navajo language helped to win World War II.

NOVEL

Toliver's Secret
by Esther Wood Brady

Ellen takes a message hidden in a loaf of bread to George Washington during the Revolutionary War.

Build Language and Vocabulary

EXPRESS OPINIONS

Study the painting. Tell what you think about it.

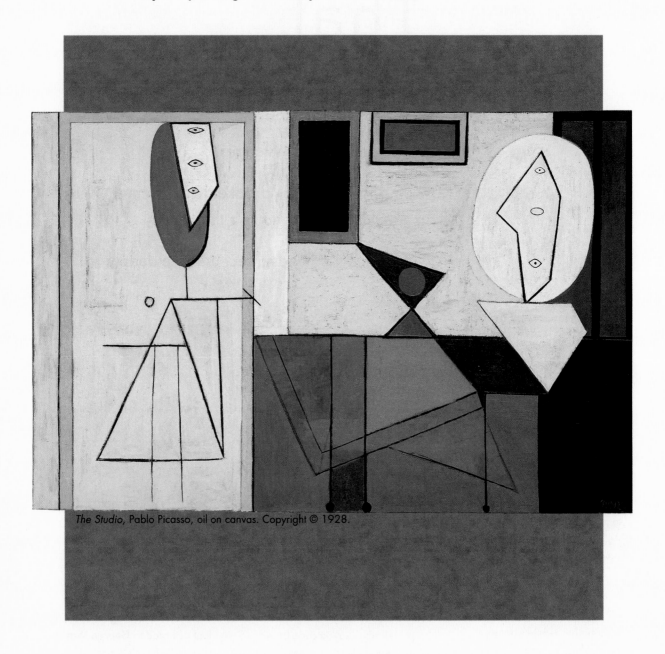

The Studio, Pablo Picasso, oil on canvas. Copyright © 1928.

TAKE NOTES IN A CHART

Listen to what one group of students had to say about the painting. Make a chart to note their opinions. Then add your own opinions.

Student	Opinions About the Painting
Kim	thinks it's great; likes the colors
Felicia	thinks it's odd; thinks the eyes are weird
Roberto	thinks it's neat; thinks grey is a dull color

BUILD YOUR VOCABULARY

Words About Communication Painting is just one way to communicate. Collect other words about ways to communicate. Add words to the web as you read this unit.

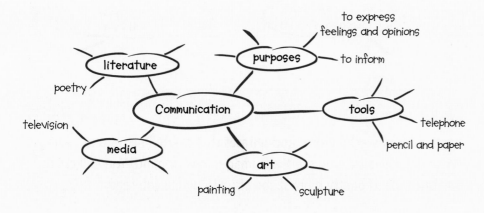

USE LANGUAGE STRUCTURES ▶ COMPLETE SENTENCES

Writing: Express Opinions Write one or two complete sentences that tell what you think about the painting.

Example:
I like all the triangles.
I think the colors are great, too.

The POWER of POETRY

poems
by Gary Soto
and interview
with the poet

Prepare to Read

THINK ABOUT WHAT YOU KNOW

Idea Exchange Is a poem a good way to communicate? Why or why not?

---

attention care and thoughtfulness

concentrate focus on or think about only one thing

creativity ability to think of new ideas and to express them

experience something that happens to a person

inspired filled with ideas, encouraged to create

inventive able to think of new ideas, creative

memory the ability to remember, something remembered from the past

motive reason for doing something

routine something that is done the same way all of the time

LEARN KEY VOCABULARY

Relate Words Study the new words and their definitions. Use the words to fill in the webs. Some words can be used in both webs. Then write a sentence about each web.

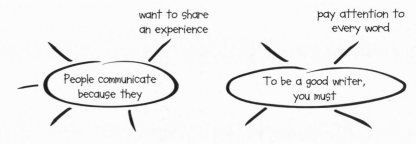

want to share an experience

People communicate because they

pay attention to every word

To be a good writer, you must

LEARN TO VISUALIZE

Poetry uses powerful words and phrases that create images and feelings. When you **visualize**, you see these images in your mind. You will enjoy and understand poetry more if you visualize while you read.

> ### READING STRATEGY
> **How to Visualize**
> 1. Read the poem once to get the general feeling of it.
> 2. Look back through the poem for words that create images.
> 3. Use those words to make a picture in your mind of the images.
> 4. Reread the poem.

Now listen to "The Power of Poetry." As you listen, visualize the images the poet creates in each poem.

The *POWER* of *POETRY*

three poems by
Gary Soto

Poet Gary Soto likes to write about
messages that matter to everyday
people. In these three poems,
a boy communicates, or expresses,
his feelings to people in his life.

Big Eaters

I stepped into the cold rush
Of a river until I was waist deep.
I screamed, "Check out this 20-foot trout,"
But the people on the shore
Kept eating their hotdogs and hamburgers.
I called, "There's a mermaid down here!"
But they only pushed their hands into bags
Of potato chips and sucked on ice.
I shouted, "Hey, a shark almost bit my toes!"
They lapped their ice creams
And bit into cookies.

No one seemed excited.
When I stepped out of the water
And looked at the sandy shore,
I called, "Hey, the steaks are almost done!"
Everyone came running with their forks.

—*Gary Soto*

BEFORE YOU MOVE ON...

1. **Details/Character's Motive** How does the boy try to communicate? Why does he say things that aren't true?

2. **Conclusions** Which message matters most to the people on the shore? Why?

---

rush fast-moving water
waist deep in the water up to my waist
Check out Look at

mermaid creature that is half fish, half woman
lapped licked, ate with their tongues

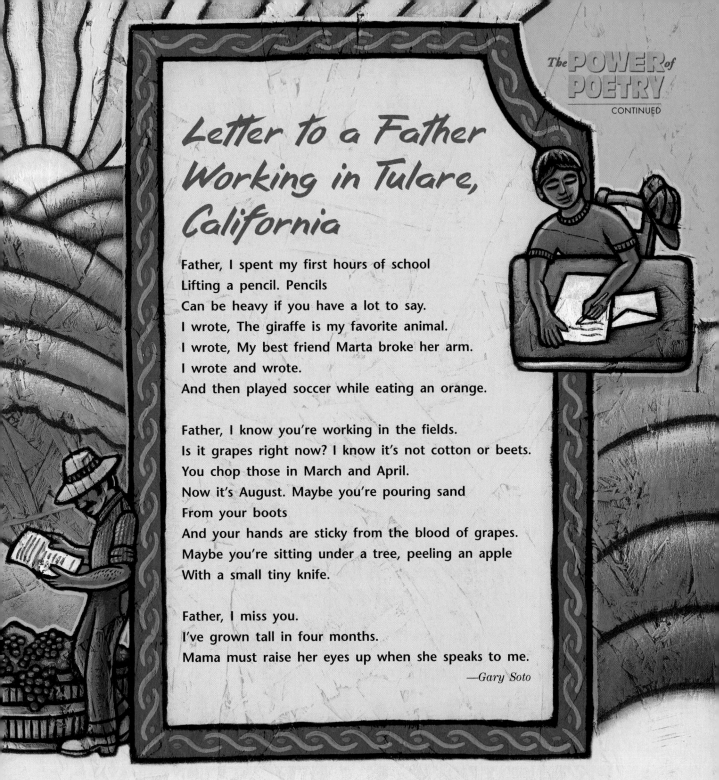

Letter to a Father Working in Tulare, California

Father, I spent my first hours of school
Lifting a pencil. Pencils
Can be heavy if you have a lot to say.
I wrote, The giraffe is my favorite animal.
I wrote, My best friend Marta broke her arm.
I wrote and wrote.
And then played soccer while eating an orange.

Father, I know you're working in the fields.
Is it grapes right now? I know it's not cotton or beets.
You chop those in March and April.
Now it's August. Maybe you're pouring sand
From your boots
And your hands are sticky from the blood of grapes.
Maybe you're sitting under a tree, peeling an apple
With a small tiny knife.

Father, I miss you.
I've grown tall in four months.
Mama must raise her eyes up when she speaks to me.

—*Gary Soto*

fields farmlands
chop cut
sticky gummy
blood juice
raise her eyes up look up

BEFORE YOU MOVE ON...

1. **Paraphrase** What does the boy tell his father in the letter?

2. **Inference** How does the boy feel about his father? Explain your answer.

WHAT THEY DON'T TELL YOU ABOUT CEREAL

In love, I ate three bowls of cereal,
The flakes so full of energy.
I put down my spoon and raced around the house.
There was rocket fuel in my heart.

Then I sat down to write a love note to Marta,
A girl in the second row, you know, by the window.
Marta, I wrote, I have a secret:
I LOVE YOU! I LOVE YOU! I LOVE YOU!

When my rocket fuel burned off,
I poured another bowl so that I could finish my note.
Again, I raced around the house,
Then sat down to write: I DO! I DO! I DO! I DO!

By the end of this note, all the cereal was gone.
My fingers were blistered from holding the pencil,
Sharpened so many times it was a nub
When I finally signed my name: JOSÉ, JOSÉ, JOSÉ.

—*Gary Soto*

---

flakes flat, thin pieces of cereal
rocket fuel high energy, excitement
burned off was used up, was gone
blistered red and hot
nub small, pointed object

BEFORE YOU MOVE ON...

1. **Character's Motive** Why is the boy writing a letter to Marta?

2. **Prediction** What would Marta say in a letter back to José?

An Interview with Poet Gary Soto

A poem is a personal message from the poet to readers. Where do poets get their ideas? What is the best way to read poetry? Find out the answers to these questions and much more about communication in this interview with Gary Soto.

Q Where do your poems come from?

A They come from my **memory** or from a story someone told me; they come from feelings and the **inventive** side of the mind. Most of my poems come from real **experiences**. But, like other artists, I treat the experiences with **a measure** of **creativity**.

Q Do you have to get **inspired** to write?

A When I began writing fifteen years ago, I waited to be "inspired," which for me was a **physical sensation**—my body **tingled**. Now I get this feeling less frequently. I **doodle** a few phrases or lines, and **a nice feeling settles on my shoulders**. This is a sign that I'm ready to write.

Q When do you write?

A Each poet has a **routine**. I write in the morning because **my mind is clear** and I can **concentrate**. After breakfast, I go out to my garage, which I've turned into a **study**, and write for two or three hours; then I have lunch, and do something else in the afternoon.

---

a measure a certain amount
physical sensation feeling in my body
tingled felt like it was full of electricity
doodle write without thinking very much

a nice feeling settles on my shoulders I feel good, I start to get comfortable
my mind is clear I can think clearly
study room for reading and writing

Q Do you write the titles of your poems first?

A I usually come up with a title when I'm about halfway through a poem. A title often **hints** to the reader what the poem is about. At times, however, poets will use wild titles that they may not wholly understand but may like for the way they sound or the way they look on the page.

Q Should I read a poem more than once?

A Yes, by all means. Read it again and again. One poet **remarked** that "poetry is **an act of** attention"—you have to concentrate when you read a poem.

I also like to think of a poem as a new person. Just because you say hello once doesn't mean that you never want to see this person again. Of course, you do. A poem also needs to be seen again and again.

Q Do you have to change any of your words?

A Since most poems are short, compared to other kinds of literature, every line needs **a great deal** of **attention**. I once worked on a single fourteen-line poem for a week, changing verbs, **reworking line breaks**, cutting out unnecessary words.

BEFORE YOU MOVE ON...

1. **Details** Where does the poet say his ideas come from?
2. **Opinion** Do you agree that a poem is like a new person? Explain.

---

a great deal a lot
reworking line breaks changing where the lines end

hints gives a clue
remarked said, made the comment
an act of an effort or action involving

Q Why don't your poems rhyme?

A Most poets today don't use rhyme; they write "free verse"—poetry that has **no regular rhyme or rhythm**. Poetry has changed over the years, but poets' **motives** for writing poetry haven't changed. Most poets write because they feel something and want to share it with others.

Q When did you decide to become a poet?

A I decided to become a poet after I read a funny/sad poem by Edward Field called "Unwanted." It's about a lonely man who feels sad that no one wants him. He hangs a picture of himself at the post office next to **posters** of dangerous criminals. He wants people to **recognize** him and love him. I was inspired by this poem and **identified with** it because it

seemed to speak about my own life. I read the poem over and over, and even **typed it out** to see what it looked like. I read this poet's book and began to read other poets. After a while, I decided to write my own poems, and have been doing it ever since.

BEFORE YOU MOVE ON...

1. **Personal Experience** Think of a poem that impressed you. Describe the poem and how it made you feel.

2. **Making Decisions** Think of a question you would ask Gary Soto if you were the interviewer.

---

no regular rhyme or rhythm no patterns for the sounds at the end of the lines or the beat of the lines

posters pictures placed for people to see or read

recognize see or know

identified with understood or shared in

typed it out used a machine or a computer to print the words

ABOUT THE POET

Gary Soto started writing poetry when he was twenty years old. One of his very first poems was a love poem he wrote for a girl he knew at school. Unfortunately, the girl rejected him and his poems, but Gary Soto continued writing poetry anyway. Since then, he has written eleven books of poetry and many plays, novels, and short stories.

Respond to the Poems and Interview
Check Your Understanding

SUM IT UP

Visualize and Summarize Make a web of the words that helped you see what happened in each of the poems.

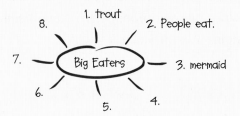

Then write one or two sentences that summarize the poem.

Example:

No one paid attention to the boy because everyone was busy eating. Then the boy said the steaks were almost ready, and all the people came over.

Determine the Author's Message Review your summaries. Make a chart to show what the poet has to say about communication.

Poem	Poet's Message About Communication
Big Eaters	People listen to the things they want to hear.
Letter to a Father...	
What They Don't Tell You About Cereal	

THINK IT OVER

Discuss and Write Talk about these questions with a partner. Write the answers.

1. **Conclusions** What did you learn about poetry and communication from the interview with Gary Soto?

2. **Author's Style** Who is the narrator of each poem? What else can you say about the author's style?

3. **Author's Purpose** Why do you think Gary Soto chose these topics for his poems? What do the topics say about him?

4. **Opinion** Which is your favorite poem? Why?

EXPRESS YOURSELF
▶ EXPRESS FEELINGS AND IDEAS

Work with a partner. Role-play an imaginary conversation between characters in the poems. Choose one of the following:

- a conversation between the boy and one of the people eating steak in "Big Eaters"

- a telephone conversation between the boy and his father in "Letter to a Father Working in Tulare, California"

- a conversation between the boy and Marta in "What They Don't Tell You About Cereal"

Language Arts and Literature

LITERARY ANALYSIS
SPEAKING/LISTENING

RECOGNIZE MOOD

Learn About Mood The feeling of a poem or story is its **mood**. Mood can be happy, sad, excited, angry, or any other feeling.

Gary Soto chose words and phrases to create a mood for each of the three poems. For example, he creates a playful mood in "Big Eaters" by using words like these:

> 20-foot trout
>
> shark almost bit my toes

Practice Reread "Letter to a Father Working in Tulare, California" and "What They Don't Tell You About Cereal." Pay attention to mood as you read. Make a list of key words that create the mood. Share your words with your classmates.

Express Mood Work with a group. Tape record yourselves reading the poems. Express the mood of each poem with your voice. Listen to the tape and talk about ways to improve the reading. Record the poems again.

TECHNOLOGY/MEDIA
LITERARY ANALYSIS

COMPARE POETS

Choose another poet you like. Compare that poet to Gary Soto. Write a paragraph to compare each poet's subject matter, style, and way of working.

1 **Locate Information** Use poetry anthologies to find several poems by the poet you chose. Start with this Web site and use key words to find biographical information.

INTERNET

INFORMATION ON-LINE

Key Word:
poets

Web Site:
➤ Poets
 • www.poets.org/index.cfm

Take notes and download useful information.

2 **Write a Paragraph** Write a paragraph that compares Gary Soto with the other poet. Then read your paragraph to your class and share the poetry that you found.

For more information on using the **Internet**, see Handbook pages 392–393.

TALKING WALLS

essay
by Margy Burns Knight

Prepare to Read

THINK ABOUT WHAT YOU KNOW

Study Walls in Your School What do the walls in your school say to you? What do they say about your school?

history story of a country and its people

legacy thing or idea handed down from the past

memento reminder of the past, souvenir

memorial something that keeps alive the memory of a person or event

monument something built to last a long time that honors a person or an event

mural large picture painted on a wall or other large surface

portray make a picture of

represent be an example or model of something

tribute something given to show thanks or respect

LEARN KEY VOCABULARY

Relate Words Study the new words and their definitions. In a chart, give an example of each kind of message. Check the boxes that apply.

Messages:	Mural	Monument	Memento
Examples:	workers' mural		
Does it portray people and places?	✓		
Does it provide a legacy?			
Is it a memorial?			
Does it represent an event in history?			
Does it honor a living person or people?	✓		

LEARN TO RELATE MAIN IDEA AND DETAILS

A **topic** is what a writer writes about. It is the writer's subject. A **main idea** is the most important idea about the topic. **Details** are pieces of information that tell more about the main idea.

READING STRATEGY
How to Relate Main Idea and Details

1. Read the title to see what the topic is.

2. Take notes as you read.

3. Review your notes. Ask yourself: What is the most important idea about the topic? This is the main idea. Then find the details that go with the main idea.

Read "Talking Walls." Find the main idea and details about each wall.

TALKING WALLS

BY MARGY BURNS KNIGHT
WITH TEXT SUPPORT BY MICHAEL RYALL

Some people tell stories with pictures and others paint with words. Both can communicate important messages to preserve history, to honor heroes, or to express personal feelings. Whether they contain words or pictures, the walls on these pages tell their own moving stories.

DIEGO RIVERA'S MURALS

This mural is called *The Mechanization of the Country.* It was painted in 1926 on a wall in the **stairwell** of the Ministry of Education in Mexico City. In it, Rivera shows that Mexico's economy was changing from one based on farming to one based on industry and technology.

The Mechanization of the Country, Diego Rivera, mural. Copyright © 1926.

The walls that Diego Rivera painted are like the pages of a large picture book. Many of the huge **murals** that he painted on walls throughout Mexico show the **glorious** and painful **history** of his country. Women **hard at work** with babies on their backs, farmers bending over in the fields, and people fighting for their **rights** are just some of the characters that Rivera **portrayed** in his murals.

An artist of tremendous energy and passion, Rivera worked for ten, twelve, sometimes fourteen hours a day. He painted to share **his vision of** Mexico's history with his people.

---

stairwell part of a building where stairs are located

glorious proud, beautiful, impressive

hard at work working very hard

rights fair and equal treatment, legal and moral justice

his vision of what he thought was important in

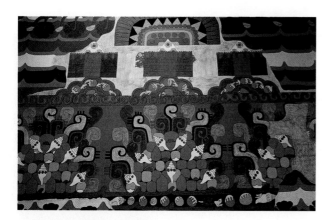

Diego Rivera

Gulf of Mexico

MEXICO

Mexico City

PACIFIC OCEAN

What Murals by Diego Rivera

Where Mexico City

Message Celebrate the people and history of Mexico.

Wall paintings, like the one above, were common in the **ancient** city of Teotihuacán in Mexico. Diego Rivera helped to **revive** this **art form** in the 1930s. His murals show what daily life was like in Mexico then. Rivera believed that working people **represented** the real Mexico.

BEFORE YOU MOVE ON...

1. **Context Clues** What special meaning does the word *characters* have here? What characters are in Rivera's mural?

2. **Viewing/Comparison** How is the mural in Teotihuacán like Rivera's mural? How is it different?

---

ancient very old
revive bring back to life
art form kind of art

THE VIETNAM VETERANS MEMORIAL

Flowers, letters, candles, and boots are lovingly placed under the names written on the Vietnam Veterans **Memorial**, in Washington, D.C. Each day these **mementos** and many others are left at the long, black **reflective wall** that rises out of the earth. The **monument** is about **one hundred sixty-five giant steps** long and was designed by Maya Lin, a twenty-one-year-old **architecture student**. She chose black **granite** for her design because she felt you could **gaze** into it forever. Every day people come to visit the wall, and many cry as they look at, touch, and remember the names of American men and women who were killed or are still missing as a result of the war in Vietnam.

Many more men, women, and children died during this war. If the names of these Vietnamese, Cambodian, and Laotian dead were **chiseled** into the wall, it would **extend** for at least another seven thousand giant steps.

In 1954, Vietnam **gained independence** from France. Two separate governments formed and fought a **civil war** that kept the country divided. In the late 1950s the United States began supporting South Vietnam in its fight against North Vietnam. In 1975, North Vietnam won the war. When it was over, more than 58,000 Americans had been killed. At least 2,000,000 Vietnamese, 200,000 Cambodians, and 100,000 Laotians were also killed during the fighting.

---

reflective wall wall that shines like a mirror
one hundred sixty-five giant steps 493.5 feet
(One giant step is about three feet long.)
architecture student student who studies how buildings and other structures are made
granite stone that is very hard

gaze look deeply
chiseled carved
extend go on, continue
gained independence became free
civil war war between two groups of people in the country

Walls Around the World

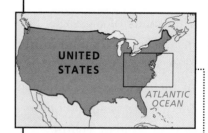

Maya Lin is an American architect well known for her design for the Vietnam Veterans Memorial shows the names of 58,156 American men and women chiseled into black granite. It was chosen over 1,400 other entries. Lin also designed the Civil Rights Monument in Montgomery, Alabama.

What The Vietnam Veterans Memorial by Maya Lin

Where Washington, D.C.

Message Honor the Americans who died in the Vietnam War.

BEFORE YOU MOVE ON...

1. **Cause and Effect** How did the Vietnam War start?

2. **Opinion** Do you think the Vietnam Veterans Memorial sends a message that matters? Explain your answer.

PABLO NERUDA'S GATE

Thousands of messages have been written on the fence that **surrounds** the Isla Negra home of Chilean poet Pablo Neruda. Many of the messages **praise** and thank Neruda for writing beautiful poetry and for speaking out for **human rights**.

Neruda didn't like it when a military government **took over** his country on September 11, 1973. A few weeks later he died, and the new military leader of Chile **warned** people to stay away from Neruda's home. However, for seventeen years people came **secretly** to write on the fence of the poet who as a child was known to say he was "hunting for poems."

When he was ten, Neruda showed one of his poems to his father. The father was so surprised by the beautiful words that he asked his son who really wrote the poem. Neruda's father thought that his son spent too much time writing poetry, and Pablo's schoolmates often made fun of him. But Pablo couldn't stop writing, and at thirteen, his first poems were **published**. Three years later, he **took the pen name** Pablo Neruda. He chose Neruda after one of his favorite Czechoslovakian poets.

Today, the government of Chile is freely elected and is proud of Neruda's **legacy**. Neruda's admirers continue to visit his home to write **tributes** to the boy who grew up to become one of the greatest poets in the world.

Pablo Neruda won the Nobel Prize for Literature in 1971. This prize is awarded each year to the writer or poet who has given "the greatest **benefit to mankind**" through his or her work.

---

surrounds goes around

praise say nice things about, give many compliments to

human rights equality, justice, and fair treatment for all people

took over took control of

warned said in a way that caused fear in

secretly without anybody seeing or knowing about it

published printed in a book

took the pen name changed his name as a poet to

benefit to mankind gift to all people in the world

**Walls Around
the World**

What The gate to Pablo
Neruda's House

Where Isla Negra, Chile

Message Honor and respect
one of the world's great
poets.

SALUDOS, GRAN POETA!
LOS DRUMMOND-ARAYENA
TE SALUDAN. (LA LIBERTAD SE GANA)
Reua. 22-06-98.   NO SE REBALA....

BEFORE YOU MOVE ON...

1. **Main Idea and Details** Find three details
   to support this main idea: Neruda began to
   write at an early age.
2. **Inference** Why do you think the people
   of Chile still love and admire Neruda?

**ABOUT
THE
AUTHOR**

Margy Burns Knight is from Winthrop, Maine,
where she teaches English as a Second Language.
She served as a Peace Corps Volunteer in Nigeria
and as a teacher in Switzerland. Her concern for
her students' need for geographical knowledge
and understanding of other cultures led her to
write the book *Talking Walls*.

Respond to the Essay
Check Your Understanding

SUM IT UP

Relate Main Ideas and Details Make a main idea diagram for each section of the essay.

Main Idea Diagram

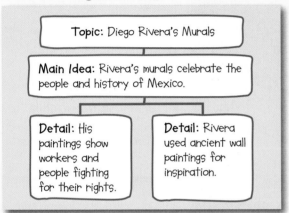

Topic: Diego Rivera's Murals

Main Idea: Rivera's murals celebrate the people and history of Mexico.

Detail: His paintings show workers and people fighting for their rights.

Detail: Rivera used ancient wall paintings for inspiration.

Write a Paragraph Use the main idea diagram to write a paragraph. A paragraph is a group of sentences that all tell about the same idea. One sentence gives the **main idea** of the paragraph. The other sentences give details that support the main idea.

Example:

Diego Rivera's Murals

   Diego Rivera painted walls to celebrate Mexico's history. He painted people hard at work. He also painted people fighting for their rights. Rivera got some of his inspiration from ancient murals of Teotihuacán.

THINK IT OVER

Discuss and Write Talk about these questions with a partner. Write the answers.

1. **Cause and Effect** Why have people in the past and in the present created talking walls? Why are they important?

2. **Comparison** How do you think viewers feel about each of the talking walls in the essay? How are each of their messages similar?

3. **Conclusions** If you were a painter or architect, how would you represent the people of the U.S. in a mural? Why?

4. **Judgments** Imagine that you could leave a message on the fence of someone whom you admire. Whose fence would it be? Explain what tribute you would write and why.

EXPRESS YOURSELF   EXPRESS OPINIONS

Tell a group about your favorite wall from the essay. Give three reasons that tell why you like that wall. Think about the way it looks, how it makes you feel, and the message it gives.

Language Arts and Literature

USE SUBJECTS AND PREDICATES

Learn About Simple Subject and Simple Predicate Every sentence has two main parts—the subject and the predicate.

- The **subject** tells whom or what the sentence is about. The **complete subject** includes all the words that tell about the subject. The simple subject is the most important word in the complete subject.

    Some painters create murals.

- The **predicate** tells what the subject is, has, or does. The **complete predicate** includes all the words in the predicate. The simple predicate is the verb.

    A mural **is a painting on a wall**.
    It **has a lot of room for big scenes**.
    Diego Rivera **painted many murals**.

Practice Write each sentence. Add a subject for each black line and a verb for each red line.

1. Maya Lin _____ the Vietnam Veterans Memorial.
2. The long, black _____ rises out of the earth.
3. Every day, many people _____ the wall.
4. Some _____ leave mementos at the foot of the wall.

USE CONTEXT CLUES

Learn About Context Clues Sometimes you can use **context clues** to understand new words. One type of context clue gives an example of the word:

    Farmers are some of the **characters** that Rivera portrayed in his murals.

The word *farmers* is an example of a character. *Characters* must mean "people in a painting."

Another type of context clue contrasts one word with another. Signal words such as *but, however,* and *instead* can introduce a contrast:

    Rivera showed the people's **fortitude** instead of their weak side.

Fortitude is in contrast with the word *weak*. It must mean "strength."

Practice Use context clues to figure out the meanings of the underlined words. Then tell which kind of clue you used for each word.

1. The farmers planted, weeded, and watered the crops. They labored all day long.
2. In Rivera's time, many people lived in the countryside. Today, however, the majority of people live in urban areas.
3. Life in Mexico City is very mechanized, but people still do some chores by hand.

Respond to the Essay, continued
Content Area Connections

FINE ARTS
MATHEMATICS

CREATE CLASSROOM WALL ART

Follow these steps to create a "talking wall" in your classroom.

1 **Plan Your Wall Project** Answer these questions:

- What topic do we want to explore?
- What message do we want to communicate?
- Will we communicate with pictures or words or both?

Have a volunteer record decisions.

2 **Prepare the Space** Measure the area of your talking wall. Cover the area with paper. Divide it into equal spaces for each group. Then draw light pencil lines on the paper to show each group's space.

3 **Design and Create** With your group, draw a sketch of your part of the mural. Work with other groups to plan how the different parts will go together. Each group should take turns creating its part of the talking wall.

4 **Present Your Mural** Invite visitors to view the wall. Explain what each part means.

MATHEMATICS
SOCIAL STUDIES

CREATE A MINIATURE MONUMENT

Make a monument to honor a person or event.

1 **Choose a Subject** Work with a group. Choose a person or event that you would like to honor. It should be an event or person that you feel strongly about.

2 **Think About Form** Think about the effect that the form of your monument will have on viewers. For example, the designer of the Vietnam Veterans Memorial chose polished black stone to create a sense of peace and provide a quiet space to think about the loss of lives.

3 **Design the Monument** Draw a sketch of the monument. Give measurements for all its sides. If you want an inscription (short text) to appear on your monument, be sure to write the text and to show where it goes.

4 **Make and Display a Model** Use your sketch to build a model of the monument. Each group can display its model in a "gallery." Invite visitors to take a guided tour of the gallery.

The Washington Monument

MAKE A PRESENTATION ABOUT FAMOUS WALLS

Use the Internet or other resources to learn about more walls around the world. Then make a presentation to share what you learned. Follow these steps.

1 **Locate Information** These Web sites might be good places to start, but remember that new sites appear every day! Use key words in your search and look for links.

INTERNET

INFORMATION ON-LINE

Key Words:
murals
monuments
memorials

Web Sites:
➤ **Murals**
  • www.diegorivera.com
  • www.lamurals.org

➤ **Information about Monuments and Memorials**
  • www.britannica.com
  • www.yahooligans.com

Download information, take notes, and draw sketches to prepare your presentation.

2 **Organize Your Information** Make a chart that gives information about each wall:

Walls Around the World

Name	Location	Date	Purpose
Ka'aba	Mecca, Saudi Arabia	about 1500 BCE	to protect a sacred stone
Great Wall	China	about 204 BCE	to protect China from invaders
Berlin Wall	Berlin, Germany	1961	to separate West Berlin from East Berlin

3 **Present Your Findings** Evaluate the information in your chart and make comparisons. Find pictures or make sketches of each wall. Add captions. Then display the pictures and point to them as you talk about the walls.

For more information on the **research process**, see Handbook pages 394–399.

Messages Across Time and Space

- What kinds of messages have been left behind from other times and other places?

- What forms do messages take today? How do they connect us to other people?

- Why do you think some messages remain important for many years while others are forgotten?

THEME-RELATED BOOKS

Radio Man
by Arthur Dorros

The radio keeps Diego connected to the world while he's on the move. In English and Spanish.

Aesop's Fox
retold by Aki Sogabe

Several of Aesop's timeless fables are combined into a single tale about a day in the life of Aesop's fox.

The Adventures of Sojourner
by Susi Trautmann Wunsch

The story of the spacecraft *Sojourner*: its historic trip to Mars and the images it sent back to Earth.

Build Language and Vocabulary
MAKE COMPARISONS

View the photo and read the poem. Hundreds of years ago, Native Americans drew images on rocks and on the walls of caves. What message do you get from this poem?

from

Before You Came This Way

Did they ever
wonder
who
in some far later time
would stand
in their
canyon
and think of them
and ALMOST hear
the echo of those voices
still in the wind?

—Byrd Baylor

MAKE A COMMUNICATION CHART

Think about the ways people send and leave messages for others. Work with a group to make a chart. List both old and new forms of communication.

Forms of Communication

Written	Spoken	Other
e-mail	tape recording	time capsule
letter	storytelling	cave painting

BUILD YOUR VOCABULARY

Words About Communication Collect words to compare two different forms of communication. You may want to compare written and spoken forms of communication. Or you may choose to compare a form used in the past with one used today.

Form of Communication	Tools Used	Where Message Is Found	How Sent
cave paintings	sticks, plants	cave walls	can't be sent
e-mail	computer	computer, printer	Internet

USE LANGUAGE STRUCTURES ▶ COMPOUND SENTENCES

Writing: Compare Forms of Communication Write compound sentences to tell how two forms of communication are alike and different. Use conjunctions from the **Word Bank**.

Examples:

Drawings are often used to communicate. Cave paintings were made up of drawings, **and** even today's e-mail can include them.

Messages on the walls of caves could not be sent to anyone, **but** e-mail messages can be sent to many people in the world.

Word Bank

and
but
or
nor
yet

Tales Across Time

folk tales retold
by Dawn Lippert and
Margaret H. Lippert

Prepare to Read

THINK ABOUT WHAT YOU KNOW

Share Folk Tales Work with a group. Each person tells a folk tale. How are the folk tales alike? How are they different?

grain seed of wheat or other cereal grasses

granary place where grain is stored

harvest gather crops when they are ripe

kernel seed of corn or wheat

kingdom country controlled by a king or queen

palace home of a king or queen

plantation large farm with many workers

storyteller person who tells stories

village community that is smaller than a town

villager person who lives in a village

LEARN KEY VOCABULARY

Relate Words Study the new words and their definitions. Make a chart. Write each vocabulary word in the correct column.

People	Places	Things	Actions
storyteller	palace		

LEARN TO MAKE COMPARISONS

When you **make comparisons**, you look to see how things are alike and how they are different. This strategy will help you organize information.

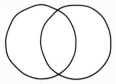

READING STRATEGY

How to Make Comparisons

1. A Venn diagram is one way to show how two things compare.

2. In the space where the circles overlap, list the ways the two things are alike.

3. List the differences in the two outer spaces.

4. Write a summary statement that explains how the two things are alike and different.

As you read, think about how the two folk tales in "Tales Across Time" are alike and different.

Tales Across Time

by Dawn Lippert and
Margaret H. Lippert

Stories and storytellers are as old as time. Though they may travel across many cultures, some stories can be surprisingly similar. The folk tales that follow have been retold by a modern mother-and-daughter storytelling team, yet they carry ideas and values from the past that are still important today.

THE FARMER'S TALE

When an Ethiopian king holds a storytelling contest, a farmer uses her skill to tell a never-ending story. She then wins half the kingdom.

The Storyteller

a folk tale from Ethiopia retold by Dawn Lippert

Long ago in Ethiopia, there lived a king who loved nothing more than listening to stories. Eventually, the **storytellers** in the **kingdom** ran out of stories. So, the king sent out **a proclamation**. It said that if anyone could tell him a story until he cried "Enough, no more!" she or he would receive half the kingdom. Many storytellers came, but none could make the king shout "Enough!"

Then one day, a farmer came to the **palace** gates. The guards tried to send her away, but she **insisted on telling** the king her story. She walked up to the king's throne and began: "Once, long ago, it was harvest time on a huge wheat **plantation**. The whole **village** helped the farmer **harvest** his wheat. On the farm was a **granary** so tall you could hardly see the top. The **villagers** began to fill the granary with wheat. They were all so busy that nobody noticed a small hole at the bottom of the granary. An ant came through it and took a

---

a proclamation an important message
insisted on telling said again and again that she must tell

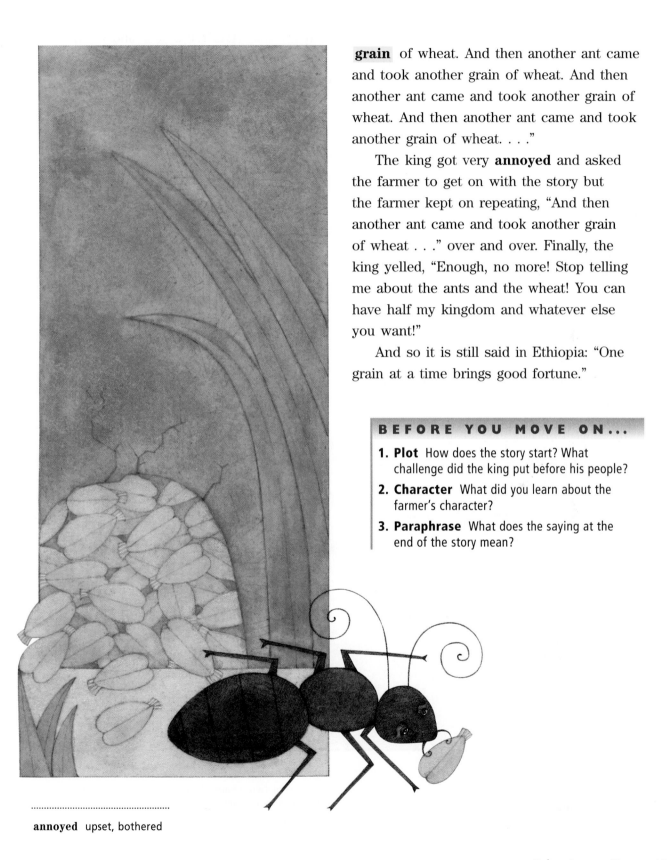

grain of wheat. And then another ant came and took another grain of wheat. And then another ant came and took another grain of wheat. And then another ant came and took another grain of wheat. . . ."

The king got very **annoyed** and asked the farmer to get on with the story but the farmer kept on repeating, "And then another ant came and took another grain of wheat . . ." over and over. Finally, the king yelled, "Enough, no more! Stop telling me about the ants and the wheat! You can have half my kingdom and whatever else you want!"

And so it is still said in Ethiopia: "One grain at a time brings good fortune."

BEFORE YOU MOVE ON...

1. **Plot** How does the story start? What challenge did the king put before his people?
2. **Character** What did you learn about the farmer's character?
3. **Paraphrase** What does the saying at the end of the story mean?

annoyed upset, bothered

THE GOATHERD'S TALE

A lonely goatherd learns of a contest for a story that lasts for a year and a day.
The goatherd tells his tale, wins the contest, and marries the king's daughter.

The Clever Goatherd

a folk tale from Spain retold by Margaret H. Lippert

Long ago there lived a village **goatherd** named Manuel. Every morning he led his goats to a **meadow** outside the village. Although Manuel loved his goats, he was often lonely. So sometimes he invented stories **to fill the time**.

One evening he **overheard two women talking** at the village **well**. "The king has a daughter. She will agree to marry the man who can tell her a story that lasts for a year and a day."

"I can tell such a story," Manuel thought. "Then I will never be lonely again."

The next morning he walked to the palace.

goatherd person who takes care of goats
meadow flat grassy area, field
to fill the time so that he would not get bored

overheard two women talking heard two women talking to each other
well water supply

"I can tell a story that lasts for a year and a day," he **announced**. The guards took him into the palace.

Manuel bowed low before the princess, then he began:

"Last year in my village, the people harvested so much corn that their **corncribs** couldn't hold it all. So they stacked the corn in a huge barn. But there was a hole under the **eaves**. One day a **dove** flew through the hole and ate a <mark>kernel</mark> of corn."

The princess smiled. She had not heard this story, and she liked the young man telling it.

Manuel continued, "The next day another dove came and ate another kernel. And the next day another dove came and ate another kernel. . . ."

"Go on," said the princess. "What next?"

"Well, the next day another dove came and ate another kernel. . . ."

The princess laughed, "I understand. You could go on for a year and a day! You have proved yourself **worthy of my hand**."

BEFORE YOU MOVE ON...

1. **Setting** Where and when does this tale take place?
2. **Character's Motive** Why does Manuel decide to tell the princess a story?

---

announced said in an important way

corncribs small buildings for storing corn

eaves part of the barn where the roof joins the wall

dove small white or light-colored bird

worthy of my hand good enough to marry me

A Note from the Storytellers

Stories connect us to the past. Every culture has its own **distinct** stories, but sometimes the stories are based on a similar **plot** or idea. Look at these two tales, for example. The basic plot is the same: the **main character** uses his or her intelligence and skill at storytelling to meet a challenge. However, some differences in the tales **reflect** the cultures they come from. In "The Storyteller," the granary is filled with wheat, which is an important crop of Ethiopia. In "The Clever Goatherd," the barn contains corn, which Spaniards use in their cooking. These stories illustrate the **similarities** between cultures while also celebrating the differences between them.

—*Margaret H. Lippert*

ABOUT THE STORYTELLERS

Dawn and **Margaret Lippert** live with their family in Mercer Island, Washington. They have been telling stories together, and with Dawn's sister Jocelyn, since the two girls were first able to talk. They tell stories at schools and libraries near Mercer Island and around the country. Both Dawn and Margaret also enjoy reading in their spare time. Margaret usually curls up with historical novels and biographies. Dawn's favorite genres include adventure and mystery novels.

---

distinct special, different
plot chain of events in the story
main character most important person in the story

reflect tell us about, show us about
similarities things that are almost the same

Respond to the Folk Tales
Check Your Understanding

SUM IT UP

Make Comparisons Make a Venn diagram to compare "The Storyteller" and "The Clever Goatherd." Then share it with a group.

Venn Diagram

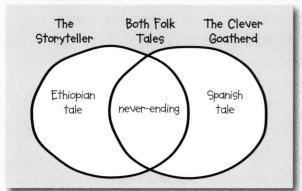

The Storyteller — Ethiopian tale

Both Folk Tales — never-ending

The Clever Goatherd — Spanish tale

Write a Summary Tell how the two folk tales are alike and how they are different. Here are some ways that you might start your sentences:

Both folk tales...
In one tale...
However, in the other tale...

THINK IT OVER

Discuss and Write Talk about these questions with a partner. Write the answers.

1. **Judgments** Which folk tale did you like best? Why?

2. **Conclusions** How are folk tales like messages across time?

3. **Comparison** How are some of the characters and plot elements similar to the folk tales you know?

4. **Opinion** Some people say storytelling is not important now because of television, books, and movies. What do you think?

EXPRESS YOURSELF
▶ RETELL AND LISTEN TO A STORY

Retell one of the folk tales in "Tales Across Time" to a partner. Then switch roles and listen as your partner retells the other folk tale.

Respond to the Stories, continued
Language Arts and Literature

▶ GRAMMAR IN CONTEXT

USE NOUNS

Learn About Nouns A **noun** is a word that names a person, place, thing, or idea. A **common noun** names any person, place, thing or idea. A **proper noun** is the name of one particular person, place, thing, or idea.

	Common Noun	Proper Noun
Person	storyteller	Margaret Lippert
Place	country	Spain
Thing	story	The Clever Goatherd

Use Specific Nouns You can use nouns to give a clear picture of what you mean.

NO: **Things** flutter on the **building**.
YES: **Flags** flutter on the **castle**.

Replace each **noun** in these sentences with a more specific noun.

The huge **thing** was full of **stuff**.

Two **birds** flew around the **place**.

Practice Write this paragraph. Add a noun in each blank. Circle the three proper nouns.

Long ago the night sky in Arizona was very dark. The _____ shone in the daytime, but at _____ there were no stars. Eagle wanted to solve the _____. He flew up to the _____ and asked the Great Spirit for _____ to shine at night.

▶ LITERARY ANALYSIS
▶ SPEAKING/LISTENING

TELL A NEVER-ENDING STORY

Learn About Fiction Folk tales, like other stories, are **fiction**. They are made up from a person's imagination. They include **characters** and a **setting**. The characters are the people or things that speak in the story. The setting is the time and place in which the story happens. For example:

- The characters in "The Storyteller" are a king, a farmer, and some guards.

- The setting is in Ethiopia a long time ago.

Most stories end when a problem gets solved, but in "The Storyteller" and "The Clever Goatherd," the farmer and the goatherd tell never-ending tales. The last line of each story is repeated over and over again.

Tell Your Story Plan your own story. Think about the setting, characters, and events. Think of a way to make your story go on "forever."

Then take turns telling your new story to a partner. Stop your partner when you think you hear "the ending that never ends."

For tips on how to **tell a story**, see Handbook page 402.

Content Area Connections

SOCIAL STUDIES

COMPARE POLITICAL LEADERS

A king is the leader of the country in both of the folk tales. Today, there are many other kinds of leaders. Find out how the roles and responsibilities of today's leaders are different from country to country.

1 **Research World Leaders** Choose several countries. Look them up in an encyclopedia, almanac, or other reference sources. Find the title for each country's leader and tell what roles the leader takes. Scan the text for words like these: *emperor, king, president, prime minister, prince, premier,* and *queen.*

2 **Make a Chart** Record your information.

Country	Leader's Title	Roles
United States	President	1. enforces laws 2. gives orders to the military 3. appoints judges to the Supreme Court
Japan	Emperor	1. symbol of national unity 2. preserves traditions 3. welcomes foreign leaders

3 **Share Information** Review your chart. Discuss how the leaders' roles are alike and different.

SPEAKING/LISTENING
HEALTH

LEARN ABOUT GRAINS AND DIET

Grains are the seeds of plants such as rice, corn, quinoa, and wheat. Most countries produce one or more grains that are an important part of the food supply. Find out about a grain and give an oral report.

1 **List Research Questions** Choose a grain to research. Brainstorm questions such as:

- Where is this grain grown?
- How is it prepared in different countries?
- What important nutrients—vitamins, minerals, or carbohydrates—does it provide?

2 **Gather Information** Look at encyclopedias, science books, health magazines, and the Internet. Take notes to answer your questions.

3 **Give an Oral Report** If possible, show a sample of the grain. Use your notes to tell about it.

Example:
"Corn grows in many places, including the U.S., Canada, and Brazil. It contains vitamins A and B...."

Learn how to give an **oral report**.
See Handbook pages 401–402.

science fiction
by Daniel Manus Pinkwater

Prepare to Read

THINK ABOUT WHAT YOU KNOW

Share Experiences Have you ever visited a dentist? In a group, talk about what happens in a dentist's office.

LEARN KEY VOCABULARY

Relate Words Study the new words and their definitions. Then look at each group of words. Two words in each group go together. Write one sentence using the two words that go together.

cavity hole in a tooth

dentist doctor who cleans and repairs teeth

filling metal or other material used to fill a cavity

invader person who enters a country by force to attack it or to steal

invasion act of entering a country by force

launch send into the air by force

receive get

spaceman man who comes from another planet

station place that sends out radio signals

stay tuned stay on the same radio station

dentist filling launch	invasion cavity spaceman	invader stay tuned station

LEARN ABOUT PLOT

The order of events in a story is its **plot**. In many stories, the first event begins with a problem that the main character has. Each following event in the story carries the plot to its conclusion, or end. If you understand the plot, you know the beginning, middle, and end of a story.

READING STRATEGY
How to Identify Events in the Plot
As you read, ask yourself:
1. Who is the main character?
2. What is the character's problem?
3. What events lead to the conclusion of the story?

As you read "Fat Men from Space," look for the events in the plot.

Fat Men from Space

from

adapted from the book by
Daniel Manus Pinkwater

When William visits his dentist, he gets a new filling in his tooth. Soon he discovers that the filling can pick up messages from the radio—and even from outer space.

THE FIRST SIGNAL

William goes to the dentist to get his tooth filled.
That night, he hears a radio program coming from his new filling.

William went to the **dentist**. It wasn't so bad—just a **filling**. The dentist said it wouldn't hurt a bit, and it was almost true. William went home **feeling a little bit numb**. There was a funny sour taste in his mouth. It made him think of electricity. When he sucked in his breath, the tooth with the new filling felt cold. He was able to eat his supper without any trouble. After watching television with his mother and father, he went to bed.

This particular night, William was lying in bed listening to the radio. He was listening to a talk show. A man said he had taken a ride in a flying saucer. He was telling how the people from outer space were crazy about **potato pancakes**. They had come to Earth **in search of** millions of them, which they planned to freeze and take back to their own **galaxy**. It was a good show, and William was enjoying it. He was ready to **drift off** to sleep. Then he realized that he had never turned the radio on.

William lay very quietly, trying to figure out where the radio program was coming from. It seemed to be coming from inside his head. "Maybe I'm imagining the whole thing," he thought. "Maybe I'm going crazy." He rubbed the tip of his tongue against the new filling. The **volume dropped** very low. Wait a second! He did it again. The volume dropped. He pressed his tongue against the tooth. No radio program at all! It was the tooth! The one with the new filling was **receiving** radio programs!

---

feeling a little bit numb without much feeling in his mouth

potato pancakes thin round cakes made with potatoes

in search of looking for

galaxy very large group of stars and planets

drift off slowly go

volume dropped level of sound went down

After a while, William **noticed** that his tooth was not receiving. At first, he thought the tooth **had gone completely dead**. Then he was able to hear **some faint static**. The static was kind of rhythmical, like music. It was interesting. William thought it was almost like a language.

BEFORE YOU MOVE ON...

1. **Vocabulary** List all of the words in the first paragraph on page 52 that describe a feeling or a taste.

2. **Details** What did William hear as he was lying in bed? What happened when he touched his tooth with his tongue?

3. **Fact and Fantasy** Which parts of the story so far could happen in real life? Which parts could not really happen?

....

noticed knew for the first time

had gone completely dead was no longer getting any radio signals at all

some faint static a low sound of crackling and hissing on the radio

THE INVASION

Radio messages from William's tooth tell about spacemen coming to take potato pancakes from Earth. And they know that William can hear their plans!

The more William listened to the strange static, the more he felt that he could almost understand it. The static was starting to make sense. It wasn't like anything William had ever heard. He knew what the noises meant. He could tell the directions they came from. The noises were **spacemen** talking to one another.

William was listening to twenty or thirty conversations at once. Some of the conversations were about potato pancakes. Some spacemen were **assembling** huge piles of potato pancakes in **remote places** on Earth. Spaceships would come and collect the potato pancakes and speed away with them. Other conversations were about **navigation**, and spaceships keeping in touch with one another. Some of the conversations were about a boy, an Earth boy who was listening in. The spacemen knew that William was listening! It made him shiver.

Spaceships would come and collect the potato pancakes and speed away with them.

*"Flash—the millions of round objects falling slowly through space are not meteorites as previously thought. They have now been identified as fat men, wearing **plaid sport jackets**, falling slowly into our atmosphere.* **Stay tuned** *to this* **station** *for further reports on the amazing story."*

The **invasion** had started. William hoped his mother and father weren't too scared.

BEFORE YOU MOVE ON...

1. **Inference** Why do you think that William could hear the spacemen's messages from his filling?

2. **Summary** What were the conversations about?

3. **Mood** Do you think this story is serious or funny? Explain your answer.

---

assembling putting together, gathering
remote places places that were hard to get to
navigation ways of finding directions

plaid sport jackets jackets with a large, bold pattern of lines and squares

3

BACK TO NORMAL

The spacemen land on Earth. Luckily, the invasion ends quickly, and life returns to normal. But on certain nights William can still hear the spacemen.

R*eports from our **affiliated stations** seem to **indicate** that the fat men have started to land. **It is estimated** that there are hundreds of millions of them still in the sky. The fat men are landing in all parts of the world, but the **greatest concentrations** appear to be in California and New Jersey.*

*"What do these fat men from space want? Is this the beginning of a war? Do they want to conquer the people of Earth? . . . It appears that, for the moment, they want hamburgers. . . . Crowds of fat men have surrounded roadside hamburger stands throughout the civilized world. . . . They are also **consuming great quantities** of pizza, and cupcakes wrapped in cellophane . . . and hot dogs . . . and ice cream bars . . . and jelly doughnuts . . . halvah . . . chocolate-covered marshmallows. . . . It*

Do they want to conquer the people of the Earth?

seems that the **invaders** *from space are after every sort of **junk food**. . . . Stand by for further bulletins."*

William was starting to get the picture now. The news bulletins were coming faster and faster.

*"**Conditions of panic exist** in many parts of the United States. **Residents of most areas** cannot get anything to eat but lean meat, fish, fruit, and vegetables."*

William could see that the **situation** was very serious. The fat men from space were eating up all the junk food on Earth **at a fantastic rate**. William thought there would be nothing left for the next day's snacks. Then he heard that a giant potato pancake had been **launched** into space near the planet Ziegler. The spacemen were off for another solar system.

---

affiliated stations radio offices with which we share information

indicate show, suggest

It is estimated Experts think

greatest concentrations largest numbers

consuming great quantities eating a lot

junk food food that is full of fat and sugar

Conditions of panic exist A lot of people are afraid

Residents of most areas People living in most cities and neighborhoods

situation problem

at a fantastic rate very quickly

In the morning, William's radio tooth still worked, although not as well as it had the night before. Sometimes the tooth would be **silent** for days at a time. Sometimes it would play fairly well. When William went to the dentist a year later, the tooth hadn't played for almost a month. Dr. Horwitz thought it would probably stop playing altogether after a while. He also told William that he had no new **cavities** —**a common occurrence** worldwide, since sugar was still scarce.

But the radio tooth **was not entirely dead**. Some nights it would play quite well. And on special nights—ones that were clear and cold—William could hear a kind of rhythmic static that was almost like a language.

---

silent completely quiet
a common occurrence an everyday happening
was not entirely dead still worked a little bit

BEFORE YOU MOVE ON...

1. **Details** What were some of the things the fat men from space wanted?
2. **Cause and Effect** Why couldn't most people on Earth get anything to eat but lean meat, fish, fruit, and vegetables?
3. **Paraphrase** In your own words, tell how the story ends.

ABOUT THE AUTHOR

Daniel Manus Pinkwater communicates with an old friend as he writes. That "old friend" is the younger Daniel who still lives inside his head and heart. He says, "I can vividly remember portions of my own childhood. I can see, taste, smell, feel, and hear them." Perhaps that's why the amusing "messages" in Pinkwater's books come through to young people so clearly. He has written many weird and wonderful books, including the ALA Notable *Lizard Music*.

Respond to the Story
Check Your Understanding

SUM IT UP

Identify Events in the Plot Think about the events in the story and complete a Story Staircase Map. Begin at the bottom "step" and move up to the top to show when events happened.

Story Staircase Map

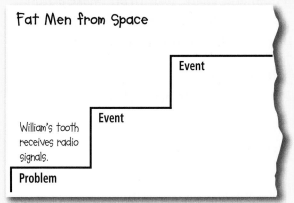

Fat Men from Space

Event

Event

William's tooth receives radio signals.

Problem

Write a Summary Use the information from the map to complete this summary.

William's problem was that _____. The first thing that happened was that _____. Then, _____. After that, _____. The story ended when _____.

THINK IT OVER

Discuss and Write Talk about these questions with a partner. Write the answers.

1. **Judgments** What would you do if you heard about an invasion from space?

2. **Prediction** William can still hear the rhythmic static through his filling. Do you think William will hear the spacemen again? What might they say?

3. **Author's Purpose** Why do you think Daniel Manus Pinkwater wrote this story?

4. **Comparison** What other stories do you know about visitors from space? Compare one other science fiction story with "Fat Men from Space."

EXPRESS YOURSELF
▶ ASK FOR AND GIVE ADVICE

Work with a partner. One of you is William, and the other is the dentist. William tells the problem and asks for advice on how to solve it. The dentist suggests a solution for the problem. Use words like these:

William:
"Hello, doctor. This is William. I have a problem..."

Dentist:
"Oh, my. That's quite a problem. I think you should..."

Respond to the Story, continued
Language Arts and Literature

▶ GRAMMAR IN CONTEXT

USE VERBS

Learn About Verbs An **action verb** tells what the subject does.

> The dentist **fills** William's tooth.

A **linking verb** connects, or links, the subject of a sentence to a word in the predicate. The word in the predicate can describe the subject.

> The noises **are** strange.

Or, the word in the predicate can be another way to name the subject.

> Now William's tooth **is** a radio.

Learn About Subject-Verb Agreement The **verb** must agree with the subject of the sentence. A singular subject and verb tell about one thing. A plural subject and verb tell about more than one thing.

> **Singular:** William **listens**. He **is** surprised.
> **Plural:** The spacemen **listen**. They **are** hungry.

Practice Choose words from each column to make as many sentences as you can.

Subject	Verb	Rest of Sentence
The invaders	are	on Earth.
The filling	collect	potato pancakes.
The situation	is	serious.
The spacemen	receives	signals from space.

▶ WRITING
▶ SPEAKING/LISTENING

WRITE A SCIENCE FICTION STORY

Use your imagination to write a science fiction story about William's next filling.

1 **Plan and Write Your Draft** Make a Story Staircase Map to plan your story. Use the events to write a rough draft of your story.

2 **Edit Your Work** Does your story have events that create excitement? Check your sentences for correct spelling and punctuation.

3 **Share Your Work in a Group** Take turns reading your stories aloud in a group. Talk about the events in each story.

Sample Story

> ### William's New Filling
> William got a new filling in the back of his mouth. Now the tooth was like a radio, and beautiful music from outer space came out of it. So many people wanted to listen to the music that William decided to ask them for food in exchange for listening. One day, the spacemen found out about the large quantities of food William had received.

Develop your skill in the **writer's craft**. See Handbook pages 414–423.

Content Area Connections

HEALTH

ANALYZE YOUR DIET

Learn About the Food Pyramid Do you eat a healthier diet than the spacemen? The food pyramid shows how much you should eat from each food group every day.

The Food Pyramid

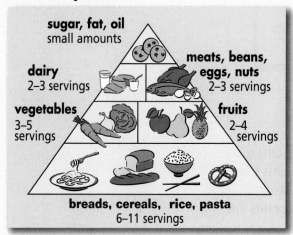

- sugar, fat, oil
  small amounts
- dairy
  2–3 servings
- meats, beans, eggs, nuts
  2–3 servings
- vegetables
  3–5 servings
- fruits
  2–4 servings
- breads, cereals, rice, pasta
  6–11 servings

Conduct a Study Keep track of the foods you eat for a day. Compare the number of your servings to those in the pyramid. What did you learn about your eating habits?

SCIENCE
MATHEMATICS

EXPLORE THE SOLAR SYSTEM

Prepare a research report on space travel.

1 Brainstorm Questions Work with a group. Think of at least three questions about space travel. Here are some ideas:

- What is the distance between each of the planets in our solar system?

- How long would it take to reach one of the planets in our solar system? At what speed?

- Have we sent spacecraft to other planets? What did we learn from those missions?

2 Gather Information and Take Notes Use an encyclopedia, the Internet, and other sources to find answers. The NASA Web site **www.nasa.gov** is one good source. Write an outline to organize your information.

3 Prepare a Report Use your outline to write a report. Present your findings to the class.

The surface of Mars

Writing That Tells a Story

Narrative writing tells a story. Some stories are about real places and real people. Others tell about people, places, or events that are made up.

PROFESSIONAL WRITING MODELS

"Fat Men from Space" is a science fiction **fantasy**—a story that could never happen in real life. It begins with an everyday character in a real-life setting, but events soon become unbelievable!

from **Fat Men from Space**

> This particular night, William was lying in bed listening to the radio. . . . Then he realized that he had never turned the radio on.
> William lay very quietly, trying to figure out where the radio program was coming from. It seemed to be coming from inside his head. "Maybe I'm imagining the whole thing," he thought. "Maybe I'm going crazy."

ELEMENTS OF A STORY

Stories are usually set in a specific time and place. In the beginning of a story, you get to know the setting and the characters. Often, one of the characters has a problem. The story tells the events that happen next. The events lead to a conclusion. Discuss the story elements in "Fat Men from Space." Which characters and events are real? Which are unbelievable?

Story Chart

CHARACTERS	SETTING	BEGINNING	EVENTS IN THE MIDDLE	CONCLUSION
William fat men from space	**Time:** Now **Place:** William's hometown in the U.S.	**The Problem:** William gets a filling at the dentist's. William's filling receives radio messages from spacemen about to invade Earth.	Hundreds of millions of spacemen fall from space to Earth, eat up all the junk food, and leave for another solar system.	William's filling rarely receives messages. He has no more cavities to fill because the fat men have eaten most of all the world's sugar.

STUDENT WRITING MODEL

Fantasy

A Textbook Adventure

by Darya Litvinchuk

Sheila's World Studies class was studying ancient Egypt, but she had been sick and missed school. Now she had to catch up. The test was the next day, and she hadn't learned anything about Egypt.

The teacher said Sheila could catch up by taking the textbook home. She read the chapters on ancient Egypt twice. Then the most amazing thing happened to her.

She was sitting at the kitchen table looking at a picture of an ancient Egyptian woman. The woman's lips moved! Then she spoke to Sheila, and Sheila jumped out of her chair!

"I will take you to ancient Egypt," said the woman as she lifted herself off the page. She pointed to a machine in the kitchen. She and Sheila stepped into it, and the woman pressed the button for ancient Egypt. A couple of seconds later, they stepped out. Sheila knew she was in Egypt because she saw pyramids.

The woman gave Sheila ancient Egyptian clothes to wear: a short-sleeved linen dress, an elaborate necklace, and sandals of braided reeds.

Sheila learned everything about ancient Egypt—how the people farmed, what the pyramids were for, and how to read hieroglyphics.

The visit was exciting, but Sheila began to wonder how she would get home. The woman seemed to read Sheila's mind, "We have to go back now."

Sheila packed up the Egyptian clothes to take home. They went back into the machine, the woman pressed U.S.A. 21st Century, and the next thing Sheila knew she was sitting at her kitchen table again.

"You won't believe what happened," she said to her mother. Sheila told her about the trip. She wanted to show her mom the ancient clothes, but for some reason, she couldn't find them.

Sheila did bring back a lot of information on ancient Egypt, however. By the way, she got an A on her World Studies test!

BEGINNING
The first paragraph introduces Sheila, the **main character**. We also learn about her **problem**.

MIDDLE
The **events** in the middle move the story along. Many of the events **could not really happen.**

The characters are **realistic but do unbelievable things.**

The **setting** changes from Sheila's kitchen in the present time to ancient Egypt and back again.

CONCLUSION
The ending tells how Sheila's problem got resolved.

Writing That Tells a Story, continued

The Writing Process

PREWRITE

1 **Collect Ideas** What settings, characters, and story ideas could you write about? Brainstorm with a partner. Write your ideas in a web.

FATP Chart

HOW TO UNLOCK A PROMPT
Form: *fantasy*
Audience: *classmates and friends*
Topic: *boy gets caught inside a video game*
Purpose: *to tell an entertaining story*

Choose the characters, setting, and story idea you like the best.

2 **Unlock the Writing Prompt** Before you begin, fill out an **FATP** chart to help guide your writing.

- Name the **form**, or what type of story you are writing.
- Name the **audience**, or who will read your writing.
- Name the **topic**, or what you are writing about.
- Tell the **purpose**, or why you are writing.

3 **Plan and Organize Your Writing** What problem will get your story started? What will happen next? Make a list of events. Plan some that are realistic and some that could never happen. You may want to draw the events in sequence on a storyboard.

Reflect and Evaluate

- Why do you think your story idea is a good choice?
- How will you introduce the problem your character faces?
- How can you make your writing interesting for your audience?

DRAFT

Use your **FATP** chart to focus on what you are writing, whom you are writing for, and why. Write quickly to get yourself involved in the action.

1 **Write the Beginning** Grab your reader's interest with a good introduction. Describe the characters and setting. Begin the plot by introducing the problem.

> **Writer's Craft: Introductions**
>
> **Grab your reader's interest.**
>
> I had just become a high level Desert Destroyer when Mom walked in. "If you don't stop playing video games, you're going to turn into a video game."
>
> I ignored her and kept playing. Suddenly, it seemed like I really was in the game. At first, I thought it was a really neat effect, but then I realized I was IN THE GAME!

2 **Write the Middle** Tell what happens next. Include some events that cannot really happen. Use descriptive words and phrases that show rather than tell.

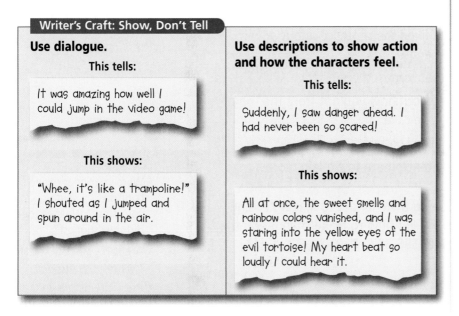

> **Writer's Craft: Show, Don't Tell**
>
> **Use dialogue.**
>
> This tells:
>
> It was amazing how well I could jump in the video game!
>
> This shows:
>
> "Whee, it's like a trampoline!" I shouted as I jumped and spun around in the air.
>
> **Use descriptions to show action and how the characters feel.**
>
> This tells:
>
> Suddenly, I saw danger ahead. I had never been so scared!
>
> This shows:
>
> All at once, the sweet smells and rainbow colors vanished, and I was staring into the yellow eyes of the evil tortoise! My heart beat so loudly I could hear it.

Reflect and Evaluate

- Did you introduce the characters and a problem in the beginning?
- Did you show most of the details, rather than tell about them?
- Does your fantasy include unbelievable characters, settings, or events?

3 **Write an Ending** Tell how the problem gets resolved.

Writing That Tells a Story, continued

REVISE

1 **Reread Your Draft** Review your **FATP**. Are your form, audience, topic, and purpose clear? Does your story include enough events that cannot really happen?

2 **Conduct a Peer Conference** Talk to a partner or group about your writing.

Here is part of the conference that a writer, Luca, had with his reviewers, Yoshi and Sarita.

Sarita and Yoshi tell what they like about Luca's story.

Yoshi: I liked the part about how you realized you were inside the video game. You made me feel like I was right there!

Sarita: When you dropped into the dark tunnel, you used clear, descriptive words. I liked the sentence about how it smelled like rotten eggs.

Luca: Is there any part that confused you?

Sarita: Well, I wasn't sure about how you got from the top of the brick wall into the cave.

Yoshi: That happened a little too fast.

Luca: OK. I can add a sentence there to explain more.

3 **Mark Your Changes** Decide on the changes to make. Revising Marks appear on Handbook page 411. For how to make changes on the computer, see Handbook pages 386–387.

Reflect and Evaluate

- Were your peer reviewers confused by anything in your story? What changes did they suggest?
- Are there parts of the story that you can drop?
- Are there details you can add to make your fantasy even more lively?

COMPLETE SENTENCES

A complete sentence has two main parts: the subject and the predicate. The verb in the predicate must agree with the subject.

- The subject tells whom or what the sentence is about. The **complete subject** includes all the words that tell about the subject. The simple subject is the most important word in the complete subject.

  Examples: Some people love video games.

  They play for hours.

  The mall in our neighborhood has a great video arcade.

- The predicate tells what the subject is, does, or has. The **complete predicate** includes all the words in the predicate. The simple predicate is the most important word in the predicate. It is the verb.

  Examples: Some people have fun with the adventure games.

  Others prefer athletic games.

  My brother's favorite is a snow-boarding game.

- The verb must agree in number with the simple subject.

  Examples: His board glides down the video mountains.

  The mountains are under a blanket of snow.

The simple subject and verb must agree even if other words come between them.

  Examples: Conditions during the game change often.

  A mudslide in the mountains is around the next curve.

Irregular Verbs

Singular	Plural
is	are
has	have
does	do

Practice Make up predicates to add to the subjects in column 1. Make up subjects to add to the predicates in column 2.

Subjects
1. My favorite game
2. The object of the game
3. My friends
4. The most popular games in the arcade

Predicates
5. like the Jungle Adventure.
6. isn't a fun game.
7. costs a lot.
8. has a good time at the mall.

Writing That Tells a Story, continued

EDIT AND PROOFREAD

1 **Check for Mistakes** Look through your writing to correct any mistakes in capitalization, punctuation, and spelling. If you need help, see Handbook pages 459–469.

2 **Check Your Sentences** Make sure every sentence has a subject and a predicate. Check that every verb agrees in number with its subject.

3 **Make a Final Copy** If you are working on a computer, print out the final, correct version of your story. If you are writing, carefully copy a final version.

PUBLISH

Use these ideas for publishing your writing or come up with your own.

- Collect everyone's stories to make a class anthology. Add a cover and a table of contents. Include a short author biography and author photograph at the end of each story.

> "I NEED TO GET OUT!" I screamed. I shut my eyes tight as an echo bounced around the dark cave: *GET OUT, GET OUT, GET OUT*. When I opened my eyes, I was back in my living room. I stared at the video screen. "I think I'll go outside to play after all," I said to myself. And that's just what I did.
>
> *THE END*
>
> ### ABOUT THE AUTHOR
>
> Luca Benini is in the seventh grade. In addition to writing stories, he likes playing soccer, listening to music, and playing video games. The idea for this story came to him because his mother says he plays video games too much!

- Illustrate your story and display it on a bulletin board.

- Submit your story to a teen magazine.

Key In TO **Technology**

After you've checked your spelling, double-check by using the spell-check feature of your word-processing program.

Reflect and Evaluate

- Are you pleased with your fantasy? Does it
  - ☑ introduce the characters and a problem in the beginning?
  - ☑ include unbelievable characters, settings, or events?
  - ☑ have events that lead in sequence to a conclusion?
- What do you like best about your story? What do you like least?
- Will this work go in your portfolio? Why or why not?

Get the Message!

1 Look Back at the Unit

Rank Messages In this unit, you read about many different messages. Talk with a partner about the messages in each selection. What ideas and information did each one communicate?

The Power of Poetry

Talking Walls

Tales Across Time

Fat Men from Space

Write the titles and a brief summary of the messages on index cards. Put the cards in order from most important to least important message. Tell why some messages are more important than others.

2 Show What You Know

Sum It All Up Expand and organize your ideas on this chart. Share your ideas about communication with a partner.

Reflect and Evaluate Make a list of things you discovered about communication from this unit. Add this list to your portfolio, along with work that shows what you learned.

Communication			
Verbal	Nonverbal	Temporary	Lasting

3 Make Connections

To Your Community Explore your community. Try to find a place that has some historical importance. Tell your class about the message that has been preserved by that historical landmark.

Rhythm, Joie de Vivre, Robert Delaunay, oil on canvas. Copyright © 1930.

A Sense of Place

Draw some large circles and put them on your classroom wall. Name them with words like brother, sister, American, good at sports, teenager, over five feet tall, speak Spanish and English, and so on. Write your name in each circle you fit in. How many groups do you belong to? Are there groups that everyone belongs to? In five years, could you add your name to more groups?

THEME **1**
Fitting In
When you find a place to belong in the world, you can connect with people from other times and other places.

THEME **2**
Bridging the Gap
You can overcome cultural differences by looking beyond the surface and finding your common interests.

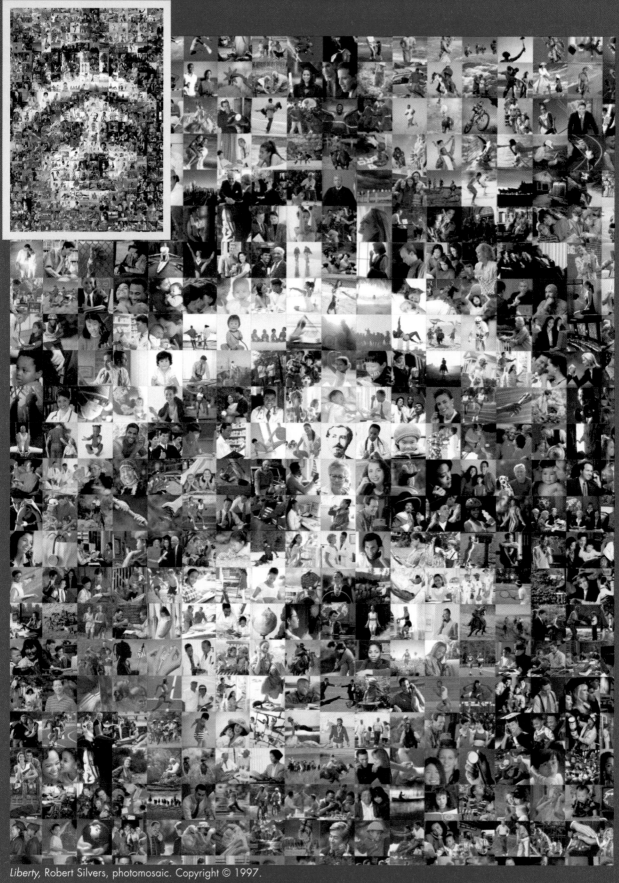

Liberty, Robert Silvers, photomosaic. Copyright © 1997.

Fitting In

- What groups do you belong to? Think about your family, friends, and cultural background.

- How do people learn to fit in and become members of a new cultural group?

- What do they keep from the old culture? What do they add from the new one?

THEME-RELATED BOOKS

Going Home
by Eve Bunting

Mexico doesn't seem like home to Carlos until he realizes home can be anywhere you are loved.

Journey to Ellis Island
by Carol Bierman

Ellis Island authorities want to send Yehuda back to Russia, but Yehuda proves that he is strong enough to be an American.

NOVEL

Yang the Third and Her Impossible Family
by Lensey Namioka

Yingmei Yang adapts to life in America while keeping her Chinese customs.

Build Language and Vocabulary

ASK AND ANSWER QUESTIONS

Listen to the following poem, then recite it with your classmates.

We're All in the Telephone Book

We're all in the telephone book,
Folks from everywhere on earth—
Anderson to Zabowski,
It's a record of America's worth.

We're all in the telephone book.
There's no priority—
A millionaire like Rockefeller
Is likely to be behind me.

For generations men have dreamed
Of nations united as one.
Just look in your telephone book
To see where that dream's begun.

When Washington crossed the Delaware
And the pillars of tyranny shook,
He started the list of democracy
That's America's telephone book.

—Langston Hughes

MAKE A TELEPHONE BOOK

Make a telephone book for your class. List your names in alphabetical order, and write your last name first. Then make up a telephone number for yourself:

- Think of a short word that describes you.

- Use the code to turn the word into numbers.

- Put a dash between each number.

> **Example:**
> Gonzales, Hector.............1-20-8-12-5-20-9-3
> Lee, Ming.......................13-21-19-9-3-1-12

CODE			
A	1	N	14
B	2	O	15
C	3	P	16
D	4	Q	17
E	5	R	18
F	6	S	19
G	7	T	20
H	8	U	21
I	9	V	22
J	10	W	23
K	11	X	24
L	12	Y	25
M	13	Z	26

BUILD YOUR VOCABULARY

Words About People and Places Copy the Personal Data Chart. Complete it with information about yourself.

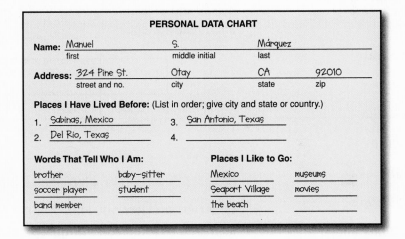

PERSONAL DATA CHART

Name: Manuel <u>first</u>   S. <u>middle initial</u>   Márquez <u>last</u>

Address: 324 Pine St. <u>street and no.</u>   Otay <u>city</u>   CA <u>state</u>   92010 <u>zip</u>

Places I Have Lived Before: (List in order; give city and state or country.)
1. Sabinas, Mexico
2. Del Rio, Texas
3. San Antonio, Texas
4. _____

Words That Tell Who I Am:
brother
soccer player
band member
baby-sitter
student

Places I Like to Go:
Mexico
Seaport Village
the beach
museums
movies

USE LANGUAGE STRUCTURES

▶ QUESTIONS: PRESENT AND PAST TENSE VERBS

Speaking: Interview a Classmate Work with a partner. Exchange charts. Review your partner's chart. Then come up with questions to ask your partner in an interview. Ask about the past and the present. Use words like *when*, *what*, *how*, *who*, *where*, *can*, and *is*.

> **Examples:**
> How old were you when you left Mexico?
> What is your favorite movie?

The Keeping Quilt

family history
by Patricia Polacco

Prepare to Read

THINK ABOUT WHAT YOU KNOW

Brainstorm Traditions What traditions does your family have? Think about births, weddings, and holidays. Make a web naming traditional objects and activities.

traditions

apron

babushka

bouquet

bride

celebrate

engaged

husband

nightdress

quilt

tablecloth

wedding huppa

LEARN KEY VOCABULARY

Locate and Use Definitions Study the new words. Work with a group. Predict the category for each word. Look up the words in the Glossary and correct your predictions. Use the words to write one or two sentences about each category.

Weddings	Clothing	Household Objects
bride	apron	tablecloth

LEARN TO PREVIEW AND MAKE PREDICTIONS

When you **preview**, you look over parts of the story before you read it. This helps you **predict**, or guess, what the story is about.

READING STRATEGY

How to Preview and Make Predictions

1. Read the title and the introduction.
2. Look at the pictures and think about how they relate to the title.
3. Predict what you think will happen in the story.
4. Read the story. Then check to see if your predictions were correct.

Make a chart to preview each section of "The Keeping Quilt" and check your predictions.

The Keeping Quilt

by Patricia Polacco

Anna and her mother make a quilt from
old clothes that belonged to family members
in their homeland. When the quilt is used
at Anna's wedding, a tradition begins. The
quilt connects Anna and her family to their
past, to their culture, and to one another.

1

THE QUILT IS MADE

When Great-Gramma Anna moves from Russia to New York City,
she makes a quilt to remember her family in the homeland.

When my Great-Gramma Anna came to America, she wore the same thick **overcoat** and big boots she had worn for farm work. But her family weren't dirt farmers anymore. In New York City her father's work was **hauling** things on a **wagon**, and the rest of the family made **artificial flowers** all day.

Everyone was in a hurry, and it was so crowded, not like in backhome Russia. But all the same it was their home, and most of their neighbors were just like them.

When Anna went to school, English sounded to her like **pebbles** dropping into **shallow water**. *Shhhhhh. . . . Shhhhhh . . . . Shhhhhh.* In six months she was speaking English. Her parents almost never learned, so she spoke English for them, too.

The only things she had left of backhome Russia were her dress and the **babushka** she liked to throw up into the air when she was dancing.

And her dress was getting too small. After her mother had sewn her a new one, her mother took her old dress and babushka. Then from a basket of old clothes she took Uncle Vladimir's shirt, Aunt Havalah's **nightdress**, and an **apron** of Aunt Natasha's.

---

overcoat long coat worn in the winter
hauling carrying
wagon cart with wheels
artificial flowers flowers made of plastic, cloth, or wire

pebbles small stones
shallow water water that is not deep

"We will make a **quilt** to help us always remember home," Anna's mother said. "It will be like having the family in backhome Russia dance around us at night."

And so it was. Anna's mother invited all the neighborhood ladies. They cut out animals and flowers from the **scraps** of clothing. Anna kept the needles threaded and handed them to the ladies as they needed them. The **border** of the quilt was made of Anna's babushka.

On Friday nights Anna's mother would say the **prayers** that started **the Sabbath**. The family ate **challah** and chicken soup. The quilt was the **tablecloth**.

BEFORE YOU MOVE ON...

1. **Main Idea and Details** Support this main idea with details: Life in New York was very busy for Anna and her family.

2. **Conclusions** Think of two reasons Anna's mother decided to use old clothes for the quilt.

3. **Inference** Why do you think Anna's mother asked the neighborhood women to help make the quilt?

---

scraps small pieces
border edge
prayers words spoken to God

the Sabbath Saturday, the Jewish day of rest and worship
challah bread that is shaped by twisting

The quilt is used as a huppa at Anna and Sasha's wedding. Many years later, the quilt becomes a wedding huppa for their daughter's wedding.

*A*nna grew up and **fell in love with** Great-Grandpa Sasha. To show he wanted to be her **husband**, he gave Anna a gold coin, a dried flower, and a piece of **rock salt**, all tied into a **linen handkerchief**. The gold was for **wealth**, the flower for love, and the salt so their lives would **have flavor**.

She accepted the **hankie**. They were **engaged**.

Under the **wedding huppa**, Anna and Sasha promised each other love and understanding. After the wedding, the men and women **celebrated** separately.

---

fell in love with started to care very deeply about
rock salt salt in the shape of a small rock
linen handkerchief square piece of strong cloth

wealth plenty of money and nice things
have flavor be interesting
hankie handkerchief

When my Grandma Carle was born, Anna wrapped her daughter in the quilt to welcome her warmly into the world. Carle was given a gift of gold, flower, salt, and bread. Gold so she **would never know poverty**, a flower so she would always know love, salt so her life would always have flavor, and bread so that she would never know **hunger**.

Carle learned to **keep the Sabbath** and to cook and clean and do washing.

"Married you'll be someday," Anna told Carle, and again the quilt became a wedding huppa, this time for Carle's wedding to Grandpa George. Men and women celebrated together, but they still did not dance together. In Carle's wedding **bouquet** was a gold coin, bread, and salt.

BEFORE YOU MOVE ON...

1. **Details** What did Sasha give Anna for their engagement? What did each of these items mean?
2. **Personal Experience** When Carle was born, she was given traditional gifts. Describe traditions you know about that welcome babies into the world.
3. **Comparison** How were Anna's and Carle's weddings alike and how were they different?

would never know poverty would always have enough money

hunger the pain of not eating

keep the Sabbath always remember that the Sabbath is a special day

3

THE TRADITION CONTINUES

Through the years, the quilt is used to celebrate marriages, welcome babies,
and comfort the family in times of sickness.

arle and George moved to a farm
in Michigan and Great-Gramma Anna came
to live with them. The quilt once again
wrapped a new little girl, Mary Ellen.

Mary Ellen called Anna, Lady Gramma.
She had grown very old and was sick a lot
of the time. The quilt kept her legs warm.

On Anna's ninety-eighth birthday, the
cake was a kulich, a **rich cake** with **raisins**
and candied fruit in it.

When Great-Gramma Anna died, prayers
were said to **lift her soul** to heaven. My
mother Mary Ellen was now grown up.

When Mary Ellen left home, she took the
quilt with her.

When she became a **bride**, the quilt
became her huppa. For the first time, friends
who were not **Jews** came to the wedding.
My mother wore a suit, but in her bouquet
were gold, bread, and salt.

The quilt welcomed me, Patricia, into the
world, and it was the tablecloth for my first
birthday party.

At night I would **trace my fingers**
around the edges of each animal on the quilt
before I went to sleep. I told my mother

---

rich cake heavy, sweet cake
raisins dried grapes
lift her soul help her go

Jews people whose religion is Judaism
trace my fingers follow with the tips of
my fingers

stories about the animals on the quilt. She told me whose **sleeve** had made the horse, whose apron had made the chicken, whose dress had made the flowers, and whose babushka went around the edge of the quilt.

The quilt was **a pretend cape** when I was in the **bullring**, or sometimes a **tent** in the **steaming Amazon jungle**.

At my wedding to Enzo-Mario, men and women danced together. In my bouquet were gold, bread, and salt.

Twenty years ago I held Traci Denise in the quilt for the first time. Someday she, too, will leave home and she will take the quilt with her.

---

sleeve arm of a shirt

a pretend cape an imagined piece of clothing worn around my shoulders

bullring arena in which men fight bulls

tent small temporary shelter made of cloth

steaming Amazon jungle hot, humid, thick forest near the equator in South America

BEFORE YOU MOVE ON...

1. **Sequence** What happened after Carle and George moved to Michigan? Tell the main events in the order in which they happened.

2. **Narrator's Point of View** Who is telling this story? How do you know?

3. **Generalization** What are all the different ways the quilt is used? What do they have in common?

ABOUT THE AUTHOR

Remembering her childhood home in Oakland, California, **Patricia Polacco** says, "All my neighbors came in as many colors, ideas, and religions as there are people on the planet. How lucky I was to know so many people that were so different and yet so alike." As a young girl, she had a learning disability that made it difficult for her to learn to read. She could draw very well, however. Now her drawing and writing come together in her books. Some of them were inspired by listening to the storytellers in her family.

Respond to the Family History
Check Your Understanding

SUM IT UP

Confirm Predictions Work with a group. Review your preview-and-prediction chart. Tell how previewing and predicting helped you understand the story.

Review and Retell a Story Create a family tree for Patricia Polacco's family.

Family Tree

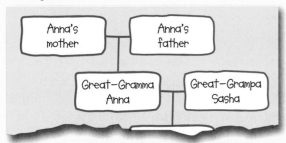

Anna's mother — Anna's father

Great-Gramma Anna — Great-Grampa Sasha

Use the family tree to retell the story to a partner. For each generation, tell how the quilt was used.

THINK IT OVER

Discuss and Write Talk about these questions with a partner. Write the answers.

1. **Conclusions** Why is the quilt important? Why do you think it is called the "keeping quilt"?

2. **Inference** The men and women celebrated separately at Anna's wedding. How did this custom change over time? Why do you think it changed?

3. **Author's Purpose** Why do you think the author wrote this story?

4. **Personal Experience** What tradition would you like to start with your family? How would this tradition give your family members a sense of belonging?

EXPRESS YOURSELF

▶ASK AND ANSWER QUESTIONS

Work with a partner. Make up questions about details in the story. Ask and answer each other's questions. Here are some sample questions:

• Whose clothes were used to make the quilt?

• What did Anna give Carle when she was born?

• What were some of the things in Mary Ellen's wedding bouquet?

Language Arts and Literature

▶ GRAMMAR IN CONTEXT

USE VERB TENSE

Learn About Verb Tense The tense of a verb shows when an action happens.

The **present tense** shows that the action is happening now.

> Anna **wears** a dress.

The **past tense** shows that the action happened in the past. To form the past tense of most verbs, add **-ed**.

> Anna **learned** English in school.

Some verbs form the past tense in different ways. These are called **irregular verbs**. See Handbook pages 450–451 for a list of irregular verbs.

> Anna **wore** a thick overcoat.

The **future tense** shows a time in the future. There are two ways to form the future tense:

> We **will make** a quilt.

> We **are going to** make a quilt.

Practice Copy the sentences. Choose the correct verb to complete each sentence.

1. Long ago, Anna and her mother makes / made a quilt.

2. Now, Patricia Polacco owns / owned the quilt.

3. Twenty years ago, Patricia holds / held her daughter in the quilt.

4. Someday, Traci will take / took the quilt with her.

▶ LITERARY ANALYSIS
▶ SPEAKING/LISTENING

LEARN ABOUT SYMBOLISM

A **symbol** is an image or object that represents an idea or value. When Sasha asked Anna to marry him, he gave her gold as a symbol of wealth. Follow these steps to create your own symbols.

❶ **Think of a Symbol** Work with a partner. Choose an important value, such as strength, happiness, or friendship. Think of a symbol that best represents or stands for that value.

❷ **Make the Symbol** Use cloth, clay, paper, or other materials to create your symbol. You may also use objects you find around your home or classroom, such as a food or a plant.

❸ **Explain Your Symbol** Show your symbol to the class. Explain the meaning of the symbol, and tell why it is a good symbol. Make a chart to show all the symbols created by the class.

Symbol	Represents	Reason
a rock	strength	Rocks are hard and can't be broken easily.

For tips on giving an **oral presentation**, see Handbook pages 401–402.

Respond to the Family History, continued

Content Area Connections

 FINE ARTS
TECHNOLOGY/MEDIA

MAKE A KEEPING QUILT

Making quilts is a tradition in many parts of the world. Quilts are often passed from generation to generation. Make a keeping quilt that represents your class.

1 **Research Quilts** Use sewing books and magazines to research the kind of quilt you want to make. Also check the Internet. New Web sites appear every day, but these sites are good places to start. Take notes and download photos of quilts.

INTERNET

INFORMATION ON-LINE

Key Word:
quilt

Web Sites:
➤ **Quilts**
  • www.historic-american.com
  • quiltorama.com

2 **Create a Class Quilt** Follow these steps:

• Choose a special experience you had in class to be the subject of your quilt square.

• Cut a square out of paper, and then draw your special memory with markers.

• Tape the squares together to make one large quilt. If possible, create a pattern.

Display the quilt in the classroom.

SOCIAL STUDIES
TECHNOLOGY/MEDIA

COMPARE WEDDING TRADITIONS

With a group, research wedding ceremonies and traditions across cultures. Prepare a multimedia report to share with your class.

1 **Gather Information** Make a list of the questions you want to answer. Use encyclopedias and books about wedding traditions. You might also want to interview married couples from different backgrounds. Organize your information into categories such as **symbols**, **customs**, **vows**, and **clothing**. Record your findings on a chart.

2 **Prepare a Multimedia Report** Use a combination of written text, pictures, videotapes and audiotapes, charts, and items used in different weddings to create your report.

3 **Make Generalizations** Listen to each group's report. Make a list that summarizes the information. Tell what the wedding traditions from different cultures have in common.

Examples:
Most weddings use symbols.
Many weddings involve a religious ceremony.

 For help with **multimedia presentations**, see Handbook pages 390–391.

Human Family

poem
by Maya Angelou

Prepare to Read

THINK ABOUT WHAT YOU KNOW

Make a Venn Diagram With a partner, make a Venn diagram. Show how you are the same and different.

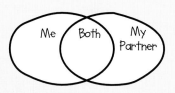

alike like one another

common ordinary

delight make very happy

obvious clear

serious thoughtful

thrive grow or do well

unalike different

variety number of different kinds

LEARN KEY VOCABULARY

Relate Words Study the new words and their definitions. Choose a synonym and an antonym for each word in the chart.

> **Synonyms** have the same meaning: **alike, same.**
> **Antonyms** have opposite meanings: **alike, unlike.**

Vocabulary	Choose from these words:			Synonym	Antonym
common	special	small	ordinary	ordinary	special
delight	show	please	anger		
obvious	clear	serious	hidden		
variety	size	likeness	difference		

LEARN TO READ POETRY

A **stanza** is a group of lines in a poem. Each stanza expresses an idea. If you understand each stanza, you will understand the whole poem.

> ### READING STRATEGY
> **How to Read a Poem with Stanzas**
> 1. Read the poem to yourself.
> 2. Stop reading after each stanza.
> 3. Ask yourself: What does the stanza mean?
> 4. Think about what the whole poem means.

Now read "Human Family." Stop after each stanza and think about what it means.

from Human Family

by Maya Angelou

I note the obvious differences
in the human family.
Some of us are serious,
some thrive on comedy.

The variety of our skin tones
can confuse, bemuse, delight,
brown and pink and beige and purple,
tan and blue and white.

I've sailed upon the seven seas
and stopped in every land,
I've seen the wonders of the world,
not yet one common man.

I know ten thousand women
called Jane and Mary Jane,
but I've not seen any two
who really are the same.

comedy funny things, humor
our skin tones the shades or colors of our skin
confuse puzzle us, seem unclear
bemuse make us think
seven seas seven great oceans of the world

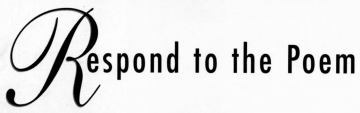

Respond to the Poem

I note the obvious differences
between each sort and type,
but we are more alike, my friends,
than we are unalike.

We are more alike, my friends,
than we are unalike.

We are more alike, my friends,
than we are unalike.

....

sort kind of person
type kind of person

ABOUT THE POET

Maya Angelou has enjoyed a long career as an actress, a film director, a poet, and an author. She often writes about characters trying to make connections with other people. In this poem, she invites you to see beyond the differences and understand that we all belong to a larger family.

THINK IT OVER

Discuss Talk about this question with a partner.

1. **Summary** What is the poet's message? Do you agree with the poet? Explain.

> **LITERARY ANALYSIS**

SOUNDS OF POETRY

Learn About Alliteration and Assonance Poets choose words for the way they sound together. Sometimes they use words that begin with the same sound:

*I've **s**ailed upon the **s**even **s**eas*

This is called **alliteration**.

Sometimes they choose words with the same vowel sound:

*S**o**me **o**f **u**s are seri**ou**s*

This is called **assonance**.

Recite the Poem Form five groups. Each group recites one stanza. All of you recite the last two stanzas. What other examples of assonance and alliteration did you hear?

BEYOND the COLOR LINES

self-portraits
by Janell, Jenny,
and Christian

Prepare to Read

THINK ABOUT WHAT YOU KNOW

Idea Exchange Think about people you know from different cultures. What words, customs, and ways of life have you learned from them?

adjust

ceremony

culture

custom

elder

feast

privilege

respect

right

tradition

LEARN KEY VOCABULARY

Locate and Use Definitions Study the new words. Work with a partner to make a vocabulary log for each word.

Vocabulary Log

> Word: ceremony
>
> Definition Prediction: church service
>
> Dictionary Definition: formal event on a
> special occasion
>
> Examples: wedding, graduation, birthday
>
> Sentence: A wedding ceremony marks the
> beginning of a marriage.

LEARN ABOUT FACTS AND OPINIONS

A **fact** is a true statement that can be proven. An **opinion** is a person's belief. It cannot be proven. When you read an opinion, you can decide if you agree or disagree with what the writer says.

> ### READING STRATEGY
> **How to Distinguish Between Facts and Opinions**
> 1. Ask yourself: Can the information in the statement be checked?
>
> 2. Ask yourself: Does the statement express a person's thoughts, ideas, or feelings? Are there signal words like *think*, *feel*, or *believe*?

As you read "Beyond the Color Lines," decide which statements are facts and which are opinions. Do you agree with the opinions?

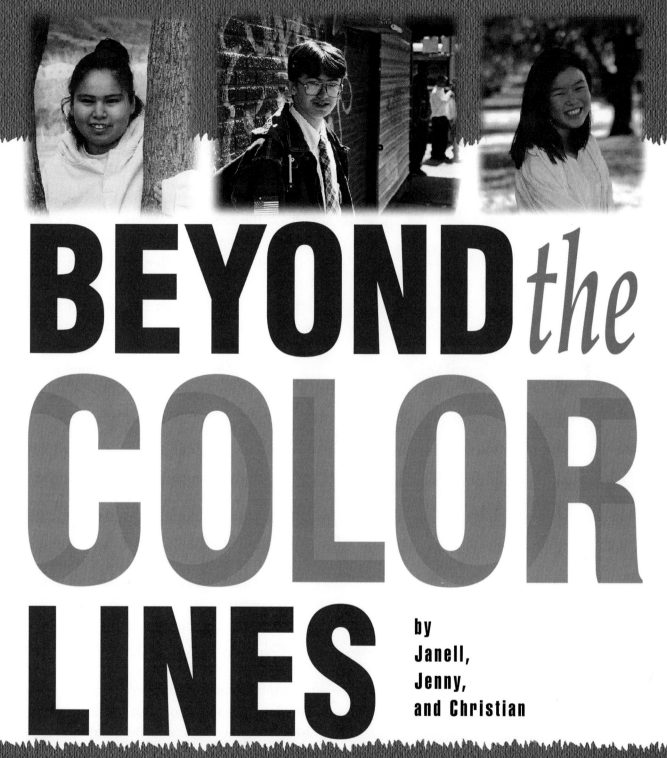

BEYOND *the* COLOR LINES

by
Janell,
Jenny,
and Christian

Three teens look beyond the obvious differences in color and national origin in order to fit in and get along with others.

Janell: "THE SAME AS ANYONE ELSE"

Janell dances in traditional Native American dress at powwows.

I'm Native American, or Indian. Usually, I say Indian. I have an Indian name I got in the **sweat lodge** when I was **an itty bitty baby**. It means something like *Mother Earth*. I'm proud to be Indian, because that's what **the Creator** brought me down to be. I really enjoy the **traditions** and **customs**, the

feasts, and the **ceremonies**, like the salmon ceremony. You can't go fishing for salmon unless you have the ceremony first. And I love being at the **powwows**.

I've been dancing since I first learned to walk. My mom said she made me little outfits to dance in, and I started bouncing around on my tippy toes. I learned by watching how the older girls moved their feet and arms. They are as beautiful as a butterfly. When I dance, I wear moccasins and leggings, and a dress with a belt, and cape and a shawl. There are bead designs on them. My Auntie Danell made one I wore. It maybe took three months to make.

All my aunties and uncles know how to do beadwork. And my grandma. She beads way different than anyone else. I know how to bead, but I want to do more, maybe when I'm older.

I think that Native American people have had dance as a part of their life from their **elders** to their elders to their elders, way

---

sweat lodge Native American shelter used for religious ceremonies

an itty bitty baby a very small child

the Creator God, the Great Spirit, the one who created the universe

powwows ceremonial meetings of Native Americans

back. When I grow up, I'd like to take my kids to powwows so they'll **get the hang of** dancing. Then they'll be at home bouncing around.

I find I can get along with anyone no matter what color or race. At middle school I have friends from different groups. A lot of my Mexican friends ask questions like, "What do you do down there on the **reservation**?" I tell them about the powwows, and watching TV or movies, or **shooting baskets** at the elementary school. I tell them that mainly we like to talk and have running races, that we're no different than anyone else.

You've got to get to know people first. Then you'll understand what they're like, that they are just the same as anyone else.

Janell with her uncle, Foster Kalama.

BEFORE YOU MOVE ON...

1. **Viewing** What colors, patterns, designs, and materials do you see in Janell's outfit?
2. **Inference** Why is dancing an important part of Janell's life? How does Native American dance connect to her past and her future?
3. **Vocabulary** Make a list of words related to Native American culture.

---

get the hang of get good at, get used to

reservation area of land set apart by the U.S. government for use by a Native American tribe

shooting baskets throwing a basketball through a hoop

Jenny: "DIFFERENT ON THE OUTSIDE"

In addition to playing the piano, Jenny has recently started taking clarinet lessons.

I was born in the Guangdong area of China, in the southern tip, pretty close to Hong Kong. I don't have any brothers or sisters. You're only supposed to have one child in China.

I've been in America about four years and am now in middle school. I like to play softball and volleyball and other sports. I play the piano, too, and I'm going to be taking clarinet. Bach's my favorite **composer**. I like to **collect** stamps and have a collection of Chinese stamps because we get mail from China sometimes.

When I get home from school I have to do homework. Afterwards, I like to **curl up** in my bedroom and read. I love mysteries. Sometimes I like ghost story mysteries.

I can't read in Chinese, though. I have this **special** book that my mom teaches me out of. I'm memorizing the **characters**. I know probably one hundred. You need to know about two thousand to be able to read the Chinese newspaper.

It's different being Chinese. I feel special. It gives me **privileges**. I can go to different special things that are Chinese, like the Chinese New Year, or special holidays.

I think of myself as more American than Chinese, though. I used to use my Chinese name, Yingyi. But sometimes **I was teased** about it. I tried to just either ignore it, or I said to them, "I bet if you went to China people would tease you about your name, because your name would seem different." Maybe then they'd find out how bad teasing is. But then I thought, Jenny sort of sounds like Yingyi. If I was Jenny, nobody would tease me. So now when people ask, I say my name is Jenny.

---

composer person who writes music
collect find and save
curl up get comfortable on a bed or sofa

special uncommon, particular
characters Chinese letters
I was teased others made jokes

Some people just don't accept you for who you are. Since you don't look like them, they think you don't belong with them, like you're different inside, too. I look Chinese, and I might have **an accent**. Some people **make fun of** others because they have an accent. I think it's unfair. What would they think if they were trying to speak, and they had a little accent? Would they want everybody to laugh at them like they laugh?

Everybody's personality is different. The way they think is different, and their culture is different. But just because they look different on the outside, they are still human beings. You just have to respect other people's rights. If you see someone who is really different, you should try to be friends. It might be really interesting. It might open you to another world.

Jenny's family celebrates traditional Chinese holidays, such as the Chinese New Year. She likes to compare her traditions with those of her friends who come from different countries.

BEFORE YOU MOVE ON...

1. **Summary** What is Jenny's background and family history?
2. **Paraphrase** According to Jenny, why do some people have trouble accepting others? What advice does she give?
3. **Making Decisions** What might you say or do if you saw people laughing at someone?

---

an accent a different way to pronounce certain words

make fun of laugh at, make jokes about

Christian: "THE TEAM SPIRIT"

Christian takes the subway home from school.

My father's grandmother was Greek and his father was Albanian. I'm Romanian, but I should say I'm Romanian American. My father and his family moved to Romania after World War II.

We try to keep some Romanian customs like going to the **Greek Orthodox church** where they have a **mass** in the Romanian **liturgy**. I speak Romanian at home, but it's hard to find others to speak with outside my home.

Next year, instead of going to twelfth grade, I'll be going to St. John's University. I'm in this program that lets me take advanced classes my junior year so I'm able to go into college my senior year. I'm excited about it. After school I play sports, do some reading, play a little guitar—I'm pretty bad actually—and I write. I love writing, especially poetry.

I think if an immigrant family leaves a country that is politically undesirable and their kids are young, the kids will **adjust** pretty easily. For **an adult**, it's something totally different. You come as an adult, you

---

Greek Orthodox church Christian church to which most of the people in Greece belong
mass Christian religious service

liturgy forms or rituals for public worship
an adult a fully grown person

don't know the language, and you are trying so hard to support a family. There is a lot of—a tremendous amount of—stress parents go through trying to adjust and fit into American culture, and at the same time **earn a living**.

I think in general too many people spend their energies on looking at what the differences are between us instead of what the similarities are.

Sport is **the great equalizer**. When I'm playing soccer, we have to play and communicate as a team. We are black, Spanish, Greek, Irish, Romanian, Polish and Indian on the team. I don't care what anyone eats at home, what church they go to, or what their skin color is, if they can't **dribble the soccer ball** or defend a goal they are no help to us.

In many sports, like soccer, every player has an important role.

BEFORE YOU MOVE ON...

1. **Comparison** According to Christian, how do children and adults differ in adjusting to a new country?

2. **Details** On a soccer team, skin color is not important. What is?

3. **Vocabulary** Write all the words on pages 96–97 that are related to culture and national origin.

---

earn a living make money by working at a job

the great equalizer something that makes all people feel they are the same

dribble the soccer ball move the ball toward the goal with their feet

Respond to the Self-Portraits
Check Your Understanding

SUM IT UP

Distinguish Between Facts and Opinions
Use a chart to record the authors' opinions about living in two cultures. What signal words helped you distinguish between the facts and opinions? Did you agree with all of the opinions? Why or why not?

Author	Opinion	Signal Words	Do you agree? Why or Why Not?
Jenny	I think it's unfair that some people make fun of others because they have an accent.	I think	I agree. You should respect other people's feelings.

Write an Opinion The authors expressed their opinions about living in two cultures. Use the signal words *think, feel, believe, should, agree,* and *disagree* to write your own opinions. How is living in two cultures difficult? What are the benefits of living in two cultures?

THINK IT OVER

Discuss and Write Talk about these questions with a partner. Then write the answers.

1. **Conclusions** What is the main message of each self-portrait?

2. **Comparison** What do Janell, Jenny, and Christian have in common? How is each person different from the other two?

3. **Generalization** What are some ways that people adjust to new cultures?

4. **Judgments** Why is it important to respect other people's rights and feelings?

EXPRESS YOURSELF ▶DRAMATIZE

Form small groups. Take turns pretending that you are Janell, Jenny, or Christian. Give more details about your self-portrait. See if your group members can guess who you are.

Language Arts and Literature

▶ GRAMMAR IN CONTEXT

USE HELPING VERBS

Learn About Helping Verbs Some verbs are made up of more than one word. The last word is the **main verb**. The verb that comes before it is the **helping verb**. The helping verb agrees with the subject. The main verb shows the action.

Some helping verbs have a special purpose. Study the examples in this chart.

Helping Verb	Purpose	Example
can, could	to tell about an ability	Janell **can get** along with anyone.
may, could, might	to tell about a possibility	There **might be** a powwow tonight.
must	to tell about a need	We **must prepare** for the powwow.
would	to tell what someone wants to do	I **would like** to know Janell.
should	to tell what someone ought to do	You **should respect** other people's rights.

Practice Answer these questions.

1. Janell can dance well. What can you do well?

2. Janell would like to take her future children to powwows. What would you like to do?

3. Jenny must do her homework after school. What must you do after school?

4. Christian might go to a university. What might you do after high school?

▶ WRITING
▶ TECHNOLOGY/MEDIA

WRITE A SELF-PORTRAIT

Use the self-portraits you have read as a model for writing your self-portrait. Include three paragraphs:

- Tell who you are, where you are from, and what activities you enjoy.

- Describe traditions and customs that are unique to your culture.

- Express your opinions about the advantages and difficulties of living in two cultures.

1 **Write a Draft** Use the outline to write your draft. Use the words *I think, I feel,* and *I believe* to signal some of your opinions.

2 **Edit and Publish Your Self-Portrait** Check your draft for mistakes. Then prepare a final draft. Include photos or drawings to illustrate your self-portrait. If you have a scanner, you may want to scan in a photo of yourself or a picture of an object that is meaningful to you. Include captions for your visuals.

All About Anil
by Anil Naik

Learn to use **word-processing software** to write your self-portrait. See Handbook pages 383–389.

The Golden Gate Bridge connects San Francisco to other cities in northern California.

Bridging the Gap

- How do people create connections with each other and find a sense of belonging?

- What kinds of thoughts, feelings, words, and actions put distance between people? What helps people bridge the gap?

- What is one step you can take toward bridging the gap with people who are different from you? Explain your answer.

THEME-RELATED BOOKS

The Bicycle Man
by Allen Say
Not long after World War II, two American soldiers make friends with a group of children at a school in Japan.

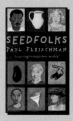

Seedfolks
by Paul Fleischman
People of different backgrounds get together and change an ugly city lot into a beautiful garden.

Oh, Freedom!
by Casey King and Linda Barrett Osborne
Young people interview adults about their involvement in the civil rights movement.

Build Language and Vocabulary

EXPRESS LIKES AND DISLIKES

Listen to the song and sing it together as a group.
Let your voices "meet" in the music!

In Music Meeting

Amid the sound,
the silent,
unsung greeting:
we sing together
and our voices touch,
in music meeting.

—*Victoria Forrester*

MAKE CLASS GRAPHS

Fold a sheet of paper into thirds. Use the sections to tell:

1. one thing you like to do
2. one thing you do not like to do
3. your most important value

Then compare your papers and make bar graphs to summarize the class's likes, dislikes, and values.

Bar Graph

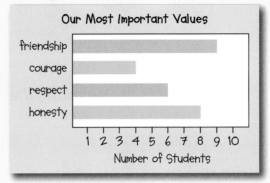

BUILD YOUR VOCABULARY

Ways to Tell About Your Likes and Dislikes Form groups according to the value you have in common. Then brainstorm different ways to say that you like or do not like something. Make a long list.

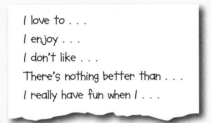

I love to . . .
I enjoy . . .
I don't like . . .
There's nothing better than . . .
I really have fun when I . . .

USE LANGUAGE STRUCTURES ▶ PRONOUNS

Writing: Express Likes and Dislikes Work with a partner. Write a short paragraph telling about the likes, dislikes, and values you both have. Use at least three pronouns in your paragraph.

Example:
We both like team sports. **I** enjoy baseball most, but **my** partner prefers volleyball. **We** agree with **our** classmates that good sportsmanship is an important value.

Prepare to Read

biography
by Peter Golenbock

THINK ABOUT WHAT YOU KNOW

Quickwrite What does it mean to "stand by your teammate"? Write a few sentences to tell what you think.

abuse mean words or treatment

challenge disagree with, take a stand against

compete try to win a contest or game

cruel mean

hostility hateful actions, mean thoughts

humiliation feeling of shame or embarassment

intimidate frighten

petition form asking for change

racial prejudice dislike of people because of their race

threat words that tell of future harm

LEARN KEY VOCABULARY

Use Context Clues Study the new words and their definitions. Write this paragraph and replace the bold words with vocabulary words.

In the 1940s, black baseball players were allowed to join white players on Major League teams. Still, black players had to live with a lot of **hateful actions** from fans and other players. Some tried to **scare** them. Much of the **mean treatment** did hurt the black players. But by the 1950s, blacks and whites began to **take a stand against** this treatment. They thought blacks should be able to compete in sports and other jobs. Some even sent a **form that asks for change** to the government. In the United States many people are still working to stop **bad feelings toward people because of their race**.

CONNECT NEW INFORMATION TO WHAT YOU KNOW

You will learn new information more easily when you **connect** it to what you already know. Use a K-W-L chart to make these connections.

> **READING STRATEGY**
> **How to Connect New Information to What You Know**
> 1. Read the title and look at the illustrations.
> 2. Write what you know in the first column of your chart.
> 3. Write questions in the second column.
> 4. After you read, write the answers in the last column.
> 5. Review what you wrote to see the connections.

Complete a K-W-L chart as you read "Teammates."

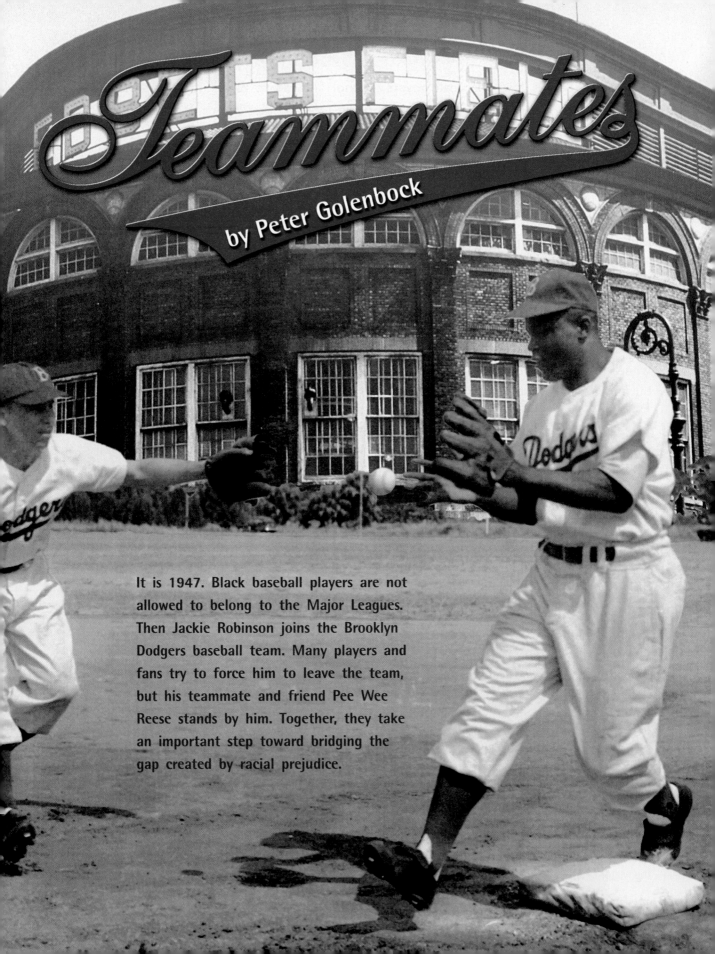

Teammates

by Peter Golenbock

It is 1947. Black baseball players are not allowed to belong to the Major Leagues. Then Jackie Robinson joins the Brooklyn Dodgers baseball team. Many players and fans try to force him to leave the team, but his teammate and friend Pee Wee Reese stands by him. Together, they take an important step toward bridging the gap created by racial prejudice.

BASEBALL BEGINS TO CHANGE

In the 1940s, black baseball players are not allowed to play in the Major Leagues.
The general manager of the Brooklyn Dodgers decides to change things.

Once upon a time in America, when automobiles were black and looked like tanks and laundry was white and hung on clotheslines to dry, there were two wonderful **baseball leagues** that no longer exist. They were called the Negro Leagues.

The Negro Leagues had **extraordinary** players, and **adoring fans** came to see them wherever they played. They were heroes, but players in the Negro Leagues didn't make much money and their lives **on the road** were hard.

Life was very different for the players in the Major Leagues. They were the leagues for white players. Compared to the Negro League players, white players were very well paid. They stayed in good hotels and ate in fine restaurants. Their pictures were put on baseball cards and the best players became famous all over the world.

Satchel Paige was an outstanding pitcher. However, he was not allowed to play in the Major Leagues for many years.

TED WILLIAMS

Baseball cards show photos of baseball players and give information about them. Baseball fans collect cards and, sometimes, trade or sell them. This card shows Ted Williams, a player who joined the Boston Red Sox in 1939.

baseball leagues groups of professional baseball teams

extraordinary extremely good, excellent

adoring fans people who loved the players on the teams

on the road while traveling

Many Americans knew that **racial prejudice** was wrong, but few dared to **challenge** openly the way things were.

The general manager of the Brooklyn Dodgers baseball team was a man by the name of Branch Rickey. He was not afraid of change. He wanted to treat the Dodger fans to the best players he could find, regardless of the color of their skin.

To do this, the Dodgers needed one special man.

Branch Rickey **launched a search** for him. He was looking for a star player in the Negro Leagues who would be able to **compete** successfully despite **threats** on his life or attempts to injure him. He would have to possess the self-control not to fight back when **opposing players** tried to **intimidate** or hurt him. If this man **disgraced himself** on the field, Rickey knew, **his opponents** would use it as **an excuse** to keep blacks out of Major League baseball for many more years.

Rickey thought Jackie Robinson might be just the man.

Jackie Robinson joined the Brooklyn Dodgers in 1947. He is shown here with Branch Rickey, general manager of the Dodgers.

BEFORE YOU MOVE ON...

1. **Comparison** How was life for baseball players in the Negro Leagues different from life for players in the Major Leagues?

2. **Cause and Effect** Why did Branch Rickey look for black players to join his team?

3. **Character's Traits** What kind of player did Branch Rickey want to find?

---

launched a search started to look
opposing players players on the other team
disgraced himself made himself look bad
his opponents the people against him
an excuse a reason

JACKIE MAKES THE TEAM

Jackie Robinson joins the Brooklyn Dodgers. Many players and fans treat him badly. His teammate Pee Wee Reese, however, supports him.

At spring training with the Dodgers, **Jackie was mobbed by blacks**, young and old, as if he were **a savior**. He was the first black player on a Major League team in almost fifty years. If he **succeeded**, they knew, others would follow.

Initially, life with the Dodgers was for Jackie a series of humiliations. The players on his team who came from the South, men who had been taught to **avoid** black people since childhood, moved to another table whenever he sat down next to them. Many opposing players were cruel to him, calling him nasty names from their dugouts. A few tried to hurt him with their spiked shoes. Pitchers aimed at his head. And he received threats on his life.

Despite all the **difficulties**, Jackie Robinson didn't give up. He made the Brooklyn Dodgers team.

Making the Dodgers was only the beginning. Jackie had to face abuse and hostility throughout the season, from April through September. His worst pain was inside. Often he felt very alone. On the road he had to live by himself, because only the white players were allowed in the hotels in towns where the team played.

A team photo of the Brooklyn Dodgers, taken in 1947.
Pee Wee Reese and Jackie Robinson are circled.

Jackie was mobbed by blacks black fans crowded around Jackie

a savior someone who could keep bad things from happening to them

succeeded accomplished this goal

Initially At first

avoid stay away from

difficulties problems

The whole time Pee Wee Reese, the Dodger **shortstop**, was growing up in Louisville, Kentucky, he had **rarely** even seen a black person, unless it was in the back of a bus. Most of his friends and relatives hated the idea of his playing on the same field as a black man. In addition, Pee Wee Reese **had more to lose** than the other players when Jackie joined the team.

Jackie had been a shortstop, and everyone thought that Jackie would take Pee Wee's job. Lesser men might have felt anger toward Jackie, but Pee Wee was different. He told himself, "If he's good enough to take my job, he deserves it."

When his Southern teammates **circulated** a **petition** to throw Jackie off the team and asked him to sign it, Pee Wee responded, "I don't care if this man is black, blue, or striped"—and **refused to sign**. "He can play and he can help us win," he told the others. "That's what counts."

Harold "Pee Wee" Reese, the shortstop for the Brooklyn Dodgers, was only 5 feet 9 inches tall and weighed 140 pounds when he began his professional baseball career.

BEFORE YOU MOVE ON...

1. **Details** What happened to Jackie during spring training?
2. **Character's Traits** What words can you think of to describe Jackie Robinson?
3. **Character's Motive** Why did Pee Wee refuse to sign the petition?

shortstop player who stands between second and third bases on the baseball field

rarely almost never

had more to lose had more reasons to be against Jackie

circulated passed around

refused to sign would not write his name on it

PEE WEE TAKES A STAND

When the Dodgers play against Cincinnati, fans scream hateful things at Jackie. Pee Wee supports Jackie, and their friendship causes baseball to change forever.

Very early in the season, the Dodgers traveled west to Ohio to play Cincinnati. Cincinnati is near Pee Wee's hometown of Louisville.

Cincinnati played in a small ballpark where the fans sat close to the field. The players could almost feel the breath of the fans on the backs of their necks. Many who came that day screamed terrible, hateful things at Jackie when the Dodgers were on the field.

More than anything else, Pee Wee Reese believed in doing what was right. When he heard the fans yelling at Jackie, Pee Wee decided to **take a stand**.

With his head high, Pee Wee walked directly from his shortstop position to where Jackie was playing first base. The **taunts** and shouting of the fans were ringing in Pee Wee's ears. It saddened him, because he knew it could have been his friends and neighbors. Pee Wee's legs felt heavy, but he knew what he had to do.

As he walked toward Jackie wearing the gray Dodger uniform, he looked into his teammate's **bold, pained eyes**. The first baseman had done nothing to **provoke the hostility** except that he sought to be treated as an equal. Jackie was **grim with anger**. Pee Wee smiled broadly as he reached Jackie. Jackie smiled back.

Pee Wee Reese and Jackie Robinson shocked the nation through their simple acts of friendship, causing many people to rethink their prejudices.

....

take a stand do what he thought was right
taunts mean words
bold, pained eyes eyes that showed hurt
provoke the hostility make people angry
grim with anger very upset and mad

Jackie Robinson

Crosley Field baseball stadium in Cincinnati. This stadium was the
scene of one of the most historic moments in baseball history.

"Pee Wee" Reese

Stopping beside Jackie, Pee Wee put his arm around Jackie's shoulders. **An audible gasp rose up** from the crowd when they saw what Pee Wee had done. Then there was silence.

Outlined on a sea of green grass stood these two great athletes, one black, one white, both wearing the same team uniform.

"I am standing by him," Pee Wee Reese said to the world. "This man is my teammate."

Today's Major League teams have players of different races and players from around the world.

BEFORE YOU MOVE ON...

1. **Paraphrase** In your own words, tell how the fans treated Jackie. Tell how Pee Wee reacted.

2. **Character's Motive** Why did Pee Wee take a stand?

3. **Conclusions** Why did the fans gasp when Pee Wee put his arm around Jackie's shoulders?

An audible gasp rose up The sound of people sucking in their breaths could be heard

Outlined on a sea of green grass stood Plainly seen on the baseball field were

I am standing by him I will be his friend no matter what happens

ABOUT THE AUTHOR

Peter Golenbock, one of America's best-selling sportswriters, has written several books about legendary baseball players and teams, including histories of the Brooklyn Dodgers, the New York Yankees, and the Boston Red Sox. In "Teammates," he shows us that star athletes are also ordinary human beings, facing life's challenges and trying to connect with people who may be different from themselves.

Respond to the Biography
Check Your Understanding

SUM IT UP

Connect New Information to What You Know Review your K-W-L chart. Share your chart with a group.

K What I Know	W What I Want to Learn	L What I Learned
There used to be separate baseball leagues for black players and white players.	Who was the first African American player for the Brooklyn Dodgers?	Jackie Robinson left the Negro Leagues and joined the Brooklyn Dodgers.

Ask More Questions What do you still want to know about Jackie Robinson, the Negro Leagues, or the Major Leagues? Brainstorm questions with a group. Discuss ways that you can find answers to your questions. Then get the answers and share those with your group.

THINK IT OVER

Discuss and Write Talk about these questions with a partner. Write the answers.

1. **Conclusions** How did Branch Rickey, Jackie Robinson, and Pee Wee Reese change baseball today?

2. **Judgment** What is the most important idea in this selection?

3. **Inference** The Shawnee leader Tecumseh said "Show respect to all men, but grovel to none." How does this quote apply to "Teammates"?

4. **Opinion** In your opinion, does racial prejudice still exist today? Give reasons to support your answer. What can people do to bridge the gap of racial prejudice?

EXPRESS YOURSELF ▶ DESCRIBE

Take the role of a sportscaster at the game in Cincinnati. How would you describe Pee Wee's actions to your listeners? Tape record your sportscast, and then play it for your classmates.

Respond to the Biography, continued
Language Arts and Literature

▶ GRAMMAR IN CONTEXT

USE PRONOUNS

Learn About Pronoun Agreement A **pronoun** is a word that takes the place of a noun. The noun that it replaces is called its **antecedent**. See Handbook pages 437–440 for a complete list of pronouns.

> **Jackie** tried out for the Brooklyn Dodgers. **He** made the team.

> Many did not want **Jackie** on the team. Some players were cruel to **him**.

> Pitchers aimed at **Jackie's** head. Jackie received threats on **his** life.

Replace Nouns with Pronouns Write the paragraph. Use pronouns in place of the underlined nouns.

> Jackie faced abuse throughout the season. Jackie's worst pain was inside. Jackie often felt very alone.

Practice Copy these sentences. Complete each sentence with the correct pronoun.

1. Some fans hated Jackie, and it / they yelled hateful things.

2. When Pee Wee heard the fans, he / she decided to take a stand.

3. Pee Wee walked with his / their head high.

4. Pee Wee went up to Jackie. Then Pee Wee smiled at him / you .

▶ WRITING
▶ LITERARY ANALYSIS

EVALUATE LITERATURE

Do you think "Teammates" is well written? Write a five-paragraph essay to give your opinion.

1 Write Use this plan for your draft.

- In the first paragraph, give your **opinion** of the biography. Is it interesting and informative?

- In the second paragraph, discuss the **background information** at the start of the biography. Is there enough information? Is there too much? Explain.

- In the third paragraph, discuss how the author uses **facts and opinions**. Are there enough facts? Do the facts support the opinions? Give examples.

- In the fourth paragraph, discuss the **photos and other illustrations**. Do they add information? Do they help tell the story?

- The fifth paragraph is the **conclusion**. Sum up your opinion of the biography.

2 Edit Your Work Check for correct spelling and pronoun agreement. Write the final draft.

3 Share Your Work in a Group Read your essay aloud. Discuss your opinions.

Review **pronouns** on Handbook pages 437–440.

Content Area Connections

SOCIAL STUDIES
REPRESENTING/SPEAKING

MAKE AN HISTORICAL EVENTS CHART

Find out what was happening in the 1940s and 1950s. Put your findings in a chart.

1 Gather Information and Take Notes You can use a variety of sources to do research:

- Encyclopedias, almanacs, or history books
- Old newspapers and news magazines
- Documentary videos about the 1940s and 1950s
- People who were young adults during those years

2 Organize Your Information Make a chart to show the important events.

Historical Events, 1940s–1950s

Year	Historical Event
1945	World War II ends.
1947	Jackie Robinson joins the Dodgers.
1954	Singer Elvis Presley begins recording his first songs.
1955	Rosa Parks refuses to give up her bus seat, an important event in the Civil Rights movement.

3 Give an Oral Report Show your chart to your class. Tell about the events in each year.

For tips on giving an **oral report**, see Handbook pages 401–402.

TECHNOLOGY/MEDIA
SPEAKING/LISTENING

INVESTIGATE MEDIA

Television programs have sound and moving pictures. A radio broadcast uses sound only. News articles use printed words, photographs, and other graphics. How do these differences affect a news report? Find out in a group project.

1 Form Media Discussion Groups Group 1 will research TV and videos; Group 2, radio; and Group 3, newspaper and other print.

2 Choose a Media Event Choose an event such as a sports game that is covered by all three types of media. Then, take notes on how your type of media helps you understand the event.

3 Compare Media Was one report more factual than the others? How did each type of media help you know what happened? Which was most effective? What differences did you find between a live report and one that was produced later?

Sports events are covered by all types of media.

Amir

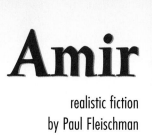

realistic fiction
by Paul Fleischman

Prepare to Read

THINK ABOUT WHAT YOU KNOW

Create a Chart How are city and country life different? Think of where food comes from or the buildings, for example. Write your ideas in a chart.

LEARN KEY VOCABULARY

benefit good result or reward for doing something

community group of people who live in the same neighborhood

conversation friendly talk between two or more people

excuse reason given for doing something

harvest festival celebration that takes place when harvest is over

provide give or supply

recognize know someone when you see him or her again

trade give one thing and take another in its place

Use New Words in Context Study the new words and their definitions. Then match the beginning of each sentence with its ending.

1. Everyone in my **community**	to eat, dance, and sing.
2. The garden **provides**	with friends about the garden.
3. After the growing season	a place for neighbors to meet.
4. My friends **recognize**	works in the city garden.
5. We **trade** vegetables	me even though I cut my hair.
6. The festival is a good **excuse**	we have a **harvest festival**.
7. We have **conversations**	a **benefit** of having a garden.
8. Good, fresh food is	for fruit.

LEARN TO SEQUENCE EVENTS

When you **sequence** events, you put them in time order. This helps you remember when the events in the story happened.

> ### READING STRATEGY
> **How to Sequence Events**
> 1. Look for words that tell, or signal, when something happens.
>   Examples: *first, second, before, next, now, later, still*
>   dates, days of the week, and months
> 2. As you read, use signal words to put story events in order.

Now read "Amir." Make a time line and put the events in order.

Amir

from **Seedfolks** by **Paul Fleischman**

A community garden sprouts up in Cleveland, Ohio. Amir, an immigrant from India, and his neighbors start to work in the garden. As they do, they learn to appreciate one another. By harvest time, Amir and his neighbors find themselves belonging to a community of friends.

THE WORLD IS FULL OF NEIGHBORS

Even in a large city Amir feels alone. After he gets to know his neighbors, they become part of his world.

In India we have many **vast** cities, just as in America. There, too, you are one among millions. But there at least you know your neighbors. Here, one cannot say that. Here you have a million crabs living in a million **crevices**.

When I saw the garden for the first time, so green among the dark brick buildings, I thought back to my parents' Persian rug. It showed climbing vines, rivers and waterfalls, grapes, flower beds, singing birds, everything a desert dweller might want. The garden's green was as **soothing to the** eye as the deep blue of that rug. I'm aware of color—I **manage** a fabric store. But, the garden's greatest **benefit**, I feel, was not **relief to the eyes**, but to make the eyes see our neighbors.

I grew eggplants, onions, carrots, and cauliflower. When the eggplants appeared in August they were **pale** purple, a strange and eerie shade. Very many people came over to ask about them and talk to me. I **recognized** a few from the neighborhood. Not one had spoken to me before—and now how friendly they turned out to be.

> I grew eggplants . . . many people came over to ask about them.

---

vast huge, big
crevices cracks
soothing to the eye nice to look at
manage am in charge of
relief to the eyes being nice to look at
pale light

BEFORE YOU MOVE ON...

1. **Inference** How do you think Amir feels at the beginning of the story? Explain.
2. **Visualizing** Amir says that the garden reminded him of a Persian rug. Write a sentence to describe how you imagine the garden looked.
3. **Foreshadowing** What hint does Amir give about what the garden will come to mean to him?

GOOD NEIGHBORS BECOME A COMMUNITY

Amir and his neighbors catch a thief near the garden. They help
each other and, in the process, form a community.

Those **conversations** **tied us together**. In the middle of summer someone **dumped a load** of tires on the garden at night, as if it were still filled with trash. A man's four rows of young corn were crushed. In an hour, we had all the tires by the curb. We were used to helping each other by then. A few weeks later, early in the evening a woman screamed, down the block from the garden. A man with a knife had taken her purse. Three men from the garden ran after him. I was surprised that I was one of them. Even more surprising, we caught him. A teenager named Royce held the man to a wall with his pitchfork until the police arrived. I asked the others. Not one of us had ever chased a criminal before. And most likely we wouldn't have except near the garden. There, you felt part of a **community**.

In an hour, we had all the tires by the curb. We were used to helping each other by then.

I came to the United States in 1980. Cleveland is a city of immigrants. The **Poles** are especially well known here. I'd always heard that the Polish men were tough **steelworkers** and that the women cooked lots of cabbage. But I'd never known one—until the garden. She was an old woman whose space bordered mine. She had a seven-block walk to the garden, the same **route I took**. We spoke quite often. We both planted carrots. When her hundreds of seedlings came up in a row, I was very surprised that she did not thin them—pulling out all but one healthy-looking plant each few inches, to give them room to grow. I asked her. She looked down at them and said she knew she ought to do it, but that this **task** reminded her too closely of her

---

tied us together brought us closer to one another
dumped a load dropped a lot, left a lot
Poles people from Poland, Polish people
steelworkers people who work in places where steel is made

route I took way I walked
task job, chore

concentration camp, where the prisoners were inspected each morning and divided into two lines—the healthy to live and the others to die. Her father, an orchestra violinist, had spoken out against the Germans, which had caused her family's arrest. When I heard her words, I realized how **useless** was all that I'd heard about Poles, how much **richness** it hid, like the **worthless shell** around an almond. I still do not know, or care, whether she cooks cabbage.

BEFORE YOU MOVE ON...

1. **Sequence** Three events take place here. Describe them in the order in which they happen.
2. **Cause and Effect** Why did Royce and the others run after the man who took the purse?
3. **Generalization** What did Amir learn after working in the garden with the Polish woman?

....

useless unimportant, of little value
richness goodness, value, worth
worthless shell shell that is good for nothing

STRANGERS CAN BE NEW FRIENDS

The gardeners celebrate the end of harvest. Amir's circle of friends grows and even includes a woman who was once angry at him.

In September Royce and a Mexican man collected many bricks from up the street and built a big **barbecue**. A bit later their friends began arriving. One brought a guitar, another played violin. They filled a folding table with food.

It was a <mark>harvest festival</mark>, like those in India, though no one had planned it to be. People brought food and drinks and drums. I went home to get my wife and son. Watermelons from the garden were **sliced open**. The gardeners proudly showed off what they'd grown. We <mark>traded</mark> harvests, as we often did. And we gave food away, as we often did also—even I, a businessman, **trained** to give away nothing, to always **make a profit**. The garden <mark>provided</mark> many <mark>excuses</mark> for breaking that **particular** rule.

The gardeners proudly showed off what they'd grown.

Many people spoke to me that day. Several asked where I was from. I wondered if they knew as little about Indians as I had known about Poles. One old woman, Italian I believe, said she'd admired my eggplants for weeks and told me how happy she was to meet me. Something bothered me. Then I remembered. A year before she'd claimed that she'd received **the wrong change** in my store. She'd gotten quite angry and called me—despite her own accent—a dirty foreigner. Now that we were so friendly with each other I **dared** to **remind her of this**. Her eyes became huge. She **apologized to me** over and over again. She kept saying, "Back then, I didn't know it was you. . . ."

---

barbecue outdoor fire used for cooking
sliced open cut open with a knife
trained taught
make a profit make more money than I spend
particular specific

the wrong change an incorrect amount of money given back after buying something
dared was brave enough
remind her of this cause her to remember it
apologized to me told me she was sorry

BEFORE YOU MOVE ON...

1. **Visualize** Imagine you are at the harvest festival. What do you hear? What are people doing? What foods do you see?

2. **Inference** How is the harvest festival an example of neighbors becoming a community?

3. **Cause and Effect** The Italian woman told Amir, "Back then, I didn't know it was you." Why did her opinion of Amir change?

ABOUT THE AUTHOR

Paul Fleischman is familiar with gardening—he grew up in a family of gardeners in Santa Monica, California. "Amir" is a chapter from *Seedfolks*, a book he wrote while spending a summer in North Carolina growing rows and rows of green beans. Paul Fleischman is a native of Monterey, California, and has written many award-winning novels, poems, short stories, and picture books, including *Joyful Noise: Poems for Two Voices*, winner of the Newbery Award.

Amir **123**

SUM IT UP

Sequence Events Read this list of events from "Amir."

- Someone dumped a load of tires in the garden.
- Men from the garden stopped a thief.
- Amir started working in the garden.
- Amir came to the United States.
- Royce and a friend built a barbecue.
- The Italian woman said she got the wrong change.

Pretend that Amir started gardening in 1982. Put the events in order on a time line.

Time Line

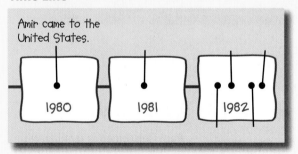

Analyze How Characters Change Look at the time line and think about the story. What changes does Amir experience? How do other characters change? Share your ideas with a group.

Make a Generalization How do you think the garden changed the way Amir looks at people? Do you think he sees strangers in the same way as before? Explain your answer.

THINK IT OVER

Discuss and Write Talk about these questions with a partner. Write the answers.

1. **Conclusions** Why is the garden important to Amir? What did he learn?

2. **Prediction** How might the community garden change in the next year?

3. **Character's Point of View** Imagine what other people in the community would say about the garden. What would Royce, the Polish woman, or the Italian woman say?

4. **Generalization** How could you get to know other people in your community?

EXPRESS YOURSELF

▶EXPRESS LIKES AND DISLIKES

Work with a partner. Tell what you liked about this selection. Tell what you didn't like. Explain why.

Language Arts and Literature

▶ GRAMMAR IN CONTEXT

USE INDEFINITE PRONOUNS

Learn About Indefinite Pronouns When you don't know the name of a specific person, place, or thing, use an **indefinite pronoun**.

Most indefinite pronouns are singular. Use them with a **singular verb**.

> **Everything** **looks** good to eat.
> **Someone** **picks** the beans every morning

A few indefinite pronouns are plural. Use them with a **plural verb**.

> **Several** of the tomatoes **are** ripe.
> **Many** of us **work** in the garden.

See Handbook page 440 for a list of more indefinite pronouns.

Practice Choose one word or phrase from each column. Use the words to make as many sentences as you can.

Indefinite Pronouns	Verbs	Phrases
Someone	is talking	green beans
Everything	can grow	very friendly
Anybody	is	tasty vegetables
Many	might be	ready to eat
Several	is cutting	about the garden

▶ LITERARY ANALYSIS
▶ WRITING/SPEAKING

WRITE A STORY

A story's **point of view** is the position or angle from which the story is told. In "Amir," the author tells the story from Amir's point of view, so we get to know Amir's thoughts and opinions. Retell the story using another character's point of view.

1 **Write Your Draft** Make sure to use the pronouns *I*, *me*, and *my* in your story.

2 **Edit Your Work** Did you give lots of details to make your story believable? Did you use the correct pronouns? Make sure you used capital letters for the names of people, countries, months, and days.

3 **Share Your Work in a Group** Read your story aloud. Ask your group to tell whose point of view you have described.

Sample Story

> Emily's Story
> I was scared when the man took my purse. Then Royce, Amir, and Marcus ran after the thief. They were so brave! Royce is the nicest teenager I know. I'm lucky to have such caring neighbors.

Develop your skills in the **writer's craft**.
See Handbook pages 414–423.

Respond to the Story, continued

Content Area Connections

TECHNOLOGY/MEDIA
SCIENCE

RESEARCH FOOD CHAINS

The plants and animals in the community garden are part of a **food chain**. A food chain is a kind of sequence in which each plant or animal is eaten by the one above it. Learn more about food chains, and report your findings in a multimedia presentation.

1 Gather Information and Take Notes

Research the answers to these questions:

- What do plants need to grow? Where do these things come from?

- Which animals eat plants, and which animals eat animals? Do any animals eat both?

- When plants and animals die, how are they still part of the food chain?

Choose an environment such as the desert, ocean, mountains, or your backyard! Research food chains in that environment. Use science books, encyclopedias, and the Internet. Take notes as you read. Make copies of helpful charts and illustrations.

2 Create a Model Draw a food chain, or use a drawing program on a computer. Make sure you show how living things in the food chain are all connected.

Sample Poster

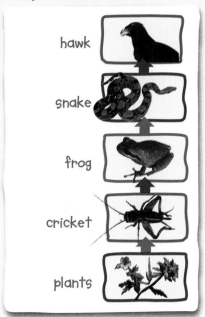

3 Prepare a Multimedia Presentation Here are some ways to present your food chain:

- Write a report and create graphics on the computer. You can create a class Web site to post your report.

- Make a diorama. Play recordings of animals and other sounds from nature.

- Draw a poster. Play a videotape of the plants and animals shown on the poster.

For more about the **research process**, see Handbook pages 394–399. For help with **multimedia presentations**, see pages 390–391.

Starting a Community GARDEN

how-to article
by DyAnne DiSalvo-Ryan

Prepare to Read

THINK ABOUT WHAT YOU KNOW

Idea Exchange In a group, talk about gardens you have grown or seen.

fee money paid to do something

imagine see something in your mind

information facts

interested caring

local close to where you live, work, or go to school

lot small piece of land

owner person to whom something belongs

permission approval to do something

steer direct, guide

LEARN KEY VOCABULARY

Use New Words in Context Study the new words and their definitions. Write these sentences. Replace each boldface word with a new word.

1. In my mind, I could **see** a beautiful garden.

2. My friends made a community garden on that **small piece of land**.

3. Mr. Gupta, **the man who owns the land,** gave his **approval**.

4. He said there would be no **money charged** for using the land.

5. The **neighborhood** newspaper printed **facts** about our garden.

6. Caring people in the community got involved.

7. I can **guide** you toward resources you will need to plant a garden.

LEARN TO SET A PURPOSE AND READING RATE

Sometimes you read to get information. Other times you read for entertainment. Your reason for reading is your **purpose**. Once you know your purpose, you can decide how fast to read.

> ### READING STRATEGY
> **How to Set a Purpose and Reading Rate**
> **1.** Preview the selection.
> **2.** Ask yourself: Will I read this selection to get information?
>   If so, you may want to read more slowly and take notes.
> **3.** Ask yourself: Will I read this selection for entertainment?
>   If so, you can probably read the selection faster.

Now preview "Starting a Community Garden." Will you read this selection quickly or slowly? Why?

Starting A Community GARDEN

a how-to article by DyAnne DiSalvo-Ryan

All across America people have joined together to turn ugly lots into beautiful gardens. You may not imagine that you can do it— but you can. If there is already a community garden in your neighborhood, ask your neighbors how they got started. If you are the first on your block to "make something happen," this is what you can do:

1. Find an **interested** grown-up who wants to help you: a parent or **guardian**, a teacher, a librarian, or a neighbor.

2. Find out the address of the **lot**. This is very important. You may have to talk to neighbors or look at the address of the buildings next door. Example: The lot I am interested in is on Main Street. It is between 75 and 81 Main Street.

3. While you are finding out the address of the lot, **get in touch with** the **local** gardening program in **your area**

....

guardian person who takes care of you
get in touch with call or write, contact
your area the place where you live

(see end of this note). Say that you are interested in starting a garden. Since every city is different, your local program will be able to **steer you in the right direction.**

4. Find out who the **owner** is. The Department of Records at your local **city hall** can help. Look in the telephone book for the address of city hall in your area.

5. If the lot is owned by the city, the people at city hall can help you get **permission** to use the lot. **Usually** there is a small **fee**. If the lot is owned by an individual person or group, you will need to get permission from that person or group to use the lot.

6. Once you get permission to use the lot, **it's yours to name!**

There are hundreds of gardening programs that are ready to help community gardeners with **information**, soil, seeds, **fencing**, and more.

To find out the community gardening program that is nearest you, write to:

American Community Gardening Association
100 N. 20th Street, 5th Floor
Philadelphia, PA 19103-1495
web address: www.communitygarden.org

Community gardens bring people together. Join the work and join the fun!

BEFORE YOU MOVE ON...

1. **Author's Purpose** What reason did the author have for writing this article?
2. **Viewing** What do the photographs add to the information you read?

---

steer you in the right direction tell you what you need to do to get started
city hall building where your city's government is located

Usually Most of the time
it's yours to name you get to decide what to call it
fencing materials for building a gate or a fence

Respond to the How-to Article
Check Your Understanding

SUM IT UP

Distinguish Between Important and Unimportant Information You and your friends have decided to start a community garden. You've found a good lot, and you have made this list to show the things you need to do.

List of Things to Do

> **How to Start a Community Garden**
>
> Find an interested grown-up who wants to help you.
>
> Make two entrances to the garden.
>
> Find out the address of the lot.
>
> Find out who the owner is.
>
> Name the garden.
>
> Buy gardening shoes and hats.

Which things on your list are important to getting your garden started? Make a T-chart. Work with a partner to compare charts. Do you agree on which information is important and which is not important?

Important Things	Unimportant Things
Find out who the owner is.	

THINK IT OVER

Discuss and Write Talk about these questions with a partner. Write the answers.

1. **Conclusions** What are some good reasons for starting a community garden?

2. **Judgments** What would you name a community garden? Why would you give it that name?

3. **Personal Experience** Have you ever been involved in a community project? What was the project about? Describe your role in it.

EXPRESS YOURSELF ▶ DESCRIBE

Work with a group. List different vegetables and flowers that grow in a garden. Take turns describing one of them. See if anyone in the group can guess what you are describing.

Language Arts and Content Area Connections

▶ REPRESENTING/SPEAKING
▶ TECHNOLOGY/MEDIA

GIVE A SPEECH ABOUT FOOD BANKS

Food banks give food to people who need it. With a group, use the Internet or other resources to prepare a speech about a food bank.

1 Find Information This Web site is a good place to start, but new sites appear every day! Use key words and look for links.

INTERNET

INFORMATION ON-LINE

Key Words:
"food bank"
"second harvest"

Web Site:
➤ **Information About Food Banks**
  • www.secondharvest.org

2 Choose Roles Some members can make posters and other visuals. Others can write the speech.

3 Give Your Speech Here are some tips:

• Say your name and tell your topic.

• Speak in a loud, clear voice. Look at your audience when you talk.

• At the end of the talk, ask if there are any questions. Thank the audience for listening.

For tips on giving a **speech**, see Handbook pages 401–402.

▶ SCIENCE
▶ SOCIAL STUDIES

COMPARE COUNTRY AND CITY GARDENS

Work in teams of four. Two members research city, or urban, gardens. The other two research country, or rural, gardens. Each set of partners makes a chart to show what they find out.

Answer questions like these:

• Where is a good place to start the garden?

• How big can the garden be?

• What grows best in this kind of garden? What combination of plants is possible?

• What kinds of insects or animals exist in this habitat? How do they affect the plants?

• Can pesticides be used? Why or why not?

• What steps must be taken to protect the plants?

• How does pollution affect the plants?

Compare the charts and define the three most important considerations in planting a garden in each place.

Learn about **charts** on Handbook pages 370–371.

Writing for Personal Expression

Expressive writing tells a writer's personal feelings about a subject. Some expressive writing, like a journal or diary entry, is private. Poems and memoirs are published to share with everyone.

PROFESSIONAL WRITING MODELS

In "The Keeping Quilt," Patricia Polacco expresses her feelings about a special family quilt that has been passed down for many generations. Notice that she uses the first person because she is part of the story.

from **"The Keeping Quilt"**

> When my grandma Carle was born, Anna wrapped her daughter in the quilt to welcome her warmly into the world. . . .
>
> The quilt welcomed me, Patricia, into the world, and it was the tablecloth for my first birthday party.
>
> At night I would trace my fingers around the edges of each animal on the quilt before I went to sleep. . . .

AN EXPRESSIVE PERSONAL HISTORY

When writers express their feelings in a personal history, they may write about events that take place over a long period of time. To help readers follow the order of events, the writer uses words that signal sequence, such as *after, then, many years later, when,* and *now.* Discuss the sequence of events in "The Keeping Quilt."

A Time Line of Personal History

Anna and her mother make a quilt to remind them of Russia.

Grandma Carle uses the quilt at her wedding and when her daughter Mary Ellen is born.

Patricia uses the quilt at her wedding and when her daughter Traci Denise is born.

Traci Denise will get the quilt next.

Great-Gramma Anna uses the quilt at her wedding and when her daughter Carle is born.

Mary Ellen uses the quilt at her wedding and when her daughter Patricia is born.

STUDENT WRITING MODEL

Personal History

The Two Worlds of Imara

by Imara Guerrero

I am sitting in my room in my house in America with a photo album on my lap. I look out the window at a bright full moon shining down on silvery snow. This is the world I live in now. But at this moment, I am dreaming about my first world—Nicaragua.

I grew up in a town called José Dolores, in a big house with six rooms and a garden. I lived there with my parents and my grandmother Socorro. All around us was family.

When I was five, my parents left our home and came to the U.S.A. I stayed in Nicaragua with my grandmother. I missed my mother and father so much. I didn't understand why they had left me behind. Now I know they were working hard to send back money and gifts for me and other family members.

Two years later, I came to the U.S.A., too. I was sad to leave my friends and family, especially my grandmother and my cousin María. But I was very happy to be with my parents again in an exciting new land—at first.

Then came my first day at school. I had no friends. I had a hard time understanding what the teacher said and what I was supposed to do. That night, I cried.

As time passed, things got better. I made new friends. I learned to be comfortable with English. I learned to eat new foods, like pizza, and to listen to new music, like Britney Spears. But I still enjoy things from my first world. I often ask my mother to make *gallopinto* and *maduro frito*, my favorite Nicaraguan foods. I listen to Selena sing in Spanish. She is still my favorite singer.

So here I am in my second world, sitting in a room in a house in America. My name is Imara, and I love both my worlds.

Imara tells about her own experiences and feelings. She speaks directly to the reader, using **first-person point of view.**

Time order words help the reader follow the sequence of events.

Past tense verbs show which actions happened earlier. **Present tense verbs** show what Imara does today.

Writing for Personal Expression, continued

The Writing Process

> **WRITING PROMPT**
>
> Write a personal history to tell an elementary school class about your experiences. Be sure to express your feelings.

PREWRITE

① **Brainstorm Ideas** Get together with a partner, and discuss some things you might include in your personal history. As you talk, take notes in a chart.

People, Places, and Events	Why They Are Important	My Feelings
Ajay, my friend in India	We liked the same things. We played sports and helped each other.	He was my best friend. I miss him the most of all my friends.
New Delhi, India	My first home. I lived there until I was nine.	I miss my family there. I miss playing cricket. I don't miss the noisy, crowded city.
going to a professional cricket match	It was a special trip with my mom and dad.	I miss going to games with Mom and Dad. I also miss watching and playing cricket. No one in the U.S. even knows how to play the game!

FATP Chart

HOW TO UNLOCK A PROMPT
Form: *personal history*
Audience: *3rd grade class*
Topic: *things I used to do in India and things I do now in the U.S.*
Purpose: *to tell about my experiences and how I feel about them*

② **Unlock the Writing Prompt** Before you begin your personal history, fill out an **FATP** chart to help guide your writing.

③ **Organize Your Ideas** The way you organize your ideas depends on what you plan to write about. Here are some possibilities:
- Use a time line to list important events in your life.
- Use a chart to compare your life in the U.S. with your life in the country you came from.
- Make a list of things you liked as you were growing up.

See pages 370–375 of the Handbook for more graphic organizers.

Reflect and Evaluate

- How did listening to your partner's ideas help you form your ideas?
- Have you listed enough information?
- Are your dates, place names, and people's names correct? Check with a family member.

DRAFT

Use your **FATP** chart to help you focus your writing. Write quickly to capture your ideas. Don't worry about making mistakes. If you think of new ideas and details, add those to your draft.

1 **Write the Beginning** In your first paragraph, introduce yourself. Write in the first person, using the pronouns *I, my, me, we, our,* and *us*.

2 **Tell About Your Life** Come up with a topic for each paragraph. State your topic in a topic sentence. Then give the details.

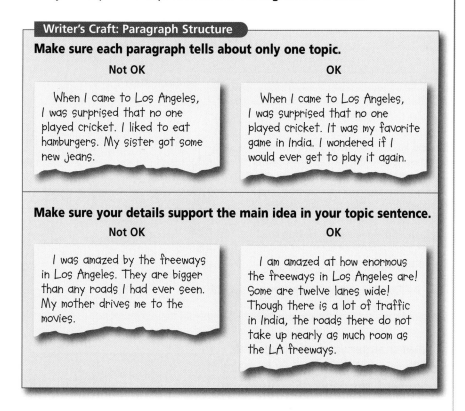

Writer's Craft: Paragraph Structure

Make sure each paragraph tells about only one topic.

Not OK

> When I came to Los Angeles, I was surprised that no one played cricket. I liked to eat hamburgers. My sister got some new jeans.

OK

> When I came to Los Angeles, I was surprised that no one played cricket. It was my favorite game in India. I wondered if I would ever get to play it again.

Make sure your details support the main idea in your topic sentence.

Not OK

> I was amazed by the freeways in Los Angeles. They are bigger than any roads I had ever seen. My mother drives me to the movies.

OK

> I am amazed at how enormous the freeways in Los Angeles are! Some are twelve lanes wide! Though there is a lot of traffic in India, the roads there do not take up nearly as much room as the LA freeways.

3 **Write an Ending** As you finish your personal history, leave your reader with a final thought to sum up your experiences. Express your feelings about them.

Reflect and Evaluate

- Read through your draft. Does it let your reader know how you feel about your experiences?

- Are your paragraphs well-organized, with topic sentences and supporting details?

Writing for Personal Expression, continued

REVISE

1 **Reread Your Draft** Review your **FATP**. Is your form, audience, topic, and purpose clear? Did you express your feelings?

2 **Conduct a Peer Conference** Share your writing with a partner or group. Did you use first person throughout your writing? Did you use correct verb tenses? The guidelines on Handbook page 411 can help you conduct peer conferences.

Look at the questions a partner asked Babu during a Peer Conference. Read what he thinks about the changes he will make.

Key In TO **Technology**

During your peer conference, insert notes, questions, or comments in another color to make them easy to see.

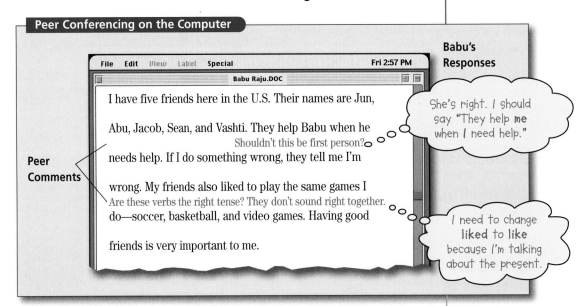

Peer Conferencing on the Computer

File Edit View Label Special   Fri 2:57 PM

Babu Raju.DOC

I have five friends here in the U.S. Their names are Jun,

Abu, Jacob, Sean, and Vashti. They help Babu when he
Shouldn't this be first person?
needs help. If I do something wrong, they tell me I'm

wrong. My friends also liked to play the same games I
Are these verbs the right tense? They don't sound right together.
do—soccer, basketball, and video games. Having good

friends is very important to me.

Peer Comments

Babu's Responses

She's right. I should say "They help me when I need help."

I need to change liked to like because I'm talking about the present.

3 **Mark Your Changes** Decide what changes you will make. See Handbook page 411 for a list of Revising Marks. For how to make changes in a word-processed document, see pages 386–387 in the Handbook.

Reflect and Evaluate

- Did your peers like what you wrote? What did they suggest you change?
- Did you find that you had to do a lot of rewriting?
- Did you include all the thoughts and feelings you wanted to?

> GRAMMAR IN CONTEXT

VERB TENSES

The tense of a verb shows when an action happens.

I play cricket
with my friend.

- Use the **present tense** to talk about something that is happening now or that happens all the time.

    Examples: I **live** in the U.S.A.

    I **walk** to school every day.

- Use the **past tense** to talk about something that happened earlier, or in the past. Past tense verbs are often formed by adding **-ed**.

    Examples: I **lived** in New Delhi, India, before.

    My best friend and I **played** sports together.

    Some verbs have special forms to show past tense.

    Examples: We **went** to cricket games together, too.

    We **knew** the name of every cricket player.

- Use the **future tense** to talk about something that will happen later, or in the future.

    Examples: I **will visit** India this summer.

    We **are going to stay** with my grandparents.

Irregular Verbs

Present	Past
are	were
bring	brought
go	went
is	was
know	knew
say	said
send	sent

Practice Write each sentence and add the correct form of the verb in parentheses.

1. When I was in India, I _____ to play cricket. (like)

2. I also _____ soccer. (play)

3. Now that I am in America, I _____ to be a basketball star. (want)

4. Today I _____ to practice my foul shots. (need)

5. Next summer, I _____ to basketball camp. (go)

6. At basketball camp, I _____ my cousin Manjeet. (see)

7. He _____ me an e-mail with information about the camp. (send)

8. In the message, Manjeet _____ he practices every day, too. (say)

Writing for Personal Expression, continued

EDIT AND PROOFREAD

1 **Check for Mistakes** Look through your writing and correct any mistakes in capitalization, punctuation, and spelling. If you need help, see Handbook pages 459–469.

2 **Check Your Verbs** Check to see that you used the correct verb tense.

3 **Make a Final Copy** Copy your personal history, making all the corrections you need to make. If you are working on a computer, make your final edits and print out a clean copy.

PUBLISH

Use one of these ideas for publishing your writing, or come up with an idea of your own.

- If you are using a computer, scan in photos from your family photo album. Import them into your personal history. Be sure to include a caption for each picture. The caption should identify who, what, and where.

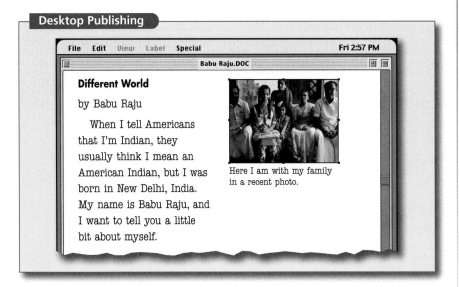

Desktop Publishing

| File | Edit | View | Label | Special | | Fri 2:57 PM |

Babu Raju.DOC

Different World

by Babu Raju

When I tell Americans that I'm Indian, they usually think I mean an American Indian, but I was born in New Delhi, India. My name is Babu Raju, and I want to tell you a little bit about myself.

Here I am with my family in a recent photo.

- Make a copy of your personal history to send to a friend or relative who lives in your native country.

I will go everywhere and see everything. I will meet all the people I can. I will think all the thoughts, feel all the emotions I am able, and I will write, write, write . . .

— Thomas Wolfe

Reflect and Evaluate

- Do you feel you did a good job "expressing yourself"? Does your personal history
  - ☑ have well-organized paragraphs with topic sentences?
  - ☑ tell important events in your life in a sequence that is easy to follow?
  - ☑ express your feelings?
- What did you learn about yourself from writing your personal history?
- Will this work go in your portfolio? Why or why not?

 A Sense of Place

▶ 1 Look Back at the Unit

Make a Word Quilt In this unit you read these selections about belonging.

The Keeping Quilt

Beyond the Color Lines

Teammates

Amir

Work with a group. Choose a quote from each selection that tells about belonging. Write each one on a square of colored paper. Then read your quotes to the class. Connect the squares to make a word quilt. Talk about how the quotes work together to make a statement about belonging.

▶ 2 Show What You Know

Sum It All Up Expand and organize your ideas on this mind map. Share your ideas about belonging with a partner.

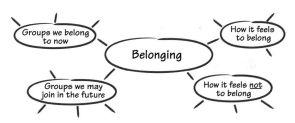

Reflect and Evaluate Write a sentence about a place where you feel like you belong. Then tell why you belong there. Add this writing to your portfolio, along with work from the unit that shows what you learned.

▶ 3 Make Connections

To Your School Think of ways to help new students feel a sense of belonging. Make care packages that include maps of your school, lists of teachers, and school activities. Offer your help as a tour guide or translator for new students.

Another Place, Another Time, Chris Van Allsburg, pencil. Copyright © 1996.

FOLLOW YOUR DREAMS

Imagine that what matters most to you is locked up in the castle in this picture. You must get to the castle and unlock it. Work with a partner to create a map of your journey. Include problems along the way. What decisions must you make to get beyond them? What does it take to reach your dreams?

THEME **1**

What Matters Most

Knowing what is important in life can help you reach your dreams and achieve your goals.

THEME **2**

Toward a Better Future

Courage and determination can help build a better future.

Family Group, Henry Moore, bronze. Copyright © 1948–49.

What Matters Most

- How do life's experiences help us find out what matters most?

- How do other people influence what we think is important?

- How do you think people's dreams affect their decisions?

THEME-RELATED BOOKS

The Lotus Seed
by Sherry Garland

A lotus seed that travels from Vietnam to America helps a family remember its heritage.

Mandela
by Floyd Cooper

The story of Nelson Mandela, who has spent his life making a better future for South Africa.

NOVEL

Going Home
by Nicholasa Mohr

While on vacation in Puerto Rico, Felita realizes that what matters most is family and friends.

Build Language and Vocabulary

TELL A STORY

Listen to this tale from Vietnam about a rooster who learns what matters most to him.

The Rooster and the Jewel
A VIETNAMESE TALE

MAKE A STORY MAP

Work with a group to plan a story about something that matters most to you. Choose the object or event. Then fill out a story map to name the characters, tell the setting, and outline the events in the plot.

Characters	Setting

Beginning

Middle

Ending

BUILD YOUR VOCABULARY

Descriptive Words Think of words you will use to describe the story's characters and setting. Collect them in the charts.

Character	What is the character like?	What does the character do?	How, when, and where does the character do things?
Yolanda	young smart	She skates. She seems to fly.	quickly before dark through the park

Setting	What can you see?	What can you hear?	What can you smell?	What can you taste?	What can you touch?
an afternoon in a park	trees lake	birds traffic	smoke food cooking	hamburger	earth grass

USE LANGUAGE STRUCTURES

▶ ADJECTIVES, ADVERBS, AND PREPOSITIONAL PHRASES

Speaking: Tell a Story Use your story map and the descriptive words in your charts to tell your story. Divide the story into parts so that each member of your group will have a part to tell.

Example:

Yolanda **quickly** gathered her skates and went **to the park**. She wanted to skate all **around the lake before dark**. She seemed to fly **through the park**, but then made a **sudden** stop. There **in the trees** she saw flames and smelled smoke. . . .

Ginger for the Heart

historical fiction
by Paul Yee

Prepare to Read

THINK ABOUT WHAT YOU KNOW

Discuss Dreams and Goals Talk about how a person's dreams and goals show what matters to that person.

craftsmanship skill or ability to do special work

debt money that is owed to another person

epidemic sickness or disease that affects most of the people in a place

garment piece of clothing

ginger root part of ginger, a spice plant, that grows underground

gold field place where gold is found

merchant person who sells things to make money

miner worker who digs in the earth for minerals

tailor person who makes and mends clothes to earn money

tower tall and narrow structure or building

LEARN KEY VOCABULARY

Use New Words in Context Study the new words and their definitions. Then write the paragraph, adding the missing words.

In 1849, gold fever spread like an ____(1)____ around the world. Chinese immigrants and many others rushed to California. They worked as ____(2)____ in the gold fields. Some of them had to repay huge ____(3)____ when they arrived. In their dreams, they saw gold coins stacked as high as a ____(4)____. Some of the new immigrants did not become miners, however. ____(5)____ opened stores and sold goods. Tailors used their ____(6)____ to sew ____(7)____.

LEARN TO RELATE GOALS AND OUTCOMES

In a story, a **goal** is what a person wants to do. The **outcome** tells if the person reaches the goal. When you know the goals and outcomes of a story, you understand the main events of the plot.

READING STRATEGY
How to Relate Goals and Outcomes
1. Look for what the people want to do.
2. Pay attention to the actions they take to reach their goals.
3. Predict the outcome. Then see if the outcome at the end of the story matches your prediction.

As you read "Ginger for the Heart," take notes on the characters' goals, their actions, and the final outcome of the story.

Ginger for the Heart

by Paul Yee

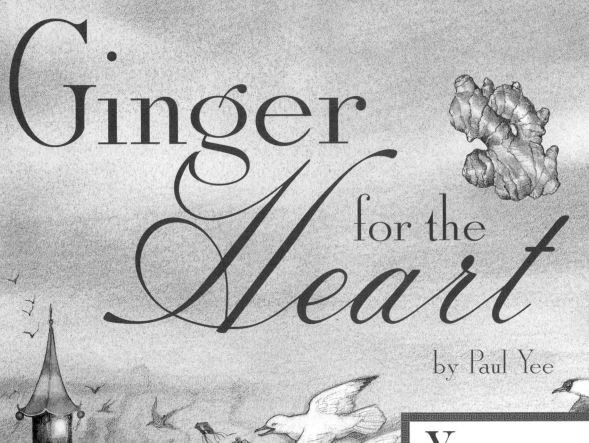

Yenna and a young man fall in love. Before he leaves on a journey, she gives him a ginger root to remind him of her. When he returns four years later, they are both amazed that the ginger has remained firm and fragrant—a symbol of their love and devotion. They learn that what means the most to them is always being together.

YENNA FALLS IN LOVE

Yenna meets a young man in the store where she works, and he visits her often.
They fall in love, but he must leave for the gold fields so he can earn money.

The buildings of **Chinatown** are **stoutly constructed** brick. While some are **broad** and others thin, they rise no higher than four solid **stories**.

Only one building stands above the rest. Its **tower** **is visible** even from the harbor, because the cone-shaped roof is made of copper.

In the early days, Chang the **merchant tailor** owned this building. He used the main floor for his store and rented out the others. But he kept the tower room for his own use, for the sun filled it with light. This was the room where his wife and daughter worked.

His daughter's name was Yenna, and her beauty was **beyond compare**. She had ivory skin, sparkling eyes, and her hair hung long and silken, shining like **polished ebony**. All day long she and her mother sat by the tower window and sewed with silver needles and **silken** threads. They sang songs while they worked, and their voices **rose in wondrous harmonies**.

In all Chinatown, the **craftsmanship** of Yenna and her mother was considered the finest. Buttonholes never stretched out of shape, and **seams** were **all but invisible**.

One day, a young man came into the store **laden with** **garments** for **mending**. His shoulders were broad and strong, yet his eyes were soft and caring. Many times he came, and many times he saw Yenna. For hours he would sit and watch her work. They fell deeply in love, though few words

Chinatown the part of town where Chinese people live and work

stoutly constructed well built

broad wide

stories floors in a building

is visible can be seen

beyond compare greater than any other's

polished ebony very smooth dark wood

silken smooth, very fine

rose in wondrous harmonies sang beautiful, enjoyable music

seams the parts of clothing where two pieces of cloth are sewn together

all but invisible very hard to see

laden with carrying a lot of

mending sewing, patching up, or restoring

were spoken between them.

Spring came and boats bound for the northern **gold fields** began to sail again. It was time for the young man to go. He had borrowed money to pay his way over to the New World, and now he had to repay his **debts**. Onto his back he threw his blankets and tools, food and warm jackets. Then he set off with **miners** from around the world, clutching **gold pans** and shovels.

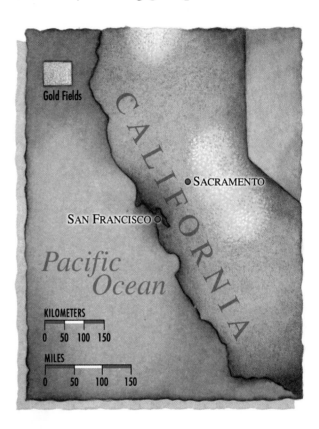

gold pans metal dishes used to separate gold from water, gravel, and dirt

BEFORE YOU MOVE ON...

1. **Details** What special skills and qualities did Yenna have?
2. **Inference** Did Yenna and her mother enjoy working together? How do you know?
3. **Cause and Effect** Why did the young man have to go to the gold fields?

THE GINGER ROOT

Yenna gives the young man a ginger root as a goodbye gift. He promises to come back. For four years she works hard and waits patiently for his return.

Yenna had little to give him **in farewell**. All she found in the kitchen was a **ginger root** as large as her hand. As she stroked its brown **knobs** and bumpy eyes, she whispered to him, "This will warm you in the cold weather. I will wait for you, but, like this piece of ginger, I, too, will age and grow dry." Then she pressed her lips to the ginger, and turned away.

"I will come back," the young man said. "The fire burning for you in my heart can never be **extinguished**."

Thereafter, Yenna lit a lamp at every nightfall and set it in the tower window. Rains **lashed against** the glass, snow piled low along the ledge, and ocean winds rattled the frame. But the flame did not **waver**, even though the young man never sent letters. Yenna did not weep uselessly, but continued to sew and sing with her mother.

---

in farewell to say goodbye, as a goodbye gift
knobs bumps, hard lumps
extinguished put out

lashed against hit hard on
waver seem to go out, flicker

There were few unmarried women in Chinatown, and many men came to seek Yenna's hand in marriage. Rich gold miners and sons of successful merchants bowed before her, but she always looked away. They gave her grand gifts, but still she shook her head, until **finally** the men grew weary and called her crazy. In China, parents arranged all marriages, and daughters became the property of their husbands. But Chang the merchant tailor **treasured** his daughter's happiness and let her be.

One winter, an **epidemic ravaged** the city. When it was over, Chang had lost his wife and his **eyesight**. Yenna led him up to the tower where he could feel the sun and drifting clouds move across his face. She began to sew again, and while she sewed, she sang for her father. The lamp continued to burn **steadily** at the tower window as she worked. With twice the amount of work to do, she labored long after **dusk**. She fed the flame more oil and sent her needle **skimming** through the heavy **fabrics**. **Nimbly** her fingers **braided shiny cords** and **coiled** them into **butterfly buttons**. And when the **wick sputtered** into light each evening, Yenna's heart soared **momentarily** into her love's memories.

Nights passed into weeks, months turned into years, and four years quickly flew by.

Nights passed into weeks, months turned into years...

BEFORE YOU MOVE ON...

1. **Character's Motive** Why did Yenna give the young man the ginger root?
2. **Character** How did Yenna and her father show how much they cared for each other?
3. **Comparison** How were the burning lamp and Yenna's love for the young man similar?

---

finally at last
treasured valued, cared a lot about
ravaged destroyed, did great damage to
eyesight ability to see
steadily all the time
dusk the time between sunset and night
skimming moving quickly
fabrics cloth

Nimbly Easily and quickly
braided shiny cords wove or wrapped together three or more bright strings
coiled twisted and turned
butterfly buttons buttons made with twisted string
wick sputtered flame on the candle began to burn
momentarily for a very short time

The young man asks Yenna to marry him, but she can't leave her father.
The still-fresh ginger is a sign that they should stay together.

One day a dusty traveler came into the store and flung a bundle of **ragged** clothes onto the counter. Yenna shook out the first shirt, and out rolled a ginger root. Taking it into her hand, she saw that pieces had been nibbled off, but the core of the root was still firm and **fragrant**.

She looked up. There stood the man she had promised to wait for. His eyes appeared older and wiser.

"Your gift saved my life several times," he said. "The fire of the ginger is powerful indeed."

"Why is the ginger root still firm and heavy?" she wondered. "Should it not have dried and **withered**?"

"I kept it close to my heart and my sweat **coated** it. In lonely moments, my tears soaked it." His **calloused** hands

"Your gift saved my life several times."

reached out for her. "Your face has not changed."

"Nor has my heart," she replied. "I have kept a lamp burning all these years."

"So I have heard," he smiled. "Will you come away with me now? It has taken many years to gather enough gold to buy a farm. I have built you a house on my land."

For the first time since his departure, tears **cascaded** down Yenna's face. She shook her head. "I cannot leave. My father needs me."

"Please come with me," the young man pleaded. "You will be very happy, I promise."

Yenna swept the **wetness** from her cheeks. "Stay with me and work this store instead," she **implored**.

ragged torn and ripped
fragrant had a strong, pleasant smell
withered lost its firm shape
coated covered

calloused rough, hard
cascaded fell, poured
wetness tears
implored begged

The young man stiffened and stated proudly, "A man does not live in his wife's house." And the eyes that she remembered so well gleamed with determination.

"But this is a new land," she cried. "Must we forever follow the old ways?"

She reached out for him, but he brushed her away and **hurled** the ginger root into the fireplace. As the flames leapt up, Yenna's eyes **blurred**. The young man **clenched and unclenched** his fists in anger. They stood like stone.

At last the man turned to leave, but suddenly he knelt at the fireplace. Yenna saw him reach in with the tongs and pull something out of the flames.

"Look!" he whispered in amazement. "The ginger refuses to be burnt! The flames cannot touch it!"

....

hurled angrily threw
blurred could not see clearly
clenched and unclenched tightened and let go

Yenna looked and saw black burn marks charring the root, but when she took it in her hand, she found it still firm and moist. She held it to her nose, and found the **fragrant sharpness** still there.

The couple embraced and vowed to stay together. They were married at a **lavish banquet** attended by all of Chinatown. There, the father passed his fingers over his son-in-law's face and nodded in satisfaction.

Shortly after, the merchant Chang died, and the young couple moved away. Yenna

sold the business and locked up the tower room. But on nights when boats pull in from far away, they say a **flicker** of light can still be seen in that high window. And Chinese women are reminded that ginger is one of their best friends.

BEFORE YOU MOVE ON...

1. **Opinion** Was it fair for the young man to ask Yenna to leave her father? Explain your answer.
2. **Character's Motive** Why did Yenna refuse to leave her father?
3. **Summary** Tell how the story ends.

ABOUT THE AUTHOR

Paul Yee grew up in Chinatown in Vancouver, British Columbia, Canada, where he felt "caught between two worlds." His stories are a mix of history and his imagination. The Chinese folk tales he heard as a child blend with his true accounts of Chinese immigrants' contributions to settling North America. Yee says that in his writing, he looks ahead with hope. His motto is "From the past, for the future."

---

fragrant sharpness strong smell

lavish banquet large meal served to entertain and celebrate a special event

flicker small or faint glow

Respond to the Story
Check Your Understanding

SUM IT UP

Relate Goals and Outcomes in a Retelling
Complete a Goal-and-Outcome Chart like this one and use it to retell the story to a partner.

Character	Goal	Actions	Outcome
Yenna			
the young man			

Generate Ideas Discuss actions the characters could have taken. How might these new actions change the outcome of the story? Choose your best idea, think of a new story ending, and share it with the class.

THINK IT OVER

Discuss and Write Talk about these questions with a partner. Write the answers.

1. **Summary** Tell what matters most to Yenna. How do you know? Is it the same for the young man? Use details from the story to support your answer.

2. **Conclusions** Why do you think this story is called "Ginger for the Heart"? What would be another good title?

3. **Opinion** Do you think Yenna and the young man will have a long and happy marriage? Identify details in the story that support your opinion.

4. **Judgment** Yenna had to wait four years for the young man to return. What things do you think are worth waiting for?

EXPRESS YOURSELF ▶ AGREE OR DISAGREE

As a class, act out part of the story in which two characters disagree and later agree on something. Take turns with different actors playing the scene. You might also choose different scenes for different pairs of actors. If possible, bring some ginger root and other props to include in your dramatizations.

Respond to the Story, continued
Language Arts and Literature

USE ADJECTIVES

Learn About Adjectives An **adjective** is a word that describes, or tells about, a noun.

Adjectives can tell how many or how much.

> Yenna waited **four** years.
> Yenna had **little** interest in marrying.

Adjectives can tell which one.

> Yenna shook out the **first** shirt.

Adjectives can tell what something is like.

> The ginger was **fragrant** and **moist**.
> The **young** man asked Yenna to marry him.

Proper adjectives come from proper nouns. They begin with a capital letter.

> Chang was from China. He was **Chinese**.

Add Adjectives Expand these sentences with adjectives.

1. Yenna sewed with _____ needles and _____ thread.
2. The _____ man held the _____ ginger in his _____ hand.

Practice Write this paragraph. Add an adjective in each blank.

> The _____ streets of Chinatown are interesting to see. There are _____ buildings. Some have _____ walls and _____ windows. One building has a _____ tower with a _____ roof.

WRITE AN OUTCOME

Think of the new endings to the story you discussed with your group in the Sum It Up activity on page 155. How would the characters' actions change in order to cause a new outcome? Would their goals also change? Make a chart to organize your ideas. Then write the new outcome.

1. **Complete a Chart** Fill in a new Goal-and-Outcome Chart like the one you made on page 155.

2. **Write a Draft** Write the main events of the beginning, middle, and end of the new story. Include dialogue that shows what the characters' goals are.

3. **Edit Your Work** Add, change, or take out text to make your story more interesting. Do the characters have believable goals? What is the final outcome? Finally, check for correct spelling, punctuation, and grammar.

4. **Read and Discuss** Read your work in a group. Discuss the goals and actions that caused the new outcomes.

 For more about the **writing process**, see Handbook pages 408–413.

Content Area Connections

RESEARCH THE GOLD RUSH

Learn About the Gold Rush A gold rush is the sudden movement of people to a place where gold has been discovered. Chinese immigrants were among those who came to California in the 1800s in search of gold. Create a class bulletin board display about this event in U.S. history.

Write Questions What would you like to know about the California gold rush? Write questions such as:

- Where did people come from?
- How long did the gold rush last?
- How did the gold rush change California?

Display Answers Work in groups. Use reference books and the Internet to find answers to your questions. Make a poster with the information you find. Include art and photos. Then display your poster.

Prospectors panned for gold in rivers and streams.

COMPARE TRAVEL RATES

In the 1800s, many Chinese immigrants came from Hong Kong to San Francisco by boat. Today you can travel between the two cities by plane. With a partner, calculate the rates of travel.

1 **Set Up a Data Grid** In 1851, the *Solida* reached San Francisco from Hong Kong, a distance of over 6,955 miles. The trip took 48 days or about 1,152 hours.

Contact an airline and ask how long a flight from Hong Kong to San Francisco takes. Ask the distance (miles or kilometers) of the flight. Use this information to make a data grid.

Means of Travel	Distance	Time	Rate
Boat— 1851			
Plane— today			

2 **Calculate the Rate of Travel** To get the rates, divide the distance by the time. Add the rates to your chart.

$$\frac{500 \text{ miles}}{5 \text{ hours}} = 100 \text{ miles per hour}$$

3 **Make Comparisons** Share your charts with another pair. How many times longer did it take to travel in the 1800s than it does today? What other conclusions can you reach?

Ginger for the Heart **157**

TWINS

article
by Debra and Lisa Ganz,
with Alex Tresniowski

Prepare to Read

THINK ABOUT WHAT YOU KNOW

Pantomime Take turns drawing an index card with the names of different activities on it. Act out each word. Discuss how people communicate without speaking.

advanced up-to-date, the most recent

condition health or physical state

confident feeling sure of yourself, believing in yourself

determined have one's mind set on doing something

excel do something extremely well and better than others

extraordinary very unusual, special

hearing-impaired unable to hear or hear well

independent able to do things alone or without help

opportunity chance to do something

secure safe, without worry or fear

LEARN KEY VOCABULARY

Use New Words in Context Study the new words and their definitions. Choose two words that go together, and write them in the same sentence.

Sample Sentence

> There are many advanced technologies to help hearing-impaired people.

LEARN TO PARAPHRASE

When you **paraphrase** something, you repeat it in your own words. Use this strategy to help you understand difficult words or phrases.

> **READING STRATEGY**
> **How to Paraphrase**
> 1. As you read, think about what the words and phrases mean.
> 2. Use your own words to tell what you just read.

As you read "Twins," stop and paraphrase each section of the article.

T W I N S

by Debra and Lisa Ganz, with Alex Tresniowski

What matters most to twins Neshmayda and Suzette is staying close to each other. Born deaf, they helped each other learn sign language to communicate. They went to school and played sports together. Now that they are both married and will soon live in different cities, their goal is to maintain their extraordinary closeness.

The twins' parents discover that Suzy and Neshy are deaf. They all learn sign language so everyone in the family can communicate with each other.

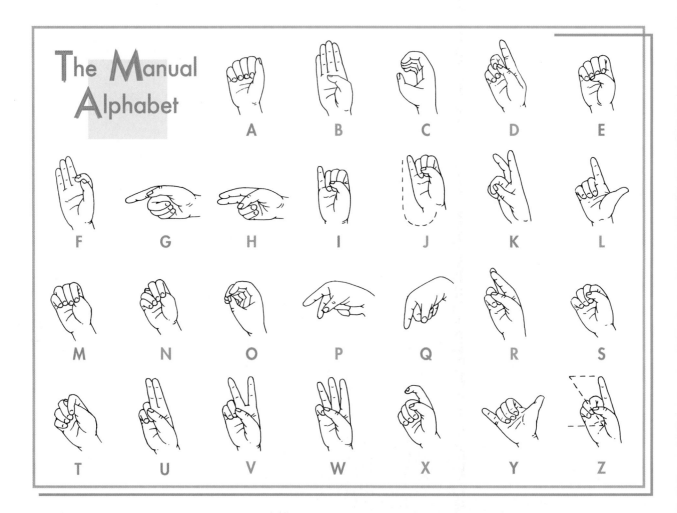

The Manual Alphabet

A B C D E
F G H I J K L
M N O P Q R S
T U V W X Y Z

Early on they knew they were different from other children, because they were the only ones who shared a face. "They loved that about themselves," says Maria Aguayo, mother of Neshmayda and Suzette. "They had a way of communicating that no one else understood. One of them would point at something or make some noise and the other would go and get what she wanted." Two kids **cavorting through** a happy world of their own, experiencing life's surprises as one—in other words, twins.

But Suzy and Neshy were different for a much greater reason—they were born **deaf**.

---

cavorting through having fun in

deaf without the ability to hear

"We did not know it for their first two-and-a-half years," says Maria, who **contracted** German measles during her first **trimester**. The technology in her native Puerto Rico was not as **advanced** as it is today, so her twins' deafness was not **diagnosed** until they were nearly three. "And when we first discovered they were deaf, I did not want to believe it. It was a mother's denial."

Maria soon accepted her daughters' **condition**, and as soon as she and her husband, Joaquin, heard about the Gallaudet school for the deaf in Washington, D.C., they moved their family and enrolled the twins,

then five years old. "We all learned **sign language** so we could communicate with the girls," says Maria. "We started to talk about all the things that had happened to them in their first five years. I learned all these things that I had not known. For instance, Suzette had once been with her grandmother and **wound up** in the emergency room **getting stitches**. Her grandmother didn't know how she got hurt. Suzy later told me that she had fallen, that she was scared, that she wanted me there with her in the hospital **so badly**. When I discovered these things, I cried and cried."

Suzette (left) and Neshmayda (right) at age six. The twins are wearing hearing aids strapped to their chests as they enjoy a day at Baltimore's Inner Harbor.

BEFORE YOU MOVE ON...

1. **Inference** What do you think helped the twins form their own way of communicating?
2. **Cause and Effect** What caused the twins' deafness, and why did it take so long to diagnose?
3. **Prediction** Do you think the twins will remain close as they grow up? Why or why not?

---

contracted got, caught
trimester three months of being pregnant
diagnosed discovered by doctors
sign language a way to communicate with our hands

wound up in the end was
getting stitches having her cut or wound closed by sewing
so badly so much

The twins are never lonely because they have each other. They learn
to play sports and to mix in with other children.

The twins helped each other learn signs—more and more signs—**ecstatic** at the **opportunity** to explore each other's feelings in a new way. "Being deaf twins is a very special thing," explains Neshy. "A deaf child in a hearing world can feel very lonely and **secluded**, but we never experienced that. We were always together, never alone. We learned from each other every day, and we still do."

Their parents **exposed them to** hearing children from a very early age, **determined** to **foster their self-sufficiency**. "We would take them to soccer practice, and they would stay behind a little, not daring to go on the field," remembers Maria. "They put up this wall between them and the rest of the world. But after a while they would feel more comfortable. They might get a ball and start kicking it between them, and then before we knew it they were mixing in with the other children."

The twins **excelled** at a number of sports, particularly soccer, and together they helped **establish** a women's varsity team at Gallaudet. They tried waterskiing, they hit the mountain slopes, they talked about one day diving from a plane. "They feel that they can do anything that they want to do, **except** hear," says their mother. "They are very **secure** and **confident** about who they are, and that has come from them being two."

Suzette, age 14, uses a TDD (Telecommunication Device for the Deaf) to talk with a friend. Messages sent and received appear on the screen below the receiver.

BEFORE YOU MOVE ON...

1. **Opinion** Do you think that being deaf helped the twins become closer to each other? Explain.

2. **Evidence and Conclusion** How did playing sports help the twins become secure and confident?

---

ecstatic very happy

secluded cut off from others

exposed them to kept them around, brought them into contact with

foster their self-sufficiency encourage their ability to take care of themselves

establish start

except but not

CLOSER THAN EVER

Even as they prepare to live apart for the first time, the twins know
they will always maintain their special closeness.

It is a closeness that will be tested now that the twins are facing their first **separation**. Suzy and Neshy—who both **earned master's degrees** in social work— were also both recently married, Suzy to a **hearing-impaired** teacher, and Neshy to a deaf legal assistant. Suzy and her husband will live in Wisconsin, while Neshy plans to stay behind in Washington, D.C. "Of course, we'll miss each other terribly," says Neshy. "When one of us is not present, we feel half empty, so it's going to be really difficult." For the last few months, "they have been **preparing themselves** for the separation," says Maria. "To even start talking about it was **extremely** painful, but they have been getting ready."

Not long ago, when Suzy spent a few weeks in Wisconsin, the twins got a chance to see how the separation would go. "It was really **tough** not being able to communicate with her **regularly**," says Suzy. "I would write her letters, but by the time she'd read them, it was old news. Thank goodness for the Internet. Now we talk for hours and hours on the computer. We need to be able

Suzette (left) and Neshmayda (right) on their wedding day in 1999. In a double ceremony conducted both by speaking and in signing, each twin married a man who is deaf.

to share our feelings all the time, and this way we can."

Busy social lives, dreams of having children, a **passion** for the Internet—perhaps the Aguayo twins are not so different after all. "They are so incredibly **independent**," says their mother. "I can't remember the last time I had to do something for them."

---

separation time of not being together
earned master's degrees completed advanced college courses
preparing themselves getting ready
extremely very

tough difficult, hard
regularly every few days or every week, often
passion love

Neshmayda (left) and Suzette (right) at Gallaudet University in their first year of graduate school.

A life without sounds has had no **impact** on the **extraordinary** love that **exists** between them—they simply found a way to share the quiet music of their souls. What chance do time and distance have of changing the way they feel? "It's true we are becoming more independent of each other," Neshy says. "But it really doesn't matter. The longer we are apart, the closer we become."

---

impact effect
exists is

BEFORE YOU MOVE ON...

1. **Character's Point of View** Why will separation be so difficult for Suzy and Neshy?

2. **Comparison** Compare writing letters with "talking" by computer. How are they alike, and how are they different?

3. **Prediction** Do you believe the twins will always remain close? Why or why not?

ABOUT THE AUTHORS

Identical twins **Debbie and Lisa Ganz** know a lot about the special joys and challenges of twinship. They share their experience with other twins, multiples, and their parents through their website and helpline. In addition, they raise funds for twins in need and help reunite twins who have grown up apart. When they opened Twins, a New York City restaurant that is staffed entirely by identical twins, critics called it a silly idea. The Ganzes were determined, however, and today their restaurant is a success.

Respond to the Article
Check Your Understanding

SUM IT UP

Paraphrase What mattered most to the Aguayos? Make a chart to paraphrase the information in the selection. Then add specific examples to support your statements.

The Aguayo Family	What Matters Most?	How Do You Know?
María and Joaquin Aguayo		
Neshy and Suzy Aguayo		

Compare and Evaluate Literature Use your charts to compare "Twins" with another selection you have read. You might:

- Compare Yenna from "Ginger for the Heart" with the twins.
- Compare the genre with "Talking Walls."
- Compare the problem and solution with "Teammates."

Write three paragraphs. In the first paragraph, tell how the two selections are alike. In the second, tell how they are different. In the last paragraph, tell which selection you think is stronger and why.

THINK IT OVER

Discuss and Write Talk about these questions with a partner. Write the answers.

1. **Prediction** Do you think Suzy and Neshy will be happy living in two different cities? How might their relationship change?

2. **Opinion** What are the advantages and disadvantages of being a twin?

3. **Inference** Do you think the twins feel that they are "missing out" because they are deaf? How can you tell?

4. **Characters' Motives** What are the twins' dreams? What kinds of decisions did they have to make to follow their dreams?

EXPRESS YOURSELF

▶ DEMONSTRATE NON-VERBAL COMMUNICATION

People around the world use gestures to give extra meaning to their words. In a group, demonstrate different kinds of movements and ways of standing. Discuss the meanings of these gestures. How do eye contact and physical closeness affect communication? Compare these gestures with those from other countries.

Respond to the Article, continued
Language Arts and Literature

 GRAMMAR IN CONTEXT

USE ADJECTIVES THAT COMPARE

Learn About Comparative Adjectives A **comparative adjective** compares two things. To make the comparison, add **–er** to the adjective and use the word **than**.

> Neshy's hair is **longer than** Suzy's.

If the adjective is a long word, use **more** or **less**.

> Neshy is **more independent than** Suzy.

Learn About Superlative Adjectives A **superlative adjective** compares three or more things. Add **–est** to the adjective. Use **the** before the adjective.

> Suzy is **the fastest** runner in her class.

If the adjective is long, use **the most** or **the least**.

> **The most important** thing to the twins is staying in touch.

Practice Write these sentences. Use the correct form of the adjective in parentheses.

1. Some hearing-impaired people have a (great) hearing loss than others do.

2. Gallaudet is perhaps the (fine) school in the world for hearing-impaired students.

3. When they learned sign language, the twins were (confident) than before.

4. The (difficult) time of all came after the twins were separated.

TECHNOLOGY/MEDIA

WRITING

WRITE TO A TWIN

With a partner, take the roles of Suzy and Neshy. Pretend that you have been apart for one month. Write a series of letters or e-mails to each other.

1 **Choose a Topic** Here are some possible topics for your first letters:

- future dreams or plans
- life in your new city or home
- an upcoming visit
- family and friends

2 **Start the Series** One partner writes the first letter or e-mail. The other partner reads it and writes back. Write several more letters or e-mails back and forth.

3 **Check Your Work** Check your work before sending it to your "twin." Check for correct spelling and punctuation.

For more about **e-mail**, see Handbook page 382.

Content Area Connections

RESEARCH CONTRIBUTIONS OF THE HEARING IMPAIRED

Create a class book with the information you find about the contributions of the hearing impaired.

1 Choose a Person With a group, choose a hearing-impaired artist, teacher, or leader that you would like to know more about. Here are a few suggestions:

- Ludwig van Beethoven, composer
- Helen Keller, author
- I. Jordan King, President of Gallaudet University
- Pete Townsend, musician
- Marlee Matlin, actress and spokesperson

2 Gather Information You can find information about the person you chose in books and encyclopedias or through a search on the Internet.

3 Make a Class Book Write a short biography or article about the person. Tell about his or her challenges and achievements. Then put all of the groups' papers together in a class book. Give the book a cover, table of contents, and title page.

TECHNOLOGY/MEDIA
SCIENCE

RESEARCH TWINS

Use the Internet and other resources to learn interesting facts about twins. Present your findings in a question-and-answer fact sheet.

1 Plan Your Research With a group, brainstorm questions such as:

- What is the difference between fraternal twins and identical twins?
- What percentage of the population is twins?
- Is a twin likely to be the parent of twins?

2 Locate Information Use key words in your search and look for links. Download helpful information.

INTERNET

INFORMATION ON-LINE

Key Word:
twins

Web Sites:
➤ **Information about Twins**
- www.eblast.com
- encarta.msn.com

3 Make a Fact Sheet Write your questions in one column and the answers in another column. Share your fact sheet with the class.

Learn to use the **Internet** on Handbook pages 392–393.

THEME 2

Toward a Better Future

- Who are the people that you admire for reaching their goals? Explain how they did it.

- What does it take to reach an important goal?

- What decisions can you make to build a rewarding future for yourself?

THEME-RELATED BOOKS

Follow the Drinking Gourd
by Jeannette Winter

The story of Peg Leg Joe, an old man with a wooden leg who leads slaves north to freedom.

The Milkman's Boy
by Donald Hall

A family crisis convinces a family to update their dairy business using the new pasteurization process.

NOVEL

The House on Mango Street
by Sandra Cisneros

Young Esperanza dreams of leaving her rundown neigborhood to make a better life for herself.

Build Language and Vocabulary

DESCRIBE

Study the painting. Then read the quotation. What do you think the future holds for these people?

Pioneers of the West, Helen Lundeberg, oil on canvas. Copyright © 1934.

WE ARE SUCH STUFF AS DREAMS ARE MADE ON.

—*William Shakespeare*

MAKE A DRAWING OF THE FUTURE

Look at the painting again. At a signal from your teacher, start drawing all the different things that might be in the future for these pioneers. Stop when you are given the next signal. You will have three minutes.

BUILD YOUR VOCABULARY

Synonyms A synonym is a word that has the same or almost the same meaning as another word. Study the chart. The pairs of words about the pioneers are synonyms. Work with a partner to list more pairs of synonyms about the painting. Take turns adding words to the chart and writing a synonym for each.

Subjects	Adjectives	Verbs	Adverbs
pioneers	brave courageous	traveled journeyed	boldly fearlessly

USE LANGUAGE STRUCTURES ▶ COMPLEX SENTENCES

Writing: Describe in Detail Write complex sentences to describe the pioneers in your drawing. Use conjunctions from the **Word Bank**.

Examples:
When the brave pioneers got to Oklahoma, they built their homes. They made them out of sod **because** there were few trees for lumber.

Word Bank

Some Subordinating Conjunctions
although
because
if
since
unless
until
when
where
while

art essay
by Jacob Lawrence

Prepare to Read

THINK ABOUT WHAT YOU KNOW

Quickwrite Why do people move from one area to another?

adversity hard times, difficult situation

exodus move of a very large number of people from an area

migration move from one place to another by a group of people

newcomer person who has recently come to an area

population shift change in the number of people living in a certain area

replace put one thing in place of another

segregation separation of one group of people from another

shortage too small a number or amount

triumph success, victory

LEARN KEY VOCABULARY

Relate Words Study the new words and their definitions. With your group, use the vocabulary words to complete a word map.

Word Map

What is it? The **migration** of people from one place to another.

Word: exodus

What are some reasons for it?

What happens?

LEARN TO MAKE COMPARISONS

When you **make comparisons**, you see how things are alike and different. This strategy will help you understand information.

> ### READING STRATEGY
> **How to Make Comparisons**
>
> 1. Preview the selection by looking at pictures, captions, and headings. Decide what you want to compare.
> 2. Set up a comparison chart. Show what you plan to compare in the headings.
> 3. Read each part of the selection. Take notes on your chart.
> 4. Look over your chart. How are things alike and different?

As you read "The Great Migration," compare life for African Americans in the South and in the North.

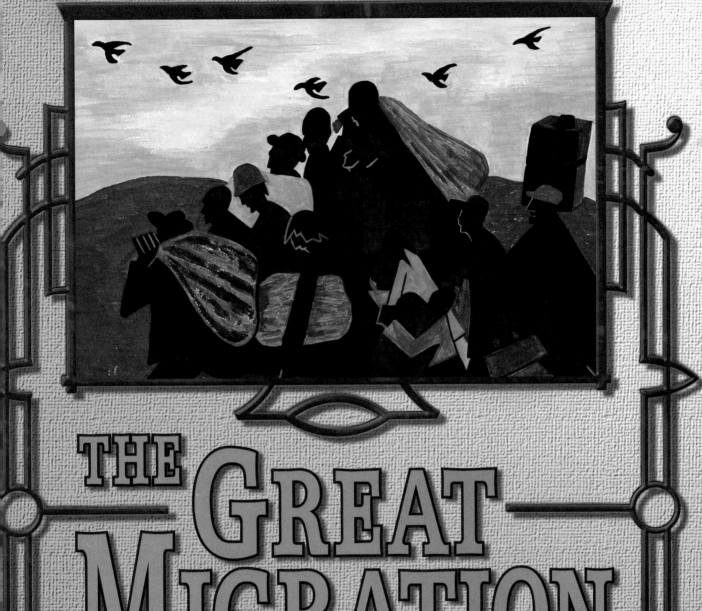

THE GREAT MIGRATION

AN AMERICAN STORY

by JACOB LAWRENCE

It is 1916. Segregation divides the South. Living conditions are difficult for all southerners, but especially for blacks. Many African Americans travel north in search of a better life. This chapter of American history, known as the "Great Migration," inspired painter Jacob Lawrence to tell the story of this journey.

AN AMERICAN STORY

Jacob Lawrence's family moves to the North during the great migration.
Many years later, he decides to paint the story to share with all Americans.

———

This is the story of an **exodus** of African Americans who left their homes and farms in the South around the time of World War I and traveled to northern **industrial cities** in search of better lives. It was **a momentous journey**. Their **movement** resulted in one of the biggest **population shifts** in the history of the United States, and the **migration** is still going on for many people today.

The great migration is a part of my life. I grew up knowing about people on the move from the time I could understand what words meant. There was always talk in my house of other families arriving from the South. My family was part of the first **big wave of the migration**, which occurred between the years 1916 and 1919.

To me, migration means movement. While I was painting, I thought about trains and people walking to the stations. I thought about field hands leaving their farms to become factory workers, and about the families that sometimes got left behind. The choices made were hard ones, so I wanted to show what made the people get on those northbound trains. I also wanted to show just what it cost to ride them. **Uprooting** yourself from one way of life to make

Jacob was born in 1917 in New Jersey after his family moved to the North. Here he is with his mother, baby brother, and sister.

····························

industrial cities cities with large factories
a momentous journey an important trip
big wave of the migration movement of a large number of people
Uprooting Moving

This is a self-portrait by Jacob Lawrence. It shows the artist in his studio, surrounded by his paintings and tools.

The Studio, Jacob Lawrence, lithograph. Copyright © 1996.

your way in another involves conflict and struggle. But out of the struggle comes a kind of power, and even beauty. I tried to **convey** this in the rhythm of the pictures, and in the repetition of certain images.

"And the migrants kept coming" is a **refrain** of **triumph** over **adversity**. My family and others left the South on a **quest** for freedom, **justice**, and **dignity**. If our story **rings true** for you today, then it must still **strike a chord** in our American experience.

—*Jacob Lawrence, 1992*

----

convey show
refrain repeated saying, common phrase
quest search
justice fair treatment
dignity sense of honor and worth
rings true has the sound of truth
strike a chord be deeply felt, be understood

BEFORE YOU MOVE ON...

1. **Setting** When and where did the great migration take place?
2. **Context Clues** What does *migration* mean to the author? Give examples from the text.
3. **Artist's Purpose** Why did Jacob Lawrence decide to paint the story of the great migration?

THE SEGREGATED SOUTH

Life in the South is difficult for African Americans. They begin leaving in great numbers in search of a better life in the North.

This painting captures the feeling of a busy train station during the great migration. The travelers are crowded together, and they are all leaning toward their destination. You can almost hear their scuffling feet and feel their bodies pressing close together.

Around the time I was born, many African Americans from the South left home and traveled to cities in the North in search of a better life. My family was part of this great migration.

There was a **shortage** of workers in northern factories because many had left their jobs to fight in the First World War. The factory owners had to find new workers to **replace** those who were marching off to war. Northern industries offered southern blacks jobs as workers and lent them money, to be repaid later, for their railroad tickets. The northbound trains were packed with **recruits**.

....

recruits new workers

These paintings show the damaging effects of floods and boll weevils on southern crops.

Nature had ravaged the South. Floods ruined farms. The boll weevil destroyed cotton crops.

The war had **doubled the cost of** food, making life even harder for the poor. Railroad stations were so crowded with migrants that guards were called in to **keep order**. The flood of migrants northward left crops back home to dry and **spoil**. For African Americans, the South was **barren** in many ways. There was no justice for them in the courts, and their lives were often in danger. Although slavery had long been **abolished,** white landowners treated the black tenant farmers **harshly** and unfairly.

And so the migration grew.

....

doubled the cost of made the price twice as high for
keep order make sure everyone followed the rules
spoil go bad, rot
barren lifeless, without happiness, empty
abolished ended
harshly in a mean or cruel way

For much of the twentieth century, many African Americans did not own cars. Most traveled to the North by train. Some even walked part of the way.

Trains were an important means of transportation in the early part of the twentieth century. The trip to the North took a long time, so many travelers took plenty of food and extra clothing.

Here Lawrence shows what life was like under segregation. He uses a river to divide the painting in order to show how blacks and whites were separated in their daily activities. In the two parts of the painting, black women and white women drink at separate water fountains.

Segregation divided the South. The black newspapers told of better housing and jobs in the North. **Agents** from northern factories **flocked** into southern counties and towns, looking for laborers. Families often gathered to discuss whether to go north or to stay south. The promise of better housing in the North **could not be ignored**. The railroad stations were crowded with migrants.

And the migrants kept coming.

In the South there was little opportunity for education, and children **labored** in the fields. These were more reasons for people to move north, leaving some communities **deserted**. There was much excitement and discussion about the great migration.

Many migrants arrived in Chicago. In Chicago and other cities they labored in the **steel mills** . . . and on the railroads.

Agents People acting for others
flocked came in great numbers
could not be ignored attracted attention
labored worked

deserted without any people
steel mills factories where steel, a very strong metal, is produced

LIFE IN THE NORTH

African Americans continue migrating to the North. Many of them find the jobs they were looking for, but they also find that there are many problems and prejudices to overcome.

And the migrants kept coming. Southern landowners, **stripped of** cheap labor, tried to stop the migration by jailing the labor agents and the migrants. Sometimes the agents disguised themselves to avoid arrest, but the migrants were often taken from railroad stations and jailed until the trains departed. Black and white southern leaders met to discuss ways to improve conditions to stop the flow of workers north.

Although life in the North was better, it was not **ideal**. Many migrants moved to Pittsburgh, which was a great industrial center at the time.

Although they were promised better housing in the North, some families **were forced** to live in overcrowded and unhealthy **quarters**. The migrants soon learned that segregation was not **confined to** the South.

Many northern workers were angry because they had to compete with the migrants for housing and jobs. There were **riots**. Longtime

African American residents living in the North did not welcome the **newcomers** from the South and often treated them with **disdain**. The migrants had to **rely on** each other.

Newcomers were excited about the opportunities waiting for them in steel mills in the North. As they approached the great northern cities, they eagerly looked out the train windows at the exciting new landscapes.

---

stripped of left without any
ideal perfect
were forced had no other choice but
quarters places to live or sleep

confined to found only in
riots violent actions by a crowd of people
disdain disapproval
rely on depend on or trust

Children could go to better schools in the North. Notice how each girl is reaching higher than the one to her left. Lawrence wanted to show that better schools provided the education needed to open up new opportunities.

parents told it to me, because their struggles and triumphs ring true today. People all over the world are still on the move, trying to build better lives for themselves and for their families.

BEFORE YOU MOVE ON...

1. **Inference** Why didn't African Americans move to other farmlands in the South?
2. **Cause and Effect** How did southern landowners and leaders react to the great migration?

The **storefront church** was a **welcoming** place and the center of their lives, in joy and in sorrow. Black professionals, such as doctors and lawyers, soon followed **their patients** and **clients** north. Female workers were among the last to leave.

Life in the North brought many challenges, but the migrants' lives had changed for the better. The children were able to go to school, and their parents gained the freedom to vote.

And the migrants kept coming.

Theirs is a story of African American strength and courage. I share it now as my

....

storefront church small church in a building that is used as a store at other times

welcoming warm and inviting

their patients the people they (doctors) cared for

clients customers; people who pay for the services of other people

ABOUT THE AUTHOR

When he was thirteen, **Jacob Lawrence** moved with his family to New York City. He began taking art lessons after school. He decided then that he wanted to use painting to tell the history of African Americans. In his long career, Jacob Lawrence has created many paintings of famous African Americans such as Frederick Douglass and Harriet Tubman. He was an art professor at the University of Washington before he retired.

Respond to the Essay
Check Your Understanding

SUM IT UP

Make Comparisons Work with a partner to review the comparison chart you made while reading. Be sure to consider elements such as employment, education, and financial situations. Add any missing details.

Life for African Americans

In the South	In the North
not many jobs	many job openings

Summarize Use the details in your chart to write a short paragraph that compares what life was like for African Americans in the South and those in the North.

THINK IT OVER

Discuss and Write Talk about these questions with a partner. Write the answers.

1. **Inference** Why do you think some African Americans in the North treated the newcomers badly?

2. **Evaluate Information** From the details in the selection, do you think the migrants were better off in the South or in the North? Explain your answer.

3. **Conclusions** What do people move to get away from? What do people move toward?

4. **Prior Knowledge** What other large migrations of people do you know about?

EXPRESS YOURSELF ▶ DESCRIBE

Which painting in the selection do you like most? Describe it to a group of classmates. Tell about the colors, how people and things appear in the painting, and how it makes you feel.

Respond to the Essay, continued
Language Arts and Literature

USE PHRASES AND CLAUSES

Learn About Phrases A **phrase** is a group of related words that does not have a subject and a predicate.

> **in the South**

A phrase can be part of a complete sentence.

> Many blacks lived **in the South**.

Learn About Clauses A **clause** is a group of words that has a subject and a verb. An **independent clause** can stand alone as a sentence.

> The **South experienced** a drought.
> **Pests ruined** the cotton crop.

Two independent clauses can be combined into a **compound sentence**. Join the clauses with a **conjunction** : *and, but, or, for, nor,* or *yet.*

> The South experienced a drought, **and** pests ruined the cotton crop.

A **dependent clause** is not a complete sentence.

> although slavery was abolished

A dependent clause can be combined with an independent clause to make a **complex sentence**.

> Although slavery was abolished, white landowners treated black farmers harshly.

Practice Work with a partner to write three compound sentences and three complex sentences.

DESCRIBE AN EVENT

Imagine that you are a character in one of Jacob Lawrence's paintings. Write a description of the event shown in the painting.

1. **Write Your Draft** Put yourself in the painting. What are you doing? Describe what you see, hear, and smell. How does the scene make you feel? Write a colorful, interesting description.

2. **Edit Your Work** Does your description make the event seem like it really happened? Did you use descriptive words and phrases? Check for correct spelling and punctuation. Check that all your sentences are complete.

3. **Share Your Work** Take turns reading your description aloud to a partner. Guess which painting you each described. Then look at the paintings together.

Sample Description

> It's cold outside, but I feel warm because we are all pressed close together. The smell of hot chocolate is mixed with the smell of burning coal. I can't wait for the trip to start!

Review **sentences** on Handbook pages 424–430.

Content Area Connections

SOCIAL STUDIES

RESEARCH CITY JOBS

Find out about jobs in today's large cities. Use what you learn to make a career notebook.

1 Choose a Category Select one of these fields to research:

communications/publishing
education
hospitality/service
manufacturing
retail
transportation
technology

2 Research Jobs in Your Category Use the Internet, the "Help Wanted" section in your local newspaper, or library books about careers. Take notes as you read.

3 Make a Career Notebook Summarize your research in a paragraph. Put copies of all your classmates' paragraphs in your own career notebook.

REPRESENTING/SPEAKING
FINE ARTS

CREATE A MESSAGE WITHOUT WORDS

How shapes and figures are arranged in a picture is called the **composition**. A good composition can clearly express the picture's message without words. Draw your own picture that speaks for itself.

1 Choose a Subject Decide what you want to draw. Think about a subject that is important or meaningful to you. What message do you want to convey about it?

2 Create the Composition Experiment by sketching different compositions. Choose one. Then use pencils, crayons, chalk, or paint to draw your final picture.

3 Take a Gallery Walk Display your picture with those of your classmates. Walk around the room, and discuss how the composition in each picture helps convey the message of the artist.

 For tips on **representing**, see Handbook pages 404–405.

Respond to the Essay, continued
Content Area Connections

TECHNOLOGY/MEDIA

SOCIAL STUDIES

STUDY POPULATION SHIFTS

Many African Americans moved north during the early 1900s. Use the Internet, encyclopedias, and almanacs to learn about other population shifts in U.S. history. Make a class chart of what you learn.

1 **Choose an Event** Find out about population shifts in U.S. history like the Westward Movement, the California gold rush, and the Dust Bowl. Be sure to find out when the migration occurred, too. Choose a topic that interests you.

2 **Prepare to Research** Write questions you'd like to answer such as:

- Why did the migration happen?
- Who migrated?
- What were the effects of the migration?

3 **Gather Information and Take Notes** These Web sites might be good places to find answers. Use the name of the migration as a key word in your search. Download helpful information.

INTERNET

INFORMATION ON-LINE

Web Sites:
➤ **Search Engine**
- www.yahooligans.com

➤ **Encyclopedia Articles**
- www.encarta.com

4 **Make a Class Chart** Combine the information you and your classmates learned into a class chart. Discuss the effects of the migrations.

Population Shifts in U.S. History

Name of Migration	Time Period	Reasons	Effects
Great Migration			
Gold Rush			

Learn more about **charts** on Handbook pages 370–371. For more about the **research process**, see pages 394–399.

FOLLOW THE DRINKING GOURD

traditional song
with text support
by Jeanette Winter

Prepare to Read

THINK ABOUT WHAT YOU KNOW

Idea Exchange Tell about groups of stars you know. Do you know how to find the Big Dipper? Why is it called that?

capture take or catch by force

conductor leader or guide on a trip

escape break loose or get free

freedom state of not being under the control of another person

journey trip

network group of people or things that work together as one

reward money or a prize given for something a person does

runaway slave person who tries to get away from someone who owns him or her

slavery custom or practice of owning slaves

LEARN KEY VOCABULARY

Use New Words in Context Study the new words and their definitions. Then write the paragraph, adding the missing words.

In the early history of the United States, ____(1)____ was legal. Some African American slaves tried to ____(2)____. A ____(3)____ often used the Underground Railroad. It was a ____(4)____ of people and places that helped these slaves. The ____(5)____ on the Underground Railroad was dangerous. Slave hunters tried to ____(6)____ some slaves. So the slaves needed a ____(7)____ to guide them north. There, they hoped to find ____(8)____. This was the ____(9)____ that waited for them at the end of their long journey.

LEARN TO ASK QUESTIONS AND CLARIFY MEANING

When you read, you can stop and **ask questions**. This helps you **clarify**, or understand what you read.

READING STRATEGY
How to Ask Questions and Clarify Meaning

1. Read part of the selection.
2. Ask yourself: What does this mean? What questions do I have about it?
3. Use resources to answer your questions.
4. As you read the next part, look for answers to your questions, and ask new questions about what you've read.

Now read "Follow the Drinking Gourd." Stop after each verse or section and ask questions to clarify meaning.

FOLLOW THE DRINKING GOURD

A TRADITIONAL SONG
WITH TEXT SUPPORT BY JEANETTE WINTER

The migration of African Americans began long before the Great Migration. From the earliest days of slavery, African Americans traveled north to find a life of freedom and opportunity.

CHORUS

Fol-low the drink-ing gourd! Fol-low the drink-ing gourd. For the old man is a-wait-ing for to carry you to free-dom If you fol-low the drink-ing gourd.

VERSE

When the sun comes back, and the first quail calls, Fol-low the drink-ing gourd. For the old man is a-wait-ing for to carry you to free-dom If you fol-low the drink-ing gourd.

The riverbank makes a very good road,
The dead trees will show you the way.
Left foot, peg foot, traveling on,
Follow the drinking gourd.

(*repeat chorus*)

The river ends between two hills,
Follow the drinking gourd.
There's another river on the other side,
Follow the drinking gourd.

(*repeat chorus*)

When the great big river meets the little river,
Follow the drinking gourd.
For the old man is a-waiting for to carry you to freedom
If you follow the drinking gourd.

---

riverbank ground by the side of the river
peg foot wood used in place of the missing right foot

a-waiting ready and waiting; an old-fashioned way of saying "waiting"
for to carry to carry

A Note About the Song

In the early days of **slavery** in the United States many slaves tried to **escape** their cruel **bondage** by fleeing north— usually to Canada—to **freedom**. By the 1840s a loosely organized group of free blacks, slaves, and white **sympathizers** formed a secret **network** of people and places that hid escaped slaves on their dangerous **journey** to freedom—a network that came to be known as the Underground Railroad.

Traveling along darkened roads at night, hiding out by day, moving slowly upriver along hundreds of miles of **connecting waterways,** the **fugitive** slaves **endured many hardships**. Slave catchers hunted them down with dogs. Many were shot or hanged. And even after crossing into the "free" states, **runaway slaves** could still be **captured** and returned to their masters for a **reward**.

The most famous **conductor** on the Underground Railroad was Harriet Tubman, a runaway slave herself, who led hundreds of her people to freedom. Among other conductors, there was a one-legged sailor named Peg Leg Joe. Joe hired himself out to plantation owners as a handyman. Then he made friends with the slaves and taught them what seemed a harmless folk song—

---

bondage slavery, enslavement
sympathizers people who cared about the slaves
connecting waterways rivers and streams that are a short distance apart yet joined together

fugitive escaping
endured many hardships had to put up with many problems and hard times

"Follow the Drinking Gourd." But hidden in the **lyrics of the song** were directions for following the Underground Railroad. The Drinking Gourd is the Big Dipper, which points to the North Star. "When the sun comes back, and the first **quail** calls" meant spring, when travel might be least **hazardous**. As the runaway slaves followed the stars north, they would come across marks Peg Leg Joe had made in mud or in charcoal on dead trees—a left foot and a peg foot—and they would know they were on the right trail.

The river that "ends between two hills" was the Tombigbee River. The second was the Tennessee River and the "great big river" was the Ohio River, where Peg Leg Joe would be waiting to **ferry** them across to the free states on the other side. From there the fugitives were guided from one hiding place to the next until—with luck—they made it to Canada or other safe places in the North.

— Jeanette Winter

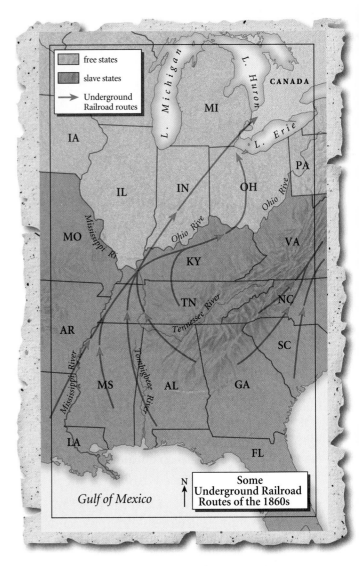

Some Underground Railroad Routes of the 1860s

BEFORE YOU MOVE ON...

1. **Characters' Motives** What mattered most to the slaves who tried to escape?
2. **Details** What could happen to runaway slaves who were captured?
3. **Inference** What can you tell about the character of the conductors?

---

lyrics of the song words in the song

quail bird; small, fat bird with brown feathers and white spots

hazardous dangerous

ferry carry; carry in a small boat

ABOUT THE AUTHOR

Jeanette Winter is an award-winning children's book author and illustrator. Among her many books are *Cowboy Charlie: The Story of Charles M. Russell* and *My Name Is Georgia: A Portrait by Jeanette Winter*. Both are stories about artists who traveled long distances to achieve their goals and live their dreams. Jeanette Winter lives with her husband in Pipe Creek, Texas.

Respond to the Song

Check Your Understanding

SUM IT UP

Distinguish Between Apparent Message and Hidden Agenda An **apparent message** is the exact meaning of the words in a selection. This song appears to be about a river through the woods.

Sometimes a selection also has a **hidden agenda**, or another meaning. The hidden agenda for this song is a series of directions for the Underground Railroad.

Make a chart that shows the details of the apparent message and hidden agenda.

Apparent Message	Hidden Agenda
The riverbank makes a very good road,	Walk along the riverbank

Draw Conclusions Tell why knowing the hidden agenda in the song would be important to a slave. Why would it be important to a slave owner? Share your ideas in a group.

THINK IT OVER

Discuss and Write Talk about these questions with a partner. Write the answers.

1. **Inference** Why was the Underground Railroad given that name? How was it like a real railroad?

2. **Comparisons** What did the Underground Railroad and the Great Migration have in common?

3. **Inference** Songs were one way for slaves to communicate. What might have been other ways for them to communicate their hidden agenda for escaping to freedom?

4. **Judgments** Peg Leg Joe and other conductors on the Underground Railroad were in great danger. Why do you think they took such risks to help runaway slaves?

EXPRESS YOURSELF ▶ STATE A GOAL

What were the goals of the people you have learned about in this selection? Role-play Harriet Tubman, Peg Leg Joe, a runaway slave, or a slave owner. Tell about your goal to a group.

A House of My Own

story
by Sandra Cisneros

Prepare to Read

THINK ABOUT WHAT YOU KNOW

Describe Places Draw a picture of your dream home and describe it to a partner. Tell about all the details that make it perfect for you.

LEARN KEY VOCABULARY

flat apartment

landlord person who owns a building and takes money from others who live in it

laundromat place of business with self-service washing machines and dryers

ordinary not special, regular

own have, possess

real true, not imagined

rent money paid to live in an apartment or house that another person owns

temporary not permanent, for a limited time

washroom bathroom or small room with a sink

Relate Words Study the new words and their definitions. Then use the new words to complete these charts.

Antonyms	
false	
permanent	
	borrow
special	

Synonyms	
apartment	
bathroom	
laundry	
	payment

LEARN TO CONFIRM WORD MEANINGS

When you read, stop to figure out the meanings of words you don't know.

READING STRATEGY
How to Confirm Word Meanings
1. Look for parts of the word that you know. Use these word parts to help you guess what the word means.
2. Read the words around the new word. Do they give you clues about the meaning of the new word?
3. Predict the meaning of the word.
4. Look the word up in a dictionary, glossary, or thesaurus. Find the meaning that fits the sentence you are reading.

Confirm the meaning of the new words you read in "A House of My Own."

A House of My Own

from The House on Mango Street
by Sandra Cisneros

Esperanza wants a
house of her own, a
space for herself,
a place where she
can dream and write.
With courage, spirit,
skill, and determination,
she sets out to build
a better future.

A HOUSE BUT NOT A HOME

Although Esperanza and her family finally own a house, it's not the large, beautiful one they had hoped for. It doesn't feel like home.

The House on Mango Street

We didn't always live on Mango Street. Before that we lived on Loomis on the third floor, and before that we lived on Keeler. Before Keeler it was Paulina, and before that I can't remember. But what I remember most is moving a lot. Each time it **seemed** there'd be one more of us. By the time we got to Mango Street we were six— Mama, Papa, Carlos, Kiki, my sister Nenny and me.

The house on Mango Street is ours, and we don't have to pay **rent** to anybody, or share the yard with the people downstairs, or be careful not to make too much noise, and there isn't a **landlord** banging on the ceiling with a broom. But even so, it's not the house we'd thought we'd get.

We had to leave the **flat** on Loomis quick. The **water pipes** broke and the landlord wouldn't fix them because the house was too old. We had to leave fast. We were using the **washroom** next door and carrying water over in empty milk gallons. That's why Mama and Papa looked for a house, and that's why we moved into the house on Mango Street, far away, on the other side of town.

They always told us that one day we would move into a house, a **real** house that would be ours for always so we wouldn't have to move each year. And our house would have running water and pipes that worked. And inside it would have real stairs, not **hallway stairs**, but stairs inside like the houses on TV. And we'd have a **basement** and at least three washrooms so when we took a bath we wouldn't have to tell everybody. Our house would be white with trees around it, a great big yard and grass growing without a fence. This was the house Papa talked about when he held a **lottery ticket** and this was the house Mama dreamed up in the stories she told us before we went to bed.

---

seemed looked as if
water pipes metal or plastic tubes used for directing water through the building
hallway stairs outside stairs like in an apartment building

basement storage room under the house
lottery ticket numbered piece of paper in a contest to win money

But the house on Mango Street is not the way they told it at all. It's small and red with **tight** steps in front and windows so small you'd think they were holding their breath. Bricks are **crumbling** in places, and the front door is so **swollen** you have to push hard to get in. There is no front yard, only four little **elms** the city planted by the **curb**. Out back is a small garage for the car we don't **own** yet and a small yard that looks smaller between the two buildings on either side. There are stairs in our house, but they're **ordinary** hallway stairs, and the house has only one washroom. Everybody has to share a bedroom—Mama and Papa, Carlos and Kiki, me and Nenny.

Once when we were living on Loomis, a nun from my school passed by and saw me playing out front. The **laundromat** downstairs had been boarded up because it had been robbed two days before and the owner had painted on the wood YES WE'RE OPEN so as not to **lose business**.

Where do you live? she asked.

---

tight small or narrow
crumbling breaking off in little pieces
swollen big beyond its normal size

elms shade trees
curb edge of the street
lose business have fewer customers than before

There, I said pointing up to the third floor.

You live *there*?

There. I had to look to where she pointed—the third floor, the paint **peeling**, wooden bars Papa had nailed on the windows so we wouldn't fall out. You live *there*? The way she said it made me feel like nothing. *There.* I lived *there.* I nodded.

I knew then I had to have a house. A real house. One I could point to. But this isn't it. The house on Mango Street isn't it. **For the time being**, Mama says. **Temporary**, says Papa. But I know how those things go.

BEFORE YOU MOVE ON...

1. **Comparison** How is the house on Mango Street better than the flat on Loomis? How is it similar?

2. **Character's Point of View** Does it matter to Esperanza what other people think about her house? Explain.

3. **Inference** Does Esperanza believe her parents when they say the Mango Street house is temporary? Explain your answer.

----

peeling coming off in pieces and strips
For the time being For right now

Esperanza compares herself to the skinny trees that survive by the city street.
She listens to the advice her mother gives about life.

Four Skinny Trees

They are the only ones who understand me. I am the only one who understands them. Four skinny trees with skinny necks and pointy elbows like mine. Four who do not belong here but are here. Four **raggedy** excuses planted by the city. From our room we can hear them, but Nenny just sleeps and doesn't appreciate these things.

Their strength is secret. They send **ferocious** roots beneath the ground. They grow up and they grow down and grab the earth between their hairy toes and bite the sky with violent teeth and never quit their anger. This is how they **keep**.

Let one forget his reason for **being**, they'd all droop like tulips in a glass, each with their arms around the other. Keep, keep, keep, trees say when I sleep. They teach.

When I am too sad and too skinny to **keep keeping**, when I am a tiny thing against so many bricks, **then it is** I look at trees. When there is nothing left to look at on this street. Four who grow **despite concrete**. Four who reach and do not forget to reach. Four whose only reason is to be and be.

---

raggedy unevenly shaped
ferocious mean and angry
keep stay alive
being living

keep keeping go on trying
then it is at that time
despite concrete even though the ground around them is covered with rock-hard material

A Smart Cookie

I could've been somebody, you know? my mother says and sighs. She has lived in this city her whole life. She can speak two languages. She can sing **an opera**. She knows how to fix a TV. But she doesn't know which subway train to take to get downtown. I hold her hand very tight while we wait for the right train to arrive.

She used to draw when she had time. Now she draws with a needle and thread, little knotted rosebuds, tulips made of silk thread. Someday she would like to go to the ballet. Someday she would like to see a play. She borrows opera records from the public library and sings **with velvety lungs powerful as morning glories**.

Today while cooking oatmeal she is **Madame Butterfly** until she sighs and points the wooden spoon at me. I could've been somebody, you know? Esperanza, you go to school. Study hard. That Madame Butterfly was a fool. She stirs the oatmeal. Look at my *comadres*. She means Izaura whose husband left and Yolanda whose husband is dead. Got to take care all your own, she says shaking her head.

Then **out of nowhere**:

Shame is a bad thing, you know. It keeps you down. You want to know why I quit school? Because I didn't have nice clothes. No clothes, but I had brains.

Yup, she says **disgusted**, stirring again. I was a smart cookie then.

BEFORE YOU MOVE ON...

1. **Comparison** In what ways is Esperanza like the four skinny trees?
2. **Inference** What does Esperanza's mother mean when she says, "Got to take care all your own"?
3. **Opinion** Do you think that "shame is a bad thing"? Why or why not?

---

an opera a musical play in which words are sung rather than spoken

with velvety lungs powerful as morning glories smoothly, beautifully, and forcefully

Madame Butterfly the main character of a famous opera

out of nowhere suddenly

disgusted unhappy at the thought of it

ESPERANZA'S DREAM

Esperanza dreams of having a wonderful house all her own, and she sets her goals. She plans to go away from Mango Street, but she won't forget her past.

A House of My Own

Not a flat. Not an apartment in back. Not a man's house. Not a daddy's. A house all my own. With my **porch** and my pillow, my pretty purple **petunias**. My books and my stories. My two shoes waiting beside the bed.

Nobody to shake a stick at. Nobody's garbage to pick up after.

Only a house quiet as snow, a space for myself to go, clean as paper before the poem.

---

porch covered area in front of the entrance
petunias flowers that are shaped like trumpets

Mango Says Goodbye Sometimes

I like to tell stories. I tell them inside my head. I tell them after the mailman says, Here's your mail. Here's your mail he said.

I make a story for my life, for each step my brown shoe takes. I say, "And so she **trudged** up the wooden stairs, her sad brown shoes taking her to the house she never liked."

I like to tell stories. I am going to tell you a story about a girl who didn't want to belong.

We didn't always live on Mango Street. Before that we lived on Loomis on the third floor, and before that we lived on Keeler. Before Keeler it was Paulina, but what I remember most is Mango Street, sad red house, the house I belong but do not belong to.

I put it down on paper and then the ghost does not ache so much. I write it down and Mango says goodbye sometimes. She does not hold me with both arms. She sets me free.

---

trudged walked slowly, as if she were tired

One day I will pack my bags of books and paper. One day I will say goodbye to Mango. I am too strong for her to keep me here forever. One day I will go away.

Friends and neighbors will say, What happened to that Esperanza? Where did she go with all those books and paper? Why did she march so far away?

They will not know I have gone away to come back. For the ones I left behind. For the ones who cannot out.

BEFORE YOU MOVE ON...

1. **Details** Describe the house that Esperanza wants.

2. **Conclusions** Look at the photographs on page 199. How has Esperanza fulfilled her mother's dream as well as her own?

3. **Inference** What do you think Esperanza means when she says, "They will not know I have gone away to come back"?

ABOUT THE AUTHOR

As a girl, **Sandra Cisneros** moved frequently with her family between Mexico City and Chicago. She didn't have much chance to make friends, so books became her friends. Her favorite book described the kind of house she wanted. Unlike the large apartment houses she was used to, it was a single-family house. Later, the books Sandra Cisneros wrote about her experiences as a Mexican American woman helped her move to the home of her dreams. She now lives and writes in her Texas home that is painted a vivid purple.

Respond to the Story

Check Your Understanding

SUM IT UP

Confirm Meanings and Make Inferences
Look at the chart. Confirm the meanings of the
underlined words. Write how you confirmed
each meaning. Then, once you understand the
words, reread each passage. What inferences
can you make about the characters?

Story Passage	How I Confirmed Meaning	Inference
Out back is a small garage for the car we don't own yet.		
And so she trudged up the wooden stairs, her sad brown shoes taking her to the house she never liked.		
But she doesn't know which subway train to take to get downtown.		

Predict Outcomes Use what you learned
about Esperanza to predict what will happen
when she grows up. Will she come back to
Mango Street? Why or why not? Share your
ideas in a group.

THINK IT OVER

Discuss and Write Talk about these questions
with a partner. Write the answers.

1. **Conclusions** What did Esperanza discover
   about herself? Why is it so important for her
   to have a place of her own?

2. **Theme** How does this selection relate to the
   theme Dreams and Decisions?

3. **Opinion** Think about this selection and "The
   Great Migration." How do you think people
   make a home wherever they go?

4. **Author's Background** Sandra Cisneros was the
   only girl among seven children. Her six
   brothers were so bossy that she says she felt as
   if she had "seven fathers." In what ways do
   you think the author's background influenced
   her life and her work as a fiction writer?

EXPRESS YOURSELF ▶ EXPRESS PROBABILITY

Do you think Esperanza will get the house she
wants? How will she find her dream home? Form
a group to discuss your ideas.

Respond to the Story, continued
Language Arts and Literature

LITERARY ANALYSIS

USE SIMILES

Learn About Similes Writers often use adjectives to describe a person or thing:

> The house was **small**.

To help the reader get a better picture of the house, a writer might compare the size to something else:

> The house was **as small as a closet**.

> The house was **like a box**.

These comparisons, which use the words *like* and *as*, are called **similes**. A simile compares two different things that are alike in some way.

Find Similes What two things are compared in this sentence?

> The bricks crumbled like stale cookies.

Practice Create similes to complete these sentences.

1. The yard was as _____ as _____ .

2. The front door was as _____ as _____ .

3. The water pipes burst like _____ .

WRITING

WRITE A HOUSE POEM

Look at how Sandra Cisneros uses a poetic quality in her writing on page 198. Write a poem with lines like these about your dream house. Tell what it is and isn't.

Sample Poem

> ### A House of My Own
>
> Not an apartment.
> Not a trailer.
>
> Not a landlord's.
>
> A big house.
>
> With my dog and my sofa,
> My books stacked high.
>
> My door opened to greet me.
>
> Nobody to tell me to get off the phone.
>
> Nobody's toys to trip over.
>
> Only a big house as cozy as fuzzy slippers.

Develop your skill in the **writer's craft**, see Handbook pages 414–423.

Content Area Connections

CREATE A DREAM HOUSE

Form a team and design a dream house.

1 Choose an Architectural Style As a class, collect pictures of various homes and decorated rooms in magazines. Cut out the pictures and note the various styles you found. Then select the style to use as a model for your home.

2 Organize Your Design Team Have each member of your team choose a task:

- Draw the outside of the home in the architectural style you have chosen.

- Use graph paper to draw the floor plan of each room. Also decide how many square feet the house has.

- Use photos of furniture and other furnishings to decorate each room.

- Write a description of the special features, such as a patio or skylight.

- Include some facts about the distinguishing features of the style.

3 Share Your Design Paste drawings, photos, and descriptions on a large poster. As a class, conduct a "dream house conference." Listen to each presentation. Then discuss the advantages of each team's design.

EVALUATE WEB SITES

Where do you dream of living? Find Web sites with information about two cities you'd like to live in. Then compare and evaluate the sites.

1 Visit Sites Work with a partner to choose your two dream cities. Use the names of the cities and their states as key words, for example "Tallahassee, Florida."

Find sites that are about the city itself and not about specific businesses or organizations in the city. Explore links through the sites. Take notes about features, such as how the site looks, the amount of information presented, and the value of the links provided.

INTERNET

INFORMATION ON-LINE

Web Sites:
➤ **Some Search Engines**
- www.google.com
- www.goto.com
- www.altavista.com

2 Evaluate Sites Use your notes to make a comparison chart. Present the information to the class.

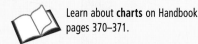

Learn about **charts** on Handbook pages 370–371.

Writing That Describes

In descriptive writing the author uses words to help the reader picture what someone or something is like.

PROFESSIONAL WRITING MODEL

Descriptive writing uses sensory details. Then readers can see, smell, hear, taste, and touch things in the story. They can imagine that they are standing right beside the characters.

from **"Ginger for the Heart"**

> His daughter's name was Yenna, and her beauty was beyond compare. She had ivory skin, sparkling eyes, and her hair hung long and silken, shining like polished ebony. All day long she and her mother sat by the tower window and sewed with silver needles and silken threads. They sang songs while they worked, and their voices rose in wondrous harmonies.

A DESCRIPTION OF A CHARACTER

In a description of a character, a writer tells what the character is like. Sometimes an author uses similes—comparisons using *like* or *as*—to help the reader understand the character. Study the character map and discuss the description of Yenna in "Ginger for the Heart."

Character Map

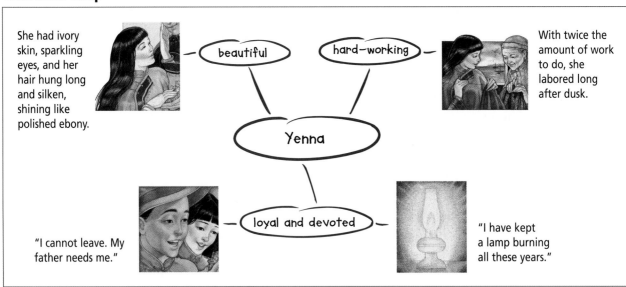

STUDENT WRITING MODEL

Character Sketch

A Dream Come True

by David Yoo

Jun Kim could tackle the most difficult computer games. He easily slipped through twisted mazes, glided around threatening opponents, and swooped up the glittering treasure. He wanted to design a new, harder computer game.

However, Jun had just come to the United States from Korea and did not speak English well. Because Jun wanted to study with the best American computer programmers, he needed to know how to speak English.

Like a runner in a long distance race, Jun pushed himself harder than he sometimes thought possible. His fingers were cramped and throbbing by the time he dropped into bed every night. As he slept, Jun dreamed of the game he would design one day.

One summer, Jun stayed in his dark room with his fingers glued to the keyboard until late at night. Slowly, his Technicolor dream game became vivid three-dimensional computer images flashing on the screen.

After three months of hard, lonely work, Jun presented his masterpiece to the world. In an instant, the game became a golden trophy everyone wanted. Several computer programmers asked to work with him.

The morning Jun heard of his game's success, he smiled. Then he turned his head back to the computer screen and continued designing his next game.

A **character sketch** uses colorful words and descriptive details to tell what someone is like.

SENSORY DETAILS
Some of the details appeal to the reader's senses. This sensory imagery tells how Jun Kim's fingers felt after studying.

COMPARISONS
David uses a simile and a metaphor to help the reader imagine what's being described.

Writing That Describes, continued

The Writing Process

> **WRITING PROMPT**
>
> Now you will write a character sketch—a description of someone. You can write about a real or an imaginary person. Your audience will be your classmates. Make the person come alive for them!

PREWRITE

1 **Collect Ideas and Choose a Subject** Think about people you know or would like to know. Or, imagine an unusual character you may meet someday. Make a chart to show your ideas.

People I Know Today	People I Remember	People I'd Like to Meet	Imaginary People
friend Aman cousin Hector baby sister	grandmother first teacher	NFL quarterback U.S. President	120-year-old man myself in the future an alien

Then choose the subject you can describe in the most interesting way.

2 **Unlock the Writing Prompt** Before you begin writing, fill out an FATP chart to help guide your writing.

3 **Collect the Details** What does your character like to do or say? What does he or she look like? Observing someone is a great way to gather details. If you can, interview the person you are writing about. Then use a Character Map like the one on page 204 to list character traits and examples.

4 **Choose a Focus** Check off the details that you think are most important. Decide what you will describe first, next, and last, and then number your details.

FATP Chart

HOW TO UNLOCK A PROMPT
Form: *character sketch*
Audience: *classmates*
Topic: *cousin Hector*
Purpose: *to describe Hector's traits*

Reflect and Evaluate

- Why do you want to describe this character?
- Do you have enough examples of your character's traits?
- How do you want your readers to feel about your character?

DRAFT

Use your **FATP** chart to remind you of whom and why you are writing. A first draft is not supposed to be final, so write just to get your ideas down. Expect to make changes later.

1 **Introduce Your Character** The beginning should introduce your character in a way that grabs your readers' attention.

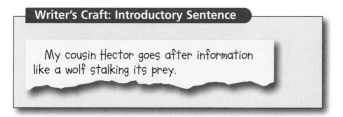

Writer's Craft: Introductory Sentence

My cousin Hector goes after information like a wolf stalking its prey.

2 **Develop the Details** Turn the details from your Character Map into sentences and paragraphs. To make your character come alive, use lots of descriptive details.

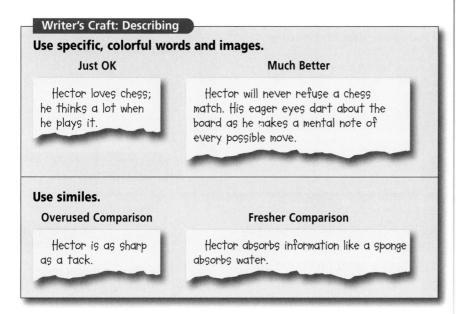

Writer's Craft: Describing

Use specific, colorful words and images.

Just OK	Much Better
Hector loves chess; he thinks a lot when he plays it.	Hector will never refuse a chess match. His eager eyes dart about the board as he makes a mental note of every possible move.

Use similes.

Overused Comparison	Fresher Comparison
Hector is as sharp as a tack.	Hector absorbs information like a sponge absorbs water.

3 **Make It Personal** Put yourself in your writing so your character can be seen through your eyes. Your personal voice and style come from the words you choose and the kinds of sentences you write.

The best advice on writing I've ever received is, "Knock 'em dead with that lead sentence."

— Whitney Balliett

Reflect and Evaluate

- Read your draft. How well do you think you've captured your character's traits?

- Does your draft have an interesting beginning?

- Have you included descriptive details that will help your readers form sharp pictures?

Writing That Describes, continued

REVISE

1 **Reread Your Draft** Review your **FATP**. Does your writing match your form, audience, topic, and purpose? Have you given a clear picture of your character?

2 **Conduct a Peer Conference** Talk to a partner or group about your writing. Discuss word choice. How can you make your descriptions more colorful and exact? Should you add or change describing words or phrases? Use the guidelines on Handbook page 411 for help.

Look at the question a reviewer asked during a Peer Conference. Then read what Tina thinks about the changes she will make.

Key In ⟨TO⟩ Technology

Your word-processing software may have a **Comments** feature that allows your reviewers to add their comments. The comments remain hidden until you point to the highlighted words.

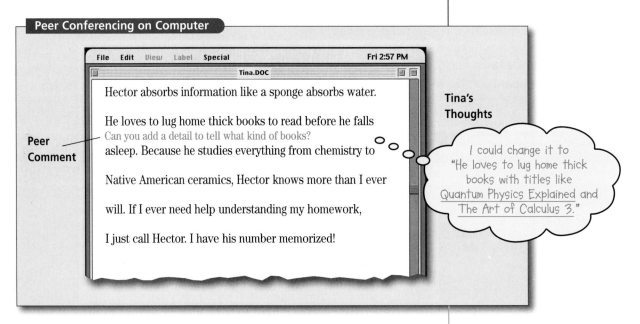

Peer Conferencing on Computer

| File Edit View Label Special | Fri 2:57 PM |

Tina.DOC

Hector absorbs information like a sponge absorbs water.

He loves to lug home thick books to read before he falls
Can you add a detail to tell what kind of books?
asleep. Because he studies everything from chemistry to

Native American ceramics, Hector knows more than I ever

will. If I ever need help understanding my homework,

I just call Hector. I have his number memorized!

Peer Comment

Tina's Thoughts

I could change it to "He loves to lug home thick books with titles like Quantum Physics Explained and The Art of Calculus 3."

3 **Mark Your Changes** Look at your notes and decide how you want to change your writing. Revising Marks appear on Handbook page 411. For how to make changes in a word-processed document, see Handbook pages 386–387.

Reflect and Evaluate

- Were your peer reviewers able to picture your character clearly?
- Did you include all the descriptive details and examples you wanted to?
- Are you pleased with your writing?

> **GRAMMAR IN CONTEXT**

ADJECTIVES, ADVERBS, AND PREPOSITIONAL PHRASES

Adjectives, adverbs, and prepositional phrases add details to sentences. They can make your descriptions stronger.

- **Adjectives** describe nouns and tell more about a person, place, thing, or idea.

    Examples: My cousin is **hilarious**.

    His **outrageous** jokes make everyone laugh.

- **Adverbs** usually describe a verb. They can also tell more about an adjective or another adverb.

    Examples: My cousin **always** makes funny comments.

    He is **really** clever.

- **Prepositional phrases** begin with a preposition and end with a noun or a pronoun. Prepositional phrases may act as adjectives or adverbs.

    Example: A joke <u>about some penguins</u> made me laugh <u>for ten minutes</u>!
                            adjective phrase   **adverb phrase**

Questions Answered by Adjectives

What is it like?
Which one?
How many?
How much?

Questions Answered by Adverbs

How?
Where?
When?
How much?
How often?

Practice Choose the correct word or phrase from the box at the right. Then write the whole sentence.

1. _____ my cousin told me a joke.

      adverb

2. It was a story _____ .

              prepositional phrase

3. The man was supposed to take the penguins _____ .

                                   prepositional phrase

4. The next day a friend saw the man _____ .

                          prepositional phrase

5. "We had an _____ time at the zoo. So today we're going to the beach!"   **adjective**

Word Box

to the zoo

incredible

about a man and two penguins

with the penguins

Yesterday

Writing That Describes, continued

EDIT AND PROOFREAD

1 **Check for Mistakes** Look through your writing and correct any mistakes in capitalization, punctuation, and spelling. If you need help, use Handbook pages 459–469.

2 **Check Your Sentences** Have you used adjectives, adverbs, and prepositional phrases correctly? Make sure you haven't used an adjective where an adverb belongs.

3 **Make a Final Copy** If you are working on a computer, print out the corrected copy of your work. If not, make the corrections as you rewrite a neat, final version.

PUBLISH

Use these ideas for publishing your writing, or come up with your own idea.

- If you are using a desktop publishing program, scan a photo of your subject into your document. Add a caption. Also think of a great title for your work, and show it in a display font.

Desktop Publishing

File   Edit   View   Label   Special   Fri 2:57 PM

Hector Vega.DOC

Hector Vega: The Human Computer

My cousin Hector goes after knowledge like a wolf stalking its prey. With a smile on his face, he untangles the most difficult math problem in a matter of minutes. To relax, Hector would rather conquer a chemical equation than watch TV. Hector prides himself on knowing all of Mozart's symphonies. He knows everything. He is a human computer.

Cousin Hector

- Read your character sketch aloud to your classmates while they close their eyes and form images. Can your classmates "see" your subject?

Key In **TO** **Technology**

Don't use the adverb *very* too often. Use the **Find** feature to look for every use of the word *very*. Then delete it or replace it with a stronger word.

Reflect and Evaluate

- Are you pleased with your character sketch? Have you
  - ☑ introduced your character in an interesting way?
  - ☑ included sharp descriptive details?
  - ☑ made some vivid comparisons?
- What do you like best about your writing? What still needs work?
- Will this character sketch go in your portfolio? Why or why not?

ᖴOLLOW YOUR DREAMS

▶ 1 Look Back at the Unit

Rank Decisions In this unit, you read about people whose decisions helped make their dreams come true.

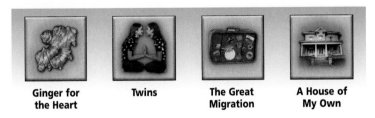

Ginger for the Heart

Twins

The Great Migration

A House of My Own

Write the title of each selection and a character's decision on an index card. Then rank the decisions according to how difficult they were to make. Share and defend your ranking.

▶ 2 Show What You Know

Sum It All Up Expand and organize your ideas on this mind map. Share your ideas about dreams and decisions with a partner.

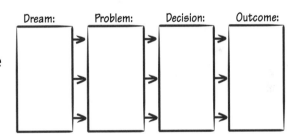

Dream: Problem: Decision: Outcome:

Reflect and Evaluate Finish these sentences:
• Something that matters a lot to me is _____.
• To make my dreams come true, I will have to _____.

Add this writing to your portfolio. Include work from the unit that shows what you learned.

▶ 3 Make Connections

To Your Community Invite friends, family, or members of the community to your class. Ask them to share dreams they have, problems they have faced, and decisions they have made in their lives.

Coming Full Circle

WE SEE DIFFERENT PHASES OF THE MOON AS IT ORBITS THE EARTH ONCE EVERY 29½ DAYS. HOW MANY TIMES DID THE FULL MOON APPEAR IN THE LAST YEAR? IN THE LAST CENTURY? IN THE LAST MILLENNIUM? WHAT DOES THIS TELL YOU ABOUT HOW NATURE WORKS IN CYCLES? WHAT CHANGES? WHAT STAYS THE SAME?

Sky and Water I, M.C. Escher, woodcut. Copyright © 1938.

The Certainty of Change

- What kinds of things change in the natural world? Describe these changes.

- What kinds of changes happen in cycles? How can we predict these changes?

- What kinds of changes happen suddenly? Can we predict these kinds of changes, too? Explain.

THEME-RELATED BOOKS

NOVEL

Cactus Hotel
by Brenda Z. Guiberson

A huge cactus grows to be nearly two hundred years old. Over the course of its long life, it provides a place to live for many small animals.

Volcanoes
by Neil Morris

This book explains everything about volcanoes. It describes how they change and how they change the areas around them.

The Time Machine
by H. G. Wells

A time-traveler explores the future, then returns to his own time to tell about the changes humankind experiences.

Build Language and Vocabulary

GIVE INFORMATION

The philosopher Heraclitus lived in ancient Greece about 2,500 years ago. He discussed many important ideas in his speeches. What do you think he meant about change being permanent?

NOTHING IS
SO PERMANENT
AS CHANGE.

—Heraclitus

Today, tourists from all over the world visit the Temple of Artemis and other ruins to learn more about ancient Greece.

MAKE A MIND MAP

Think of different kinds of changes. What kinds of changes happen in cycles? What kinds happen slowly over time? What kinds happen suddenly? Add two examples of each kind of change to the mind map.

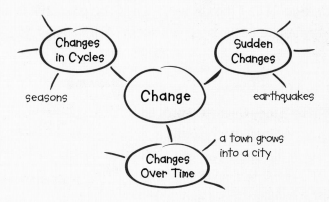

BUILD YOUR VOCABULARY

Words About Change Work with a group. Choose an example of change from your mind map and collect words that describe it. Organize your words into a chart.

Town to City

Then	Now
dirt roads	paved streets
small houses	skyscrapers

USE LANGUAGE STRUCTURES ▶ RELATIVE CLAUSES

Writing: Tell About Changes Write two complex sentences about a change. Each sentence should have a clause that begins with a word from the **Word Bank**.

Example:

The people **who** settled Chicago would be surprised to see today's skyscrapers.

Word Bank

who
whose
whom
that
which

THE MOTHER WHO LOST HER DAUGHTER

play based on a
Greek myth retold
by Anne Rockwell

Prepare to Read

Idea Exchange Skim "The Origin of Myths" on page 219. In a group, talk about what the pictures tell you about each god and goddess.

bear fruit produce ripe fruit in time for harvest

damp slightly wet, moist

dull not shiny

gloomy sad, not cheerful

shiver shake with cold, fear, or excitement

shrivel up become dry and smaller in size

sprout begin to grow

underworld to the ancient Greeks, the underground home for the dead

wither become dry

LEARN KEY VOCABULARY

Relate Words Study the new words and their definitions. Then draw a picture of summertime in the upper part of a circle and a picture of wintertime in the lower part. Write a sentence about each half of the circle. Use as many of the new words as you can.

Drawing

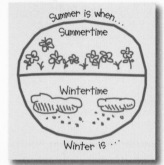

LEARN ABOUT CHARACTERS AND PLOT

A **character** is a person, animal, or imaginary creature in a story or play. The **plot** is the sequence of events that happen. The plot is often about a problem that the main character must solve. The words and actions of the characters move the plot along.

> ### READING STRATEGY
> **How to Analyze Characters and Plot**
> 1. Preview the selection and find the names of the characters.
> 2. As you read, ask yourself: What are the character's traits? What is the character's problem?
> 3. Think about how the character will act. See if these actions show up in the plot.

As you read "The Mother Who Lost Her Daughter," identify the characters. Think about how their traits and problems affect the events in the plot.

THE ORIGIN OF MYTHS

In ancient Greece, over 3,000 years ago, people did not understand events in the natural world such as the changing seasons or the rising and setting of the sun. They made up stories called myths to explain these **mysteries**. In the myths they told how different gods and goddesses made events happen.

Here are five of the Greek gods and goddesses and the parts of the world they controlled.

Athena, goddess of wisdom and war planning, had the ability to change shape and disguise herself.

Hermes, messenger of the gods and a guide for travelers, was a son of Zeus.

Demeter was goddess of growing things. She ruled over the harvest.

Zeus, king of the gods and goddesses, controlled the sky and weather. He ruled from his home on Mount Olympus.

Hades, god of the **underworld**, ruled over the dead. He was the brother of Zeus.

mysteries things not known or understood

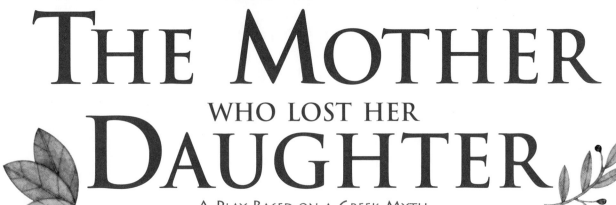

THE MOTHER
WHO LOST HER
DAUGHTER

A PLAY BASED ON A GREEK MYTH
RETOLD BY ANNE ROCKWELL

The goddess Demeter is deeply saddened when her daughter Persephone is taken from her by the god of the underworld. In her sadness, Demeter takes her gifts of fruit and flowers from Earth, but restores them when Persephone is returned to her. Demeter's joy and sadness are reflected in the cycle of the seasons.

CHARACTERS

In ancient Greek drama, the chorus provided narration and commentary on the action. These characters are in the chorus and should read their parts aloud.

FIRST CHORUS
SECOND CHORUS
SINGLE FEMALE VOICE
SINGLE MALE VOICE

These are the actors in the play. The actors should act out their parts as they say their lines.

DEMETER
PERSEPHONE
TRIPTOLEMUS
HADES
HERMES

DEMETER LOSES HER DAUGHTER

One day, Demeter's daughter Persephone sees a strange flower and picks it.
She falls through an opening in the ground into the underworld.

FIRST CHORUS: The Mother Who Lost Her Daughter

SECOND CHORUS: A play based on a Greek myth retold by Anne Rockwell

FIRST CHORUS: Demeter was the goddess of green and growing things. She was good and kind and beautiful, and she had a young daughter named Persephone. No mother ever loved a child as much as Demeter loved her Persephone.

SECOND CHORUS: In those days, it was always summertime, and people on Earth were never cold or hungry. But they did not know how to plant seeds.

FIRST CHORUS: Only Demeter could make things grow. Without her, people would have had no fruit and flowers, or wheat and barley with which to make their bread. But Demeter saw to it that the fields were high and golden with wheat and barley and the trees always bore sweet fruit.

One day, her daughter Persephone was picking flowers in a meadow.

PERSEPHONE: [*singing softly in background*]

SECOND CHORUS: Persephone danced and sang as she picked the flowers. Suddenly she stopped dancing and said, . . .

PERSEPHONE: Ohhh, how beautiful!

FIRST CHORUS: For Persephone saw a strange flower she had never seen before. She ran over to pick it, singing and dancing as she added it to her bouquet.

SECOND CHORUS: [*deep voice*] Far down below in the **chilly, dank** underworld Hades . . .

SINGLE MALE VOICE: [*heavily*] the god who ruled the land of the dead . . .

FIRST CHORUS: [*deep voice*] heard Persephone's sweet singing and the sound of her dancing feet.

He decided he wanted the young girl to be his queen. She was full of laughter and joy, and Hades often grew **gloomy** and lonely in his dark and **dismal** kingdom, with only the dead for company. He made up his mind to steal Persephone away from the flower-filled meadow.

[*Sound Effect: cracking and breaking sound in background, growing from soft to thunderous*]

---

chilly, dank cold, wet
dismal depressing

SECOND CHORUS: [*quickly*] All at once there was a terrible cracking sound. The earth where Persephone danced opened wide. Hades rose up from the dark underworld, driving a **golden chariot** pulled by black horses.

SINGLE MALE VOICE: [*forcefully*] He grabbed Persephone, lifted her into his chariot . . .

FIRST CHORUS: [*quickly*] and galloped back to the black hole where the earth had ripped open.

PERSEPHONE: [*frantic*] Mother! Mother! Help me!

SECOND CHORUS: The poor girl **shrieked** as loudly as she could. But Persephone had danced so far from where her mother was, that Demeter could not hear her calling.

SINGLE FEMALE VOICE: Only a little **swineherd tending his pigs** saw what happened.

FIRST CHORUS: He began to cry as loudly as Persephone, because all his pigs tumbled into the black opening in the earth. Then the hole closed behind them.

B E F O R E   Y O U   M O V E   O N . . .

1. **Setting** Were there seasons in this part of the myth? Explain your answer.
2. **Fantasy and Reality** Which events could happen in real life? Which could not?
3. **Character's Motive** Why did Hades take Persephone down into the underworld?

---

golden chariot kind of cart made of gold
shrieked yelled, screamed, let out a loud cry

swineherd tending his pigs boy who takes care of pigs

DEMETER LOOKS FOR PERSEPHONE

Demeter cannot find her daughter. She learns that Hades has pulled her down into the underworld. Demeter demands her return.

SECOND CHORUS: Demeter searched for her daughter.

FIRST CHORUS: [*agitated*] She ran everywhere calling for her, and when she could not find her, she began to **sob and wail**. No laughing girl's voice called back to her, . . .

SINGLE FEMALE VOICE: [*faint as if far away*] I am coming, Mother.

SECOND CHORUS: Persephone could not answer, for she was far, far away.

FIRST CHORUS: [*slow and gloomy*] Day after day she sat, sad and silent, next to Hades on the throne he had given her in the land of the dead. Her tan and rosy cheeks grew pale and cold. She ate nothing, until one day when she tasted a **pomegranate** and . . .

SINGLE MALE VOICE: [*slow and measured*] swallowed one of its tiny, blood-red seeds.

SECOND CHORUS: Demeter traveled all over the world searching for her lost child. Her beautiful golden hair, which had been the color of **ripe** wheat, turned **dull** and gray. In her **grief**, the goddess forgot to tell the wheat and barley to grow.

---

sob and wail   cry loudly without control
pomegranate   red fruit with juicy, sour-tasting seeds

ripe   ready to harvest
grief   great sadness

FIRST CHORUS: So all the stalks of wheat and barley **withered**. She forgot to tell the trees to **bear fruit**.

SECOND CHORUS: So the fruit trees **shed** their green leaves, and their apples and pears and figs **shriveled up** and died.

SINGLE MALE VOICE: The first cold winter in the world came.

SINGLE FEMALE VOICE: All the people were hungry.

ALL VOICES: Their children cried, for they had no bread or fruit to eat and they were cold, besides.

FIRST CHORUS: [*quickened pace*] Demeter kept on searching for Persephone. She asked everyone she met if they had seen her child. But everyone said no until at last the goddess met a boy called Triptolemus.

SINGLE FEMALE VOICE: Triptolemus was the older brother of the little swineherd.

SECOND CHORUS: Demeter asked Triptolemus, as she asked everyone she met, . . .

DEMETER: Have you seen my lovely child who is lost? Have you seen dear Persephone with her golden **braids** and dancing feet?

FIRST CHORUS: And Triptolemus answered, . . .

TRIPTOLEMUS: I have not seen her, but I know where she is.

SECOND CHORUS: Then he told the goddess what his brother had seen that **dreadful** day.

FIRST CHORUS: When Demeter heard what Triptolemus told her, she grew very angry. Since Hades was the brother of Zeus, she went straight up to Mount Olympus and said to **mighty** Zeus, . . .

DEMETER: Your **wicked** brother has stolen my child! Make him give her back to me!

SECOND CHORUS: And Demeter, who had always been so kind and gentle, screamed at Zeus so that even he was afraid. Besides, he was sad to see the fruits and grains and grasses of the earth all withered and gone. It was no fun for him to watch the mortals below when they just sat and **shivered** with cold and hunger.

---

shed dropped
braids hair tied and twisted like rope
dreadful bad, horrible, awful
mighty powerful
wicked bad, mean, evil

BEFORE YOU MOVE ON...

1. **Cause and Effect** Why was Demeter so sad? What changes happened on Earth because of her sadness?

2. **Foreshadowing** Do you think it is important that Persephone ate a pomegranate seed? Why or why not?

3. **Details/Sequence** How did Demeter find out where Persephone was? What happened next?

PERSEPHONE RETURNS

Zeus makes Hades return Persephone to Earth for part of every year.
When she arrives, she brings spring. When she goes back, it is winter.

FIRST CHORUS: So Zeus sent Hermes down to the underworld kingdom. Hermes told Hades that Zeus **commanded** him to return Persephone to her mother. Hades could not **refuse to obey** the orders of his brother, for Zeus was even more powerful than he. But Hades knew that the girl had eaten the pomegranate seed.

SINGLE MALE VOICE: The blood-red pomegranate was the fruit of the dead.

SECOND CHORUS: Anyone who tasted it had to return, sooner or later, to Hades' underworld kingdom.

HADES: I will let her go, since Zeus commands me, . . .

FIRST CHORUS: said Hades to the messenger god.

HADES: But because of the pomegranate seed she ate, she must return to me for part of the year to sit beside me as my wife and queen.

SECOND CHORUS: Persephone returned to her mother. [*lively*] Demeter was glad and happy again. Once more she told the wheat and barley to grow. She made red poppies **appear** among the golden wheat and made the trees bear apples and pears and figs. She made the earth **put forth** all the good things that people needed.

SINGLE FEMALE VOICE: It was the first springtime in the world. And everyone was happy again.

---

commanded told, ordered
refuse to obey say no to
appear come up, show, become visible
put forth grow

FIRST CHORUS: But after eight months, Persephone had to say goodbye to her mother and return to her throne beside her husband, King Hades. She had to **remain** in the cold, **damp**, dark underworld for four long months. While she was there, she seemed as cold and lifeless as the dead around her, and her husband did not understand why she would not dance and sing for him.

ALL VOICES: Throughout those four months of every year, Demeter **mourns** for her child. The wheat and barley wither and die. The red poppy petals fall away, and the trees bear no more fruit.

SINGLE MALE VOICE: [*heavy, deep voice*] Winter comes.

ALL VOICES: Demeter's tears fall as cold rain and **sleet** until at last the happy day arrives when her daughter returns to her and springtime begins.

SECOND CHORUS: [*lightly*] Demeter rewarded Triptolemus well for his help. She gave him a chariot pulled by dragons . . .

SINGLE FEMALE VOICE: a bag of seeds . . .

SINGLE MALE VOICE: and a wooden plow.

....

remain stay, wait
mourns shows her sadness by crying
sleet frozen raindrops

FIRST CHORUS: Then she whispered to him the secrets of how to make things grow and how to harvest them and save them so that people would have food to eat through the long winter months.

SECOND CHORUS: Triptolemus traveled all over the world in his dragon chariot. He taught the people who would listen to him how to plant and how to harvest and **preserve** what they had grown. All over the world, people planted the seeds Triptolemus gave them—

SINGLE FEMALE VOICE: the gifts of Demeter.

SINGLE MALE VOICE: The people had bread for the long winter.

ALL VOICES: When springtime comes, people on Earth **rejoice** with Demeter. Persephone returns to her mother and sings and dances through the fields. Demeter is filled with joy and all the green things **sprout** and grow again.

PERSEPHONE: [*softly singing, fade out voice*]

----

preserve keep fresh, protect
rejoice become happy or joyful, celebrate

BEFORE YOU MOVE ON...

1. **Cause and Effect** Why did Persephone have to return to the underworld?
2. **Inference** Why do you think that Persephone felt "cold and lifeless" in the underworld?
3. **Conclusions** How does this myth explain the change of seasons?

ABOUT THE AUTHOR

Anne Rockwell says that she loved rainy days as a child. "I didn't have to go outside to play. Instead, I could stay indoors reading. . . ." Her feelings about the outdoors have changed since then. Now she gets ideas for her books while walking on the beach with her dog and sketchbook. Nature's forces of waves and winds, in Connecticut, where Anne Rockwell lives, give her a different beach to observe each day.

Respond to the Play
Check Your Understanding

SUM IT UP

Analyze Characters Complete character maps for Demeter, Hades, and Persephone.

Character Map

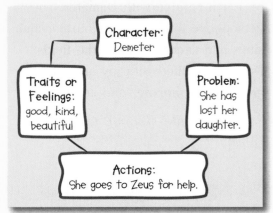

Relate Problems, Solutions, and Consequences Make a chart like this one for each character. For the last two rows, work with a partner to think of another possible solution and consequence.

Problem	Hades is lonely.
Solution	He kidnaps Persephone.
Consequence	Persephone is unhappy.
Other Solution	Hades finds a wife who wants to marry him.
Other Consequence	They live happily ever after.

Review your chart with a partner. Discuss how the characters affect the plot.

THINK IT OVER

Discuss and Write Talk about these questions with a partner. Write the answers.

1. **Plot** How is this myth like a circle?

2. **Conclusions** What are all the different ways that Demeter helped people on Earth?

3. **Judgments** In the myth, spring is a time of growth and happiness, and wintertime is sad and lifeless. Do you feel this way about the seasons? Give reasons to support your answer.

4. **Inference** Why do people create myths?

EXPRESS YOURSELF ▶ NEGOTIATE

Work with a partner. Act out a scene in which two characters from the play negotiate to reach an agreement.

Example:

Demeter: If you talk to Hades for me, I will let the crops grow again.

Zeus: I will talk to Hades if you make sure the people have food. Agreed?

Demeter: Agreed.

Language Arts and Literature

LITERARY ANALYSIS

MAKE A PLOT DIAGRAM

Learn About Plot Use a **plot diagram** to show events in a story. A plot diagram shows these main elements of the plot:

- The **conflict** is the story problem. Most stories start with or are built around a conflict.

- **Complications** are events that make the story problem harder to solve.

- The **climax** is the turning point. It is the most important or exciting part of the story where the outcome of the conflict is decided. Actions or events that lead to the climax are the **rising action**. The events that follow the climax are the **falling action**.

- The **resolution** comes at the end of the story. It answers the remaining questions.

Plot Diagram

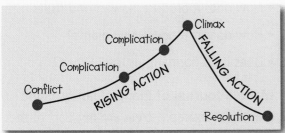

Practice Make a plot diagram for "The Mother Who Lost Her Daughter." In the diagram, write notes to show the plot's main elements.

WRITING
LITERARY ANALYSIS

WRITE A MYTH

Imagine that you are a storyteller who lives in ancient Greece. Write your own myth about how the natural world changes.

1 Prepare to Write Choose a natural event. Then choose a Greek god or goddess, or invent one as a character. Make a character map like the one you made on page 228.

2 Write Your Draft Imagine the myth in your mind. Write what you see and hear.

3 Edit Your Work Do your characters have personal traits? How is the plot or problem solved in the end? Remember to check for correct spelling and punctuation.

4 Publish a Book Put all of the class myths together in a book. Give the book a title, and share it with others.

 Develop your skill in the **writer's craft**. See Handbook pages 414–423.

Respond to the Play, continued

Content Area Connections

SCIENCE

STUDY BEHAVIOR AND NATURE

How do events in nature affect people's behavior? One way to study these events is by following the **scientific method**. The scientific method is a process for gathering information. With a group, choose one event in the living world that you would like to study.

1 **Form a Hypothesis** A **hypothesis** is a statement that you will try to prove. For example: People sleep more when the days are shorter and the nights are longer. Make a hypothesis about the natural event you chose to study.

2 **Do Your Research** Look at calendars, encyclopedias, and almanacs to get information about your topic. Make observations. If possible, interview people to gather **data**. Data is information that you get from the real, or living, world.

3 **Draw Conclusions and Explain Results** Review the data and information you collected. Draw a conclusion. Was your hypothesis proven to be true? If not, then, like other scientists, you must change your hypothesis to match the data. Explain the results of your study to a group.

SCIENCE
REPRESENTING/WRITING

CREATE A BOTANICAL JOURNAL

Scientists write and draw in botanical journals to collect information about plants. Make a class botanical journal to record information about plants in the play. Follow these steps:

1 **Sketch** Draw a detailed picture of the plant. Compare pictures of the plant to help you.

2 **Label** Use an encyclopedia or field guide to find the botanical name of the plant. The botanical name may be different from the name you use. Write the name under your drawing. Label other parts of the plant.

3 **Write** Write a short paragraph about the life cycle of the plant. Answer these questions:

- When does the plant sprout?
- How does it produce flowers and fruit?
- How does it produce new plants?
- Does it go dormant, or rest? When?

4 **Make a Journal of Plants** Classify all the plants. For example, trees are not part of the same group as cactus. Arrange them in groups in the journal. Then create a cover.

 For more about the **research process**, see Handbook pages 394–399.

Chrysalis Diary

poem for two voices
by Paul Fleischman

Prepare to Read

THINK ABOUT WHAT YOU KNOW

Discuss Life Stages Discuss the stages of human life. Use the stages to make a time line on the board.

LEARN KEY VOCABULARY

caterpillar worm-like stage in the life cycle of a butterfly or moth

cease stop

chronicle record of events in the order in which they happened, history

chrysalis stage in the life of some insects when they are enclosed in a hard shell

dangle hang down loosely

diary notebook in which private thoughts are written

dissolve disappear

fasten attach, join, connect

reshape change into a new form

shed lose by natural process

vanish disappear, fade

Use Context Clues Study the new words and their definitions. Replace each underlined word in the paragraph with a vocabulary word. You may need to change the form of some words.

The Life Story of a Butterfly

A butterfly starts as a tiny egg, then changes into a <u>worm-like creature</u>. The caterpillar <u>hooks</u> onto a plant. Then it <u>loses</u> its skin and becomes an <u>insect enclosed in a hard shell</u>. The chrysalis <u>hangs down loosely</u> from the plant. Inside, the chrysalis <u>completely changes</u> itself. Its old body parts <u>disappear</u>, and it grows wings. It <u>stops</u> being a caterpillar or a chrysalis. It is now a butterfly. It comes out, flies away, and <u>fades from view</u>.

LEARN ABOUT STEPS IN A PROCESS

A **process** is a series of steps. When you put the steps in order, you can understand the whole process.

> ### READING STRATEGY
> **How to Relate Steps in a Process**
> 1. Pay attention to the order in which the steps happen. Look for signal words such as *first, second, next, then,* and *finally.*
> 2. Make a graphic organizer that shows the order of the steps.
> 3. Reread the selection and check the order.

Complete a diagram to show a butterfly's life cycle as you read "Chrysalis Diary."

Chrysalis Diary

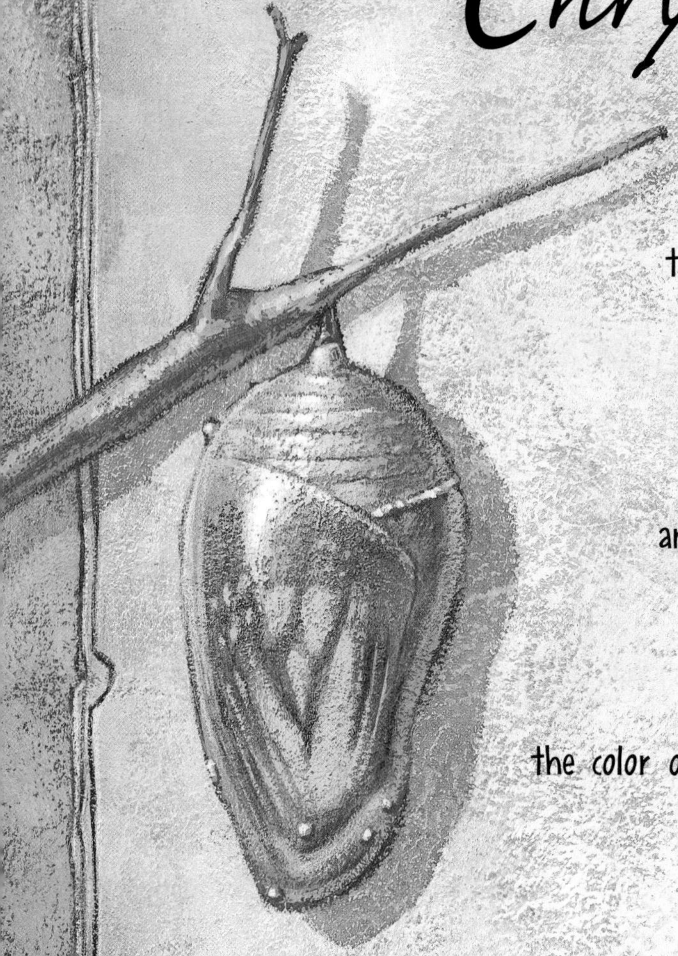

November 13:

Cold told me
to fasten my feet
to this branch,

to dangle upside down
from my perch,

to shed my skin,

to cease being a caterpillar
and I have obeyed.

and I have obeyed.

December 6:

Green,

the color of leaves and life,
has vanished!

has vanished!
The empire of leaves
lies in ruins!

lies in ruins!
I study the
brown new world around me.

I hear few sounds.

I fear the future.

Have any others of my kind
survived this cataclysm?

Swinging back and forth
in the wind,
I feel immeasurably alone.

my perch the branch where I sit

survived this cataclysm lived through this great disaster

immeasurably so very much

I can make out snow falling.

I find I never tire of
watching the flakes
in their multitudes
passing my window.

Astounding.
I enter these
wondrous events
in my chronicle

January 4:

For five days and nights
it's been drifting down.

The world is now white.
Astounding.

knowing no reader
would believe me.

February 12:

Unable to see out
at all this morning,

and branches falling.

ponder their import,

and wait for more.

An ice storm last night.

Yet I hear boughs cracking

Hungry for sounds
in this silent world,
I cherish these,

miser them away
in my memory,
and wait for more.

---

drifting down slowly falling to the ground
multitudes great numbers
wondrous events beautiful happenings
boughs large branches

cherish love, care a lot about
ponder their import wonder what
they mean
miser them away put them in a
secret place for me only

March 28:

I wonder whether
I am the same being
who started this diary.

like the weather without.

my legs are dissolving,

my body's not mine.
This morning,
a breeze from the south,
strangely fragrant,

a faint glimpse of green
in the branches.

I've felt stormy inside

My mouth is reshaping,

wings are growing
my body's not mine.

a red-winged blackbird's
call in the distance,

And now I recall
that last night
I dreamt of flying.

—*Paul Fleischman*

fragrant sweet-smelling
faint glimpse peek, brief view
recall remember

ABOUT THE POET

Paul Fleischman grew up in California, where the seasons of the year seem to blend into one another. When he moved to New Hampshire, he experienced a dramatic change of seasons for the first time. He wrote his poem "Chrysalis Diary" in a home deep in the woods. There, the ever-changing sounds of nature drifted into his poetry.

Respond to the Poem
Check Your Understanding

SUM IT UP

Relate Steps in a Process Write these steps in the life cycle of a butterfly. Add the missing steps.

1. _____

2. Each egg hatches into a caterpillar.

3. _____

4. _____

5. A beautiful butterfly emerges from the chrysalis.

Put a check beside the steps described in the poem.

Make Predictions The entry for March 18 ends with the words "And now I recall that last night I dreamt of flying." In a group, discuss why you think the poet chose to end the poem with these words. Then, choose a date later in March and write a new entry for the diary that shows what you are experiencing as a butterfly.

THINK IT OVER

Discuss and Write Talk about these questions with a partner. Write the answers.

1. **Mood** What is the mood, or feeling, of the poem? What words in the poem support your answer?

2. **Author's Style** Why do you think the poet wrote this poem as if he were the chrysalis?

3. **Personal Experience** People also go through many changes in their lives. What kinds of changes have you experienced? Compare yourself now to the way you were as a very young child or baby.

EXPRESS YOURSELF

▶RECITE A POEM FOR TWO VOICES

Paul Fleischman wrote this poem to be read aloud by two readers. Sometimes the readers take turns, and sometimes they read together.

Practice in pairs first, and then form two groups with the whole class. Each group reads one column of the poem aloud. The groups join together when the same words appear on the same line in each column. Listen to see if your voices go together and are clearly understood.

The Big
Blast

science article
by Patricia Lauber

Prepare to Read

THINK ABOUT WHAT YOU KNOW

Idea Exchange Read about volcanoes on page 237. Tell a partner one thing you learned.

avalanche sudden falling of snow or rock down a mountain

colonizer plant or animal that moves to a new place to live

crater bowl-shaped hole at the top of a volcano

dome large, round top

earthquake sudden movement of the earth

eruption strong, sudden release of something

flow stream, steady movement

force power, energy; make something move

lava hot, melted rock that comes out of a volcano

magma hot, melted rock below the earth's surface

pressure energy used to press one thing against another

survivor animal or plant that lives through a dangerous event

LEARN KEY VOCABULARY

Use New Words in Context Study the new words and their definitions. Make a four-square diagram for each word.

Word: dome	Picture
Definition: large, round top	Sentence: Mount St. Helens' dome is very large.

LEARN TO SKIM AND TAKE NOTES

When you **skim** a selection, you look at the headings, photos, and diagrams before you read the whole selection. This strategy can help you form questions and get ready to **take notes**.

> **READING STRATEGY**
> **How to Skim and Take Notes**
> 1. Read the headings.
> 2. Look at the diagrams, photos, captions, and charts. Think about how these graphics relate to the headings.
> 3. Form questions you hope to answer as you read. Write each question at the top of a notecard.
> 4. As you read, write down the answers to your questions.

Skim "The Big Blast." Prepare notecards before you read, and write the answers to your questions as you read.

Sleeping Giants

Many volcanoes are quiet and still for years, even centuries. When they do awake, or become active, the once-sleeping giants shake the earth with their great power.

WHAT HAPPENS IN AN ERUPTION

The temperature deep inside the earth is very hot—so hot that it can melt rock. Melted rock is called **magma**. When rock melts, gases are released and become mixed with the magma. Magma rises and melts surrounding rock to create and fill a **magma chamber**. Pressure then causes the magma to melt a path through rock lying above. An **eruption** occurs when magma, gases, and other materials are forced through openings to the earth's **surface**.

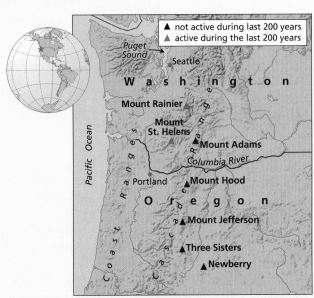

▲ not active during last 200 years
▲ active during the last 200 years

Puget Sound

Seattle

W a s h i n g t o n

Mount Rainier
Mount St. Helens
Mount Adams
Columbia River
Portland
Mount Hood

O r e g o n

Mount Jefferson
Three Sisters
Newberry

Pacific Ocean
Coast Ranges
Cascade Range

gas, ash, cinders, fragments, and dust

crater

lava

conduit

previous lava flows

magma chamber

Mount St. Helens is part of a group of mountains called the Cascade Range. The Cascade Range stretches from California to British Columbia in Canada. It took thousands of years and many eruptions to form Mount St. Helens. There were small eruptions in 1832 and 1857. The mountain then slept for more than a hundred years, but on May 18, 1980, Mount St. Helens erupted again.

magma chamber space that contains magma
surface upper or outer boundary

The Big Blast

from Volcano: The Eruption and
Healing of Mount St. Helens
by Patricia Lauber

For more than one hundred years, the volcano
Mount St. Helens lay green and silent. Then, in
the spring of 1980, it began to stir. The mountain
shook as small earthquakes took place inside
it. It blew out steam and gas. A huge bulge
formed on one side. In May the volcano erupted.
Later it looked as if all life had been wiped
out and nothing would ever grow on the
mountainside again. Yet some life was still there
and more would soon return.

The First Blast

The May 18 eruption of Mount St. Helens began with an **earthquake** that **triggered** an **avalanche**. At 8:32 A.M. instruments that were miles away **registered** a strong earthquake. The pilot and passengers of a small plane saw the north side of the mountain rippling and churning. Shaken by the quake, the **bulge** was tearing loose. It began to slide, in a huge avalanche that carried along rock ripped from deep inside Mount St. Helens.

The avalanche tore open the mountain. A **scalding blast** shot sideways out of the opening. It was a blast of steam, from water heated by rising magma.

Normally water cannot be heated beyond its boiling point, which is 212 degrees Fahrenheit at sea level. At boiling point, water turns to a gas, which we call steam. But if water is kept under **pressure**, it can be heated far beyond its boiling point and still stay liquid. (That is how a pressure cooker works.) If the pressure is removed, this superheated water suddenly turns, or flashes, to steam. As steam, it takes up much more room—it expands. The sudden change to steam can cause an explosion.

Before the eruption Mount St. Helens was like a giant pressure cooker. The rock inside it held superheated water. The water stayed liquid because it was under great pressure, sealed in the mountain. When the mountain was torn open, the pressure was suddenly **relieved.** The superheated water flashed to steam. Expanding violently, it **shattered** rock inside the mountain and exploded out the opening, traveling at speeds of up to 200 miles an hour.

The blast **flattened** whole forests of 180-foot-high firs. It snapped off or uprooted the trees, scattering the trunks as if they were straws. At first, this damage **was puzzling**. A wind of 200 miles an hour is not strong enough to **level forests of giant trees**. The explanation, **geologists** later discovered, was that the wind carried rocks ranging in size from grains of sand to blocks as big as cars. As the blast roared out of the volcano, it swept up and carried along the rock it had shattered.

---

triggered caused
registered recorded, measured
bulge huge bump
scalding blast very hot and powerful stream of air, gas, or steam
relieved let out, lessened

shattered broke up
flattened knocked down
was puzzling caused questions
level forests of giant trees make the big trees in a forest fall down and lie flat
geologists scientists who study the earth

The result was what one geologist described as "a stone wind." It was a wind of steam and rocks, traveling at high speed. The rocks gave the blast its great **force**. Before it, trees snapped and fell. Their stumps looked as if they had been **sandblasted**. The wind of stone rushed on. It stripped bark and branches from trees and uprooted them, leveling 150 square miles of countryside. At the edge of this area other trees were left standing, but the heat of the blast **scorched** and killed them.

The stone wind was traveling so fast that it overtook and passed the avalanche. On its path was Spirit Lake, one of the most beautiful lakes in the Cascades. The blast stripped the trees from the **slopes** surrounding the lake and moved on. Meanwhile the avalanche had hit a **ridge**

These photos (top to bottom) show the first few minutes of the eruption on May 18, 1980. An earthquake, an avalanche, and a violent blast closely followed one another.

....

sandblasted stripped clean by powerfully blown sand
scorched burned
slopes sides of the mountain
ridge narrow area of higher ground

and split. One part of it poured into Spirit Lake, adding a 300-foot layer of rock and dirt to the bottom of the lake. The slide of avalanche into the lake **forced** the water out. The water **sloshed** up the slopes, then fell back into the lake. With it came thousands of trees **felled** by the blast.

The main part of the avalanche swept down the valley of the North Fork of the Toutle River. There, in the valley, most of the avalanche slowed and stopped. It covered 24 square miles and averaged 150 feet thick.

POINT-BY-POINT

Change Comes to Mount St. Helens

An earthquake causes an avalanche.

Mount St. Helens loses part of its north side in the first blast.

The blast breaks off rocks and carries them at high speed. It damages everything in its path.

The blast leveled whole forests of huge firs. The tiny figures of two scientists (lower right) give an idea of the scale.

....
sloshed splashed
felled knocked down

BEFORE YOU MOVE ON...

1. **Cause and Effect** What effect did the avalanche have on the mountain?

2. **Vocabulary** Make a list of words that describe something that has been damaged or destroyed. Example: *shattered*

3. **Prediction** What might happen if material continues to flow into the lake and river?

The Upward Eruption

The blast itself continued for 10 to 15 minutes, then stopped. Minutes later Mount St. Helens began to erupt upwards. A dark column of ash and ground-up rock rose miles into the sky. Winds blew the ash eastward. Lightning flashed in the ash cloud and started forest fires. In Yakima, Washington, some 80 miles away, the sky turned so dark that streetlights went on at noon. Ash fell like snow that would not melt. This eruption continued for nine hours.

Shortly after noon the color of the ash column changed. It became lighter, a sign that the volcano was now throwing out mostly new magma. Until then much of the ash had been made of old rock.

At the same time the volcano began giving off huge **flows** of **pumice** and ash. The material was very hot, with temperatures of about 1,000 degrees Fahrenheit, and it traveled down the mountain at speeds of 100 miles an hour. The flows went on until 5:30 in the afternoon. They formed **a wedge-shaped plain** of pumice on the side of the mountain. Two weeks later temperatures in the pumice were still 780 degrees.

Finally, there were the mudflows, which started when heat from the blast melted ice and snow on the mountaintop. The water mixed with ash, pumice, ground-up rock, and dirt and rocks of the avalanche. The result was a thick mixture that was like

Melted snow and ice caused this mudflow. The smaller part of the flow went into Spirit Lake (lower left), while the larger part traveled down the Toutle River.

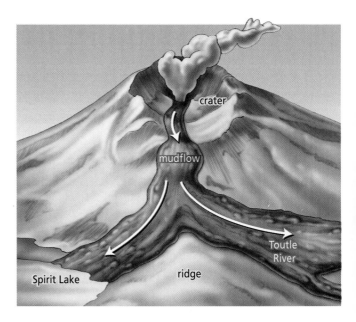

pumice rock from the volcano
a wedge-shaped plain an area shaped like a triangle

POINT-BY-POINT

Change Comes to Mount St. Helens

Mount St. Helens erupts again. This time the blast comes out of the top.

Very hot flows of volcanic rock and ash move down the mountain.

Melted snow and ice mix with rocks and dirt. These mudflows cause great damage.

The mudflow swept up and carried along huge boulders and tore out bridges.

wet concrete, a mudflow. The mudflows traveled fast, **scouring** the landscape and **sweeping** down the slopes into river valleys. Together their speed and thickness did great damage.

The largest mudflow was made of avalanche material from the valley of the North Fork of the Toutle River. It **churned** down the river valley, tearing out steel bridges, ripping houses apart, picking up boulders and trucks and carrying them along. Miles away it **choked** the Cowlitz River and blocked **shipping channels** in the Columbia River.

....

scouring clearing away
sweeping moving quickly
churned moved with great force
choked blocked, stopped
shipping channels deep areas that ships pass through

BEFORE YOU MOVE ON...

1. **Cause and Effect** How did lightning affect the forest?
2. **Paraphrase** Explain how the avalanche material became a mudflow.
3. **Summary** Compare your prediction to what actually happened as mud and rocks flowed into the lake and river.

Many Changes for Mount St. Helens

When the sun rose on May 19, it showed a greatly changed St. Helens. The mountain was 1,300 feet shorter than it had been the morning before. Most of the old top had slid down the mountain in the avalanche. The rest had erupted out as shattered rock. Geologists later figured that the volcano had lost three quarters of a cubic mile of old rock.

The north side of the mountain had changed from a green and lovely slope to a **fan-shaped wasteland**.

At the top of Mount St. Helens was a big, new **crater** with the shape of a horseshoe. Inside the crater was the vent, the opening through which rock and gases erupted from time to time over the next few years.

In 1980 St. Helens erupted six more times. Most of these eruptions were explosive—ash **soared** into the air, pumice swept down the north side of the mountain. In the eruptions of June and August, thick **pasty lava** oozed out of the vent and built a **dome**. But both domes were destroyed by the next eruptions. In October the pattern changed. The explosions stopped, and thick lava built a dome that was not destroyed. Later eruptions added to the dome, making it bigger and bigger.

During this time, geologists were learning to read the clues found before eruptions. They learned to predict what St. Helens was going to do. The predictions helped to protect people who were on and near the mountain.

Among these people were many **natural scientists**. They had come to look for **survivors**, for plants and animals that had lived through the eruption. They had come to look for **colonizers**, for plants and animals that would move in. Mount St. Helens had erupted many times before. Each time life had returned. Now scientists would have a chance to see how it did. They would see how nature **healed itself**.

May 17, 1980. Mount St. Helens before the big eruption.

---

fan-shaped wasteland large area of land, shaped like a fan, where everything is dead

soared flew high

pasty rough and sticky

natural scientists scientists that study the earth and living things

healed itself returned itself to health

September 9, 1980. Mount St. Helens after the big eruption.

BEFORE YOU MOVE ON...

1. **Comparison** After October, how did the eruptions affect the mountain differently than before?

2. **Conclusions** What could scientists learn from the eruptions of Mount St. Helens? Explain how this knowledge might be helpful.

POINT-BY-POINT

Change Comes to Mount St. Helens

 An earthquake causes an avalanche.

 Mount St. Helens loses part of its north side in the first blast.

 The blast breaks off rocks and carries them at high speed. It damages everything in its path.

 Mount St. Helens erupts again. This time the blast comes out of the top.

 Very hot flows of volcanic rock and ash move down the mountain.

 Melted snow and ice mix with rocks and dirt. These mudflows cause great damage.

 Mount St. Helens becomes 1,300 feet shorter in one day.

 The mountain erupts six more times and then stops.

 Signs of life return to the mountain.

In 1982, 110,000 acres were set aside as Mount St. Helens National Volcanic Monument. Trails, viewpoints, and information centers have been established so that visitors can enjoy the mountain.

Afterword: Twenty Years Later

After the eruption, the north side of Mount St. Helens looked as lifeless as the moon. It looked like a place where nothing could be alive or ever live again. Yet life was there, and more life would soon appear.

Some plants had **survived** under the snow. Some survived as roots, bulbs, and stems underground.

Some small animals also survived under the snow or in the ground. There were chipmunks, squirrels, deer mice, ants. Eggs laid by insects also survived underground. Fish in ice-covered lakes survived. In time, larger animals wandered through. Deer and elk fed on some of the plants, but they also brought in seeds. Some were stuck in their coats. Some were in their **droppings**.

Scientists knew that Mount St. Helens had erupted in the past and that each time life had returned to the mountain. Watching after the 1980 eruption, they were surprised at how quickly life began to come back. Someday the volcano will erupt again, and then, once again, life will return.

—*Patricia Lauber*

survived lived through the eruption
droppings waste from digested food

ABOUT THE AUTHOR

Patricia Lauber has always liked reading and writing about volcanoes. She had not, however, thought of writing about Mount St. Helens until she saw a photograph of a hardy green plant that had pushed its way through a crack in the ash and put out a pink flower. "Suddenly," she says, "I knew that I wanted to write a book about the eruption and also about the return of life." After making two research trips to the volcano, she wrote her book.

Respond to the Article
Check Your Understanding

SUM IT UP

Relate Causes and Effects An event has a cause and effect. The **cause** is what made it happen. The **effect** is the result of the event.

Review your notecards. Add more notes if you need to. Then use your notes to write causes and effects in a chart.

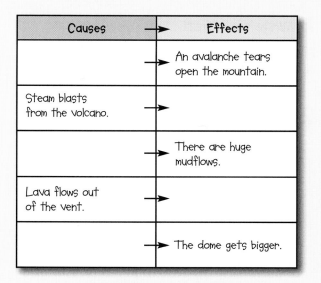

Causes	→	Effects
	→	An avalanche tears open the mountain.
Steam blasts from the volcano.	→	
	→	There are huge mudflows.
Lava flows out of the vent.	→	
	→	The dome gets bigger.

Compare Literature "The Mother Who Lost Her Daughter" is a myth, and "The Big Blast" is nonfiction. Still, they both tell about change. Write a few sentences to compare how these two selections relate to the topic of change.

THINK IT OVER

Discuss and Write Talk about these questions with a partner. Write the answers.

1. **Prediction** Do you think Mount St. Helens will look the same in the year 2100 as it did in the year 2000? Why or why not?

2. **Inference** After the big blast, how do you think life changed for people who lived near Mount St. Helens?

3. **Personal Experience** What should people know if they live near a volcano? What can people do to prepare in the event of an earthquake or eruption?

EXPRESS YOURSELF

▶ ASK FOR AND GIVE INFORMATION

With a partner, look through the article and find words about volcanoes. Write each word on a piece of paper, and put the papers in a box. Take turns drawing words and using them to ask each other questions.

Respond to the Article, continued
Language Arts and Literature

> **VOCABULARY**

USE LATIN AND GREEK ROOTS

Learn About Root Words Many words in English come from Latin and Greek, as well as other languages. **Root words** can help you understand what the whole word means in the English language. Study the chart.

Root	Meaning	Example
geo	earth	geologist
photo	light	photograph
graph	written	autograph
rupt	to break	erupt
dict	to say	predict
viv	to live	survive
sci	knowledge	scientists

Find Words Look at the vocabulary list on page 236. Which words have Greek or Latin roots?

Practice Add a word from the chart to complete each sentence.

1. A _____ studies the earth.

2. People try to _____ when volcanoes might erupt.

3. Other _____ are interested in life forms found near volcanoes.

4. They study the plants and animals that _____ volcanic eruptions.

> **WRITING**

WRITE NEWS STORIES

Write a news article about an event at Mount St. Helens before the eruption. You may want to write about an outdoor activity, for example, hiking. Then write another news story about what happened the day after the eruption.

1 **Write Your Draft** Write headlines that give the main ideas of your two stories. In the stories, answer the questions *Who? What? When? Where? Why?* and *How?*

2 **Edit Your Work** Did you answer all six questions in your articles? Did you include facts and interesting details? Check your work for correct spelling and punctuation.

3 **Publish a News Story** Rewrite or type your article on the computer in the style of a news article.

Sample Article

The Daily News
May 17, 1980

A Busy Day for Mount St. Helens
   Today was a perfect day to enjoy the outdoors at Mount St. Helens. It was 75 degrees with no wind. Hundreds of campers came to look at the beautiful scenery and breathe the fresh air.

Content Area Connections

TECHNOLOGY/MEDIA
SCIENCE

MAKE A VOLCANO REPORT

Volcanoes have erupted many times and in many different places. With a group, use the Internet or other resources to research one eruption. Present your findings to the class, using a map and chart.

1 **Gather Information** Choose a volcano like Etna, Kilauea, Krakatoa, Mauna Loa, Mount Shasta, or Vesuvius. Use the name of the volcano as the key word in your search. These Web sites might be a good place to start, but remember that new sites appear every day!

INTERNET

INFORMATION ON-LINE

Web Sites:
➤ **Volcano Sites**
  • volcano.und.nodak.edu
  • www.geol.ucsb.edu/~fisher

➤ **Online Encyclopedia**
  • www.letsfindout.com

Download helpful articles and take notes for your presentation.

2 **Make a Map** Create a map to show the location of the volcano. Label the country, closest city, and any bodies of water.

Sample Map

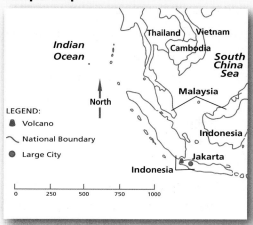

3 **Summarize Information** Present your map to the class, and tell about the effects of the eruption. Summarize each group's presentation in a class chart. Include the volcano's name, location, date of eruption, and its effects.

 Learn to use the **Internet** on Handbook pages 392–393.

D-Day: American soldiers land in Normandy during World War II.

An Enduring Legacy

- What changes in history have had a lasting effect on you? What kinds of changes can you bring about that will have a lasting effect on the future?

- Does change always represent progress? Is change always within your control?

- What can you learn about yourself by the way you respond to change?

THEME-RELATED BOOKS

Nine Spoons: A Chanukah Story
by Marci Stillerman

A few prisoners in a Nazi camp risk everything to gather together nine spoons to make a menorah for Chanukah.

So Far from the Sea
by Eve Bunting

A family brings special mementos to a grandfather who died in a Japanese internment camp.

NOVEL

Number the Stars
by Lois Lowry

During World War II, Annamarie Johansen goes on a dangerous mission to save the life of her best friend, Ellen Rosen.

Build Language and Vocabulary

DEFINE AND EXPLAIN

In 1941, the U.S. entered World War II. Americans from all parts of the country joined the war effort. Listen to the song and read the words. How do you think this song made Americans feel during the war years?

from The House I Live In

What is America to me?
A name, a map, or a flag I see
A certain word, democracy.
What is America to me?

The house I live in
A plot of earth, a street
The grocer and the butcher
Or the people that I meet.

The children in the playground
The faces that I see
All races and religions,
That's America to me.

—performed in the 1940s to support the war effort, written by Lewis Allen and Earl Robinson

MAKE A COMPARISON CHART

Make a chart to compare life in the United States in the 1940s with life in the United States today.

Life in the United States

Life in the U.S., 1940s	Life in the U.S., Today
Food and goods are in short supply.	Food and goods are readily available.
Communication is by telephone, telegraph, and letter.	E-mail, Internet, and fax are common means of communication.

BUILD YOUR VOCABULARY

Wartime Words Look at the list of words that relate to the World War II period. Find out more about these words by looking in an encyclopedia and a dictionary. Take notes.

ally	defeat	ration
buddy system	democracy	sacrifice
citizen	invade	unity
courage	join	victory

USE LANGUAGE STRUCTURES
▶ VERBS IN THE PRESENT PERFECT TENSE

Writing: Define and Explain an Historical Term Write a paragraph about America during World War II. Define and explain one of the words in the list. Use verbs in the present perfect tense.

Example:

A *sacrifice* is giving up one thing for another thing. During World War II, Americans made many sacrifices. Soldiers **have written** stories about the terrible times. If you **have read** about the war years, you know that the people at home made sacrifices, too.

Anne Frank

biography
by Yona Zeldis McDonough

Prepare to Read

THINK ABOUT WHAT YOU KNOW

Idea Exchange Read and discuss the information on pages 255–257. What were some of the key events of World War II?

annex part added to a building

concentration camp place where prisoners of war are held

declare war on tell a country of plans to fight against it

discriminate against harm or treat differently from others because of color, race, age, or religion

law rule made by the government that controls what people can and cannot do

power ability to make people do what you want

prisoner person who is held in a place and not allowed to leave

survive live through a dangerous time or event

LEARN KEY VOCABULARY

Use New Words in Context Study the new words and their definitions. Then write the paragraph and add the missing words.

After Adolf Hitler gained ____(1)____ in Germany in 1933, he took away the freedom of German Jews to live normal lives. Hitler made more than one ____(2)____ that would ____(3)____ the Jews, or treat them differently. He also sent Jews to a cruel kind of prison, or ____(4)____. In that terrible place, it was hard to ____(5)____. In 1939, Hitler invaded Poland. Great Britain decided to ____(6)____ Germany, and World War II began. During the war years, Anne Frank, a young Jewish girl, hid with her family in a building that had a secret ____(7)____ to the house. She wrote in her diary what her life was like. She described her fears of being captured and made a ____(8)____ of the Nazis.

LEARN TO USE GRAPHIC ORGANIZERS

A **graphic organizer** is a diagram that shows how information and ideas are related. It helps you to keep track of what you read.

> **READING STRATEGY**
> **How to Use a Graphic Organizer**
> 1. Think about how the ideas are related.
> 2. Create an organizer. For example, if you are reading about history, you might make a time line to show the order of events.

Look at the time line on pages 255–257. As you read "Anne Frank," think about where you would place the events in her story on the time line.

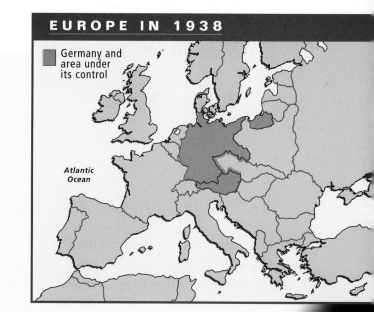

EUROPE IN 1938

Germany and
area under
its control

*Atlantic
Ocean*

REFERENCE ▼ POINT

THE YEARS
BEFORE THE WAR
1933-1938

In 1932, the people of Germany have no work and no money. Adolf Hitler blames the Jews for Germany's problems. Many Germans believe that Hitler and his Nazi Party will help them. In 1933, Hitler becomes **dictator** of Germany. He wants to rule not only Germany but the rest of Europe.

Adolf Hitler tells Germans that Jews have taken all their jobs and money. Many, but not all, Germans believe him. The Nazis force Jews to wear a yellow star with the word "Jew," shown here in Dutch.

1933

1935

1936

1938

Hitler becomes dictator of Germany.

Hitler takes away the freedoms of German Jews. He creates **laws** that **discriminate against** them.

Hitler's troops march into the Rhineland, land that is next to France.

Hitler annexes, or adds, Austria to Germany's territory.

Anne Frank   **255**

Prepare to Read, continued

REFERENCE ▼ POINT

THE WORLD AT WAR
1939–1945

In 1939, Germany invades Poland and World War II begins. Jews who live under German control try to **survive** Hitler's **anti-Jewish laws**. Many Jews find places to hide. Some Jews escape. Others fight back. However, millions of Jews are arrested and sent to **concentration camps** where they are forced to work. Many die there.

1939

Germany takes control of Czechoslovakia. Germany then invades Poland. As a result, Great Britain and France **declare war on** Germany. World War II begins.

1940

Germany invades Denmark, Norway, the Netherlands, Belgium, Luxembourg, and France.

1941

Without warning, on December 7th, Japan bombs the United States Navy at Pearl Harbor, Hawaii. The U.S. declares war on Japan the next day.

---

anti-Jewish laws rules that are unfair to people who are Jewish

German soldiers force Jews to leave their homes. Many are loaded into boxcars on trains and taken to concentration camps. Most of them starve or are killed in those camps.

1944

1945

On June 6, 1944, D-Day, more than 150,000 American, British, and Canadian soldiers land on the coast of Normandy in France. They begin to push the Germans out of France.

Germany loses the war. U.S., Soviet, and British soldiers release surviving Jews from the concentration camps.

Anne Frank

by Yona Zeldis McDonough

Anne Frank's family lives happily in Germany until Adolf Hitler becomes the leader in 1933. When Hitler begins to treat Jews unfairly, Anne's father decides to move his family to Amsterdam, the Netherlands. The Franks are safe there for a few years, but the family has to hide when Hitler's armies invade the Netherlands. Although hiding is difficult for thirteen-year-old Anne, she tries to stay cheerful and busy. She often writes about her thoughts, dreams, and feelings in a diary. On August 4, 1944, the Nazis discover the Franks' hiding place and send them to concentration camps. Everyone in the family except Anne's father dies.

1

A TIME OF CHANGE

Adolf Hitler becomes the leader of Germany and
begins to treat Jews unfairly.

Anne Frank was born in Germany. Her parents, Edith and Otto Frank, were German Jews. They came from the town of Frankfurt am Main, where Otto's family had lived **for generations**. First the Franks had a daughter named Margot. Then, on June 12, 1929, Anne was born. The Franks' house was in a pretty neighborhood where Anne played happily in her sandbox or with the many other children who lived nearby.

Otto Frank

Edith Frank

Margot Frank

About 1935. German people held up signs like this one in front of Jewish stores. The German words mean, "Germans! Watch yourselves! Don't buy from Jews!"

But outside the loving world of Papa, Mama, and Margot, bad things were happening in Germany. People lost their jobs and had no money for food and clothes. They were scared and angry. They wanted a leader who promised an end to their problems. Adolf Hitler, who **came to power** in 1933, seemed like such a leader. He told the Germans that they were better than all other people on Earth. He blamed Germany's troubles mainly on the Jews. He immediately began passing laws that discriminated against the Jews. Hitler and all the people who **supported** him were called Nazis, a shortened **version** of the German word *Nationalsozialist*, which means **National Socialist**.

> **BEFORE YOU MOVE ON...**
> 1. **Details** Where and when was Anne Frank born?
> 2. **Cause and Effect** Why did people listen to Adolf Hitler?

---

for generations since long before his birth
came to power became the leader
supported agreed with

version form
National Socialist the government that ruled Germany from 1933 to 1945

A HIDING PLACE

Anne's family moves to the Netherlands. They are happy until Hitler's armies arrive. Then the Frank family has to hide from the Nazis.

Anne's father saw that it was not safe to be a Jew in Nazi Germany so when Anne was four, he took his family to Amsterdam, in the Netherlands. The Franks liked their new home. It was not far from the shore, and they spent happy summer holidays on the beach.

When Anne started school at the age of five, she quickly learned to read and write. She was a good student and had lots of friends. Because Anne was **outgoing** and

1939. Margot, Anne, and Grandma Hollander are at the beach in Zandvoort, Holland.

lively, she often was given **lead parts** in the school plays.

In 1939 Hitler declared war on Poland. War **broke out** across Europe, and soon Hitler's armies **reached** the Netherlands, where Anne and her family lived.

Even with the war going on, Anne still had fun with her friends. History, movie stars, cats, and dogs were among her favorite things. Another favorite thing was the little red-and-white-checked diary she got from her parents as a thirteenth-birthday present. Anne was **thrilled** by the gift and thought of it as her best friend. She wanted to give it a name, so all the **entries** in the diary began with "Dear Kitty."

Writing to Kitty, Anne described how Hitler's anti-Jewish laws had spread to **Holland**. Slowly, Jews had lost their jobs and **their possessions** had been taken away. All Jews over the age of six had to wear a six-pointed yellow Star of David on their clothing. Although Anne did not know it, her father was making plans for the family to **go into hiding**.

---

outgoing very friendly, fun-loving
lead parts the most important roles
broke out suddenly began
reached arrived in
thrilled pleased, excited

entries different pieces of writing
Holland the Netherlands
their possessions the things they owned
go into hiding hide

In July 1942 the Frank family moved into a hidden apartment in the back of the building that **housed** Otto Frank's business. Anne called it the secret **annex**. The entrance to their rooms was **blocked by a movable bookcase** that was built just after they **settled in**.

Only seven people knew that the family was there. Four of them worked in Otto's office. These friends **smuggled** food and clothing to the Franks when they could. Had they been caught by the Germans, they could have been put to death.

After the Franks had been living in the secret annex for about a week, they were joined by Mr. and Mrs. van Pels and their fifteen-year-old son, Peter. Anne was glad that Peter had brought along his pet cat, Mouschi, since Anne had had to leave her own cat behind when they left home. In November the last member of their little group, a dentist named Fritz Pfeffer, came to stay as well.

> These friends
> smuggled
> food and clothing
> to the Franks . . .

1942–1944. This is the building where Anne's family was hiding.

This bookcase moved to open the way to the hidden rooms.

BEFORE YOU MOVE ON...

1. **Characters' Motives** Why did the Franks move into a hiding place?
2. **Character** How would you describe Anne's personality?
3. **Details** Who was the last person to join the Franks in the annex?

---

housed contained
blocked by a movable bookcase covered up by a bookcase that could be moved

settled in went to live there
smuggled secretly brought in

LIFE IN HIDING

Anne tries hard to stay busy and cheerful in the crowded annex. She writes in her diary and hopes that one day people everywhere will read her words.

L ife in hiding was not easy for Anne. She was often bored and lonely. She longed for her friends, her school, and most of all her freedom. Living in such **close quarters** with near-strangers was not easy either. Many times, there were arguments. Anne **quarreled** with her mother and sister. She even felt misunderstood by her beloved father. All of her sadness and **frustration** were poured out into the pages of her diary, Kitty, who was her friend **throughout**.

Anne told Kitty how strange she felt during the first few days in the secret annex. She missed her friends, the black bicycle on which she rode to school, and the room in which she had grown up. Since the Franks were frightened of being discovered, they had to whisper and tiptoe around during the day. Only at night could they relax a little, although they still had to take care not to be seen through the windows. Using scraps of different materials, Anne and her father stitched together some curtains that they pinned to the walls.

Yet Anne was brave. She tried hard to stay busy and cheerful. She spent time reading and doing schoolwork, so she wouldn't be too far behind when she was finally able to return to school. She worked on a detailed **family tree** of all the kings and queens of Europe and she learned **shorthand**.

She loved to look at photos of her favorite movie stars and paste their pictures on the walls of her bedroom. Even in hiding there were still little treats and surprises, like the time when Anne, who was growing quickly, outgrew her shoes and was given a pair of red high heels by Miep Gies, one of the **devoted** friends who knew their secret.

The **attic** was Anne's special place, since it had a small window that could be opened to let in a glimpse of the stars, sunshine, or the tower across the street. Anne and Margot often went up there to read. And

> The attic was Anne's special place . . .

---

close quarters a crowded place

quarreled argued, disagreed

frustration a feeling that nothing she could do would make any difference

throughout for the whole time

family tree chart that shows all of the family members

shorthand a shorter way to write using symbols instead of letters to show a word

devoted loving, faithful

attic room at the top of the building

Layout for the 3rd and 4th Floor of the Annex

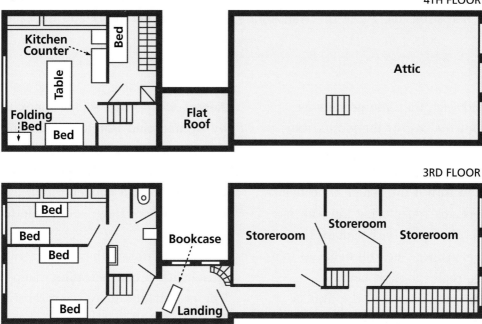

4TH FLOOR

Kitchen Counter

Bed

Table

Folding Bed

Bed

Flat Roof

Attic

3RD FLOOR

Bed

Bed

Bed

Bed

Bookcase

Landing

Storeroom

Storeroom

Storeroom

when Anne and Peter formed a special friendship, the attic was the place where they got together to talk.

Alone in the attic, Anne often thought about the life she hoped to lead when the war ended. She wanted to be a writer. In addition to her diary, she wrote fairy tales and other imaginary stories. She even began work on a book called *Stories and Events from the Secret Annex*.

And when she learned that the Dutch government hoped to **publish** all wartime diaries, she started to copy hers out neatly, on lined paper. She **cherished** the dream that someday her words would be read by people all over the world.

BEFORE YOU MOVE ON...

1. **Personal Experience** Why do you think there were quarrels among the people living in the annex?
2. **Inference** Why did Anne think of her diary as a friend?
3. **Main Idea and Details** Find details to support the main idea: Anne found many ways to keep busy in the annex.

publish print and sell to many people
cherished cared very much about

4

A TIME OF GREAT SADNESS

The Nazis find the Franks and send them to a concentration camp. Anne, her mother, and her sister die. After the war, Anne's father finds her diary and publishes it.

Although the little group was **cut off from** the rest of the world, they managed to hear news from a radio kept in Otto's office. At night, they would creep into the room and turn it on. When Anne heard that the Germans were losing the war, she felt hopeful. She wrote in her diary that, **despite everything**, she still believed that people were really good at heart.

But someone discovered the Franks' hiding place and told the police. On August 4, 1944, the secret annex was **raided** by German and Dutch Nazis. Anne and the others were now **prisoners**. The Franks, the van Pelses, and Fritz Pfeffer were sent to Westerbork, a concentration camp in Holland, where they were made to work for the Nazis.

A month later, they were sent to Auschwitz, a concentration camp in Poland. The **conditions** there were terrible. Anne, Margot, and their mother were forced to work with little food, water, or clothing. Many people around them died of hunger and sickness. Many others were killed outright by the Nazis. In October the two girls were sent to Bergen-Belsen, a camp in Germany. Their parents were left at Auschwitz, where their mother, Edith, died in the **infirmary**.

It was a long, cold winter and the girls got sick. First Margot died of **typhus** and a short while later Anne died too. She had not yet turned sixteen.

About 1944. The entrance to Auschwitz concentration camp. The words over the gate mean, "Work will make you free."

---

cut off from not part of, away from
despite everything even though so many bad things had happened
raided entered suddenly

conditions ways people lived
infirmary place where sick people are kept
typhus a painful sickness

About 1941. Anne Frank at a public hall in Amsterdam.

Anne's little book became extremely popular and it was translated into many languages. Because people were amazed by Anne's courage and maturity, the story of her life was made into a play and the building where she and her family hid **was turned into** a **museum**. Anne Frank **lives on** through her remarkable words, which **are an inspiration to** millions of people all over the world.

Anne's diary and other papers were found in the annex by Miep Gies, who kept them. After the war ended, Anne's father went back to Amsterdam. He was the only one from the secret annex who survived the hard winter at Auschwitz. When he read the diary Miep gave him, he decided it should be published.

was turned into became
museum place where important objects are kept and shown
lives on continues to live
are an inspiration to encourage, support

BEFORE YOU MOVE ON...

1. **Sequence** Tell what happened to the Franks after the annex was raided.
2. **Opinion** Do you think life in the concentration camps changed Anne's belief that people are good at heart? Explain.
3. **Character's Motive** Why do you think Anne's father decided to publish her diary?

ABOUT THE AUTHOR

Yona Zeldis McDonough was born in the Jewish state of Israel and now lives in Brooklyn, New York, with her husband and two children. Although the story of Anne Frank is not a happy one, she feels that it is important for everyone to know what the Nazis did to the Jews and other people in Europe during World War II.

Respond to the Biography
Check Your Understanding

SUM IT UP

Compare Sequences Complete a time line to show how the events in the life of the Frank family were connected to the events of World War II.

Time Line

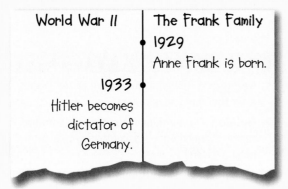

World War II	The Frank Family
	1929
	Anne Frank is born.
1933	
Hitler becomes dictator of Germany.	

Talk over your time line with a partner. Answer questions like these to compare the events.

- How old was Anne when Hitler became dictator of Germany?

- When did the Frank family leave Germany? Why?

- Why were the Franks no longer safe even in Holland?

Form Generalizations Think about the comparisons you made. Write a sentence or two to tell how world events affect the lives of individuals.

THINK IT OVER

Discuss and Write Talk about these questions with a partner. Write the answers.

1. **Conclusion** Why is it important to remember what happened to Anne and other Jews during World War II?

2. **Judgment** What is Anne Frank's legacy?

3. **Comparisons** What has changed in the world since Anne Frank's time? What has stayed the same?

4. **Personal Knowledge** Anne's diary became her connection to the world. Name other ways that people communicate their thoughts to the world.

EXPRESS YOURSELF ▶ DEFINE AND EXPLAIN

Choose one event from the time line on pages 255–257. In a group, tell about the event and then explain how it affected people like Anne. Next, put yourself in Anne's place and explain how these events made her and other ordinary people feel.

Language Arts and Content Area Connections

GRAMMAR IN CONTEXT

USE THE PRESENT PERFECT TENSE

Learn About Helping Verbs Some verbs are made up of more than one word—a **main verb** and one or more **helping verbs**. The helping verb agrees with the subject of the sentence.

Use **has** with *he*, *she*, or *it*.

Since May, Lisa **has learned** about the Franks.

Use **have** with *I*, *you*, *we*, or *they*.

I **have enjoyed** reading Anne's diary.

Learn About Present Perfect Verbs The present perfect tense can tell about an action that began in the past and may still be going on.

Millions of people **have learned** about her.

Sometimes you don't know when an action happened in the past. Use a verb in the present perfect tense to tell about this action, too.

Mark **has read** the diary twice.

To form the present perfect tense, use the helping verb **has** or **have** with the past participle. See pages 450–451 in the Handbook for the past participles of irregular verbs.

Practice Write each sentence. Choose the correct helping verb.

1. It is November, 1942. Anne and her family <u>have / has</u> been in hiding for four months.

2. The Franks <u>has / have</u> moved into a hidden apartment.

3. The young girl <u>has / have</u> started a diary.

SOCIAL STUDIES
REPRESENTING/SPEAKING

GIVE AN ORAL REPORT

What would you like to learn about World War II? With a partner, research and then report on one event from the war.

1 **Form Questions** Choose a battle or event you want to research. Use these words to form questions about your topic: *Who? What? When? Where? Why? How?*

2 **Research the Answers** Use encyclopedias, newspapers, magazines, and the Internet to find the answers to your questions.

3 **Present Your Findings** Share your questions and answers with the class. Use pictures and graphics to support your presentation.

For tips on giving an **oral report**, see Handbook pages 401–402.

Allied paratroopers fill the skies over Europe in 1942.

Respond to the Biography, continued

Content Area Connections

> SOCIAL STUDIES
> REPRESENTING

MAKE A WAR EFFORT POSTER

During World War II, the U.S. government needed help from all its citizens. While soldiers fought overseas, there was much work to do at home. The government created posters to ask citizens to join in the war effort. Look at the images and read the slogans in these posters.

In this poster, a popular character called Uncle Sam encourages men to join the U.S. Army. The poster calls to their patriotism, or love for their country.

The government encouraged women to take jobs during the war. Because of the government's slogans—messages that are easy to remember—many women worked for the first time.

Work with a small group. Follow these steps to design your own war effort poster.

1 Think of a Message Brainstorm ideas for a war effort poster. You may want to ask people to grow their own food, for example. Or, you might want to convince people to save fuel and metal products. With your group, choose one idea to develop as a message.

2 Design Your Poster Use persuasive words and images in your message. Strong colors, simple images, and direct language are very effective.

3 Display Your Poster Show your group's poster to the class. Tell about the process of brainstorming and creating your poster. Then display all of the posters in a class "gallery."

 For tips on **representing** ideas, see Handbook pages 404–405.

REPORT ON NUCLEAR WEAPONS

Like Anne Frank, the scientist Albert Einstein decided to leave Germany in the early 1930s because of Hitler's anti-Jewish laws. He warned the U.S. that Germany might develop an atomic bomb. Scientists who worked for the U.S. built their own atomic bomb first.

The atomic bomb is a very powerful weapon that is built by splitting apart an atom. Weapons that are made with this technology are called nuclear weapons. With a group, research the history and effects of the atomic bomb and other nuclear weapons. Here is a list of questions to help guide your research:

- When was the first atomic bomb developed? Who invented it?

- Where was the atomic bomb dropped during the war? What were its effects?

- What are some types of nuclear weapons?

- Which countries have nuclear weapons today?

Use the Internet and other resources to conduct your research.

1 Gather Information and Take Notes
These Web sites might be good places to start, but remember that new sites appear every day! Use key words in your search and look for links.

INTERNET

INFORMATION ON-LINE

Key Words:
"atomic bomb"
"hydrogen bomb"
"nuclear weapons"

Web Sites:
➤ **Manhattan Project**
- www.encyclopedia.com
- www.letsfindout.com

Download helpful information and take notes for your report.

2 Organize Information Write key points and facts on a large chart. Use it to present your report to the class.

3 Present Your Report Choose a member of the group to tell about the group's findings. Other members can point to related facts on the chart as the speaker gives the report.

For more about the **research process**, see Handbook pages 394–399. For help with the **Internet**, see pages 392–393.

The Diary
of a
Young Girl

diary
by Anne Frank

Prepare to Read

THINK ABOUT WHAT YOU KNOW

Brainstorm What do people write in diaries? Make a class list.

LEARN KEY VOCABULARY

agitated nervous, upset, worried

bother make an effort

call-up notice message from the Nazi police that ordered a person to be at a certain place at a certain time

exhausted very tired

impression idea

matter be important

preoccupied thinking about something else, lost in thought

shock great and sudden surprise

stunned greatly surprised

Use New Words in Context Study the new words and their definitions. Then write the paragraph, adding the missing words.

When I read Anne Frank's diary, I get the _____(1)_____ that she was a lot like me. I can feel how scared she was when her father got the _____(2)_____. Like Anne, I try to write each memory in my personal diary. Sometimes I get so _____(3)_____ over a problem that I want to scream! Instead, I write about it. That way, I am not _____(4)_____ by the situation, and I can think about other things. All of my diaries _____(5)_____ more to me than anything else. I am never too _____(6)_____ to write in them. One morning, I didn't even _____(7)_____ to eat breakfast because I was writing. That was a real _____(8)_____ to my mother! I was _____(9)_____ too when I wrote 100 pages in a month.

LEARN TO MONITOR YOUR READING

When you **monitor your reading**, you stop from time to time to be sure you understand the text.

READING STRATEGY

How to Monitor Your Reading

1. **Clarify** Make sure you understand new words and ideas.

2. **Ask Questions** Ask yourself questions about each section.

3. **Summarize** Think about the most important events or ideas. State them in a sentence or two.

4. **Predict** Think about what will happen next.

Use these strategies as you read "The Diary of a Young Girl."

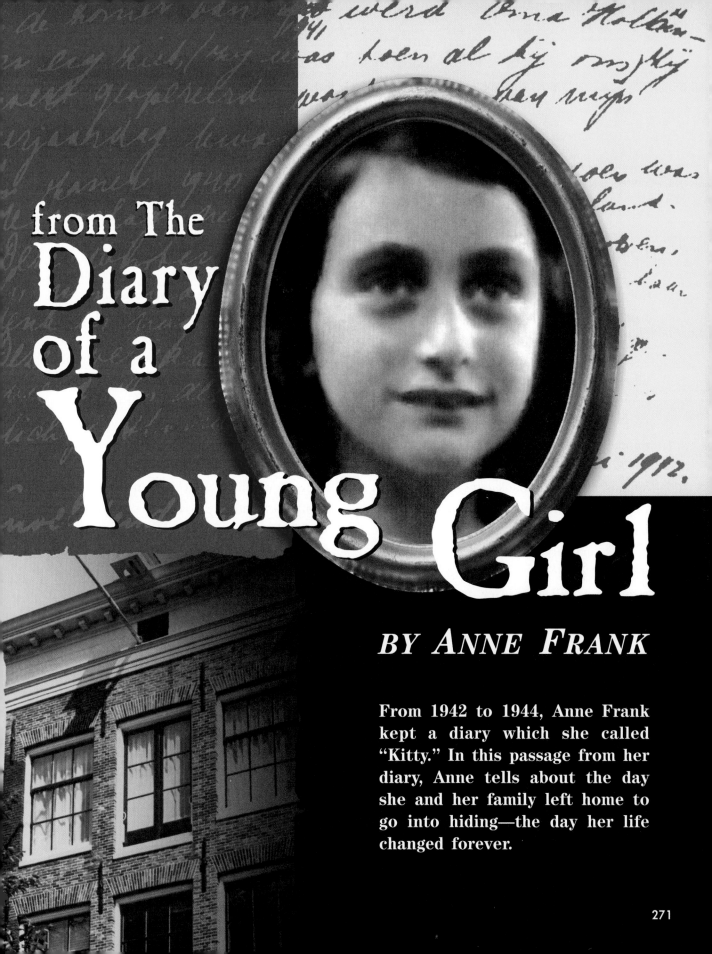

from The Diary of a Young Girl

BY ANNE FRANK

From 1942 to 1944, Anne Frank kept a diary which she called "Kitty." In this passage from her diary, Anne tells about the day she and her family left home to go into hiding—the day her life changed forever.

RECEIVING THE CALL-UP

Hitler's police call for Anne's father. His family fears that he will be taken away to a concentration camp.

WEDNESDAY, JULY 8, 1942

Dearest Kitty,

It seems like years since Sunday morning. So much has happened it's as if the whole world had suddenly turned upside down. But as you can see, Kitty, I'm still alive, and that's the **main thing**, Father says. I'm alive all right, but don't ask where or how. You probably don't understand a word I'm saying, so I'll begin by telling you what happened Sunday afternoon.

At three o'clock (Hello* had left but was supposed to come back later), the doorbell rang. I didn't hear it, since I was out on the balcony, lazily reading in the sun. A little while later Margot appeared in the kitchen doorway looking very **agitated**. "Father has received a **call-up notice** from **the SS**," she whispered. "Mother has gone to see Mr. van Daan." (Mr. van Daan is Father's **business partner** and a good friend.)

I was **stunned**. A call-up: everyone knows what that means. **Visions** of concentration camps and lonely **cells** raced through my head. How could we let Father go to such a fate? "Of course he's not going," declared Margot as we waited for Mother in the living room. "Mother's gone to Mr. van Daan to ask whether we can move to our hiding place tomorrow. The van Daans are going with us. There will be seven of us altogether." Silence. We couldn't speak. The thought of Father off visiting someone in the Jewish Hospital and completely **unaware of** what was happening, the long wait for Mother, the heat, the **suspense**—all this **reduced us to silence**.

*Hello Silberberg was Anne's close friend. He would often visit Anne at her home.

---

main thing most important point
the SS Hitler's police force, the *Schutzstaffel*
business partner partner in the work they do
Visions Pictures

cells rooms in a prison
unaware of not knowing
suspense fear, tension
reduced us to silence made us unable to speak

In her diary, Anne called the van Pels family the van Daans. These pictures show Auguste, Peter, and Hermann van Pels.

Anne, left, with her neighbor Hannah Goslar in Amsterdam before the war. They were separated when the Franks went into hiding, but they met again in Bergen-Belsen concentration camp. Hannah survived the war, and the story of her friendship with Anne was later published in a book.

BEFORE YOU MOVE ON...

1. **Cause and Effect** Why did Mrs. Frank go to see Mr. van Daan about moving into the hiding place?

2. **Details** Where was Anne's father while she and Margot waited for him to return home?

3. **Summary/Sequence** Retell the events described on page 272 in the correct time order.

The Diary of a Young Girl **273**

Anne learns that the call-up is for her sister Margot, not her father.
The Franks and their friends start packing and prepare to go into hiding.

Suddenly the doorbell rang again. "That's Hello," I said.

"Don't open the door!" exclaimed Margot to stop me. But it wasn't **necessary**, since we heard Mother and Mr. van Daan downstairs talking to Hello, and then the two of them came inside and shut the door behind them. Every time the bell rang, either Margot or I had to tiptoe downstairs to see if it was Father, and we didn't let anyone else in. Margot and I were sent from the room, as Mr. van Daan wanted to talk to Mother alone.

When she and I were sitting in our bedroom, Margot told me that the call-up was not for Father, but for her. At this second **shock**, I began to cry. Margot is sixteen—**apparently** they want to send girls her age away on their own. But thank goodness she won't be going; Mother had said so herself, which must be what Father

Otto Frank

had meant when he talked to me about our going into hiding. Hiding . . . where would we hide? In the city? In the country? In a house? In a **shack**? When, where, how . . . ? These were questions I wasn't **allowed** to ask, but they still kept running through my mind.

Margot and I started packing our most important **belongings** into a schoolbag. The first thing I stuck in was this diary, and then curlers, handkerchiefs, schoolbooks, a comb and some old letters. **Preoccupied** by the thought of going into hiding, I stuck the craziest things in the bag, but I'm not sorry. Memories mean more to me than dresses.

Father finally came home around five o'clock, and we called Mr. Kleiman to ask if he could come by that evening. Mr. van Daan left and went to get Miep. Miep arrived and promised to return later that

---

necessary needed
apparently it seems
shack small run-down building

allowed free
belongings things we own, possessions

night, taking with her a bag full of shoes, dresses, jackets, underwear and stockings. After that it was quiet in our apartment; none of us felt like eating. It was still hot, and everything was very strange.

We had rented our big upstairs room to a Mr. Goldschmidt, a divorced man in his thirties, who apparently had nothing to do that evening, since **despite** all our **polite hints** he hung around until ten o'clock.

Miep and Jan Gies came at eleven. Miep, who's worked for Father's company since 1933, has become a close friend, and so has her husband Jan. Once again, shoes, stockings, books and underwear **disappeared** into Miep's bag and Jan's deep pockets. At eleven-thirty they too disappeared.

I was **exhausted**, and even though I knew it'd be my last night in my own bed, I fell asleep right away and didn't wake up until Mother called me at five-thirty the next morning. **Fortunately**, it wasn't as hot as Sunday; a warm rain fell throughout the day.

1933. Anne Frank and her sister Margot at home in Germany during happier times.

BEFORE YOU MOVE ON...

1. **Conclusions** Why didn't Anne and Margot let anyone into the house except their father?

2. **Inference** Why do you think the Gieses took so many of the Franks' belongings away?

3. **Making Decisions** What would you take with you if you had to go into hiding today?

---

despite no matter, in spite of
polite hints gentle suggestions
disappeared were put away, went away
Fortunately Luckily

FACING THE UNKNOWN

Anne and her family leave home in a hurry. She doesn't know where the hiding place is; she knows only that they have to reach it safely.

1941. Anne and her family safe and together for a time in Amsterdam.

The four of us were wrapped in so many **layers** of clothes it looked as if we were going off to spend the night in a refrigerator, and all that just so we could take more clothes with us. No Jew in our **situation** would **dare** leave the house with a suitcase full of clothes. I was wearing two undershirts, three pairs of underpants, a dress, and over that a skirt, a jacket, a raincoat, two pairs of stockings, heavy shoes, a cap, a scarf and lots more. **I was suffocating** even before we left the house, but no one **bothered** to ask me how I felt.

Margot **stuffed** her schoolbag with schoolbooks, went to get her bicycle and, with Miep leading the way, rode off **into the great unknown**. At any rate, that's how

I thought of it, since I still didn't know where our hiding place was.

At seven-thirty we too closed the door behind us; Moortje, my cat, was the only living creature I said good-bye to. According to a note we left for Mr. Goldschmidt, she was to be taken to the neighbors, who would give her a good home.

The **stripped beds**, the breakfast things on the table, the pound of meat for the cat in the kitchen—all of these **created** the **impression** that we'd left in a hurry. But we **weren't interested in** impressions. We just wanted to get out of there, to get away and **reach our destination** in safety. Nothing else **mattered**.

More tomorrow.

Yours, Anne

---

layers pieces, coverings
situation place
dare take the chance to
I was suffocating I could hardly breathe
stuffed tightly packed, filled up
into the great unknown to where no one knew or could guess

stripped beds beds with all the sheets and covers taken off
created made, produced
weren't interested in didn't care about
reach our destination get to where we were going

Johannes Kleiman worked in the office below the Annex. He helped to hide Anne's family. When the family was discovered on August 4, 1944, Mr. Kleiman was arrested. Because of his poor health, he was released shortly afterward. He stayed in Amsterdam until his death in 1959.

Miep Gies was a friend and helper of the Franks and the van Pelses. She is still living in Amsterdam. Her husband Jan died in 1993.

BEFORE YOU MOVE ON...

1. **Inference** Explain why Anne and her family could not leave with their belongings in a suitcase.

2. **Cause and Effect** What created the impression that Anne's family left in a hurry?

3. **Main Idea and Details** List three details to support this main idea: The Franks had a lot to do before they went into hiding.

The building in which the Franks had hidden is now a museum.

ABOUT THE AUTHOR

Anne Frank is the author of one of the most famous diaries ever written. *The Diary of a Young Girl* has been published in more than fifty languages. Anne wrote her diary with the intention of having it published. During the last year of her life, she rewrote and edited it to improve its quality. She took out some passages that she didn't think were very interesting and added others from memory. In addition to her diary, Anne wrote poems and stories while she was in the annex. She had dreams of becoming a writer after the war was over.

Respond to the Diary
Check Your Understanding

SUM IT UP

Identify Important Information Review "The Diary of a Young Girl." Make a list of the important events in the selection.

Relate Causes and Effects Some events have a cause-and-effect relationship. The **effect** tells what happens. The **cause** tells why it happened.

Review your list of important events from "The Diary of a Young Girl." Write them in a chart like this one to show how they are related. Add a cause or effect, if necessary, to go with an event.

Cause	→	Effect
Father receives a call-up notice.	→	The Family decides to go into hiding.

THINK IT OVER

Discuss and Write Talk about these questions with a partner. Write the answers.

1. **Mood or Tone** How does Anne seem to feel about leaving her home and moving into the annex?

2. **Character** What words would you use to describe Anne?

3. **Comparison** Compare an event from Anne's diary to the same event in the Anne Frank biography. How are they similar? How are they different?

4. **Judgments** Why is *The Diary of a Young Girl* an important book for people to read today? What lessons can we learn from it?

EXPRESS YOURSELF ▶ GIVE INFORMATION

Work with a team. Choose facts from "Anne Frank" and quotations from "The Diary of a Young Girl." Prepare a report for a radio broadcast on the experiences of the Frank family. Take turns making the broadcast.

Respond to the Diary, continued

Language Arts and Literature

▶ GRAMMAR IN CONTEXT

USE THE PRESENT PERFECT TENSE

Learn About the Present Perfect Tense The **present perfect tense** is formed in this way:

has + past participle

have + past participle

Use the present perfect tense when you need to tell about an action that began in the past and may still be going on. You can also use the present perfect tense when you aren't sure of the exact time of the past action.

Learn About Past Participles Most verbs form the past tense and past participle by adding *-ed*.

Verb	Past	Past Participle
happen	happened	happened

Some verbs have irregular forms. Study the examples. See Handbook pages 450–451 for more irregular verbs.

Present	Past	Past Participle
go	went	gone
leave	left	left
speak	spoke	spoken

Practice Write each sentence. Add *has* or *have* and a past participle from the list above.

1. Anne's mother _____ to Mr. van Daan about going into hiding.

2. The Franks _____ to the annex.

3. The Franks _____ their home forever.

▶ WRITING

KEEP A DIARY

Anne enjoyed writing in her diary and wanted it to be published. Write in your own diary for one week. Then choose one entry that you would like to share with your classmates.

❶ Prepare to Write Think about something that is important to you. You may want to write about school, family, friends, or your feelings. Write your first entry. Put the day and date at the top. Use Anne Frank's diary as a model.

❷ Make Daily Entries Write in your diary every day for a week. Choose a quiet time and place where you can write in private. Use the correct verb tenses in your entries.

❸ Publish Choose an entry that does not give away any information you don't want to share. Publish your entry in a class diary.

Sample Entry

Tuesday, February 1, 2001

Dear Diary,
   Today I made a new friend. His name is Eric, and he's from Guatemala. He's shy but very nice. I hope we become the best of friends!

                              Yours,
                              Tara

Review **verbs** on Handbook pages 444–454.

Content Area Connections

EVALUATE AND USE WEB SITES

Web sites differ in quality. Evaluate Web sites and choose one for research.

1 **Visit Web Sites** Find at least five sites about World War II or Anne Frank. Remember that new Web sites appear every day, but these might be a good place to start.

INTERNET

INFORMATION ON-LINE

Key Words:
Anne Frank

Web Sites:
➤ **Sites about Anne Frank**
• www.annefranknm.com
• come.to/annefrank

2 **Evaluate Web Sites** What do the Web sites show? Are they easy to understand and use? Do they give enough information? Summarize your findings.

Example:

Anne Frank Center USA—shows museum exhibits; easy to use; lots of links

3 **Make an Oral Report** With a group, use the best site to conduct more research. Report your findings to the class.

Learn to use the **Internet** on Handbook pages 392–393.

EXPLORE LEGACIES

Anne Frank's life left an important legacy to the world. What other people from World War II left important legacies? Learn more about leaders from this period, then role-play these figures in a class simulation.

1 **Choose a Figure** Here is a list of key figures from World War II. Choose one to research.

• Winston Churchill, British Prime Minister

• Franklin Delano Roosevelt, U.S. President

• Eleanor Roosevelt, First Lady of the U.S.

• General Dwight D. Eisenhower, Supreme Allied Commander

• Albert Einstein, scientist

• A. Philip Randolph, labor activist

• Hirohito, Emperor of Japan

• Josephine Baker, member of French resistance

2 **Research** Use encyclopedias, history books, and the Internet to learn about your leader.

3 **Stage a Dinner** Pretend that all the leaders are having dinner together. Take the role of the leader you researched. Answer questions about your participation in the war and your legacy.

Writing That Informs and Explains

Expository writing gives information. Often the writer explains facts about a topic. The writer may also explain how something happens, how it works, and why it is important or interesting.

PROFESSIONAL WRITING MODEL

"The Big Blast" is a nonfiction article about a real event—the 1980 eruption of Mount St. Helens. The writer uses scientific facts and descriptions to explain what happened.

from "The Big Blast"

The blast flattened whole forests of 180-foot-high firs. . . . At first, this damage was puzzling. A wind of 200 miles an hour is not strong enough to level forests of giant trees. The explanation, geologists later discovered, was that the wind carried rocks ranging in size from grains of sand to blocks as big as cars. . . .

The result was what one geologist described as a "stone wind."

A CAUSE-AND-EFFECT CHART

When writing nonfiction, writers often explain causes and effects. A cause-and-effect chart can help you understand how events are related. Use the chart below to discuss some of the causes and effects in "The Big Blast."

Cause-and-Effect Chart for "The Big Blast"

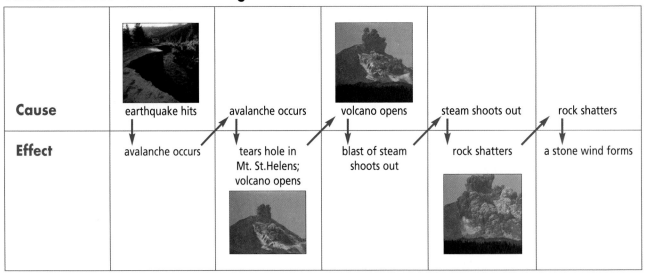

Cause	earthquake hits	avalanche occurs	volcano opens	steam shoots out	rock shatters
Effect	avalanche occurs	tears hole in Mt. St.Helens; volcano opens	blast of steam shoots out	rock shatters	a stone wind forms

STUDENT WRITING MODEL

Content-Area Report

Why Pompeii Is Famous

by Claudia Rizo

Pompeii was a city in ancient Italy. It is famous today because of a disaster that happened about two thousand years ago.

Pompeii was located near a volcano named Mount Vesuvius. For as long as the people of Pompeii could remember, Vesuvius had been quiet. Then in 62 CE, there was a sudden earthquake, causing damage to Pompeii and other nearby towns. People rebuilt the city. They thought the danger was past, but they were mistaken.

Early in the afternoon of August 24, 79 CE, disaster struck. With a loud roar, Mount Vesuvius erupted so violently that it blew its top off. It kept erupting throughout the night. Showers of hot ash, stone, and flaming cinder fell on Pompeii. Later on, poison gas filled the air.

The residents of Pompeii panicked. Many grabbed what they could and ran out of the town. The people who stayed in Pompeii did not survive. Some were killed by falling stones or hot ash. Some hid but died from the poisonous air. When the eruptions ended, Pompeii was buried under twelve feet of ash, cinder, and stone. As the years went by, grass covered the site. Pompeii disappeared.

For a while, the city was forgotten. But one of the people who had escaped, Pliny, wrote about the disaster. People wondered where Pompeii was buried. Then in 1748, the site was found. Scientists began to uncover the ancient city. The ash that buried Pompeii also preserved it. By pouring plaster into casts, scientists created "statues" of those who were left behind. Then they could see exactly what the people were like and what they were doing.

Today many people visit Pompeii to see what an ancient city looks like. Some come to study Mount Vesuvius. They hope to learn more about volcanoes so that no one else will have to suffer the way the people of Pompeii did almost 2000 years ago.

INTRODUCTION
The **introduction** tells what the report is about, the ancient city of Pompeii.

BODY
The middle paragraphs, or the **body**, give the facts. Here Claudia tells about the volcanic eruption and its effects on Pompeii.

Each paragraph starts with a **topic sentence** that tells one main idea about the subject.

The **information** presented in a report must be accurate. The writer found and checked facts in two or more reliable sources.

CONCLUSION
The **conclusion** sums up the report. Claudia tells how the eruption has affected our lives today.

Writing That Informs and Explains, continued

The Writing Process

WRITING PROMPT

Write a report for your classmates on a science or social studies topic that includes a cause and its effects. Explain what happened. Tell why it happened.

PREWRITE

1 Collect Ideas and Choose a Topic Who or what would you like to learn more about? Brainstorm a list of ideas with a partner. Cross out ideas that do not involve causes and effects. Then choose a topic that would be the most interesting to your audience.

2 Unlock the Writing Prompt Before you begin writing, fill out an FATP chart.

3 Collect Information Use at least two sources to find information on your topic. Take notes. Keep a list of your sources. Go back to them if you need to. See pages 394–399 of the Handbook for tips on doing research and taking notes.

4 Get Organized Look through your notes to identify the causes and effects you want to include in your report. Create an outline. Use Roman numerals for main ideas and capital letters for supporting details.

FATP Chart

HOW TO UNLOCK A PROMPT
Form: *report*
Audience: *classmates*
Topic: *Toussaint L'Ouverture*
Purpose: *to explain what caused him to lead a revolt and the effects of his fight for freedom*

Topic of Report ——— Toussaint L'Ouverture, Freedom Fighter
Introduction ——— I. Who was Toussaint L'Ouverture?
Main Idea ——— II. What was the early history of the French colony in Haiti?
Supporting Detail ———   A. What caused the French to set up this colony?
                         B. Why did they bring over African slaves?
                    III. What happened during the slave revolt of 1791?
                         A. What caused this revolt?
                         B. What was Toussaint's role?
                    IV. What happened as a result of this revolt?
                         A. What did the French do?
                         B. What did Toussaint do?
Conclusion ——— V. Why is Toussaint important? What is his effect today?

Reflect and Evaluate

- How did working with a partner help you choose a topic?

- Did you find all the information you need? Are your facts accurate?

- As you organized your outline, did you focus on causes and effects?

DRAFT

Use your **FATP** chart to focus your writing. Write quickly to get your ideas down on paper. Don't worry about making mistakes on your draft.

1 **Introduce Your Topic** Your title should make clear what your report is about. The opening paragraph should introduce your topic and spark your audience's interest.

2 **Write the Body of Your Report** Use your outline to write your report. Make your writing interesting and clear. If you decide you want to add more information, go back to your notes or to your sources.

Writer's Craft: Sentence Variety and Elaboration

Vary the way your sentences begin.

Just OK	Much Better
Toussaint L'Ouverture was a famous freedom fighter. Many people think he is the greatest freedom fighter of all time. Toussaint L'Ouverture was born a slave in the French colony of Saint Domingue. Toussaint led a slave revolt against the slaveholders.	To many people, Toussaint L'Ouverture is the greatest freedom fighter that ever lived. Born a slave in the French colony of Saint Domingue, he led a revolt against the slaveholders.

Add more information to your sentences to make the causes and effects clear.

Just OK	Much Better
Toussaint became the leader of Saint Domingue. The colony did well. Then, in 1802, the French ruler Napoleon sent an army to Saint Domingue.	Toussaint became the leader of Saint Domingue. The colony did well because of his wise leadership. By 1802, the French ruler Napoleon decided he wanted the colony back under French control, so he sent an army to Saint Domingue.

---

3 **Write a Conclusion** In your last paragraph, sum up your topic. Tell why it is important to know about this person or event.

Reflect and Evaluate

- Look over your draft. Do you want to add more information?
- Have you made it easy for your reader to identify causes and effects?
- Are your sentences varied and interesting?

Writing That Informs and Explains, continued

REVISE

1 **Reread Your Draft** Check your draft against your **FATP**. Does it match the form, audience, topic, and purpose you listed? Have you written about causes and effects? Have you checked your facts?

2 **Conduct a Peer Conference** Hold a roundtable discussion to read and evaluate each other's reports. Look at the flow of the sentences: Are they too short and choppy? Do any run on? Use the guidelines on Handbook page 411 to help you.

Read what Marco's group had to say during a Peer Conference. Notice how Marco decides to make changes.

Round Table Peer Conferencing

Lilia: You have 5 short sentences in a row: "It was August 22. The revolt began. Some black slaves rebelled against their owners. Then hundreds joined them. Then thousands joined." Try to combine some of them.

Marco: Is this better? "The revolt began on August 22, when some black slaves rebelled against their owners. Hundreds and then thousands joined them."

Peter: That sounds better.

Veronica: The next sentence is too long, and some of it doesn't make sense. I think it is a run-on.

Marco: You're right! I'll change it to "At first, Toussaint did not fight. He even led his master and mistress to safety. When he finally felt he had to fight, he showed that he was a good leader."

3 **Mark Your Changes** Review your notes and decide how you want to change your writing. Revising Marks appear on Handbook page 411.

Use the guidelines on Handbook page 411 to help you.

Revising Marks appear on Handbook page 411.

Reflect and Evaluate

- Did your peers find your report interesting and informative? Were their suggestions helpful?

- Did you need to revise your sentences? If so, what problems did you correct?

- Were you able to include most of the interesting facts you found about your topic?

GRAMMAR IN CONTEXT

COMPLEX SENTENCES

A complex sentence contains one independent clause and one or more dependent clauses.

Toussaint
L'Ouverture

- An **independent clause** expresses a complete thought. It makes sense by itself.

  Examples: Toussaint taught himself to read.

  He became well-educated.

- A **dependent clause** does not express a complete thought. It does not make sense by itself.

  Examples: because there were no schools for slaves

  although he was a slave for almost 50 years

- In a **complex sentence**, a subordinating conjunction connects the dependent clause to the independent clause.

  Examples:

  Toussaint taught himself to read because there were no schools for slaves.
  <u>independent clause</u> <u>dependent clause</u>

  He became well-educated although he was a slave for almost 50 years.
  <u>independent clause</u> <u>dependent clause</u>

  If the dependent clause comes first, set it off with a comma.

  Example:

  Although he was a slave for almost 50 years, he became well-educated.
  <u>dependent clause</u> <u>independent clause</u>

Some Subordinating Conjunctions

after
although
because
before
if
since
until
when
where
while

Practice Combine each pair of sentences to form a complex sentence. Use a subordinating conjunction. Add a comma after the dependent clause if it comes first.

1. Toussaint read about the American Revolution. He was a young man.

2. Toussaint was willing to fight for freedom. He did not want to use violence.

3. The slaves rebelled on August 22, 1791. Many slave owners were killed.

4. Toussaint did not join the rebellion. He first led his master and mistress to safety.

5. Later Toussaint joined the rebellion. He proved to be a great leader.

Writing That Informs and Explains, continued

EDIT AND PROOFREAD

1 **Check for Mistakes** Carefully read your report and correct any mistakes in capitalization, punctuation, and spelling. If you need help, use Handbook pages 459–469.

2 **Check Your Sentences** Did you combine short sentences to make complex sentences? Did you avoid any run-on sentences?

3 **Make a Final Copy** Neatly hand copy your report. Or, if you are working on a computer, print out a final copy.

PUBLISH

Choose one of these ideas for publishing your report, or come up with your own idea.

- Put your report in a binder. Add drawings, charts, or maps. At the back, list a variety of book titles, magazine articles, movies, and Internet sites on your subject.

To Find Out More About Toussaint...

• Read These Books	• Visit These Sites
Toussaint L'Ouverture—The Fight for Haiti's Freedom by Walter Dean Myers	www.pbs.org/wgbh/aia
	encarta.msn.com
Toussaint L'Ouverture—Lover of Liberty by Laurence Santrey	britannica.com

- Give an oral report. Create a diagram or a 3-D model to show how the causes led to the effects. As part of your report, walk your audience through your display.

Reflect and Evaluate

- Are you pleased with how your report turned out? Does it
  - ☑ clearly introduce your topic?
  - ☑ include well-organized sentences and paragraphs that tell about causes and effects?
  - ☑ present accurate facts?
  - ☑ sum up your topic at the end?
- Did you enjoy finding out about your topic? Do you want to find out more—or do you wish you had picked a different topic?
- What was the hardest part of doing research? What part was the most fun?

1▶ Look Back at the Unit

Rate the Selections In this unit, you read about events that are examples of continuity and change. You also read about people who experienced our ever-changing world.

The Mother Who Lost Her Daughter   The Big Blast   Anne Frank   The Diary of a Young Girl

Work with a partner to list the titles in order from your favorite to your least favorite. Share your list with the class. Together discuss the selection that offers the best example of continuity, the one that offers the best example of change, and the one that provides the best example of both.

2▶ Show What You Know

Sum It All Up Expand and organize your ideas on this mind map. Share your ideas about continuity and change with a partner.

Why is continuity important?
What stays the same?
Continuity
What changes?
Change
Why is change important?

Reflect and Evaluate Write about an event that has changed your life. Add this writing to your portfolio, along with the work from the unit that shows what you learned.

3▶ Make Connections

To Your Community Find a place in your community that has changed over time. Report your findings to the class. Tell whether the change was caused by natural events or by people's decisions to make changes.

Overcoming Obstacles

Few people ever reach the top of Mount Everest. Those who do have overcome many obstacles—extreme cold, fear of falling. Brainstorm other challenges. Rank them from easy to hard. Find a partner who would accept the same challenge as you. Figure out the obstacles, how you would meet the challenge, and what you would learn. What did you find out about the positive and negative sides of meeting a challenge?

Endangered Species, Andy Warhol, silkscreen. Copyright © 1983.

The Siberian tiger,
black rhinoceros, and
Grevy's zebra are all endangered
wildlife, or animals at high risk of dying
out. The Pine Barrens tree frog was once endangered
but is now at lower risk. People can make a difference by
getting involved to help save endangered animals.

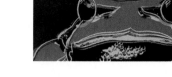

Making a Difference

- Think about our natural environment.
  What are some problems that need to be solved?

- Why is it important to take action as an individual
  or as part of a group?

- What are some ways in which you can make
  the world a better place?

THEME-RELATED BOOKS

The Shaman's Apprentice
*by Lynne Cherry and
Mark J. Plotkin*

A young boy and a scientist
work to keep the knowledge
of a traditional healer alive.

Sawgrass Poems
by Frank Asch and Ted Levin

Poems and photographs that
capture the beauty and wonder
of the Everglades and its unusual
plants and animals.

Every Living Thing
by Cynthia Rylant

A collection of stories about
animals that influence people's
lives by causing them to see
things in a different way.

Build Language and Vocabulary

PERSUADE

Look at the photos and read the quote. Then listen to a persuasive message about protecting the environment.

The time has come
when speaking is not enough,
applauding is not enough.

We have to act.

—*Jacques Cousteau*

BRAINSTORM IMPORTANT PROBLEMS AND SOLUTIONS

What other problems in the world today require action? Work with a group to make a list. Tell what actions need to be taken to solve the problems.

Problem-and-Solution Chart

Problem	What Actions Can Solve The Problem?
Sea plants and animals are harmed and killed by pollution.	clean up polluted waters pass laws to prevent further pollution

BUILD YOUR VOCABULARY

Words Used to Persuade Work as a class. Collect words that will help you get others to do something about the problem.

Words Used to Persuade

You should. . .

We really must. . .

Let's act now to prevent. . .

The world needs your help.

Time is running out.

If you will do only one small thing each day. . .

USE LANGUAGE STRUCTURES ▶ VERBS IN THE PAST PERFECT TENSE

Speaking: Give a Persuasive Talk Give a talk on a problem that concerns you. In the first sentence, state the problem. Then try to persuade others to think or act as you do. Use at least one verb in the past perfect tense.

Example:

If you **had seen** how many animals **had been** destroyed by the oil spill, you would agree that we must act now to prevent future spills.

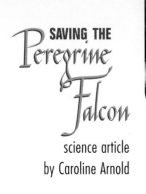

SAVING THE Peregrine Falcon

science article
by Caroline Arnold

Prepare to Read

THINK ABOUT WHAT YOU KNOW

Take a Poll Which animals do you think are in danger of dying out? Check your answers on the Internet or in an encyclopedia.

combat fight against

effect result

endangered in danger of dying out or disappearing forever

environment air, land, and water that people, plants, and animals need to live

extinct not living anymore, gone forever

ignorance not having education or knowledge about something

interfere get in the way, block

peregrine falcon, hunting bird with a dark head, gray and white feathers, and a hooked bill

pollution chemicals, dirt, smoke, and garbage that make the air, water, and soil unclean and unsafe

repair fix

LEARN KEY VOCABULARY

Relate Words Study the new words and their definitions. Then use the words to fill in a map like the one below.

Word Map

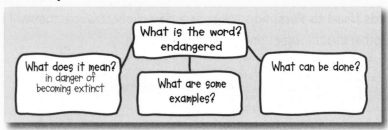

LEARN TO USE SQ3R

SQ3R is a study strategy, or plan, to use when you read nonfiction. It will help you remember what you read.

READING STRATEGY

How to Use SQ3R

1. **Survey** the selection. Look at the graphs, charts, and section titles.
2. **Question.** Turn the titles into questions. Write them down.
3. **Read** each section slowly and carefully. Look for answers to your questions.
4. **Recite.** Summarize each section in your own words.
5. **Review** what you read. Try to answer your questions.

Use the SQ3R strategy as you read "Saving the Peregrine Falcon."

SAVING THE Peregrine Falcon

In Ithaca, New York; Boise, Idaho; and Santa Cruz, California, teams of scientists make a difference every day of the year. They work to save a beautiful bird, the peregrine falcon, from extinction. The scientists help peregrine falcon eggs to hatch and then release the birds into the wild.

by Caroline Arnold

Photographs by Richard R. Hewett

THE PROBLEM: DDT

For **centuries** the **peregrine** was prized by kings and **falconers** who used it to hunt. Bird lovers too have always admired the peregrine. Yet a few years ago it was feared that soon there would be no more peregrines. **Pollution** of the **environment** with the poison DDT had **interfered** with the birds' **ability** to **produce** babies.

Most of the smaller birds that peregrines in the United States eat spend the winter in Central and South America. There they eat grains and insects that have been sprayed with DDT. DDT is a poison used by farmers to kill insects that are harmful to crops. When the birds eat food with DDT on it, the poison is **stored** in their bodies. Later, when the peregrines eat these birds, they eat the poison too. The more birds the peregrines eat, the more DDT they store.

Scientists have found that DDT causes birds to lay eggs with shells that are too thin. When they measure the shells of **hatched** or broken eggs, they find that the thinnest shells are those with the most DDT in them. When parent birds sit on these eggs to keep them warm, the thin shells often break. Thin-shelled eggs also lose moisture faster than thick-shelled eggs. Often the chick growing inside the egg dies because the egg dries out too much.

A DEADLY CHAIN

Farmers in Central and South America use DDT to kill insects.

Small birds like jays and doves eat the poisoned plants and insects. DDT stays in the birds' fatty tissue.

The small birds fly to North America. Peregrines eat the poisoned birds.

The DDT decreases the calcium in the peregrines' bodies so they lay eggs with thin shells.

The shells break and dry up quickly so the chicks growing inside do not survive.

---

centuries hundreds of years
falconers people who hunt with hawks and falcons
ability being able

produce make
stored kept
hatched empty

GIVING NATURE A HAND

By helping the eggs with thin shells to hatch, scientists can **combat** some of the **effects** of DDT.

Most wild peregrines nest on high ledges on rocky cliffs. Scientists carefully watch each peregrine nest. Then if they feel that the eggs are **unlikely** to hatch without help, they borrow them for a while, but first they let the birds sit on the eggs for five days. This seems to **improve** the eggs' chances of hatching in the **laboratory**.

Because the cliffs where peregrines nest are so steep, only a mountain climber can reach a nest. When he approaches the nest, the angry parents screech and swoop at him. The mountain climber quickly and carefully puts each speckled egg into a padded box. He then replaces the eggs he has taken with **plaster eggs** which look just

This climber is in search of a peregrine nest.

POINT-BY-POINT

HOW PEOPLE HELP THE PEREGRINE

1 Scientists search for eggs affected by DDT.
▼
2 Climbers take eggs from the nest. They replace them with plaster eggs.
▼
3 They take the real eggs to the laboratory in an incubator.
▼

like real peregrine eggs. These fake eggs will fool the parent birds. After the mountain climber leaves, the parents will return to the nest and sit on the plaster eggs as if they were their own.

It is important to keep the parent birds interested in the nest. After the eggs have hatched, the mountain climber will bring the babies back so that the parents can take care of them.

When the mountain climber gets back down from the top of the cliff, he puts the eggs into a portable **incubator**. The incubator will keep them safe and warm on their ride back to the laboratory.

BEFORE YOU MOVE ON...

1. **Cause and Effect** Why are peregrines in danger of extinction?
2. **Conclusions** Do you think it matters if all the peregrines die out? Why or why not?
3. **Judgments** Is it fair to the peregrines to put fake eggs in their nests? Why or why not?

---

unlikely not expected
improve make better
laboratory room where scientists work

plaster eggs fake eggs
incubator warm, moist case used to hatch eggs

IN THE LABORATORY

In the laboratory each egg is carefully weighed. Then it is held in front of a bright light in a dark room. This is called *candling*. When an egg is candled, the shadow of the chick growing inside and a lighter area at the large end of the egg can be seen. The lighter area is called the air pocket.

Then the egg is placed on a **rack** inside an incubator. The incubator keeps the egg warm and **moist**. Each day the egg will be weighed and candled again. As the chick grows, water slowly **evaporates** from the egg, making room for the air pocket to get bigger. The egg's weight shows how much water it is losing. If it is losing water too quickly, the incubator can be made more moist.

Wild birds turn their eggs **constantly** as they move around in the nest. But in the laboratory, people must carefully turn each egg four or five times each day. This **prevents** the growing chick from sticking to the inside of the eggshell. If the eggs are not turned, they will not hatch.

Sometimes eggs are found with shells so thin that they have already begun to crack. Then people in the laboratory try to **repair** them with glue. Sometimes eggs are also **waxed** to prevent them from losing moisture. Everything possible is done to make sure that each egg hatches into a healthy peregrine chick.

The eggs are kept in the incubator until they are 31½ days old. Then they are carefully watched for the first signs of hatching.

A scientist uses glue to repair a crack in a peregrine's egg.

rack shelf

moist slightly wet

evaporates becomes water vapor and moves into the air

constantly all the time

prevents stops

waxed covered with wax

BREAKING OUT

Each chick has a hard pointed knob on the top of its beak. This is called an *egg tooth*. The chick pushes against the inside of the shell with its egg tooth and breaks the shell.

The first crack in the egg is called the *pip*. When the pip appears, the egg is moved to a special hatching **chamber**. There the egg will take 24 to 48 hours to hatch. During this time somebody watches it all the time. Some chicks are too weak to break out of their shells. Then the scientists are there to help them.

Often two eggs begin to hatch at about the same time. Then they are put next to each other. When a chick is ready to hatch, it begins to **peep** inside its shell. The two chicks can hear each other peep. This seems to **encourage** them to move around and break their shells. Sometimes when there is only one egg, the scientists make peeping sounds for the chick to hear.

Starting at the pip, the chick slowly turns, pressing its egg tooth against the shell. Soon the crack becomes a ring around the shell. Then the chick pushes its head against the top of the shell, and the shell pops open. After hatching, the egg tooth is no longer needed, and in a week or so it falls off.

POINT-BY-POINT

HOW PEOPLE HELP THE PEREGRINE

4 The staff check the eggs' moisture levels. They turn the eggs and repair damaged shells. ▼

5 Scientists watch for signs of hatching. Sometimes they peep to encourage the chicks to hatch. ▼

BEFORE YOU MOVE ON...

1. **Summary** Tell a partner what the scientists do to take care of the eggs.
2. **Vocabulary** What words would you use to describe the work the scientists do in the laboratory? Does your partner agree or disagree?

The first crack in the egg is called the pip.

The chick breaks a ring around the entire shell.

Then the chick pushes its head against the top of shell, and the shell pops open.

---

chamber room that is very small

peep make a weak, high-pitched noise

encourage help

A newly hatched chick eats a tiny piece of meat.

CARING FOR THE CHICKS

The newly hatched chick is wet and its down feathers are **matted** together. A cotton swab is used to clean the feathers. If necessary, **ointment** is put on the chick's navel to prevent **infection**. In the shell the chick gets **nutrients** from the **yolk** through its navel. Normally, by the time a chick hatches, the yolk has been totally **absorbed** and the navel has closed.

In the wild, a mother bird **broods** her chicks by sitting on top of them to keep them warm and dry. In the laboratory, the dry chick is placed with one or more others in a small container called a brooder. A heater keeps the chicks warm. The chick will rest in the brooder for eight to twelve hours. Then it will be ready for its first meal.

In the wild, the father peregrine hunts birds and brings them back to the nest. Then he and the mother peregrine tear off small bits of meat to feed each chick. The hungry chicks beg for food by peeping and opening their mouths wide.

Bird meat is also used to feed chicks in the laboratory. First the meat is put through a meat grinder to break it into small pieces. The newly hatched chicks are then fed tiny pieces with tweezers. For somewhat older chicks the ground meat can be squeezed through a bag with a **nozzle**.

---

matted pressed down
ointment medicine
infection disease caused by germs
nutrients food

yolk yellow part of an egg
absorbed taken in
broods uses her wings to cover
nozzle cap with a small opening

PREPARING FOR FREEDOM

▶ **POINT-BY-POINT**

HOW PEOPLE HELP THE PEREGRINE

6 Scientists clean the chicks, keep them warm, and feed them.
▼

7 Scientists make sure the chicks imprint on adult birds.
▼

Even though the peregrine chicks are cared for by people, it is important that they **remain** wild. During the first week or so, the chicks cannot see very well. Then it does not matter if people feed them directly. But as they get older, their contact with people must be **limited**.

Young animals identify with the other animals they see during the first weeks of life. This is called **imprinting**. Most young animals only see their parents in early life, and they imprint on them.

Peregrines raised in the laboratory that will be returned to the wild must be imprinted on adult peregrines. One way to help them do this is to feed them with a

A peregrine chick thinks this puppet is its parent.

....

remain stay

limited as little as possible

imprinting a learning process that establishes a behavior pattern

a substitute a replacement

breeding season time for making chicks

adopted peregrine chicks chicks she has taken in

peregrine-shaped puppet. The puppet fools the peregrine chicks and they behave as if it were a real bird. When a peregrine chick is three days to a week old, it is put into the nest of an adult bird that has been imprinted on people.

Unfortunately there are not enough adult peregrines to care for all the hatched chicks. Another more common bird, the prairie falcon, is very much like the peregrine, and it is often used as **a substitute** parent for very young peregrine chicks. During the **breeding season**, a female prairie falcon will care for **adopted peregrine chicks**. She will keep them warm and feed them as if they were her own. When the chicks are one to two weeks old, they are put into nests of peregrines which are not imprinted on people. Then, at the age of three weeks, the young peregrines are ready to go back to wild nests.

BEFORE YOU MOVE ON...

1. Summary Use these words to retell how the chick hatches and how the scientists care for it: *egg tooth, pip, brooder.*

2. Details/Inference What are some things the scientists do to help the chicks after they hatch?

3. Cause and Effect Why do the scientists make sure the peregrine falcons do not imprint on people?

IN THE WILD

The chicks are put into a special wooden pack and taken to the nest **site**. There the mountain climber puts the pack on his back and climbs to the nest. He **removes** the plaster eggs and puts in the young chicks. Then he leaves as quickly as possible. He does not want to **disturb** the parent birds any more than necessary.

The parent birds soon return to the nest. Although they are surprised at first to find healthy chicks instead of eggs in their nest, the parents quickly accept their new babies. The hungry chicks beg for food, and the parents' natural response is to feed them. The chicks are finally on their way to growing up as wild peregrines.

The peregrine falcon is a beautiful bird, and it would be sad to let it become **extinct** simply through **ignorance** or **carelessness**.

Many animals that once **roamed** the earth are now gone because people destroyed or polluted their environments. For the present, the peregrine falcon has been saved from extinction. Through the work of many people around the world, its numbers are increasing each year. If you are lucky, maybe where you live, you can see one of these magnificent birds soaring high in the sky.

BEFORE YOU MOVE ON...

1. **Paraphrase** How do the scientists return the babies to the parent birds?
2. **Personal Experience** Talk to your partner about other animals that are also in danger of extinction.

ABOUT THE AUTHOR

Caroline Arnold, who lives with her husband in Los Angeles, California, has written over 100 books, mostly about natural science. She has been interested in birds and the environment for a long time. When discussing her research, she said, "Few experiences can match the thrill of seeing hawks and falcons up close and then watching them soar skyward after their release." Caroline Arnold has a web page on the Internet where people can learn more about her, her books, and her thoughts about writing. Her home page address is: http://www.geocities.com/Athens/1264/

....

site location, place
removes takes away
disturb bother
carelessness not being careful
roamed walked around

POINT-BY-POINT

HOW PEOPLE HELP THE PEREGRINE

1 Scientists search for eggs affected by DDT.
▼

2 Climbers take eggs from the nest. They replace them with plaster eggs.
▼

3 They take the real eggs to the laboratory in an incubator.
▼

4 The staff check the eggs' moisture levels. They turn the eggs and repair damaged shells.
▼

5 Scientists watch for signs of hatching. Sometimes they peep to encourage the chicks to hatch.
▼

6 Scientists clean the chicks, keep them warm, and feed them.
▼

7 Scientists make sure the chicks imprint on adult birds, not humans.
▼

8 Scientists return chicks to the wild.
■

On August 20, 1999, the peregrine falcon was officially removed from the **endangered species** list. As of that day, there were at least 1,650 breeding pairs in the United States! Although the banning of DDT made the peregrine's recovery possible, the hard work of the scientists really did make a difference: their work was the main reason the numbers of peregrines increased so quickly.

....

species plants and animals

Respond to the Article
Check Your Understanding

SUM IT UP

Review the Article Use the "Point-By-Point" feature on page 305 to review the article and check the answers you found to the questions you had before reading.

Respond to Literature Use your questions and answers about the selection to make a reflection log.

Reflection Log

The answers to the important questions are _____	I was surprised to learn that_____
It's interesting that _____	I'd like to find out more about_____

Draw Conclusions Take a class poll on this question: Is it worth the time and money it takes to save an endangered animal? Tally the yes and no answers, and then discuss reasons. Complete the following paragraph to summarize the discussion.

(number) members of our group think that it is worth it to save an endangered animal because (reason). (number) members of our group think that it is not worth it to save an endangered animal because (reason).

THINK IT OVER

Discuss and Write Talk about these questions with a partner. Write the answers.

1. **Summary** What did you learn about peregrine falcons and the effort to save them?

2. **Generalization** How does the peregrine's situation apply to endangered animals in general?

3. **Making Decisions** How can you make a difference and help save endangered animals?

EXPRESS YOURSELF ▶VERIFY INFORMATION

Take turns with a partner and make a statement based on information from the article. You can make a true statement, such as "DDT causes the birds to lay eggs with thin shells." Or, you can make a false statement, such as "Peregrines make their nests on the ground." Verify that your partner's statement is true or false. Read the text that proves your conclusions.

Language Arts and Literature

GRAMMAR IN CONTEXT

USE THE PAST PERFECT TENSE

Learn About the Past Perfect Tense Some past actions are completed before another action in the past. To tell about them, use the **past perfect tense**. It is formed in this way:

had + past participle

Study these examples.

The babies were born in the laboratory because the researcher **had taken** the eggs from the falcons' nests.

The researcher **had cared** for the chicks until she released them into the wild.

Review Past Participles Add *–ed* to form the past participle of most verbs. Memorize the past participle forms for irregular verbs. See Handbook pages 450–451 for a list.

Practice Write this paragraph. Add these verbs. Put the verbs in the past perfect tense.

eat	spray	poison

A few years ago, the peregrine falcon was almost extinct. Farmers in Central and South America ____(1)____ their fields with DDT. This pesticide ____(2)____ the smaller birds that peregrines like to eat. Once the falcons ____(3)____ the poisoned birds, the shells of their eggs became very thin.

WRITING

WRITE A THANK-YOU LETTER

Imagine that you are a peregrine falcon. Write a thank-you letter to a scientist who helped to save your chicks.

1 **Write Your Draft** Give specific details that show you know how the scientist helped your chicks.

Sample Letter

February 21, 2002

Dear Doctor Zayas,

I saw you take my eggs. You thought you tricked me, but I knew what you were doing. Thanks to you, my chicks are alive and well. Thank you again and again!

Sincerely,
P. Falcon

2 **Edit Your Letter** Did you use the words "thank you"? Have you included the date, a greeting, and a closing? Check your letter for correct spelling and punctuation.

3 **Deliver Your Letters** Take turns reading your letters aloud. Consider sending them to real scientists.

Review **punctuation marks** and **spelling** on Handbook pages 462–469.

Respond to the Article, continued
Content Area Connections

▶ MATHEMATICS
▶ REPRESENTING/SPEAKING

GRAPH POPULATION CHANGES

With a group, choose an endangered animal species, and research how its population has changed over time.

1 Collect Data Use wildlife magazines, encyclopedias, almanacs, and the Internet to find population statistics. Note why the population changed, too.

2 Create a Graph Use your data to make a bar graph that shows the population of the species over a period of time.

Graph

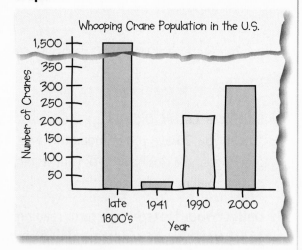

Whooping Crane Population in the U.S.

3 Draw Conclusions and Report Your Findings Present your graph as you share what you learned with the class.

▶ SOCIAL STUDIES
▶ WRITING/VIEWING

INVESTIGATE THE LEGISLATIVE PROCESS

The Endangered Species Act is a law that protects endangered animals. This law began as a bill. Make a flow chart to show how a bill becomes a law.

1 Find Information To find information:
- Use a social studies textbook.
- Call the office of a U.S. Senator or member of the House of Representatives.
- Contact an environmental group like the Sierra Club.

Take notes about each step of the process.

2 Organize Your Information Put each step on a different notecard. Put your cards in order and number them.

3 Prepare Your Report Use your notecards to make a flow chart that shows the steps a bill takes to become a law. Describe the process to a group.

Learn about **flow charts** on Handbook page 371.

MAKE AN INFORMATIONAL POSTER ON AN ENDANGERED ANIMAL

Why are animals endangered? With a group, research an endangered species and make an informational poster about it.

1 Choose a Species Decide which animal to research. Make a list of questions about it, for example: Why is it endangered? What is being done to protect it?

2 Gather Information and Take Notes Use the name of the species as a key word to search print and electronic sources. Start with these sites, but remember the Internet is always changing.

INTERNET

INFORMATION ON-LINE

Web Sites:
➤ **Endangered Species**
• endangered.fws.gov
• www.endangeredspecie.com

Download helpful images and take notes for your poster.

3 Make a Poster Write sentences that answer your research questions. Use pictures to illustrate the information. Then display your poster in the classroom or media center.

Sample Poster

WHALE REPORT

Why are Whales Endangered?
Whale hunters killed many whales for oil and other products through the 1800s and 1900s.

What is being done to protect them?
• The International Whaling Commission (IWC) told all countries to stop hunting whales from 1986 until further notice.

• In 1994, the IWC created the Southern Ocean Sanctuary as a protected place for whales.

For more about the **research process**, see Handbook pages 394–399. Learn to use the **Internet** on pages 392–393.

A Celebration of the Everglades

article
by Ted Levin

poems
by Frank Asch

Prepare to Read

THINK ABOUT WHAT YOU KNOW

Idea Exchange What do you know about the Florida Everglades? Scan pages 311–313. Tell a partner one thing you learned.

canal waterway built by people

dike wall of stone or earth that holds back water

extinction end of life for a whole category of plants or animals

levee wall of earth built along a river to prevent floods

marsh area of low, wet land with grasses

preserve keep safe, protect, keep the same from year to year

runoff rainfall that does not go into the ground but runs from higher to lower ground

temperate zone area between the Tropic of Cancer and the Arctic Circle or between the Tropic of Capricorn and the Antarctic Circle

tropics part of the earth's surface between the Tropic of Cancer and the Tropic of Capricorn

wetland wilderness low, wet land where people do not live

LEARN KEY VOCABULARY

Relate Words Study the new words and their definitions. Make a four-square chart for each word.

Word marsh	Picture
Definition low, wet land with grasses	Sentence Birds make their nests in the marsh.

LEARN ABOUT AUTHOR'S POINT OF VIEW AND PURPOSE

An author's **point of view** is how the author feels about a subject. His or her reason for writing is the **purpose**. When you know the author's point of view and purpose, you can better evaluate what you read.

> **READING STRATEGY**
> **How to Identify Author's Point of View and Purpose**
> 1. Take notes on the words or phrases that show how the author feels about a subject.
> 2. Ask yourself: Does the author want to tell me a story, explain something, or persuade me to do something?

As you read "A Celebration of the Everglades," look for clues to help you determine the authors' purposes and points of view.

Everglades: The River of Life

Many people once thought of the Florida Everglades as a useless swamp. In fact, it is a rich and unique natural resource important to the survival of the people, animals, and plants of Florida. Today Everglades National Park is a special area protected by the U.S. government.

The Source of the Everglades

Much of the Everglades' water comes from the Kissimmee River. As a slow, winding river, the Kissimmee used to travel 103 miles before it reached Lake Okeechobee. In its slow **course** south to the lake, the water was cleaned of most pollution. In the early 1960s, however, the river was changed into a canal and lost half its length. The shorter, faster river is not as clean as before. It brings polluted water into the lake and into the Everglades.

Tricolored herons stand in the water and catch fish, frogs, and other small animals.

....

course path

Why Is the Everglades Important?

The Everglades water system is **vital to** the plants and animals that live there. It is also needed for human life. The connection between the Kissimmee River, Lake Okeechobee, and the Everglades forms a great river of life that supports much of southern Florida.

The Everglades: Water for Life

Southern Florida depends upon rainfall for its fresh water. The Everglades is an important part of the water cycle that brings rain to southern Florida. Here is how the cycle works:

❺ As clouds cool more, the water vapor turns to rain and falls to earth.

❹ The vapor cools and forms clouds.

❸ Water vapor rises into the air.

❷ Heat from the sun turns water into vapor, or gas.

rain

Evaporation from Everglades

Evaporation from ocean

soil

porous rock

wetlands

ocean

❶ Rain water flows into lakes, rivers, wetlands, and oceans.

How Does the Everglades Work?

This diagram explains the importance of the Everglades to southern Florida. Without the fresh water that the Everglades provides, no plants, animals, or people could live there.

❶ Kissimmee River
The waters of the Kissimmee River still flow into Lake Okeechobee. However, not as much water feeds the lake—and the Everglades—as it did before the canal was built.

❷ Lake Okeechobee
The southern end of Florida is lower than the land to the north. Water from Lake Okeechobee flows south to the Everglades.

fresh water

soil

❸ Limestone
Underground, Florida has a layer of porous rock called limestone. Fresh water from the lake flows through the rock. People in nearby cities and towns have drilled wells into the limestone to find drinking water.

soil

soil

---

vital to needed in order to keep alive

Florida panthers once lived throughout much of the southeastern United States. Today they are found only in southwestern Florida.

A Friend of the Everglades

Marjory Stoneman Douglas understood the importance of the Everglades to both people and wildlife. She began working to gain government protection of the Everglades in the 1920s.

In her own words:

*Our most important resource and the most **imperiled** is water. It is the lifeblood on which the health of Florida's economy depends. In South Florida, protecting our water requires the destruction of the Kissimmee Canal so that water can flow down to Lake Okeechobee, which serves as nature's **filter** for the pollution from the marshlands now used for grazing and sugar growing. At all costs we must clean up the lake itself, which is now highly polluted.*

*All of our fresh water in South Florida comes from rainfall, and 80% of our rainfall comes from the **evaporation of the wet Everglades**.*

*We have the laws on the books to **prevent all this pollution**, and nothing has been done about it. We must prevent the unregulated dumping of dairy wastes into Lake Okeechobee. The best we can do is protect our great natural resources. This must be done or we will lose everything.*

—*Marjory Stoneman Douglas*, Florida Trend

4 The Everglades
The right level of fresh water helps keep salt water from flowing into the wetlands.

wetlands

5 Gulf of Mexico
If the amount of fresh water is too low, salt water from the sea will flow north into the wetlands. Salt water kills the plants and animals and poisons the wells.

salt water

imperiled in danger

filter cleaner

evaporation of the wet Everglades water of the Everglades changing into vapor

prevent all this pollution keep all this pollution from happening

A Celebration of the Everglades

from *Sawgrass Poems*

The Florida Everglades is a vast and mysterious place filled with unusual plants and animals. It is also a place in danger of extinction. In this selection, a poet and a photographer sing the praises of the Everglades.

by Frank Asch and Ted Levin

Introduction

The Everglades is a **wetland wilderness**, born in the sky and **sustained** by rain. It has no winter, summer, fall, or spring, like the rest of North America. Instead, like the **tropics**, the Everglades has two seasons— wet and dry. During the dry season, from November to April, the seemingly **endless stretches** of grassy **marshes** are brown and **brittle**, and the sky is blue, horizon to horizon. During the wet season, from May to October, the landscape is green and lush and looks like a wide, **shallow**, slow-moving river.

Nowhere else in North America do plants and animals of both the **temperate zone** and the tropics **mingle**. Nowhere else in America can you see manatees and crocodiles; or one-hundred-foot-tall royal palms; or bouquets of orchids and colorful snails. In the dry season, alligators dig holes to stay wet, and water-loving animals—otters, fish, snakes, frogs, turtles, snails, crayfish—join them. Thousands of herons, egrets, ibis, and storks feast on the trapped fish, cover the **crowns of mangroves** like fresh snow, and decorate the Florida skies in one of America's wild and wondrous **pageants**.

In 1947, Harry S. Truman dedicated the tip of south Florida as Everglades National Park. It was the first national park in the

Alligator holding a softshell turtle in its mouth at Eco Pond in the Everglades.

world to be **preserved** for its unusual gathering of plants and animals rather than its spectacular scenery. Now, almost fifty years later, the Everglades has another unique distinction. It is the most endangered national park.

Water is the very soul of the Everglades, but nearby man-made **dikes** and **levees** **interrupt its flow**. **Canals** drain water away and send it to the ocean. When water finally reaches the Everglades National Park, it often arrives at the wrong time of year, polluted by **runoff** from the farm fields.

---

sustained kept alive
endless stretches long distances
brittle dry and easily broken
shallow not very deep
mingle live together

crowns of mangroves top branches of mangrove trees
pageants shows
interrupt its flow stop the water from running

Marjory Stoneman Douglas, in her book *The Everglades: River of Grass* (1947), called the Everglades a river. The Everglades is actually the largest freshwater marsh in North America, one hundred miles long and about fifty miles wide (at its widest). Before the central and northern Everglades were diked and dammed, a high count of nearly 265,000 wading birds nested in the mangroves in Everglades National Park. Now the number of wading birds has fallen to about 18,500.

—Ted Levin

Sometimes the park gets too much water. Sometimes it gets too little. Now, teams of biologists, hydrologists, engineers, and politicians have **pledged** to help **restore** the flow of water by removing some of the levees, plugging some of the canals, and cleaning the farmland runoff. No one knows if the Everglades, which has survived for five thousand years, will survive for fifty more.

These poems and photographs are a celebration of the Everglades. Frank and I want her to speak for herself. If, after sitting with these poems, you want to **immerse yourself in** the southern tip of Florida, we have succeeded. Long may she flow and her wild winds blow.

—Ted Levin

....

pledged promised
restore bring back
immerse yourself in learn much more about

BEFORE YOU MOVE ON...

1. **Cause and Effect** What changes have canals caused in the Everglades?

2. **Inference** Why does Ted Levin want to celebrate the Everglades?

Some Rivers

Some rivers rush to the sea.
They push and tumble and fall.
But the Everglades is a river
with no hurry in her at all.
Soaking the cypress
that grows so tall;
nursing a frog,
so quiet and small;
she flows but a mile
in the course of a day,
with plenty of time
to think on the way.
But how can she cope
with the acres of corn
and sorrowful cities that drain her?
With hunters and tourists and levees
that chain and stain and pain her?
Does the other half of her that's left
think only of the past?
Or does she think of her future
and how long it will last?
Some rivers rush to the sea.
They push and tumble and fall.
But the Everglades is a river
with no hurry in her at all.

—*Frank Asch*

Soaking Covering with water
nursing protecting
flows travels
the course of a day one day's time
cope with handle, manage
drain her use up her water

BEFORE YOU MOVE ON...

1. **Mood or Tone** Describe the feeling that Frank Asch's poem "Some Rivers" creates.

2. **Inference** What does the poet mean by the phrase "the Everglades is a river with no hurry in her at all"?

Old Man Mangrove

Mangrove forests are found in quiet waters throughout the tropics worldwide. In the Everglades there are three species of mangroves that each live in water of different depths with different amounts of salt in it. Because they continually shed their nutrient-rich leaves, mangrove forests are among the most naturally productive areas in the world. The fallen leaves form a basic part of the food chain as they **decompose**.

—*Ted Levin*

Old Man Mangrove
lives by the sea.
He's a sailor, he's a farmer,
he's a rookery.

All year long he
drops green leaves,
enriching the soil
for other trees.

Shrimp and lobster
spawn on his farms.
Thousands of birds
nest in his arms.

Covered in oysters,
living on land,
he seems to creep
across the sand.

He moves at the pace
of a tired old snail,
till the tide comes in
and he sets sail.

—*Frank Asch*

decompose break down into tiny pieces
rookery place where birds and other animals build nests
enriching adding food to
spawn lay eggs
pace speed
sets sail floats away as if on a boat

Two Baby Snail Kites

Two baby snail kites
sitting in their nest,
hungry and endangered,
hoping for the best.

Apple snails for dinner.
Apple snails for lunch.
And every Sunday morning,
apple snails for brunch.

Two baby snail kites,
eyes still and steady,
waiting for a meal,
mouths wide and ready!

Snail kites are an endangered tropical member of the hawk family. Because snail kites feed mostly on apple snails that rise to the surface of the water to breathe, these kites are especially endangered by the draining of the Everglades. Anything that affects the well-being of the apple snail seriously affects the snail kite.

—Ted Levin

Apple snails for dinner.
Apple snails for lunch.
And every Sunday morning,
apple snails for brunch.

"Hey Mom! Hey Dad!
How about some meat?"
"So sorry, little ones.
Snails is what we eat."

Apple snails for dinner.
Apple snails for lunch.
And every Sunday morning,
apple snails for brunch.

—Frank Asch

....

brunch a late morning meal that combines breakfast and lunch

still and steady looking straight ahead

BEFORE YOU MOVE ON...

1. **Inference** What message does the poem about the mangrove tree tell readers?

2. **Author's Style** Identify two examples of personification in each poem.

3. **Author's Purpose** Why do you think the author wrote each of these poems? Do you think he was successful? Explain.

Manatees are plant-eating water creatures distantly related to elephants. Like whales, these gentle, friendly mammals give birth in the water. Although manatees have no known enemies, they are frequently injured or killed by speeding powerboats.

—*Ted Levin*

Hey You, Manatee!

You're no mermaid mama.
Yes, that's true!
But I can understand
how those ancient sailors
fell in love with you.
You whisker-nosed blubber blob!
You seaweed-munching sea slob!
You mossbacked moat goat,
slow-motion victim of speedboat!
Quietly munching
cow of the sea,
I confess—
I love you, manatee!

—*Frank Asch*

slow-motion slow-moving
victim of something that gets hurt by
munching chewing
confess tell the truth

ABOUT THE POET

Frank Asch grew up close to nature. "I had a brook next to where I lived ... and I could always wander around," he explains. His poems and books encourage readers to take care of the earth. He feels that the energy fueling his work comes from "a light, bright future—the future where the earth *doesn't* get blown up or drown in its own pollution."

ABOUT THE PHOTOGRAPHER

Ted Levin has visited the Everglades many times and never ceases to be amazed by its beauty. His photographs and articles have appeared in many publications such as *National Geographic Traveler* and *Natural History*. Ted Levin lives with his wife, son, a baby weasel, and a bunny in Thetford, Vermont.

Respond to the Article and Poems
Check Your Understanding

SUM IT UP

Respond to Literature Complete your charts to show how the poems made you feel.

Words that Make Me Like Plants and Animals	Words that Make Me Worry About the Everglades
Old Man Mangrove mermaid mama	sorrowful cities hunters

Evaluate Literature The poet and the photographer created this selection to make you care about the Everglades. Study your charts and think about what you learned in the selection. Then write a paragraph to tell if the poet and the photographer achieved their purpose. Give three reasons to support your answer. Include examples from the article, poems, and photographs.

THINK IT OVER

Discuss and Write Talk about these questions with a partner. Write the answers.

1. **Summary/Conclusion** How do the plants, animals, and climate of the Everglades form a connected system? What happens to the whole system if one part of it is sick or damaged?

2. **Comparisons** Marjory Stoneman Douglas and the authors of "A Celebration of the Everglades" want to persuade you to save the Everglades. How do their persuasive techniques differ?

3. **Judgments** Why is it necessary to protect the Everglades?

EXPRESS YOURSELF ▶ PERSUADE

Give a three-minute speech to persuade your classmates to do something to help preserve the Everglades.

Language Arts and Literature

USE FIGURATIVE LANGUAGE: METAPHOR

Learn About Metaphors A metaphor makes a comparison by saying one thing *is* another thing.

> The otter **is a clown**.
> The cloud **was a giant pillow**.

Metaphors paint pictures with words. They help readers create images in their minds.

Find Metaphors Read the following lines from "Old Man Mangrove." What are the metaphors? How is the tree like these things?

> Old Man Mangrove
> lives by the sea.
> He's a sailor, he's a farmer,
> he's a rookery.

Practice Create metaphors about these plants and animals in the Everglades.

- crocodiles
- turtles
- orchids
- palm trees

WRITE A RHYMING POEM

Learn About Rhyme Scheme The pattern of rhymes in a poem is called the **rhyme scheme**. You can use letters to label which lines have the same rhyme. In this stanza from "Two Baby Snail Kites," the last words in the second and fourth lines rhyme.

Two baby snail kites	*a*
sitting in their nest,	*b*
hungry and endangered,	*c*
hoping for the best.	*b*

The rhyme scheme for this poem is *abcb*.

Learn About Meter The beat of a poem is the **meter**. It makes the poem musical and fun to read aloud.

Read aloud the stanza from "Two Baby Snail Kites." Clap for each syllable, and notice the beats in each line.

Practice Now write a two-stanza rhyming poem. Develop a rhyme scheme and meter for it. You can use "Two Baby Snail Kites" and "Hey You, Manatee!" as models.

Respond to the Article and Poems, continued

Language Arts and Content Area Connections

▶ TECHNOLOGY/MEDIA
▶ REPRESENTING/SPEAKING

EVALUATE PROPAGANDA IN THE MEDIA

People often use **propaganda** in the media to convince others to think or feel a certain way. Find and evaluate different examples of propaganda.

1 **Learn About Propaganda** Here are two types of propaganda.

A **bandwagon** ad tries to convince you that everyone is doing something. The idea is that you should do it because everyone else is.

We're All Helping!

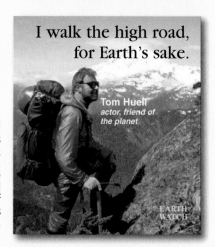

A **testimonial** ad uses a famous person to talk about an issue. Many people are influenced by the words of famous athletes and artists.

I walk the high road, for Earth's sake.

Tom Huell
actor, friend of
the planet

EARTH
WATCH

2 **Collect and View Propaganda** Study several different kinds of propaganda in newspapers and magazines. If possible, you might record radio broadcasts and TV commercials, too.

3 **Evaluate Techniques** Make a comparison chart. Identify the types of propaganda you have collected. Evaluate how effective each propaganda technique is. Use your chart to present your ads to the class.

Media	Technique	Effectiveness
magazine ad	testimonial by a famous actor	very effective, because people like and respect him

For tips on **viewing**, see Handbook page 403.

EXPLORE GEOGRAPHY

Map the Climate Zones "A Celebration of the Everglades" tells about the temperate zone and the tropics. Find out about other climate zones and show them on a map.

1 **Research Climate Zones** Earth has many climate zones including:

Desert	Tundra
Subtropical	Highland
Subarctic	Humid Continental

Use the Internet or an encyclopedia to learn where each climate zone is.

2 **Prepare and Present Your Map** Draw and label the climate zones on a world map. Use different colors to distinguish them. Highlight the Everglades section of Florida. Make a map key to tell what the colors mean. Then display your map in the classroom.

 For tips on **representing**, see Handbook pages 404–405.

MAKE A WILDLIFE REPORT

Research a plant or animal that is found in the Everglades. Report your findings to the class.

1 **Choose a Topic** Select a plant or animal from those listed on page 315.

2 **Research and Take Notes** Use an encyclopedia and other reference materials to learn about the habitat and life cycle of the plant or animal you chose. What is its place on the food chain? Take notes.

3 **Report to the Class** Choose from one of these ideas to present what you learned:

- Write a report.
- Make a poster.
- Create a diorama with models of plants and animals.
- Write a song or a rap.
- Make a plant or animal puppet and have the puppet tell about its life.

REACH BACK INSIDE YOURSELF AND GRAPPLE FOR THAT EXTRA OUNCE OF GUTS . . . .

—*Jesse Owens*

In 1936, Adolf Hitler attempted to use the Olympic Games in Berlin to establish the superiority of his race. African American athlete Jesse Owens pushed past the limits of racial prejudice to prove him wrong. This grandson of former slaves went on to win four gold medals at the Games. Jesse Owens showed the world that talent and determination, rather than race, distinguish one person from another.

Pushing Past the Limits

- What are some limits people have in their lives? Give examples of physical, intellectual, and social skills that help people push past these limits.

- What are some challenges that people face alone? How do people face challenges together?

- Who are the people you admire most for pushing past a limit? Explain.

THEME-RELATED BOOKS

Wilma Unlimited
by Kathleen Krull

Wilma Rudolph could barely walk as a child, but she overcame a crippling disease to become a gold medalist at the Olympics.

Wings
by Jane Yolen

The Greek myth of Icarus, who learned the secret of flight.

NOVEL

Call It Courage
by Armstrong Sperry

Determined to conquer his fear of the sea, Mafatu goes to sea all alone, survives a frightening ordeal, and returns to his village a hero.

Build Language and Vocabulary
ELABORATE

Study the painting and listen to the tape. Then read the quotation. What do you think Brian has learned about challenges and survival?

I might be hit but I'm not done.
When the light comes, I'll start to rebuild.

—*Gary Paulsen, from* Hatchet

MAKE A WORD WEB

Make a large copy of the word web to put up in your classroom. Think of challenges that people face, and add them to the web. Bring in pictures that illustrate a challenge or show people who have met challenges and survived. Add them to the word web, too.

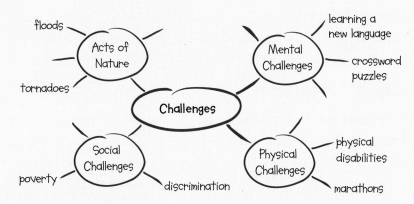

BUILD YOUR VOCABULARY

Survival Words These verbs are often used in talking about survival. Tell what each one means. Use a dictionary to find the meanings of words you don't know.

im·pro·vise (im´ pru vīz) v. to make something from whatever is available.

Word Bank

Survival Words
choose
consider
discover
exceed
exert
improvise
learn
plan
prepare
risk
strive

USE LANGUAGE STRUCTURES ▶ FUTURE PERFECT TENSE VERBS

Writing: Explain and Elaborate Write three sentences to tell what Brian will have done if he makes it through the storm. Use verbs in the future perfect tense.

Examples:
Brian **will have considered** different ways to protect himself.
He **will have chosen** the best way to survive. He **will have learned** that he can trust his own judgment.

The Circuit

autobiography
by Francisco Jiménez

Prepare to Read

THINK ABOUT WHAT YOU KNOW

Share Your Experiences Did you ever make a big change in your life? What was it? Why did you make the change? Tell a partner about it.

camp foreman

crate

enroll

grape season

labor camp

migrant worker

shack

vineyard

year-round job

LEARN KEY VOCABULARY

Locate and Use Definitions Study the new words. Write each word in a chart and guess what it means. Use the Glossary to confirm its meaning.

Word	What I Think It Means	What It Really Means	✓
camp foreman	head person in a camp	person in charge of the workers in a camp	✓

LEARN TO RELATE CAUSES AND EFFECTS

The **cause** is the reason something happens. The **effect** is what happens. If you can relate causes and effects, you can understand how one action leads to another in a chain of events.

> ### READING STRATEGY
> **How to Relate Causes and Effects**
> 1. Look for words that signal a cause *(since, because)* and words that signal an effect *(so, as a result, therefore)*.
> 2. Ask: What happened? Why did it happen?
> 3. Notice how one cause leads to another in a chain of events.

As you read "The Circuit," take notes about the causes and effects.

The Circuit

by Francisco Jiménez

The life of a migrant
family is one of constant
change, brutal poverty,
and back-breaking work.
For Panchito, the son
of migrant workers,
there is one more
challenge to face—how
to get an education as
his family moves from
place to place.

1

THE MOVE TO FRESNO

Panchito's family moves from place to place, following the crops. Once the strawberry season is over, they must move to Fresno to work in the vineyards.

A t sunset we drove into a **labor camp** near Fresno. Since Papá did not speak English, Mamá asked the **camp foreman** if he needed any more workers. "We don't need no more," said the foreman, scratching his head. "Check with Sullivan down the road. Can't miss him. He lives in a big white house with a fence around it."

When we got there, Mamá walked up to the house. She went through a white gate, past a row of rose bushes, up the stairs to the house. She rang the doorbell. The porch light went on and a tall **husky** man came out. They **exchanged** a few words. After the man went in, Mamá **clasped her hands** and hurried back to the car. "We have work! Mr. Sullivan said we can stay there the whole season," she said, **gasping** and pointing to an old garage near the **stables**.

The garage was worn out by the years. It had no windows. The walls, eaten by **termites**, **strained to support** the roof full of holes. The dirt floor, populated by earthworms, looked like a gray road map.

That night, by the light of a **kerosene lamp**, we unpacked and cleaned our

These are a few of the central California crops that **migrant workers** help to grow and harvest.

----

husky heavy, large

exchanged spoke

clasped her hands put her hands together to show happiness

gasping breathing hard

stables building where horses are kept

termites insects that eat wood

strained to support were almost unable to hold up

kerosene lamp lamp that burns kerosene oil

new home. Roberto swept away the loose dirt, leaving the hard ground. Papá plugged the holes in the walls with old newspapers and tin can tops. Mamá fed my little brothers and sister. Papá and Roberto then brought in the mattress and placed it on the far corner of the garage. "Mamá, you and the little ones sleep on the mattress. Roberto, Panchito, and I will sleep outside under the trees," Papá said.

Early the next morning Mr. Sullivan showed us where his crop was, and after breakfast, Papá, Roberto, and I headed for the **vineyard** to pick.

Around nine o'clock the temperature had risen to almost one hundred degrees. I was completely **soaked in sweat** and my mouth felt as if I had been chewing on a handkerchief. I walked over to the end of the row, picked up the jug of water we had brought, and began drinking. "Don't drink too much; you'll get sick," Roberto shouted. No sooner had he said that than I felt sick to my stomach. I dropped to my knees and let the jug roll off my hands. I remained motionless **with my eyes glued on** the hot sandy ground. All I could hear was the **drone** of insects. Slowly I began to recover. I poured water over my face and neck and watched the dirty water run down my arms to the ground.

....

soaked in sweat wet with perspiration
with my eyes glued on while staring at
drone continuous sound

I still felt dizzy when we took a break to eat lunch. It was past two o'clock and we sat underneath a large walnut tree that was on the side of the road. While we ate, Papá jotted down the number of boxes we had picked. Roberto drew designs on the ground with a stick. Suddenly I noticed Papá's face **turn pale** as he looked down the road. "Here comes the school bus," he whispered loudly **in alarm**. **Instinctively**, Roberto and I ran and hid in the vineyards. We did not want to get in trouble for not going to school. The neatly dressed boys about my age got off. They carried books under their arms. After they crossed the street, the bus drove away. Roberto and I came out from hiding and joined Papá. *"Tienen que tener cuidado,"* he warned us.

After lunch we went back to work. The sun **kept beating down**. The buzzing insects, the wet sweat, and the hot dry dust made the afternoon seem to last forever. Finally the mountains around the valley **reached out and swallowed the sun**.

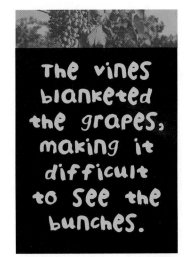

The vines blanketed the grapes, making it difficult to see the bunches.

Within an hour it was too dark to continue picking. The vines blanketed the grapes, making it difficult to see the bunches. *"Vámonos,"* said Papá, signaling to us that it was time to quit work. Papá then took out a pencil and began to figure out how much we had earned our first day. He wrote down numbers, crossed some out, wrote down some more. *"Quince,"* he **murmured**.

When we arrived home, we took a cold shower underneath a water hose. We then sat down to eat dinner around some wooden **crates** that served as a table. Mamá had cooked a special meal for us. We had rice and tortillas with *"carne con chile,"* my favorite dish.

BEFORE YOU MOVE ON...

1. **Point of View** This story is autobiographical. Which character do you think represents the author?

2. **Cause and Effect** Why did Panchito and Roberto hide when Papá said the school bus was coming?

3. **Opinion** Do you think Panchito would rather have been in school than working in the vineyard? Explain your answer.

---

turn pale lose its color

in alarm with fear and surprise

Instinctively Without having to think

Tienen que tener cuidado You must be careful (in Spanish)

kept beating down continued to shine bright and strong

reached out and swallowed the sun hid the setting sun

Vámonos Let's go (in Spanish)

Quince Fifteen (in Spanish)

murmured said softly

carne con chile meat with chili (in Spanish); a spicy meat stew

BACK TO SCHOOL

On Panchito's first day of school, his teacher offers to spend extra time to help him with his reading. Mr. Lema also offers to teach him to play the trumpet.

The next morning I could hardly move. My body **ached** all over. **I felt little control over** my arms and legs. This feeling went on every morning for days until my muscles finally got used to the work.

It was Monday, the first week of November. The grape season was over and I could now go to school. I woke up early that morning and lay in bed, looking at the stars and **savoring the thought** of not going to work and of starting school for the first time that year. Since I could not sleep, I decided to get up and join Papá and Roberto at breakfast. I sat at the table across from Roberto, but I kept my head down. I did not want to look up and face him. I knew he was sad. He was not going to school today. He was not going tomorrow, or next week, or next month. He would not go until the cotton season was over, and that was sometime in February. I rubbed my hands together and watched the dry, acid stained skin fall to the floor in little rolls.

I had not heard English for months.

When Papá and Roberto left for work, I felt **relief**. I walked to the top of a small **grade** next to the shack and watched the *Carcachita* disappear in the distance in a cloud of dust.

Two hours later, around eight o'clock, I stood by the side of the road waiting for school bus number twenty. When it arrived I climbed in. Everyone was busy either talking or yelling. I sat in an empty seat in the back.

When the bus stopped in front of the school, I felt very nervous. I looked out the bus window and saw boys and girls carrying books under their arms. I put my hands in my pant pockets and walked to the principal's office. When I entered I heard a woman's voice say: "May I help you?" I was **startled**. I had not heard English for months. For a few seconds I remained speechless. I looked at the lady who waited for an answer. My first instinct was to answer her in Spanish, but I held back. Finally, after **struggling for** English words, I **managed**

---

ached hurt
felt little control over did not have enough strength to use
savoring the thought enjoying the idea
relief calm, less worry

grade hill
Carcachita car (in Spanish slang)
startled surprised
struggling for trying hard to think of
managed found a way

to tell her that I wanted to **enroll**. After answering many questions, I was led to the classroom.

Mr. Lema, the teacher, greeted me and assigned me a desk. He then introduced me to the class. I was so nervous and scared at that moment when **everyone's eyes were on me** that I wished I were with Papá and Roberto picking cotton. After taking roll, Mr. Lema gave the class the assignment for the first hour. "The first thing we have to do this morning is finish reading the story we began yesterday," he said **enthusiastically**. He walked up to me, handed me an English book, and asked me to read. "We are on page 125," he said politely. When I heard this, I felt **my blood rush to my head**; I felt dizzy. "Would you like to read?" he asked **hesitantly**. I opened the book to page 125. My mouth was dry. My eyes began to water. I could not begin. "You can read later," Mr. Lema said **understandingly**.

During recess I went into the rest room and opened my English book to page 125. I began to read in a low voice, pretending I was in class. There were many words I did not know. I closed the book and **headed** back to the classroom.

Mr. Lema was sitting at his desk correcting papers. When I entered he looked up at me and smiled. I felt better. I walked up to him and asked if he could help me with the new words. "Gladly," he said.

The rest of the month I spent my lunch hours working on English with Mr. Lema, my best friend at school.

everyone's eyes were on me everyone was looking at me
enthusiastically with great energy
my blood rush to my head hot and embarrassed

hesitantly without being sure if I could
understandingly with knowledge of how I felt
headed started to go

One Friday during lunch hour Mr. Lema asked me to take a walk with him to the music room. "Do you like music?" he asked me as we entered the building. "Yes, I like *corridos*," I answered. He then picked up a trumpet, blew on it, and handed it to me. The sound **gave me goose bumps**. I knew that sound. I had heard it in many *corridos*. "How would you like to learn how to play it?" he asked. He must have **read my face** because before I could answer, he added: "I'll teach you how to play it during our lunch hours."

....

corridos traditional songs, ballads (in Spanish)

gave me goosebumps caused little bumps to appear on my skin because it excited me

read my face known what I was thinking by looking at my face

That day I could hardly wait to tell Papá and Mamá the great news. As I got off the bus, my little brothers and sister ran up to meet me. They were yelling and screaming. I thought they were happy to see me, but when I opened the door to our shack, I saw that everything we owned was neatly packed in cardboard boxes.

BEFORE YOU MOVE ON...

1. **Paraphrase** In your own words, tell what Panchito's first day back at school was like.

2. **Evidence and Conclusion** Did Mr. Lema care about Panchito? How do you know?

3. **Inference** When did Panchito realize that the family was about to move again? How did he feel?

EPILOGUE

Not long after this **episode**, I returned to Mexico. A few months later, I got the papers I needed to live in the United States. My brother and I moved to Santa Clara, California. We both got **year-round jobs** as janitors. This job allowed me to settle in one place and complete my education.

I always loved learning. I studied hard and did very well. I **earned several scholarships to** Santa Clara University and a Woodrow Scholarship to Columbia University.

After I finished school, I became a professor of Spanish Language and Latin American Literature at Santa Clara University.

In 1999, I began writing the **sequel** to *The Circuit*, though I never learned to play the trumpet.

—*Francisco Jiménez*, January 2000

---

episode event, time in my life
earned several scholarships to won awards of money in order to attend
sequel next part

ABOUT THE AUTHOR

Francisco Jiménez had a purpose in mind when he wrote about his experiences as the child of a migrant family. It was to fill the need for understanding about the hardships endured by migrant families in the United States. Francisco Jiménez overcame obstacles and met a personal challenge to achieve his goals. He became a successful educator and an award-winning writer of such books as *The Circuit* and *La Mariposa*, which is also about the migrant experience.

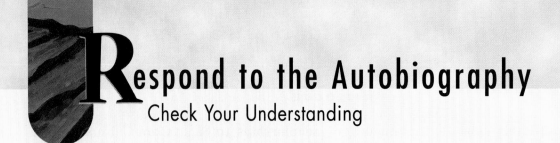

SUM IT UP

Relate Causes and Effects to Retell a Story
Show what happened when each season ended.
Then use your Cause-and-Effect Chains to retell
the story to a partner.

Cause-and-Effect Chains

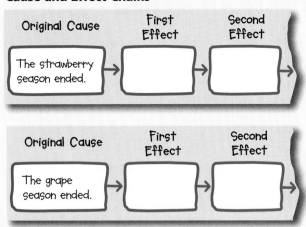

Compare Life Stories In "Twins" you read
about deaf twins who have overcome a number
of challenges. How are they and Panchito alike?
How are they different? Compare their families,
their feelings, and the changes they go through.
Discuss your ideas in a group.

THINK IT OVER

Discuss and Write Talk about these questions
with a partner. Write the answers.

1. **Author's Point of View** What does Panchito
   think about having to move from place
   to place?

2. **Prediction** How do you think Panchito will
   feel the next time he has to start over in a
   new school?

3. **Conclusions** How did Panchito's hard work as
   a migrant worker prepare him for the
   challenges of getting a college education?

EXPRESS YOURSELF
▶CLARIFY AND ELABORATE

Think about the ways in which Mr. Lema helped
Panchito. Then tell about a teacher, coach, or
other adult who has been important to you.
Give examples that show how this person has
helped you.

Language Arts and Literature

USE THE FUTURE PERFECT TENSE

Learn About the Future Perfect Tense Some actions will start and be completed at a specific time in the future. To tell about these actions, use the **future perfect tense.** It is formed in this way:

> *will have* + past participle

Study these examples.

> By sunset, the workers **will have filled** many boxes with strawberries.

The sunset will take place in the future. Filling the boxes will also happen in the future, but at a specific time—before the sunset.

Make Up Sentences Complete these sentences with a verb in the future perfect tense.

1. By lunchtime, I _____ .

2. When school ends, you _____ .

Practice Write the paragraph. Use the verb in parentheses in the future perfect tense.

> By the time his family moves on, Panchito (learn) many new English words. He (start) music lessons. Before spring, however, the family (move) to a new place. When he is grown up, Panchito (live) in many different places.

USE LOGICAL ORDER IN WRITING

Learn About Logical Order When authors present information, they often use a **logical order.** "The Circuit" follows a circle—it starts and ends with the family moving. Some other examples of logical order are:

- A news article gives the most important information first.

- A description of a place may start at the front and move to the back, or it may describe details in a left-to-right direction.

- A persuasive letter often begins with the reason for writing it, followed by supporting ideas and details.

Choose a Writing Form Choose one of these ways to rewrite the story of Panchito's life in another logical order. Then share your writing with a group.

- Write a news story about Panchito's graduation from college.

- Describe a scene from the story, such as Panchito's home, the vineyard, or the school.

- Write a persuasive letter that suggests ways to improve life for migrant farm workers.

Respond to the Autobiography, continued
Content Area Connections

SOCIAL STUDIES

EXPLORE GEOGRAPHY

Make a Circuit Map Migrant workers like Panchito and his family follow crops from place to place. They move with the harvest and the needs of the growers. Use atlases, maps, and the Internet to find the answers to these questions:

- What crops are grown in the southwestern United States?

- Where are the major areas in which these crops are grown?

- How long is the growing season of each crop? When is each crop harvested?

Use the answers to these questions to make a "circuit map." Show the circular route a typical family might take as they follow the crops thoughout the year.

Harvesters pick lettuce in California.

TECHNOLOGY/MEDIA
SOCIAL STUDIES

STUDY THE "SALAD BOWL TO THE WORLD"

With a group, make a profile map of one of the counties in the California Central Valley, the "salad bowl to the world."

1 Gather Information and Take Notes Look up the names of the Central Valley counties and choose one to research. Use its name as a key word to find out about the number of crops grown there, where the crops are shipped, and other facts. Try these Web sites to get started. Take notes and download interesting photos.

INTERNET

INFORMATION ON-LINE

Web Sites:
➤ **Information about the Central Valley**
  - www.californiacv.com

➤ **Information about California Farms**
  - www.cfbf.com

2 Make a Profile Map Draw a map of the county you choose. Write captions that list interesting facts that you found. Include pictures of the crops grown there.

Learn to use the **Internet** on Handbook pages 392–393.

Mother to Son

poem
by Langston Hughes

THINK ABOUT WHAT YOU KNOW

Share Parents' Sayings What kinds of things do your parents say to you again and again? Share these sayings with a group and explain why your parents think they are important.

board flat piece of wood

crystal very high quality glass that people value for its beauty

landing flat area at the top of a number of steps

splinter small, thin, sharp piece of wood

stair set of steps that goes from one level or floor to the next

tack small, sharp nail

LEARN KEY VOCABULARY

Relate Words Study the new words and their definitions. Make a Venn diagram to show how a crystal stair and a wooden stair are alike and different.

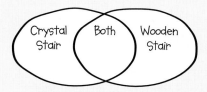

LEARN TO INTERPRET METAPHORS

A **metaphor** makes a comparison. Poets use metaphors to paint a picture with words.

READING STRATEGY
How to Interpret Metaphors
1. Ask yourself: What two things does the poet compare?
2. Form a picture in your mind of the metaphor. What does the comparison mean?
3. Restate the comparison in your own words.

As you read "Mother to Son," visualize the metaphor the poet uses.

Mother to Son

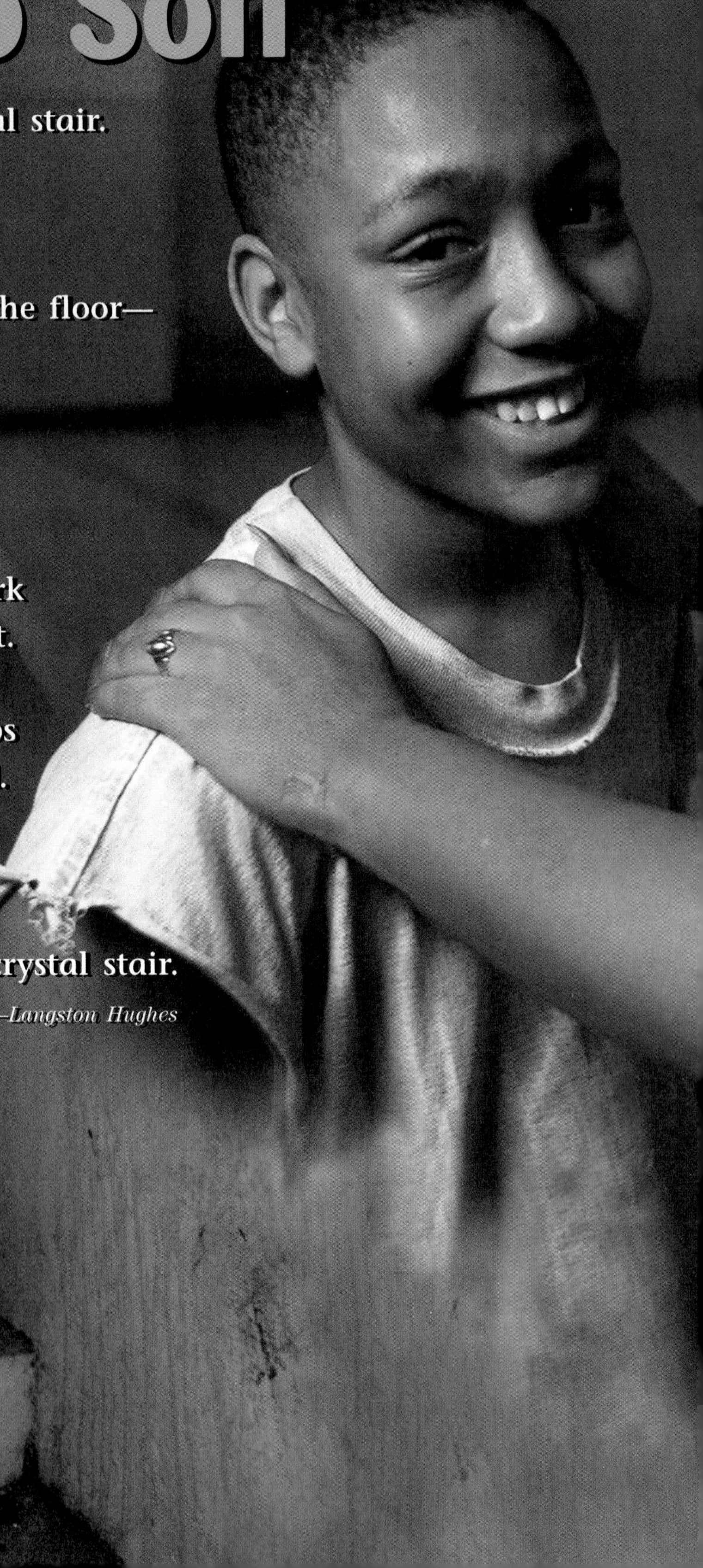

Well, son, I'll tell you:
Life for me ain't been no crystal stair.
It's had tacks in it,
And splinters,
And boards torn up,
And places with no carpet on the floor—
Bare.
But all the time
I'se been a-climbin' on,
And reachin' landin's,
And turnin' corners,
And sometimes goin' in the dark
Where there ain't been no light.
So, boy, don't you turn back.
Don't you set down on the steps
'Cause you finds it kinder hard.
Don't you fall now—
For I'se still goin', honey,
I'se still climbin',
And life for me ain't been no crystal stair.

—Langston Hughes

---

ain't been no hasn't been a
I'se I have
a-climbin' climbing
kinder kind of, sort of

Respond to the Poem

THINK IT OVER

Discuss Talk about these questions with a partner.

1. **Comparisons** What other metaphors could be used to describe life's journey?

2. **Personal Experience** What advice about life would you give to someone who is younger than you?

EXPRESS YOURSELF

▶ JUSTIFY

What experiences or situations could cause the mother in the poem to have this talk with her son? Take the role of the mother and justify her position. Explain why she feels her son needs her advice.

ABOUT THE POET

Langston Hughes earned his place as one of America's greatest poets by writing about the trials, hopes, and triumphs of ordinary black people. Langston Hughes was born at the beginning of the 20th Century, a time when African Americans had very few civil rights. He survived the Great Depression and lived to see the beginning of the civil rights movement. In one of his essays, "The Negro Artist and the Racial Mountain," he wrote, "We build our temples for tomorrow, as strong as we know how, and we stand on top of the mountain, free within ourselves." Langston Hughes died in 1967.

The Clever Wife

folk tale from
ancient China
retold by Carol Kendall
and Yao-wen Li

Prepare to Read

THINK ABOUT WHAT YOU KNOW

Quickwrite Think about folk tales you know. What kinds of challenges usually appear in folk tales? Write a few sentences about them in your journal and share your ideas with the class.

LEARN KEY VOCABULARY

appalling arrogance strong and shocking pride

boastful speaking with too much pride, bragging

braggart person who brags or praises himself or herself too much

capability ability to do something well

cleverness intelligence

conceited too proud of oneself

incomparable wisdom knowledge without equal or beyond compare

matchless wit clever and powerful mind that has no equal

remarkably proud unusually pleased or satisfied

swollen head feeling of being better than others

unusually clever more intelligent and creative than most people

Relate Words Study the new words and their definitions. Then put the words in order from the highest degree to the lowest.

Diagram

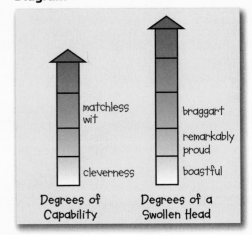

matchless wit

cleverness

Degrees of Capability

braggart

remarkably proud

boastful

Degrees of a Swollen Head

LEARN TO SUMMARIZE

A **summary** tells the most important ideas in a story and helps you remember what you read.

READING STRATEGY
How to Summarize
1. Make a list of important details in each section of the story.
2. Read through your list and put a check next to the most important details.
3. Write a summary statement that uses these important details and tells the main idea of the section.

As you read "The Clever Wife," collect important details for each section and write a summary statement.

The Clever Wife

an ancient Chinese folk tale retold by
Carol Kendall and Yao-wen Li

Fu-hsing is a simple but wealthy man, thanks to his wife's cleverness. When his pride in her is mistaken for a swollen head about himself, however, the district magistrate promises to punish Fu-hsing. Once again, Fu-hsing's wife must use her wits to help her husband face this challenge.

FU-HSING PRAISES HIS WIFE

Fu-hsing writes words in praise of his clever wife. A magistrate thinks
the words are about Fu-hsing himself and wants to punish him.

A very long time ago there lived in a far corner of China, in Sinkiang, a good and simple man named Fu-hsing, who had an **unusually clever** wife. All the day long he would run to her with questions about thus-and-such, or about such-and-thus. No

matter how difficult the problem he took to her, she always thought of a solution. Thanks to her extreme intelligence, the house of Fu-hsing enjoyed success and good **fortune**.

Fu-hsing was **remarkably proud** of his wife and often spoke of her as his **"Incomparable Wisdom,"** his **"Matchless Wit,"** or his "Dearest **Capability**." He only wished that all who passed his house could know it was her **cleverness** that had brought him such good fortune. For months he puzzled his head over a **suitable way of declaring his gratitude**. He at last created **a couplet** that **delicately conveyed** his feeling. He wrote the lines on twin **scrolls** and **posted** them on the gate before his house:

> A Matchless Wit like Fu-hsing's
> Does with ease a million things.

All who passed the house saw the scrolls. Those who knew Fu-hsing thought he was a true and honest husband to praise his wife in this way.

---

fortune luck
suitable way of declaring his gratitude way to thank her that matched all the good she had done for him
a couplet two rhyming lines of poetry

delicately conveyed used the perfect words to show
scrolls rolls of paper for writing
posted put, hung

One day, however, the **district magistrate** happened to pass that way. On reading the scrolls, he **drew** his mouth down and his eyebrows together in a terrible frown. "What a **boastful**, **conceited** fellow lives there!" he thought. "What **appalling arrogance**! Such boastfulness should not go unpunished!"

When he returned to his quarters, he ordered Fu-hsing to appear before him. This frightened Fu-hsing so much that he could hardly tell his wife of it. ". . . can't understand . . . **I'm law-abiding** . . . good citizen . . . pay taxes without cheating. . . ." He pulled at his hair, dropping strings of it on the floor. "My dear Capability, what did I do to bring this upon myself?"

His wife laid a calming hand on his before he could tear out the last of his thinning hair. "It must be," she said, after a moment's thought, "that the scrolls on the gate gave the wrong **impression**. Really, it is not worth worrying about! Go see the magistrate and have no fear. If you run into difficulty, we can talk it over when you return."

BEFORE YOU MOVE ON...

1. **Character's Motive** Why did Fu-hsing post the scrolls on his gate?

2. **Conflict** What problem did the scrolls create? How could it have been prevented?

3. **Judgment** Compare how Fu-hsing and his wife each reacted to the magistrate's order. Who would be better at pushing past limits? Why?

---

district magistrate person who carries out the law in the town
drew pulled

I'm law-abiding I follow all laws
impression idea

The magistrate tells Fu-hsing to perform three impossible tasks or he will
be punished. Fu-hsing asks his wife to help him.

Much relieved, Fu-hsing soon was standing before the magistrate. By now his eyebrows were crossing each other. He stared frowning from behind **an immense** table. His arms were folded into his sleeves.

"So!" he exclaimed "This is the braggart who posts scrolls on his gate to boast of his extraordinary **cleverness**." He **leant** forward to **glare** into Fu-hsing's face. His terrible eyebrows **bristled** like angry hedgehogs. "You think you can do anything at all, do you! No matter how difficult? Very well!"

Loosing his arms from his sleeves, he **struck** an angry fist on the table. "I have three small **tasks** for you to perform. At once! For a fellow of your remarkable talents, they should provide no difficulty. No difficulty whatsoever.

"First, then," and *pound* went the fist, "you shall make a cloth as long as a road. Second," *pound, pound,* "you shall make as much tea as there is water in the ocean. Third," *pound, pound, pound,* "you shall raise a pig as big as a mountain."

With an awful smile, the magistrate opened his fist to wave a long finger under poor Fu-hsing's nose. "Of course, if you do not complete these tasks for me one, two, three, you will soon learn how this court deals with a **swollen head!**"

Wretched and **anxious**, Fu-hsing **hastened** home to his wife and told her about the three impossible tasks.

His wife threw back her head and laughed. "Foolish husband," she said. "The hardest problems are those with the simplest answers!"

Fu-hsing continued to **wring his hands**. "But what shall I do? I know that you can accomplish anything, but this is **beyond all reason**. . . ."

Madame Fu-hsing's smile stopped him. "It is really quite simple. Rest well tonight. Tomorrow you must go back to the magistrate. You will present to him three quite ordinary tools which I shall make ready for you. I will give you certain words to take along with these tools. You must say them to the magistrate just as I tell them to you."

---

an immense a huge, a very large
leant leaned
glare stare deeply
bristled became stiff
struck pounded
tasks jobs
Wretched Very unhappy, Miserable

anxious worried
hastened hurried
wring his hands squeeze and twist his hands together
beyond all reason too much for anyone to be able to do

1. **Comparison** Compare the person Fu-hsing was with the person the magistrate believed him to be.

2. **Character's Motive** Why did the magistrate give Fu-hsing impossible tasks to perform?

3. **Prediction** Do you think Fu-hsing's wife will succeed in helping her husband? What clues does the author give?

THE CLEVER WIFE MEETS THE CHALLENGE

Fu-hsing follows his wife's plan and asks for more information about the three tasks. The magistrate cannot answer and lets Fu-hsing go without punishment.

Fu-hsing listened carefully to his wife's instructions. The next morning, carrying a ruler, a large measuring bowl, and a balancing scale, he stood in front of the magistrate once again.

When he started speaking, the magistrate's eyebrows were **as tightly knotted** as before. But when Fu-hsing laid the three tools down, his brows lifted up and up until they became flying birds of **astonishment**.

"This morning, as I was setting out to do the tasks you gave me," Fu-hsing began, "I realized that I needed **further instruction** from you before I could finish. Therefore, your Honor, I have brought these three tools to help you. I must respectfully ask you, first, to measure the road with this ruler so that I know the length of the cloth I must make. Second, measure the ocean's water with this bowl so that I know how much tea I must make. Third, weigh the mountain with this balance so that I know how big a pig I must raise."

Fu-hsing **bowed** deeply. "Just as soon as you have made the measurements, your Honor, I shall be pleased to finish the tasks."

The magistrate was so surprised by the **cunning** solution that he allowed Fu-hsing to go without punishment, and never bothered him again. Truly, the magistrate believed Fu-hsing's Matchless Wit could do a million things.

BEFORE YOU MOVE ON...

1. **Comparison** How were the three things Fu-hsing asked the magistrate to do similar to the three tasks the magistrate had asked him to do?

2. **Personal Experience** Give an example of a time when someone helped you or you helped someone push past a limit. Briefly explain what happened.

---

as tightly knotted showing as much anger
astonishment surprise
further instruction more directions

bowed leaned forward at the waist
cunning very clever

能解萬事難

吾妻智無雙

ABOUT THE AUTHOR

Carol Kendall was pleased with her first children's book, *The Other Side of the Tunnel*, but she dreamed of doing better. "I ached to write a book with meaning, a book that readers would take to their hearts and remember always." In time, she accomplished this goal and became famous for her fantasy novels. Carol Kendall is also proud of her collection of Asian folk tales. One of the books in this collection is *Sweet and Sour Tales*, which she and illustrator **Yao-wen Li** translated from Chinese into English. It includes the story of "The Clever Wife."

SUM IT UP

Summarize Each Section Use the important details to complete a summary statement for each section of the folk tale.

1 Fu–hsing Praises His Wife	2 Fu–hsing Faces a Challenge	3 The Clever Wife Meets the Challenge
Details	Details	Details
Summary Statement	Summary Statement	Summary Statement

Summarize the Selection Put your summary statements together to create a summary for the entire folk tale. Share your work with a group.

THINK IT OVER

Discuss and Write Talk about these questions with a partner. Write the answers.

1. **Authors' Purpose** Folk tales are told for many years before they are written down. Why do you think the authors chose to write down this folk tale?

2. **Judgment** Was Fu-hsing right to brag about his wife so much? Explain your answer.

3. **Comparisons** How did Fu-hsing in "The Clever Wife" and Panchito in "The Circuit" overcome obstacles? What can you learn from each of them?

EXPRESS YOURSELF ▶PERSUADE

If you were Fu-hsing, how would you convince the magistrate that you are not a braggart? Find a partner to play the role of the magistrate and deny that you are bragging about yourself.

Language Arts and Literature

LITERARY ANALYSIS

EVALUATE HOW SETTING AFFECTS CHARACTERS

Learn About Setting Where and when a story takes place is the **setting**. The setting has an impact on the way the characters think and act. "The Clever Wife" takes place in China during the Han Dynasty (206 BCE–220 CE) at a time when the class system lets the magistrates rule the people. Fu-hsing's problems seem more important and believable because of the time and place where the story occurs.

Practice Study this chart about China during the Han Dynasty. Complete the chart to tell how the setting affects the actions of the characters in "The Clever Wife."

Setting: The Clever Wife

Elements in the Setting	Effects on the Characters
The government encourages intelligent and educated thinking.	
The magistrate could punish people by killing them.	
Any family member could be punished for the actions of another family member.	

SPEAKING/LISTENING

SING YOUR PRAISES

Create a Rhyme Put your classmates' names in a box. Each person can draw out a name and write a two-line rhyme praising that person. Students can sing or say the rhymes.

Sample Rhyme

> Jennifer is so very kind,
> Her friends are always on her mind.

WRITING

WRITE A REVIEW OF A STORY

One way to tell others about a story is to write about it. Write a review of "The Clever Wife."

- In the first paragraph, tell the title, authors, and main idea. Summarize important events.

- In the second paragraph, tell how you feel about the story and why.

- In the third paragraph, tell the most important idea you learned from the story.

You may want to publish your review in a class newspaper.

Develop your skill in the **writer's craft**. See Handbook pages 414–423.

Writing That Persuades

Persuasive writing states an opinion and tries to convince readers to agree with it. Persuasive writing can be printed, or it can be delivered as a speech.

PERSUASIVE LANGUAGE IN PROFESSIONAL WRITING

"A Celebration of the Everglades" includes a persuasive speech by Marjory Stoneman Douglas. In it, she uses facts and strong words to state the problem and make her position clear.

from Marjory Stoneman Douglas's speech

Our most important resource and the most imperiled is water. It is the lifeblood on which the health of Florida's economy depends. In South Florida, protecting our water requires the destruction of the Kissimmee Canal so that water can flow down to Lake Okeechobee, which serves as nature's filter for the pollution from the marshlands . . . .

The best we can do is protect our great natural resources. This must be done or we will lose everything.

LOGICAL ORDER IN PERSUASIVE WRITING

A persuasive speech is more effective when the arguments are delivered in a logical order. For example, a speaker might present an opinion, propose an action, and then tell why the action is important. Or, a speaker might state a position and then give the arguments in order from the least important to the most important.

Diagrams of Logical Order

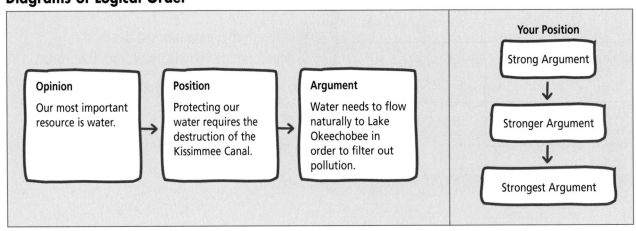

Opinion	Position	Argument
Our most important resource is water.	Protecting our water requires the destruction of the Kissimmee Canal.	Water needs to flow naturally to Lake Okeechobee in order to filter out pollution.

Your Position

Strong Argument → Stronger Argument → Strongest Argument

STUDENT WRITING MODEL

5-Paragraph Essay

Students Should Not Fight!

by Jacob Tang

We need a No Play-Fighting Rule on our school grounds. The way things are now, it's all right for kids to play-fight outside—as long as they don't have weapons and aren't trying to hurt each other. We must stop play-fighting though, and I'll give you some good reasons why.

For one thing, play-fighting can look like real fighting. Little kids at the day school across the street see the big kids fighting all the time. They might think it's all right to fight. It's not just little kids who think so. People walking by our grounds think that the kids are really fighting and that our school is not a safe place to be.

Another reason is that play-fighting can lead to real fighting. Sometimes two kids start off play-fighting, and then one of them hits the other too hard by mistake. The other one hits back. Suddenly, it's a real fight! This happened three times last month. Eight kids were involved. Two of the kids had gotten into real fights before. This happens because students' attitudes get worse after they have a real fight. Next time they play-fight, they are meaner.

Play-fighting is especially bad because other people can get injured when kids pretend to fight. Just last week, a girl was hurt when two boys who were play-fighting knocked into her. She fell and had to have five stitches. Accidents like this have happened before and will happen again.

In conclusion, play-fighting on our school grounds needs to be stopped. Tell the principal that you want a No Play-Fighting Rule at our school. If we all speak up, we may be able to change the rules. At least we will have tried!

INTRODUCTION
Jacob **presents the issue** and **states his position**.

BODY
In the body, Jacob **presents his arguments in a logical order**. He starts with his least important argument and ends with the one he thinks is most important.

He includes **facts or examples** to support his opinions.

CONCLUSION
The last paragraph **sums up his position**. Jacob uses **persuasive words** to get his readers to take action.

Writing That Persuades   **357**

Writing That Persuades, continued

The Writing Process

> **WRITING PROMPT**
>
> Choose an issue you feel strongly about. Write an essay to use for a speech that will persuade others at your school to agree with your position. Include three good arguments with strong evidence.

PREWRITE

1 **Choose Your Issue** Think about issues at your school, in your neighborhood, or among your friends. Make a chart.

What's the issue?	What's my position?	Will this issue interest others?
Should kids be allowed to use school computers for personal use?	Yes – as long as it's not during class time.	Yes, if they are interested in going on-line.
Should the City Council include a couple of students as advisors?	Yes – it's the best way for kids to have a voice in city issues.	Yes. Everyone argues about this at school.
Is there too much violence in video games for kids?	No – kids know the difference between real and make-believe violence.	Yes – except most kids agree with me already. They don't need persuading.

2 **Unlock the Writing Prompt** Before you begin writing, fill out an **FATP** chart to help guide your writing.

3 **Collect Your Arguments and Evidence** Make two lists of arguments: one in favor of your position and one against your position. This will help you see the issue from both sides. Circle the strongest three arguments in favor of your position. Gather evidence that supports these arguments.

4 **Get Organized** You might use a diagram like the one on page 356 to decide on an order for presenting your arguments.

FATP Chart

> **HOW TO UNLOCK A PROMPT**
>
> **F**orm: *speech*
>
> **A**udience: *people at school*
>
> **T**opic: *student advisors on the City Council*
>
> **P**urpose: *to persuade students to send letters to the council supporting the idea of student advisors*

> **Reflect** and Evaluate
>
> - Does this issue really matter to you? It's easier to persuade others when you believe in your topic!
>
> - Have you looked at both sides of the issue? If you know why people might disagree with you, you can make your arguments stronger.

DRAFT

Keep your **FATP** chart handy to remind you why you are writing. Focus on writing down your ideas, not on correcting your grammar.

① **Write an Introduction** Make your position clear.

② **Present and Support Your Arguments** Use your chart and lists to draft the body of your essay. For each argument, present important evidence that supports your position. Connect your arguments with good transitions.

Writer's Craft: Important Details and Transitions

Replace unimportant details with important information to strengthen your argument.

Just OK	Better
The City Council needs student representation. There have never been students on the council. Having student advisors would offer a new view of things.	The City Council needs student representation. Students have a unique point of view that is currently not represented on the council. Having student advisors would provide a new perspective.

Use transition words like *in addition* and repeat a key word or phrase like *student advisors* to connect your paragraphs.

Just OK	Better
We need to keep other students aware of and interested in city issues. It is important to keep all of our youth involved in our community.	In addition, student advisors would keep other students aware of and interested in city issues. It is important to keep all of our youth involved in our community.

③ **Write a Conclusion** Sum up your position. Remind your audience of your position, and be specific about the action you want them to take.

Writer's Craft: Effective Conclusions

Be clear and concise.

In conclusion, let me say that the City Council needs student advisors. Please join me in writing to all the council members. Urge them to vote YES for student advisors.

Reflect and Evaluate

- Read the draft of your essay. Will it hold—and keep—your audience's attention?

- Have you made your position clear in both your introduction and conclusion?

REVISE

1 **Reread the Draft of Your Essay** Does it go with your **FATP**? Is your position clear? Have you included three persuasive arguments to support your position?

2 **Conduct a Peer Conference** Read your draft to a partner or to a small group. Speak clearly and don't rush. Ask your audience to answer these questions:

- Did I include transition words to make my arguments easy to follow?

- Did I include important details that you needed to know?

- Was I persuasive?

I would like to know more about what the student advisors would actually do on the City Council.

She's right. That's an important detail I have to add.

3 **Mark Your Changes** Look over your notes and decide how you want to change your writing.

Reflect and Evaluate

- Did your peer's comments help you improve your draft?

- Does your revised essay do a better job of persuading than your draft did?

> **GRAMMAR IN CONTEXT**

PERFECT TENSES

The tense of a verb shows when an action happens. The perfect verb tenses are formed with *has, have,* or *had* and the past participle of the main verb.

City Council

- Form the **past participle** of regular verbs by adding **-ed**.

    Examples: help   help**ed**   support   support**ed**

    Irregular verbs have special forms for the past participle:

Present	Past	Past Participle
is	was	been
know	knew	known
run	ran	run

- Use the **present perfect tense** to talk about an action that began in the past and may still be going on. You can also use the present perfect tense when you aren't sure of the exact time of the past action.

    Examples: I **have supported** our City Council for a long time.
    The City Council **has talked** about the issues many times.

- Use the **past perfect tense** to talk about an action that was completed before another action in the past.

    Example: I **had supported** the Council even before last month's great decision.

- Use the **future perfect tense** to talk about an action that will be completed at a specific time in the future.

    Example: By the end of this year, I **will have supported** the Council for three years.

Helping Verbs for Present Perfect Tense

I have	we have
you have	you have
he has	
she has	they have
it has	

Practice Complete each sentence. Write the verb in the tense shown.

Verb	Tense	Sentence
plan	past perfect	1. City Council members _____ to add student advisors, but then they changed their minds.
state	present perfect	2. Some members _____ that students are really not interested in city government.
support	future perfect	3. At the end of this month, I _____ this issue for four years!
know	past perfect	4. I _____ for years that the council would be slow to act.

Writing That Persuades, continued

EDIT AND PROOFREAD

1 **Check for Mistakes** Look through your essay and correct any mistakes in capitalization, punctuation, and spelling. Remember you will be using your essay to give a speech, and a sloppy paper is hard to read aloud! If you need help editing, use Handbook page 412.

2 **Check Your Sentences** Make sure your verb tenses are correct.

3 **Make a Final Copy** Make all the corrections you marked. For your final copy, leave an extra space between each line. This will make it easier for you to find your place when you give your essay as a speech.

PUBLISH

Now it's time to deliver your essay as a speech.

- Practice reading your speech aloud in front of a mirror. Are you looking up occasionally as you talk? Do you look interested in what you're saying?

- Then practice in front of other people. Can they understand what you are saying? Do you sound persuasive?

- If you have a computer with a microphone, record yourself reading your speech. Be your own critic. Do you sound persuasive? If so, send the sound file to a friend. Ask for feedback.

Key In TO Technology

You can record yourself on the computer, but experiment with it first. Record yourself holding the microphone at different distances from your mouth. Try different tones—quiet, louder, friendly, serious. Play them back. Choose the one that sounds best.

Reflect and Evaluate

- Does your speech sound persuasive? Does it
  - ☑ have strong arguments organized in an effective order?
  - ☑ focus on the important details that listeners need to know?
  - ☑ include transition words to help listeners follow your arguments?
  - ☑ use persuasive words to get people to take action?
- Which was easier for you— writing your essay or giving it as a speech?
- Are you pleased with how your speech turned out? What is the best thing about it?

Overcoming Obstacles

1 Look Back at the Unit

Make a Literary Report Card In this unit, you read selections about overcoming obstacles.

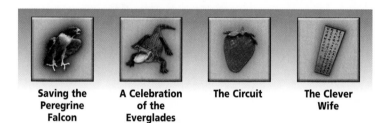

| Saving the Peregrine Falcon | A Celebration of the Everglades | The Circuit | The Clever Wife |

Write the title of each selection on an index card. Give an "A" to the selection that best describes a challenge. Then grade the other selections. On the back of each card, summarize the challenge and justify the way you graded the selection.

2 Show What You Know

Sum It All Up Expand and organize your ideas on this mind map. Share your ideas about meeting challenges with a partner.

Challenge | Obstacles | How to Meet the Challenge | What You Can Learn

hard
easy

Reflect and Evaluate

Write about obstacles in your life:

• Describe a challenge from your past. Tell how you met it.

• Describe an obstacle that is still in your way. Tell how you will overcome it. .

Add this writing to your portfolio, along with the work from the unit that shows what you learned.

3 Make Connections

To Your Community Study articles in a newspaper, a magazine, or on the Internet. Look for stories about people who are overcoming obstacles. Plan a current events day to talk about these people. Then use the stories to create a bulletin board to inspire other students.

HIGH POINT
Handbook

Strategies for Learning Language

These strategies can help you learn to use and understand the English language.

1 Listen actively and try out language.

WHAT TO DO	EXAMPLES
Repeat what you hear.	You hear: *Way to go, Joe! Fantastic catch!* You say: *Way to go, Joe! Fantastic catch!*
Recite songs and poems.	**When the Ground Shakes** When the ground shakes along the street, There's something happening beneath your feet. Earth layers are shifting, Slipping, Sliding, Bumping together. Shock waves are rising! *When the ground shakes along the street,...*
Listen to others and use their language.	You hear: "When did you know that something was missing?" You say: "I knew that something was missing when I got to class."
Add chunks of language to your speech.	You hear: "You can send the invitation by e-mail or snail mail." You think: *Snails move very slowly, and e-mail is much faster than regular mail. Snail mail must be regular mail.* You say: *I'll send it by snail mail. There's plenty of time, and I have the invitation all written out on special paper.*
Rehearse ways of speaking that match the social situation.	Formal: "Hello, Ms. Taylor. How are you?" "Fine, thank you. And how are you today?" Informal: "Hey, Paco. How's it going?" "Okay. And you?"

WHAT TO DO	EXAMPLES
Use the language you learn in one subject area in other subject areas and outside of school.	**You read this in Social Studies:** After almost two centuries of struggle, the Voting Rights Act of 1965 guaranteed all U.S. citizens the right to vote. **You write this in your reading journal:** *I wonder if The Secret of Gumbo Grove has something to do with voting rights. It'll be interesting to see what Raisin Stackhouse uncovers in the cemetery!* **At home, you might say:** Mom, did you vote? You're guaranteed the right to vote.
Explore different ways of saying things.	**All of these mean the same thing:** My teacher helps me push my thinking. My teacher makes me think before I make up my mind. My teacher helps me stretch my mind to see different viewpoints. Before I make a decision, my teacher suggests I role-play different choices in my mind.

❷ Ask for help and feedback.

WHAT TO DO	EXAMPLES
Interrupt politely.	Excuse me. Please explain what the word "habitat" means. Other options: "Pardon me, but could you say that again?" "Could you help me? I don't understand the phrase 'how precious life is.'"
Ask questions about how to use language.	Did I say that right? Did I use that word in the right way? Which is correct, "bringed" or "brought"?
Use your native language or English to ask for clarification.	You say: "Wait! Could you go over that point again, a little more slowly, please?" Other options: "Does 'have a heart' mean to be kind?" "Is 'enormous' another way to say 'big'?"

Strategies for Learning Language, continued

③ Use nonverbal clues.

WHAT TO DO	EXAMPLES
Use gestures and mime to get across an idea.	*I will hold up five fingers to show that I need five more minutes.*
Look for nonverbal clues.	*María wants me to go to the Subhumans' concert, but I think their music is awful—and downright insulting.* *I'm not sure what she said about the Subhumans' music, but I can tell she doesn't like it. Just look at her!*
Compare nonverbal and verbal clues.	*Let's give him a hand.* *Everyone is clapping. "Give him a hand" must mean to clap for him.*

④ Verify how language works.

WHAT TO DO	EXAMPLES
Test hypotheses about language.	**You try out what you learned:** I can add *-ation* to the verb *observe* to get the noun *observation*. So maybe I can make a noun by adding *-ation* to all verbs that end in *-e*. Let's see. *Prepare* and *preparation*. Yes, that works! *Preserve* and *preservation*. That works, too. *Compare* and *comparation*. That doesn't sound right. I'd better see what the dictionary says... Now I see — it's *comparison*.

④ Verify how language works, continued

WHAT TO DO	EXAMPLES
Use spell-checkers, glossaries, and dictionaries.	You just finished your draft of a story, so you think: *Now I'll run the spell-check to see what words I need to fix.*
Analyze the situation to determine the appropriate language to use.	**Formal:** "Thank you, Mr. Giacometti, for helping me enter the science fair." **Informal:** "Mom, thanks for getting the jars for my science fair exhibit." "Hey, Roberto, that was cool of you to help me set up."

⑤ Monitor and evaluate your learning.

WHAT TO DO	EXAMPLES
Assess your own language development.	*Did I use the right words? Was it correct to use "they" when I talked about my grandparents?* *Were my words all in the correct order?* *Was I polite?*
Keep notes about what you've learned. Use your notes to practice using English.	**How to Ask Questions** • I can turn a statement around to make it a question: It is a nice day. Is it a nice day? • I can put the question at the end of a statement: It is a nice day, isn't it? • If I want more than a "yes" or "no" answer, I should use "who," "what," "where," "when," "how," or "why" at the beginning of my question: What will the weather be like today?

Graphic Organizers

You can use graphic organizers to highlight important points in your reading, to organize your ideas before writing, or to represent information for your readers.

CLUSTERS

Clusters help you connect information. You can use a cluster to show

▶ **How Words or Ideas are Related**

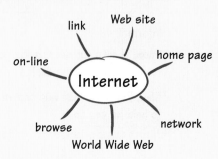

▶ **Details of an Event**

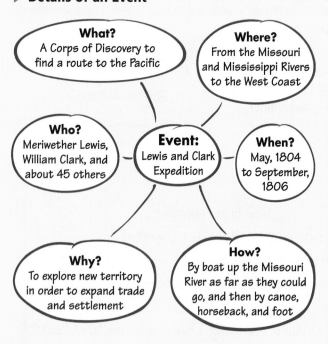

CHARTS

Charts have rows, columns, and labels to display information. Use a chart to

▶ **Picture Data**

Music Preferences Among Eighth Graders	
Rap/Hip-hop	22
Rhythm & Blues	12
Swing	10
Rock	27
Reggae	13

▶ **Relate Ideas**

Cause

President Thomas Jefferson sent Lewis and Clark to explore new territory from the Mississippi River to the West Coast.

Effects

New species of plants and animals were discovered.

The territory was mapped.

Trappers and settlers moved into the new territory.

The U.S. laid claim to land from the upper Missouri to the Pacific Northwest.

▶ **Compare and Contrast**

Stringed Instruments

Instrument	Number of Strings	How to Play	Relative Size
banjo	4, 5, or 6	pluck or strum	medium
cello	4	use bow	large
double bass	4	use bow or pluck	largest
guitar	6 or 12	pluck or strum	medium
violin	4	use bow	smallest

▶ Record Observations

Location:	Tide pools, Seaside Beach 11/15/00 10:45 a.m.
Sights:	Starfish, sea anemones, seaweed, barnacles
Sounds:	Seagulls calling, waves splashing against rocks
Smells:	Tangy salt air, seaweed
Textures:	Grainy sand, rough rocks, slimy seaweed
Comments:	The tide was out. We walked on the rocks and looked in the tidepools. Some waves splashed into the tidepools, so the living things in the pools were always wet.

▶ Show the Steps in a Process

How to Make a Mask

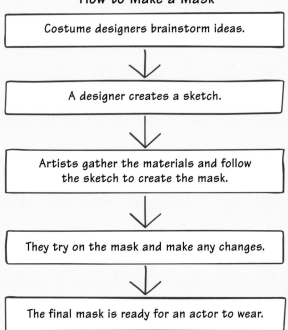

Costume designers brainstorm ideas.

↓

A designer creates a sketch.

↓

Artists gather the materials and follow the sketch to create the mask.

↓

They try on the mask and make any changes.

↓

The final mask is ready for an actor to wear.

▶ Show What You Know, What You Want to Learn, and What You Learned

Topic: The Revolutionary War		
K What I Know	**W** What I Want to Learn	**L** What I Learned
The war was between England and the American colonies. The colonies won and formed the United States.	When was it? What started it? How did the colonies defeat such a powerful country?	**Fill in this column after you read.**

▶ Show Organization or Classification

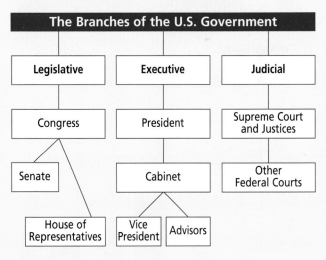

The Branches of the U.S. Government

- Legislative
  - Congress
    - Senate
    - House of Representatives
- Executive
  - President
    - Cabinet
      - Vice President
      - Advisors
- Judicial
  - Supreme Court and Justices
  - Other Federal Courts

Graphic Organizers, continued

GRAPHS

Graphs use words, numbers, lines, and other shapes to picture data. A graph can show

▶ **Parts of a Whole**

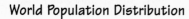

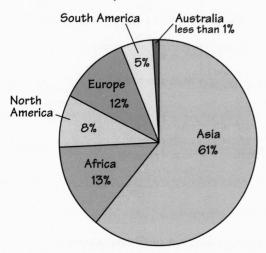

World Population Distribution

South America
Australia less than 1%
5%
Europe 12%
North America
8%
Asia 61%
Africa 13%

▶ **How Something Changes Over Time**

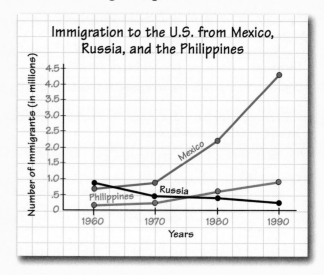

Immigration to the U.S. from Mexico, Russia, and the Philippines

▶ **Comparisons**

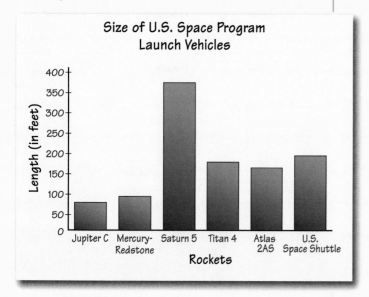

Size of U.S. Space Program Launch Vehicles

DIAGRAMS

Diagrams combine drawings and text to show where things are, how something works, or when something happens. Use a diagram to

▶ Show When Events Happen

The Founding of the English Colonies in America

1607	Virginia
1630	Massachusetts Bay
1634	Maryland
1636	Rhode Island, Connecticut
1638	New Hampshire
1663	North and South Carolina
1664	New York, New Jersey
1681	Pennsylvania
1704	Delaware (split from Pennsylvania)
1732	Georgia

▶ Show Parts of Something

The Parts of a Guitar

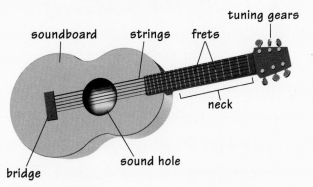

soundboard   strings   frets   tuning gears

neck

sound hole

bridge

▶ Explore the Meaning of Words

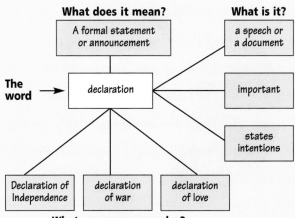

What does it mean?

A formal statement or announcement

What is it?

a speech or a document

The word → declaration

important

states intentions

Declaration of Independence | declaration of war | declaration of love

What are some examples?

▶ Show a Process that Repeats

The Carbon Dioxide-Oxygen Cycle

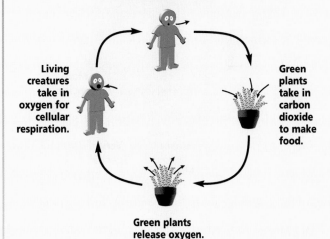

Living creatures release carbon dioxide.

Green plants take in carbon dioxide to make food.

Green plants release oxygen.

Living creatures take in oxygen for cellular respiration.

Graphic Organizers, continued

▶ Show Similarities and Differences

▶ Narrow or Develop a Topic

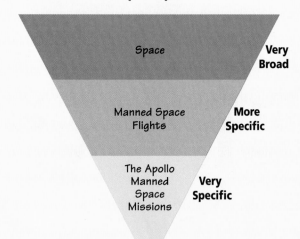

▶ Organize Details Related to the Main Idea

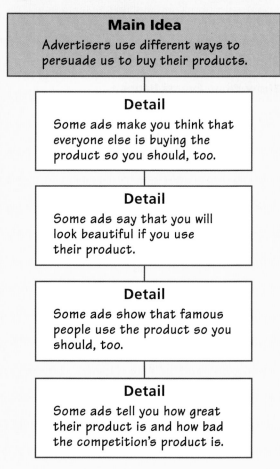

STORY MAPS

Story maps show how a story is organized.

▶ Beginning, Middle, and End

Title: User Friendly

Author: T. Ernesto Bethancourt

Beginning

Kevin's computer, Louis, started asking Kevin questions, just like a real person.

↓

Middle

1. Kevin was upset when Ginny called him a nerdy kid. He went home and told Louis.
2. Louis make creepy calls to Ginny by using its modem.
3. Ginny and her brother got upset about the calls. Kevin warned Louis to stop.
4. The next day, Ginny told Kevin about more problems her family had faced. Kevin knew Louis was responsible.

↓

End

Kevin asked his dad to help. His dad had already reformatted Louis, but he did not understand a strange print-out signed "Louise."

▶ Goal and Outcome

Title: Island of the Blue Dolphins

Author: Scott O'Dell

Goal

Karana, alone on her island when her people are killed or taken away, wants to leave.

Event 1

Karana builds a canoe, but it leaks and she has to return to her island.

Event 2

Karana finds a wounded, wild dog who becomes her friend.

Event 3

Karana decides it is all right to live alone.

Outcome

Years later, a ship stops by the island and takes Karana to the mainland.

Graphic Organizers, continued

▶ Problem and Solution

Title: The House of Dies Drear

Author: Virginia Hamilton

Characters: Thomas Small, Thomas' family, Pluto Skinner, Mayhew Skinner, Pesty, "Mac" Darrow, the Darrow family, Mr. Carr

Setting: an old house that was once a stop on the Underground Railroad

Problem: Thomas' family moves to an old house that seems to be full of secrets.

Event 1: When his family arrives at the house, Thomas' brothers start crying, as if they know the house is haunted.

Event 2: Pluto, the caretaker, rearranges the family's furniture, upsetting the family.

Event 3: Thomas falls into a hole and discovers a tunnel under the house.

Event 4: Someone enters the house at night and leaves mysterious triangles on the door frames.

Event 5: The kitchen is vandalized while the Smalls are at church.

Solution: Thomas and his father confront Pluto and learn about the treasure hidden in the house. They agree to help keep the secret of the House of Dies Drear.

▶ Causes and Effects

Title: A Wrinkle in Time

Author: Madeleine L'Engle

Characters: Meg Murry, Charles Wallace, Calvin, Mrs. Whatsit, Mrs. Which, Mrs. Who, Mrs. Murry, Mr. Murry

Causes		Effects
Meg, her friends, and Charles Wallace travel to a planet in search of Mr. Murry.		The group learns that they must overcome the dark thing that is holding Mr. Murry.
The group goes to another planet where everyone acts like a robot.	→	An evil force called "IT" influences Charles Wallace, and he begins to act like a robot.
Charles Wallace leads them to where Mr. Murry is trapped. Charles says Meg must join "IT" to help free Mr. Murry.		Meg resists and uses Mrs. Who's glasses to free Mr. Murry.
Meg, Mr. Murry, and Calvin leave the planet, but Meg must go back to rescue Charles.	→	Meg goes back alone with everyone's love and blessings.
Meg's love helps her to overcome and destroy "IT". She rescues Charles.	→	Everyone goes back to Earth to join their family and friends.

Story Staircase

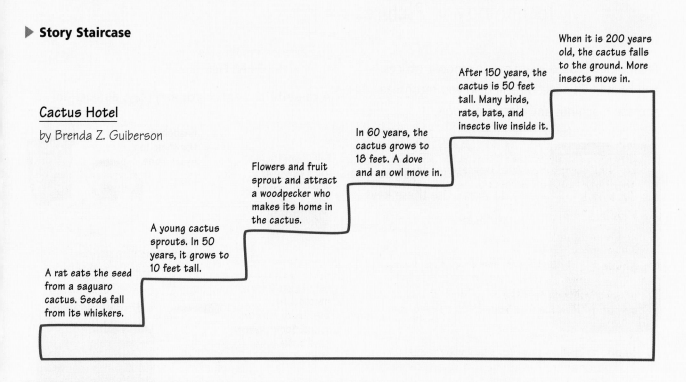

Cactus Hotel
by Brenda Z. Guiberson

When it is 200 years old, the cactus falls to the ground. More insects move in.

After 150 years, the cactus is 50 feet tall. Many birds, rats, bats, and insects live inside it.

In 60 years, the cactus grows to 18 feet. A dove and an owl move in.

Flowers and fruit sprout and attract a woodpecker who makes its home in the cactus.

A young cactus sprouts. In 50 years, it grows to 10 feet tall.

A rat eats the seed from a saguaro cactus. Seeds fall from its whiskers.

Rising and Falling Action

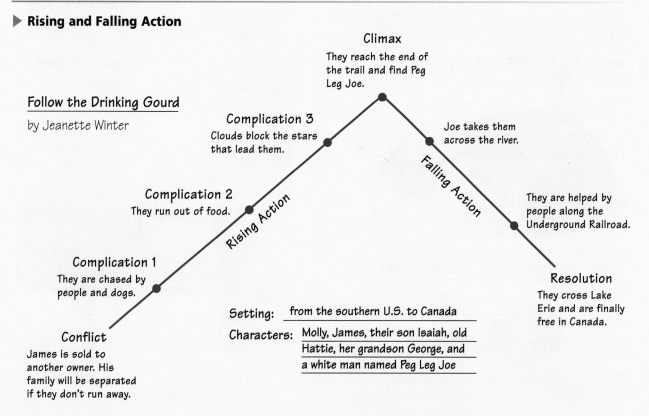

Follow the Drinking Gourd
by Jeanette Winter

Climax
They reach the end of the trail and find Peg Leg Joe.

Complication 3
Clouds block the stars that lead them.

Complication 2
They run out of food.

Complication 1
They are chased by people and dogs.

Conflict
James is sold to another owner. His family will be separated if they don't run away.

Rising Action

Falling Action

Joe takes them across the river.

They are helped by people along the Underground Railroad.

Resolution
They cross Lake Erie and are finally free in Canada.

Setting: from the southern U.S. to Canada

Characters: Molly, James, their son Isaiah, old Hattie, her grandson George, and a white man named Peg Leg Joe

Technology and Media
Technology in Pictures

Technology is used every day in schools, offices, and homes. This section will help you recognize and use machines and electronic tools.

CALCULATOR

A **calculator** helps you do math. Use these keys when you:

—— divide
—— multiply
—— subtract

—— add

COMPACT DISC PLAYER

A **compact disc (CD) player** plays compact discs with music or other sounds.

display screen
This shows information about which **track**, or selection, the machine is playing.

buttons
Use these to play, pause, or stop the recording, and to choose the track you want to hear.

compact disc
Use this to play or record music or other sounds.

CASSETTE PLAYERS

A **cassette player** records and plays audiocassettes.

audiocassette tape
Use this to play or record sound.

headphones
Use these to listen alone.

buttons
Use these to play, stop, and move the tape forward or back.

microphone
Use this to record sound. Some players have built-in microphones.

FAX MACHINE

A **fax machine** uses phone lines to send or receive a copy of pages with pictures or words.

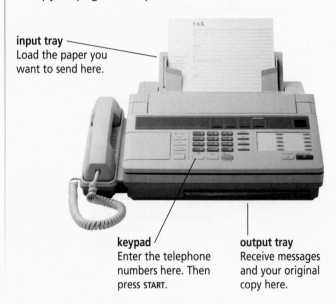

input tray
Load the paper you want to send here.

keypad
Enter the telephone numbers here. Then press START.

output tray
Receive messages and your original copy here.

WIRELESS TELEPHONE

A **wireless telephone** lets you talk to people wherever you are.

power key
Use this to turn the phone on and off.

number keys
Enter the phone number with these keys.

send key
Press TALK or SEND to dial the phone number you set.

end key
Press this when your call is finished.

CAMCORDER

A **camcorder** is a hand-held video camera. It records pictures and sounds on videotape. You can watch the videotape on a television.

microphone
This records sound.

view finder
Use this to see the picture as you record.

lens
Aim this at the action you want to record.

videotape
Use this or smaller tapes to record or play pictures and sounds.

VIDEOCASSETTE RECORDER

A **videocassette recorder (VCR)** records and plays videotapes through a television. You can record television programs or watch videos that you make, buy, rent, or check out from the library.

television
Use this to watch programs.

remote control
Use this to control the television and other machines from far away.

VCR and videotape
Use these to record and watch programs.

DIGITAL VIDEODISC PLAYER

A **digital videodisc (DVD) player** plays discs that have very clear pictures and sounds. You can watch movies by connecting a DVD player to a television or a computer.

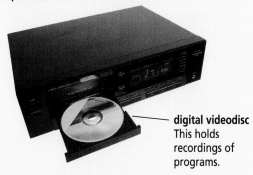

digital videodisc
This holds recordings of programs.

Technology and Media, continued
Technology in Pictures, continued

THE COMPUTER

A **computer** is an electronic tool that helps you create, save, and use information.

Compact Disc Read-Only Memory (CD-ROM)
Use this to read or play CD-ROMs with text, sound, video, photographs, and computer software.

monitor and **screen**
These show the text and pictures that are in the computer.

digital camera
Use this to take photographs you can use on the computer. You can view, print, or work on your pictures.

scanner
Use this to take a picture of words or pictures that are already on a page. You can view, print, or work on whatever you scan on your computer.

keyboard
This has letter, number, symbol, and function keys. Type here to add information and give commands to the computer.

mouse
Use this to choose and move things on your screen.

printer
Use this to make a paper copy of the information on your computer.

THE COMPUTER KEYBOARD

Use the **keys** on the **keyboard** to write, do math, or give the computer commands. Keyboards may look different, but they all have keys like these:

escape key
Press here to quit a job you are doing.

tab
Press this key to indent for a new paragraph.

function keys
Press these keys to give the computer commands.

delete or **backspace key**
Press here to erase the character to the left of the flashing cursor. You can also erase text that you highlight.

shift key
Hold this down to make a capital letter or to type the symbol on the top half of a key.

space bar
Press here to put in a space when you type.

return or **enter key**
Press here to tell the computer to do a task or move the cursor down to a new line.

arrow keys
Press these keys to move your cursor on the screen.

Technology and Media, continued
How to Send E-mail

E-mail is electronic mail that can be sent on-line from one computer to another. Anyone who has an e-mail address can send and receive messages. E-mail can travel around the classroom or around the world.

You can use e-mail to:

- write messages to one or more friends at a time
- send computer files
- save money on postage and telephone calls
- send and receive messages almost instantly.

To send an e-mail message:

1. Open the e-mail program.
2. Open a new message.
3. Enter this information:
   - Type the recipient's e-mail address in the "To" box.
   - Type a short title for your e-mail in the "Subject" box.
   - Type your message.
4. Send your message.

Each e-mail program is different. Here is one example of a "mailbox":

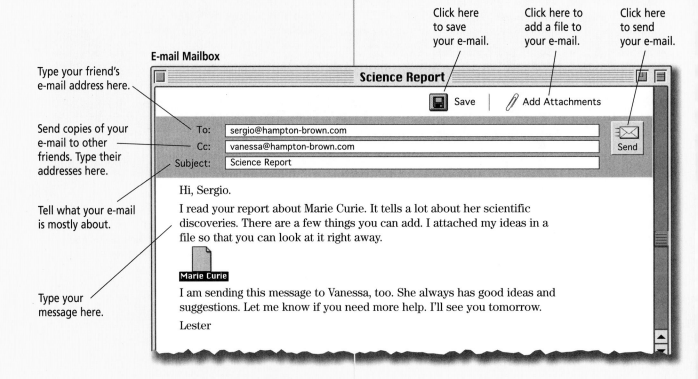

Click here to save your e-mail.

Click here to add a file to your e-mail.

Click here to send your e-mail.

E-mail Mailbox

Type your friend's e-mail address here.

Send copies of your e-mail to other friends. Type their addresses here.

Tell what your e-mail is mostly about.

Type your message here.

Science Report

Save | Add Attachments

To: sergio@hampton-brown.com
Cc: vanessa@hampton-brown.com
Subject: Science Report

Send

Hi, Sergio.

I read your report about Marie Curie. It tells a lot about her scientific discoveries. There are a few things you can add. I attached my ideas in a file so that you can look at it right away.

Marie Curie

I am sending this message to Vanessa, too. She always has good ideas and suggestions. Let me know if you need more help. I'll see you tomorrow.

Lester

How to Use a Word-Processing Program

A **computer program** is a set of directions that tells a computer what to do. A **word-processing program** helps you create and store written work. You can use it to:

• store ideas, outlines, plans, and papers
• write drafts of your work
• revise, edit, and proofread your writing
• format and publish your work
• make written work look neat and organized.

There are many kinds of word-processing programs. There are also different ways to use the computer to make each job easier. This section of the Handbook will give you some ideas. Ask your teacher or classmates for other ways they have found to use your school's word-processing program.

Working on the computer

My First Day in an American School

by Marco Quezada

My first day of school in the United States was very scary because I didn't speak English. I didn't know how I was going to talk to people. I didn't have any friends. I tried to understand the teacher, but I couldn't. I felt like a chair.

Suddenly, a very loud bell rang. The teacher opened the door, and all the kids jumped up and rushed out the door.

Why was everyone leaving? In Haiti, we stayed in the same classroom all day. I followed the class, and we went into a new room. A stranger gave me a book and some papers. I was really puzzled. Fortunately, the man spoke some Creole and explained that he was my science teacher.

Finally, I understood. In America, there are special teachers for science, music, and gym. Students also move to new classrooms. At first, it was very confusing, but now I like having different teachers for my subjects.

How to Use a Word-Processing Program, continued

GET STARTED

1 **How to Set Up a File** Before you start to write, make a **file**—a place to keep your work. Follow these steps:

1. Click **File** to see the **File Menu**. A **menu** gives you a list of choices.

File Menu and New

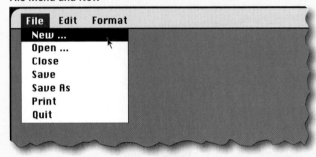

2. Click **New** to create a new document. A blank page will appear.

New Document

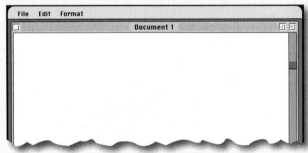

To save your new file in a folder, click **Save As** on the **File Menu**.

File Menu and New

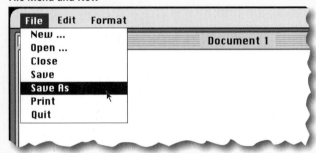

A **dialogue box** will appear to ask for information.

1. Type a short name for your file.

2. Make sure that the file name and folder are correct. If you don't have a folder for your work, ask your teacher for help to start one.

3. Click **Save** to save your file.

Save Dialogue Box

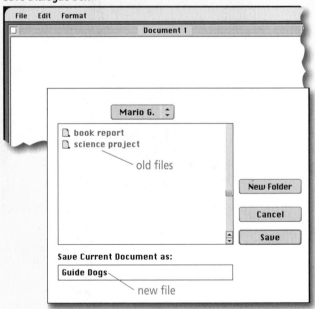

CREATE DOCUMENTS

1 How to Type a Document Now you are ready to type. Your work will appear in front of a flashing cursor. The **cursor** shows where you are working on the page.

Cursor

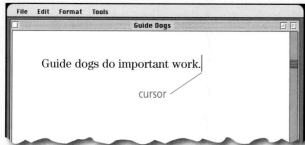

As you type, the **indicator box** shows where you are in the document. You can use the **scroll bar** to move up and down in your file.

- Click and hold the **up arrow** to move toward the top of the screen.
- Click and hold the **down arrow** to move toward the bottom of the screen.

Scrolling

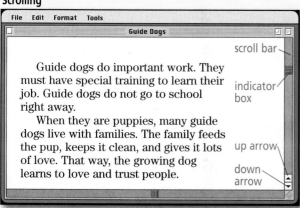

2 How to Save Your Work Remember to save your work as you write. If you do not save, you may lose the work you have done on your file. Remember:

✔ Save your work every 10 minutes!
✔ Save before you leave your computer.
✔ Save before you **Print**.
✔ Save before you **Quit**.
✔ Save, save, save!

To save your work, click **Save** in the **File Menu**.

Save

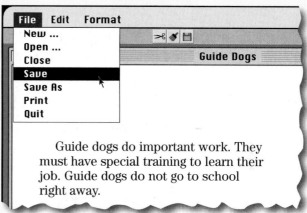

Or, click the **save icon** on the **toolbar**.

Toolbar Icons

toolbar   save icon

How to Use a Word-Processing Program, continued

MAKE CHANGES TO YOUR WORK

1 **How to Add Words** It is easy to add words to your work.

    1. Use your mouse to move the cursor to the place where you want to add words.

    2. Click the mouse once. The cursor will start to flash.

Add Words (before)

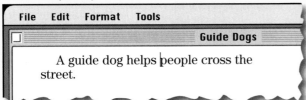

    3. Type the new words.

Add Words (after)

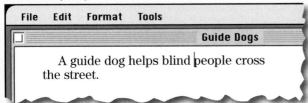

2 **How to Delete Words** When you **delete**, you take words out. Before you delete, you need to highlight the words you want to remove.

    1. To remove one word, put the cursor on the word. Click the mouse twice.

Delete Words (before)

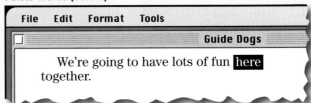

    2. You can also **click and drag** to highlight and remove words.

      • Click and hold the mouse and slide it over all the words you want to take out. The words will be highlighted.

Delete Words (after)

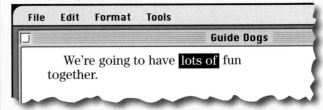

      • After the words are highlighted, press the **delete key**. The words will disappear from the screen.

Delete Words (after)

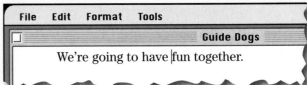

3 **How to Cut and Paste** You can **cut and paste** to move sentences or paragraphs to a different place in your paper.

When you **cut** text, the computer takes out the highlighted words. The words are not deleted. They are stored in the computer's memory to be placed somewhere new.

To cut text, click **Cut** from the **Edit Menu**.

Cut (before)

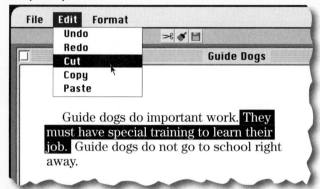

Or, click the **cut icon** on the **toolbar**.

Toolbar Icons

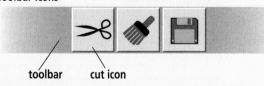

toolbar   cut icon

Your text will look like this:

Cut (after)

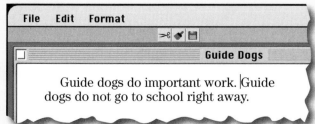

When you **paste** text, the cut words are placed at the flashing cursor. To paste text, move the cursor to where you want the text and click **Paste** from the **Edit Menu**.

Paste (before)

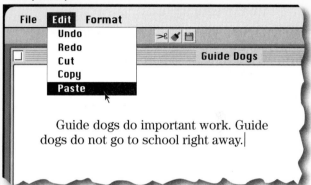

Or, click the **paste icon** on the **toolbar**.

Toolbar Icons

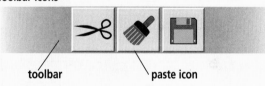

toolbar   paste icon

Your text will look like this:

Paste (after)

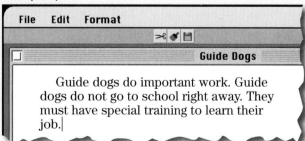

Technology and Media, continued

How to Use a Word-Processing Program, continued

④ How to Check Your Spelling Most word-processing programs have tools to check your spelling. Follow these steps:

1. Open the **Tools Menu** and choose **Spelling**. The computer will show you a highlighted word from your text.
2. Choose the correct spelling from the list of suggestions. If the word is not listed, check a dictionary.

Spell Check

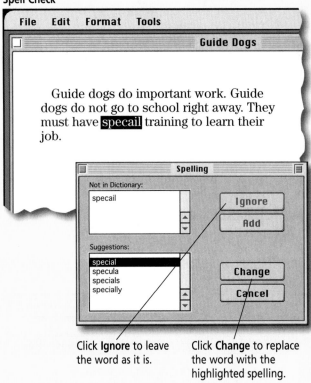

Click **Ignore** to leave the word as it is.

Click **Change** to replace the word with the highlighted spelling.

⑤ How to Find Synonyms Use the computer's thesaurus to find synonyms for words you use.

1. Highlight the word you want to change. Then open the **Tools Menu** and choose **Thesaurus**.
2. Some words have different meanings. Choose the correct one from the list of Meanings.
3. Look at the list of synonyms for that meaning. Highlight the word you want.

Thesaurus

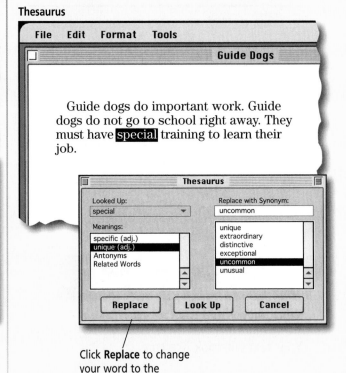

Click **Replace** to change your word to the highlighted synonym.

FORMAT YOUR PAPER

When you **format** your work, you make it look neat and organized. Here are some ways to format, or arrange, your paper.

1 How to Change the Font, Style, and Size
A **font** is a unique style for the letters and numbers that you type. Follow these steps:

* Highlight the section you want to change.
* Open the **Format Menu** and choose **Font**, or click the font, style, and size icons on your toolbar.

bold   italic   underline

* Choose the font, word style, and word size you want for your text. Then click **OK**. You can choose from many fonts. For class work, choose a font that is clear and easy to read. If you are writing to friends, you can choose more fun styles! Here are some examples:

Fonts

good for reports	good for essays
good for a friendly letter	*great for your journal*

Styles

normal	*italic*
bold	underlined

Sizes

12	14	16	18

2 How to Change Text Alignment When you set **text alignment**, you choose how words will line up on the page. You may want to put a title in the center of the page, or put your name in the right-hand corner. Follow these steps:

* Highlight the text you want to align.
* Click the icon that shows where you want the text placed. For example:

align left   center   align right   justify

3 How to Set Spacing You can choose the **spacing**—how much space comes between each line you type. Follow these steps:

* Open the **Edit Menu** and choose **Select All**.
* Click the correct spacing icon:

single space   1.5 line   double space

Ask your teacher or your friends for more ideas about how to format your work. Soon, your work will have a new style that is unique and attractive.

Technology and Media, continued
How to Create a Multimedia Presentation

A **multimedia presentation** uses technology to present ideas. Your audience can read, see, and hear your work.

LEARN ABOUT MEDIA

There are many ways to share information. Choose media that fit your purpose. Here are some possibilities:

▶ **Visuals**

- Use a computer to create slides of important points, outlines, or quotations.
- Scan tables or diagrams to show information.

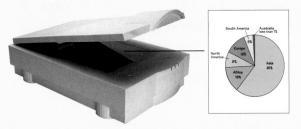

▶ **Photographs**

- Scan photographs.
- Download pictures from the Internet.
- Use pictures from a CD-ROM.

▶ **Video and Animation**

- Use videos from the news.
- Create animation to show how something changes.
- Make a videotape of yourself or others.

▶ **Sounds**

- Play music on a cassette, CD, or CD-ROM.
- Make a recording of yourself or others.
- Download sound files from the Internet.

"I have a dream..."

MAKE A MULTIMEDIA PRESENTATION

Follow these steps to give your own multimedia presentation.

1 Plan Think about how you can present your ideas creatively.

- Put your ideas into a logical order.
- Ask yourself: What pictures, videos, and sounds will help the class understand my ideas? What technology can I use?
- Use a **graphic organizer** to put the steps of your presentation in order. Here is one example:

Flow Chart

```
┌─────────────────────────────────┐
│         Show title slide:        │
│   Democracy in Ancient Greece.   │
└─────────────────────────────────┘
                 ↓
┌─────────────────────────────────┐
│    Talk about Greek city-states. │
└─────────────────────────────────┘
                 ↓
┌─────────────────────────────────┐
│   Show slide of map of ancient   │
│    Greece on the computer.       │
└─────────────────────────────────┘
                 ↓
┌─────────────────────────────────┐
│        Play 2-minute video       │
│        of Greek elections.       │
└─────────────────────────────────┘
```

2 Practice Rehearse your presentation until you are comfortable with your speech and the technology you will use.

- Practice in front of your family and friends. Ask them for ideas and suggestions.
- Unexpected things can happen when you work with technology. Before your presentation, test your equipment to be sure it works.

3 Present Remember that your goal is to give an effective presentation.

- Speak slowly and clearly.
- Give your audience time to understand the ideas you are sharing.
- Have fun!

Technology and Media, continued
How to Use the Internet

The **Internet** is an international network, or connection, of computers that share information with one another. The **World Wide Web** allows you to find, read, go through, and organize information. The Internet is like a giant library, and the World Wide Web is everything in the library including the books, the librarian, and the computer catalog.

The Internet is a fast way to get the most current information about your topic! You'll find resources like encyclopedias and dictionaries on the Internet and amazing pictures, movies, and sounds.

WHAT YOU WILL NEED

To use the Internet, you need a computer with software that allows you to access it. You'll also need a modem connected to a telephone line.

HOW TO GET STARTED

You can search the Internet in many different ways. Ask your teacher how to access the Internet from your school. Usually you can just double click on the **icon**, or picture, to get access to the Internet and you're on your way!

HOW TO DO THE RESEARCH

Once the search page comes up, you can begin the research process. Just follow these steps.

1 **Type in Your Subject** Enter your key words in the search box and then click on the Search button. You'll always see a toolbar at the top of the screen. Click on the **icons** to do things like print the page.

Try different ways to type in your subject. You'll get different results!

- If you type in **Mars**, you'll see all the sites that have the word *Mars* in them. This may give you too many categories and sites to look through!

- If you type in **"Mars exploration,"** you'll see all the sites with the exact phrase, or group of words, *Mars exploration*.

- If you type in **Mars+exploration**, you'll see all the sites with the words *Mars* and *exploration* in them.

2 Read the Search Results All underlined, colored words are links, or connections, to other sites. They help you get from page to page quickly.

- If you want to go directly to a Web page, click on a site.
- Click on a category to see more options for information related to your topic.
- Read the descriptions of the sites to save time.

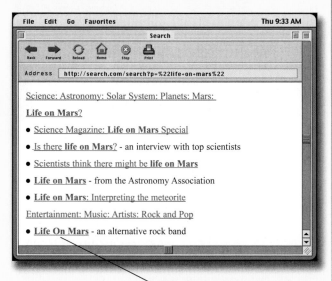

This site could be very interesting, but it probably won't help with your report.

3 Select a Site and Read You might want to pick a new site or start a new search. If so, click on the **Back** arrow to go back a page to the search results. If you want to go to another Web page, click on a link.

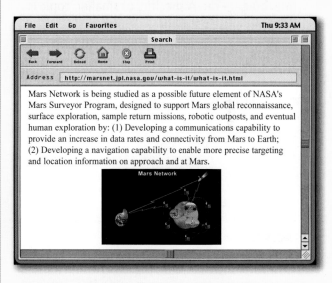

4 Locate More Resources If you already know the **URL (Uniform Resource Locator)**, or address, of a Web site, you can type it in the address box at the top of the screen.

Remember that information on Web sites changes frequently. Sometimes Web pages are not kept up. If you can't access one Web site, try another one.

The Research Process

When you research, you look up information about a topic. You can use the information you find to write a story, article, book, or research report.

❶ CHOOSE A TOPIC

Think of something you want to learn more about and something that interests you. That will be your research **topic**. Pick a topic that is not too general. A specific, or smaller, topic is easier to research and to write about. It is also more interesting to read about in a report. Look at these topics:

Outer Space
This is a big topic! There are a lot of things in outer space: stars, suns, planets, moons, and black holes. That would be too much to research or write about in one report.

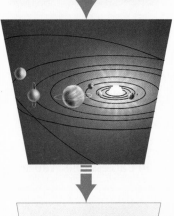

Planets
This topic is better, but it's still too big. There are nine planets in our solar system! You could do a report on the planet Mars. But what is it you want to know about Mars?

Life on Mars
The topic "Life on Mars" is more specific than "Mars." Finding out if Mars has water, plants, animals, or Martians could be VERY interesting!

❷ DECIDE WHAT TO LOOK UP

What do you want to know about your topic? Write down some questions. Look at the most important words in your questions. Those are **key words** you can look up when you start your research.

> Is there life on Mars?
>
> Is there water or oxygen on Mars?
>
> Can people, plants, or animals live on the surface of Mars?
>
> Have space missions studied Mars?
>
> Did anyone find proof of Martian life forms?

❸ LOCATE RESOURCES

Now that you know what to look up, you can go to different **resources** to find information about your topic. Resources can be people, such as librarians, teachers, and family members. Resources can also be books, magazines, newspapers, videos, or the Internet. You can find resources all around you.

Whatever your topic is, try exploring the library first. There you'll discover a world of information!

④ GATHER INFORMATION

When you gather information, you find the best resources for your topic. You look up your key words to find facts about your topic. Then you take notes.

How to Find Information Quickly Use alphabetical order to look up words in a list. In many resources, the words, titles, and subjects are listed in **alphabetical order**.

Look at these words. They are in order by the **first** letter of each word.

> **a**steroid
> **m**oon
> **p**lanet
> **s**un

If the word you are looking up has the same first letter as other words in the list, look at the **second** letters.

> M**a**rs
> M**e**rcury
> m**i**ssion
> m**o**on

If the word you are looking up has the same first and second letters as others in the list, look at the **third** letters.

> ma**g**netic
> ma**p**
> ma**r**s
> ma**s**s

Skim and scan the text to decide if it is useful. When you **skim** and **scan**, you look at text quickly to see if it has the information you need. If it does, you can take the time to read it more carefully. If it doesn't, go on to another source.

To skim:

- Read the title to see if the article is useful for your topic.
- Read the **beginning sentences** and **headings** to find out more about an article's topic.
- Skim the ending. It often sums up all the ideas in the article.

To scan:

Look for **key words** or **details** in dark type or italics. If you find key words that go with your topic, you'll probably want to read the article.

PLANETS, STARS, AND SPACE TRAVEL

LOOKING FOR LIFE ELSEWHERE IN THE UNIVERSE

For years scientists have been trying to discover if there is life on other planets in our solar system or life elsewhere in the universe. Some scientists have been looking for evidence based on what is necessary for life on Earth—basics like water and proper temperature.

WHAT SCIENTISTS HAVE LEARNED SO FAR

Mars and Jupiter. In 1996, two teams of scientists examined two meteorites that may have come from **Mars** and found evidence that some form of life may have existed on Mars billions of years ago. In 1997, in photographs of Europa, a moon of **Jupiter**, scientists saw areas with icy ridges and areas without ice. It seemed that underneath the ice there might be water—one of the essentials of life.

New Planets. In 1996, astronomers believed they found several new planets traveling around stars very far away (many light-years away) from our sun. Scientists do not think life exists on these planets, because they are so close to their sun that they would be too hot. But scientists are hoping to find other stars with planets around them that might support life.

AND THE SEARCH CONTINUES

NASA (the National Aeronautics and Space Administration) has a program to look for life on Mars. Ten spacecraft are to be sent to Mars over the next ten years. Some will fly around Mars taking pictures, while others will land on Mars to study the soil and rocks and look for living things. The first two, *Mars Pathfinder* and *Mars Global Surveyor*, launched in 1996, were scheduled to reach Mars in 1997.

Another program that searches for life on other worlds is called **SETI**. SETI (an acronym for Search for Extraterrestrial Intelligence) uses powerful radio telescopes to look for life elsewhere in the universe.

Question: Is there life elsewhere in the universe? **Answer:** No one knows yet.

The Research Process, continued

④ GATHER INFORMATION, continued

How to Take Notes Write down important words, phrases, and ideas while you are reading and researching. These notes will help you remember **details**. They'll also help you remember the **source**. The source is where you got the information.

Set up your notecards in the following way so you can easily put your information in order when you write.

1. Include your research question.

2. Write down the source so you can remember where you found your facts.
   - For a book, list the title, author, and page number.
   - For a magazine or newspaper article, list the name, date, volume, and issue number of your source. Also, write the title of the article in quotation marks.

3. List the details and facts in your own words. Use quotation marks for exact words you copy from a source.

Notecard for a Book

Is there life on Mars ?

Mars by Seymour Simon, page 27

—Viking spacecraft supposed to find out if there's life

—some think experiments showed there isn't

—others believe experiments were the wrong kind; maybe scientists looked in wrong places

Notecard for a Magazine or Newspaper

Is there life on Mars ?

Time for Kids, Sept. 13, 1996

Vol. 2, No. 1 "Next Stop: Mars"

—maybe—Mars has some features like Earth. "It has volcanoes and giant canyons."

—hard to prove, but maybe space missions like Pathfinder can find something

⑤ ORGANIZE INFORMATION

Make an Outline An outline can help you organize your report. Follow these steps to turn your notes into an outline.

1. Put all the notecards with the same research question together.

2. Turn your notes into an outline.
   - First, turn your question into a **main idea.** Each main idea follows a Roman numeral.

   > I. Life on Mars

   - Next, find details that go with the main idea. Add them to your outline. Each **detail** follows a capital letter. Each **related detail** follows a number.

   > I. Life on Mars
   >   A. How Mars is like Earth
   >   1. Volcanoes
   >   2. Giant canyons

3. Write a **title** for your outline. The title tells what your outline is all about. You can use it again when you write your report.

Sample Outline

> **Mars: Is Anyone Up There?**
>   I. Life on Mars
>   A. How Mars is like Earth
>   1. Volcanoes
>   2. Giant canyons
>   B. Fact-finding missions
>   1. Viking
>   2. Pathfinder
>   II. Signs of life on Mars
>   A. Studied by David McKay's team
>   B. Meteorite
>   1. Might contain bacteria fossils
>   2. Found in Antarctica
>   3. Probably from Mars
>   III. Continued search for life on Mars
>   A. Look underground
>   B. More study
>   1. Mission planned for near future
>   2. Gases in atmosphere
>   3. What rocks are made of

The Research Process, continued

⑥ WRITE A RESEARCH REPORT

Now use your outline to write a **research report**. Turn the main ideas and details from your outline into sentences and paragraphs.

Write the Title and Introduction Copy the title from your outline and write an interesting introduction to tell what your report is mostly about.

Outline

Mars: Is Anyone Up There?

Title and Introduction

Mars: Is Anyone Up There?

You've probably seen some pretty creepy outer space creatures in movies and on TV. Do they really look like that? Are there really living beings up there?

Write the Body Use your main ideas to write a topic sentence for each paragraph. Then use your details and related details to write sentences about the main idea.

Outline

I. Life on Mars
  A. How Mars is like Earth
    1. Volcanoes
    2. Giant canyons

Topic Sentence and Details

People have always wondered if there is **life on** other planets, especially **Mars**. **Because Mars is similar to Earth,** with features like **volcanoes and giant canyons,** it seems possible that there is life on Mars. There are lots of missions to Mars, like the spacecrafts Viking and Pathfinder, so it seems like we might find out soon!

Write a Conclusion Write a sentence for each main idea in the last paragraph of your report.

Outline

I. Life on Mars

II. Signs of life on Mars

III. Continued search for
   life on Mars

Conclusion

Basically, no one knows if there is or isn't life on Mars. It is possible that life does or did exist there. Spacecrafts that go to Mars in the future will give us more proof. Hopefully, the mystery will be solved soon for all of us!

A good research report gives facts about a topic in an organized and interesting way.

Mars: Is Anyone Up There?

You've probably seen some pretty creepy outer space creatures in movies and TV. Do they really look like that? Are there really living beings up there?

People have always wondered if there is life on other planets, especially Mars. Because Mars is similar to Earth, with features like volcanoes and giant canyons, it seems possible that there is life on Mars. There are lots of missions to Mars, like the spacecrafts Viking and Pathfinder, so it seems like we might find out soon!

David McKay and his team of scientists discovered possible signs of ancient Martian life. They think they found bacteria fossils in a meteorite that crashed into Antarctica thousands of years ago. They believe the meteorite is from Mars because it has the same chemicals in it as the Martian atmosphere. They think the fossils, which are a lot smaller than the width of a human hair, were alive on Mars from 3 to 4 billion years ago. At that time, there was water on the planet. Since the fossils were deep in the center of the meteorite, McKay's team feels that the fossils were definitely from Mars and not from Earth.

No one has seen a live Martian, but some scientists feel that we need to keep looking. Since no one has found water on the surface of Mars, maybe Martians live underground where there is water. A mission to look for Martian life and bring soil samples back to Earth is planned for the near future. Until then, scientists will continue to study the other aspects of Mars like the gases in its atmosphere and what its rocks are made of.

Basically, no one knows if there is or isn't life on Mars. It is possible that life does or did exist there. Spacecrafts that go to Mars in the future will give us more proof. Hopefully, the mystery will be solved soon for all of us!

INTRODUCTION
The **title** and **introduction** tell what your report is about. They get your reader interested.

BODY
The **body** of the report presents the facts you found. Each paragraph begins with a **topic sentence** that tells one main idea from your outline. The other sentences give **details** and **related details**.

CONCLUSION
The **conclusion** is a summary of the most important information about your topic.

Speaking and Listening

You talk, or speak, to others every day. That's how you express your ideas. You also listen to others to learn about new ideas.

HOW TO BE A GOOD LISTENER

Good listeners listen carefully to what others say.

How to Be a Good Listener

- Pay attention. Open your eyes and ears. Look at the speaker as you listen. That way you'll "hear" more.
- Be quiet while the speaker is talking.
- Don't interrupt unless you need the speaker to talk louder.
- Save your questions until the speaker is finished.

HOW TO PARTICIPATE IN A DISCUSSION

Sometimes you will discuss ideas as a class, in a group, or with a partner. You may also have a conference with a teacher or a peer to talk about your writing. Discussions are good ways to find information, check your understanding, and share ideas.

How to Participate in a Discussion

- Use good listening skills.
- Give each speaker a chance to make a statement. Wait until someone has finished speaking before you respond.
- Make positive comments about the ideas of others. Respect everyone's ideas and feelings.
- Think about the topic. Offer ideas about only that topic and not something else.
- Ask questions if you need more information.

HOW TO LISTEN CRITICALLY

There are many reasons to listen carefully. You can find out how to do something or learn more about a topic. You can also use what you hear to help you decide how you think and feel. As you listen:

- Think about what you are hearing. Try to relate what you hear to what you already know.
- Listen for key words and important details. Take notes to help you remember the ideas.

  Example:
  ecosystem: things in nature and how they work together

- Ask yourself: What is the speaker's purpose? Does the speaker want to inform or entertain the audience? Does the speaker want to persuade me to do something?
- Pay attention to the speaker's tone of voice, gestures, and expressions. What do they tell you about how the speaker feels about the topic?
- Think about who is speaking. Is the speaker an expert on the topic?
- Summarize what the speaker says in your own mind. Do you agree or disagree? What new information did you learn?

HOW TO GIVE AN ORAL PRESENTATION

What would you like to share with others? Choose an interesting topic. Then decide if you want to make a speech, give a report, recite a poem, or give a performance to share your ideas. Follow these steps to prepare your presentation.

1 Plan Your Presentation Think about your audience. What ideas do you want to share? What is the best way to present your ideas?

- Organize your information. You might use a graphic organizer to show the details and the order in which you'll present ideas.

  Example:
  I. Ecosystem
     A. Is like a community
     B. Includes all living things in nature
  II. Food Chain
     A. Is different in different places
     B. Has a sequence
        1. Microorganisms in soil
        2. Plants grow
        3. Animals eat plants

- Think of a way to grab the audience's attention and introduce your topic. You might use a quote, make a startling statement, or ask a question.

- Write your main points on notecards. Use them as you speak to help you remember what to say.

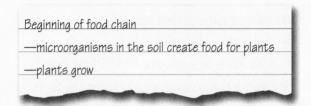

Beginning of food chain
—microorganisms in the soil create food for plants
—plants grow

- Use visuals and technology to support your ideas. Organize them to match your notes.

Food Chain Poster

hawk

snake

frog

cricket

plants

- Use your notecards, visuals, and technology to practice your presentation in front of a mirror or your family. Videotaping or tape recording your presentation may give you ideas about how to improve.

Speaking and Listening, continued

❷ Choose Appropriate Language and Tone
Are you speaking to your friends, to young kids, or to adults you don't know? Think about your topic, audience, and purpose to help you decide how to give your presentation.

To give a persuasive speech:
- Use a strong, clear tone of voice. Change your tone to emphasize important points.
- Use formal language to present the facts. Use persuasive words to give opinions.

To tell a story:
- Use informal language to make the characters seem real. Change your voice to show when a new character is speaking.
- Use facial expressions, gestures, and other movements to show the characters' feelings and actions.

To give a formal report:
- Use formal language to present the facts and information.
- Speak slowly and clearly so everyone can understand the information.
- Present the information in a logical order.
- Use examples and visuals that support your main points.

Use formal language to give a report.

❸ Give Your Presentation Now you can stand up and be heard! As you present your ideas:
- Stand up straight.
- Make eye contact with the audience.
- Speak slowly and clearly in a loud voice so everyone can hear you.
- Use expressions and movements that go with the information you are presenting.
- Point to or hold up any visuals so your audience can follow along.
- Try to stay calm and relaxed.
- Thank the audience when you're done. Ask for questions when you are finished.

Viewing and Representing

You can get information from the things you see, or view. You can also use visuals to help you communicate and represent your ideas.

HOW TO EVALUATE WHAT YOU SEE

There are many things to view—photographs, videos, television commercials, graphs and charts, Web sites, and people who use gestures and movements to send messages without words. Here's how to evaluate what you see. Try out the process with the visual below.

1 View and Look for Details Take a minute or two to study the visual. Ask yourself:

- Who or what does the image show? Are there other details that tell when, where, why, or how?

- How does the visual make me feel? Do I enjoy looking at it? Does it scare me, make me laugh, or give me a good feeling?

- Do I like the colors? How does the size or shape of the visual affect me?

2 Think About the Purpose and the Message What you see can influence the way you feel about a topic. Ask yourself:

- What message does the visual convey?

- Why did the artist create the visual? Does it make me want to do something? Does it give me new information?

- Does the visual represent the complete picture of the topic, or was it chosen to control my understanding of it?

3 Look for Stereotypes A stereotype is a general opinion that doesn't consider individual differences. It's like saying that because one dog is mean, all dogs are mean. Try to identify any stereotypes in the visual.

Persistent Sea No. 2, by O. Louis Guglielmi, oil on canvas.

Viewing and Representing, continued

HOW TO REPRESENT YOUR IDEAS

There are many resources that can help you make your point more clearly. Choose media that match your purpose and your topic. Strong visual images will make a strong impression.

A beautiful **illustration** can add creativity and make a story come alive.

Illustration

A **flow chart** can show steps in a process.

Flow Chart

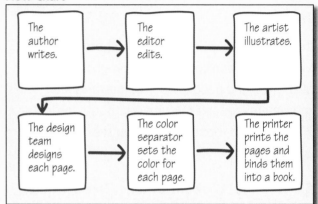

A **chart** or a **graph** can show comparisons.
Look for more graphic organizers on pages 370–377.

Chart

Number of Endangered Species in the United States	
Classification	**Number of Species**
Mammals	61
Birds	75
Reptiles	14
Fishes	69
Insects	28

Graph

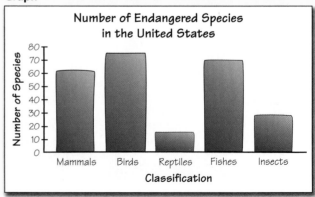

HOW TO MATCH MEDIA TO YOUR MESSAGE

Choose the best media to help you get your point across. It will help you get your audience's attention. Take a look at the different media you can use on Handbook pages 378–381. Here are a few examples.

1 **To Entertain** Include props, illustrations of the setting, or slides for a backdrop. Create a film strip, animation, or a video.

2 **To Inform** Include maps and charts to support your topic. You might make a time line to show chronological events or use a transparency to display information on an overhead projector.

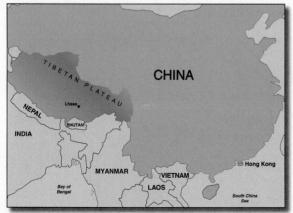

Most Giant Pandas originated in China.

3 **To Persuade** Show images that will change people's opinions. You might use slides or photographs that appeal to people's emotions.

Fewer than 1,000 pandas live in the wild.

Strategies for Taking Tests

These strategies will help you learn how to take tests and show what you know.

MULTIPLE-CHOICE TEST

For a multiple-choice test, you will mark the best answer from a list of choices.

1 **Read the Directions Carefully** The test directions tell you what you need to do. Words like *best, always, only, all,* and *never* will help you find the correct answer. There may be more than one correct answer, but only one is the "best" answer.

> **Directions: Read each question. Circle the best answer.**
>
> **4.** Which type of transportation causes the least air pollution?
> A a bus   **C** a bike
> B a car   **D** a motorcycle

2 **Mark Your Answers** You may need to fill in a bubble on an answer sheet, circle an answer, or write your answer on a separate sheet of paper. When you use an answer sheet, be sure to match the item number on the test to the item number on the answer sheet.

> **Read the sentence. Mark the answer that gives the best meaning for the underlined word.**
>
> **5.** People can <u>recycle</u> to help save the Earth.
> **F** use products over again
> **G** go backwards on a bicycle
> **H** throw away all their trash
> **J** keep trash in a special place
>
> 4. Ⓐ Ⓑ Ⓒ Ⓓ
> 5. Ⓕ Ⓖ Ⓗ Ⓙ

3 **Plan Your Time** Skip over any hard questions. Don't spend too much time on one question. If you have time, you can go back to it later.

4 **Read Items Again** If you are not sure about an answer, read the item again. Think about all the answer choices. Which one seems best?

TRUE-FALSE TEST

In a true-false test, you will decide if a statement is true or false.

1 **Read Carefully** If *any* part of the statement is false, the answer is false. If you're still not sure after reading an item, make your best guess!

2 **Look for Key Words** Watch for words like *never, always, all,* and *no.* Statements with those words are often false.

> _false_   **1.** Businesses never monitor the dirty air from their factories.

SHORT-ANSWER TEST

Often a test item will ask for a short answer. Look for key words like *who* or *what* that tell you the information to include in the answer.

> **12.** What do farmers put on their crops to kill insects? _____*pesticides*_____

ESSAY TEST

For an essay test, you will need to write one or more paragraphs to answer a question.

1 Study the Item and Key Words Read the question at least two times. Look for key words that tell you exactly what to do. You might see prompts like these on an essay test:

- Compare the rainforest and the tundra.
- Summarize how the transcontinental railroad influenced western expansion.
- Describe the main events that led to the Civil War.

2 Plan Your Answer Think about the key words and the topic. Write facts or details you know in a web, chart, or another graphic organizer. Add numbers or make an outline to show how you will organize your writing.

3 Write the Essay Use the words in the prompt to help you write an introduction. Then use your notes and details to write your essay.

- Write a topic sentence for each paragraph.
- Include all the important details.
- Sum up your essay with a concluding sentence.
- Before you turn in your essay, read it over. Be sure that you have written about what was described in the prompt.

Prompt

> **1.** Explain three ways that people can reduce air pollution.

Sample Answer

> People can reduce air pollution in three main ways. One way is to carpool. If people share rides, they can reduce the amount of car exhaust. A second way is to walk or ride a bicycle for short trips. That doesn't cause any air pollution! Finally, people can encourage businesses to stop the air pollution caused by their factories. If we do these things today, we'll have cleaner air in the future!

The Writing Process

Writing is one of the best ways to express yourself. The steps in the Writing Process will help you say what you want to say clearly, correctly, and in your own unique way.

PREWRITE

Prewriting is what you do before you write. During this step, you collect ideas, choose a topic, make a plan, gather details, and organize your ideas.

1 Collect Ideas Writing ideas are everywhere! Think about recent events or things you've read or seen. You can brainstorm more writing ideas with your classmates, friends, and family. Collect your ideas in a computer file, a notebook, or a journal. Then when you're ready to write, check your idea collections.

2 Choose a Topic Sometimes you have a lot of ideas you want to write about. Other times, your teacher may give you a **writing prompt**, or a writing assignment. You will still need to decide exactly what to write about. Make a list of possible writing ideas. Then circle the one that is the most important or interesting to you. That idea will be your **topic**.

> I could write about...
>
>   a concert my friends and I went to
>
>   when my grandparents arrived in the U.S.
>
>   why we need more school dances
>
>   why the eagle is a popular symbol

3 Plan Your Writing An **FATP** chart can help you organize your thoughts and focus on the details that you'll need for your writing.

FATP Chart

HOW TO UNLOCK A PROMPT
Form: _personal narrative_
Audience: _my teacher and classmates_
Topic: _when my grandparents arrived in the U.S._
Purpose: _to describe a personal experience_

Here are the ways an **FATP** chart can help you:

- The **form** tells you the type of writing. Study examples of the form to help you decide how to craft your writing.

- If you know your **audience**, you can choose the appropriate style and tone. For example, if you are writing for your friends, you can use friendly, informal language.

- A specific **topic** will help you collect only those details you need.

- The **purpose** is why you are writing. Your purpose can be to describe, to inform or explain, to persuade, or to express personal thoughts or feelings.

For more about writing for a specific audience or purpose, see pages 414–415.

4 **Gather Details** To write about a personal experience, you can just list the things you remember about an event. For other kinds of writing, you may need to talk about your topic with others or do research to gather information.

There are many ways to show the details you've gathered. You can

- make charts, lists, or webs
- draw and label pictures
- take notes on notecards
- make a story map
- use a gathering grid to write down answers to your questions

Gathering Grid

Topic: Vietnam	Get to Know Vietnam (book)	Internet
What is the population?		
What fuels the economy?		

Show your details in a way that works best for you and for your topic.

5 **Get Organized** Review your details and plan an interesting way to write about your topic. Put the details in the best order for your writing.

- Sometimes you can organize the details as you write them down.
- Other times, you can use numbers to order events in time sequence or to order the details from most to least important.
- You could also make an outline to show main ideas and supporting details.

The Writing Process, continued

DRAFT

Now you are ready to start writing. At this stage, don't worry about making mistakes—just get your ideas down on paper! Turn your details into sentences and paragraphs. As you are writing, you'll probably think of new ideas. Add those to your draft.

Trang Bui's Draft

> My family stood by the windows and watched the plane land at SeaTac Airport in Seattle on October 28, 2000. We were so excited to see the plane. The people started coming through the door. We lined up so we could see. I had to lift my little sister up so she could see.
>
> Suddenly everyone was hugging and crying. "I see them," my mother cried. My little sister tried to hide. My sister didn't know my grandparents. She was feeling shy.

Write your ideas in a first draft.

REVISE

A first draft can always be improved. When you revise a draft, you make changes to it.

1 **Read Your Draft** As you read your draft, ask yourself questions about the most important ideas. Make sure your ideas are clear, complete, and presented in the best way.

Revision Checklist

☑ Did I follow the plan on my FATP chart? Is the language appropriate for the writing form and audience? Did I stick to the topic?

☑ Is my writing interesting? Did I use different kinds of sentences? Did I vary the sentence beginnings?

☑ Does my writing have a beginning, a middle, and an ending?

☑ Are my details organized in the best way? Should I change the order of any details?

☑ Did I include details to make my ideas clear? Should I add or cut any details?

☑ Did I use the best words to say what I mean? Did I avoid using the same words over and over again?

2 Discuss Your Writing with Others Arrange a time to meet with your teacher to talk about your writing. Ask for suggestions for what you can do to improve it. Make any changes your teacher suggests, and then meet again to see how you are doing.

You might also have a **peer conference** with your classmates. Their comments can help you identify things that you might not notice yourself.

Guidelines for Peer Conferences

When you're the writer:

1. Tell your purpose for writing. Then read your writing aloud, or give copies to the group.

2. Ask for help on specific points:
   • Should I add any details about...?
   • Does the ending make sense?
   • Did I leave anything out?

3. Listen carefully to suggestions and take notes. Use the comments that you think will improve your writing.

When you're the reader:

1. Read the writing twice, or listen once and read it once. Make notes as you read. If you don't understand something, ask questions.

2. Look for the strongest parts of the writing. Why do they work? Tell the writer:
   • I like the way you...
   • One part you described well was...
   • You caught my interest when you wrote...

3. Make specific suggestions. Tell how the writer can improve the details, sentences, or organization.

---

3 Mark Your Changes What changes do you want to make to your draft? Use the Revising Marks or special features in your computer's word-processing program to show the changes.

Trang Bui's Revisions

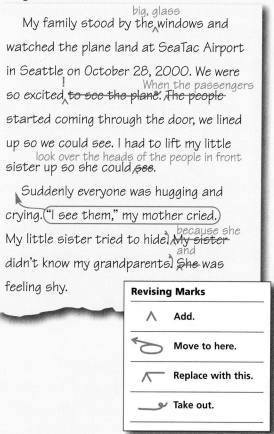

The Writing Process **411**

The Writing Process, continued

EDIT AND PROOFREAD

After you revise your draft for content, it's time to check it for mistakes.

1 Check Your Sentences When you edit, check that your sentences are clear, complete, and correct. Ask yourself:

- Does each sentence have a subject and a predicate?
- Did I break up run-on sentences?
- Are there any short sentences that I can combine into longer sentences?

2 Check for Mistakes Proofread to find and correct errors in capitalization, punctuation, grammar, and spelling. Look especially for:

- capital letters, end marks, apostrophes, and quotation marks
- subject–verb agreement
- use of pronouns
- misspelled words.

3 Mark Your Corrections Use the Proofreading Marks to show your corrections or make the corrections when you find them in your document on the computer.

4 Make a Final Copy Rewrite your work and make the corrections you marked. If you are using a computer, print your corrected copy. For more ideas about formatting your paper, see page 389.

Trang Bui's Proofread Draft

¶ When we left vietnam, my grandparents had to stay behind. "We are too old to go someplace new," my grandfather said. My grandmother cooked ~~a special~~ *an incredible* dinner for us before we left, but ~~he~~ *she* could not eat. We didnt know how long it would be before we would see each other again.

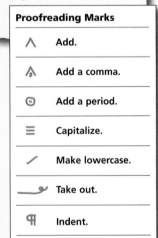

Proofreading Marks	
∧	Add.
⩘	Add a comma.
⊙	Add a period.
≡	Capitalize.
/	Make lowercase.
⟿	Take out.
¶	Indent.

PUBLISH

Now that you have corrected your work, share it with others! Here are just a few ideas for publishing your writing.

- E-mail it to a friend or family member.
- Make a home video of you reading it.
- Put it on a poster, add pictures, and display it in your classroom.
- Send it to your favorite magazine for publication.

The Best Day of My Life
by Trang Bui

My family stood by the big, glass windows and watched the plane land at SeaTac Airport in Seattle on October 28, 2000. We were so excited! When the passengers started coming through the door, we lined up so we could see. I had to lift my little sister up so she could look over the heads of the people in front.

"I see them," my mother cried. Suddenly everyone was hugging and crying. My little sister tried to hide because she didn't know my grandparents and was feeling shy.

When we left Vietnam, my grandparents had to stay behind. "We are too old to go someplace new," my grandfather said. My grandmother cooked an incredible dinner for us before we left, but she could not eat. We didn't know how long it would be before we would see each other again.

My family came to Seattle to start a new life. My parents worked in the donut shop and sent some of the money they earned each month to my grandparents. It took four long years, but my grandparents finally arrived, and we're all together again.

EVALUATE YOUR WRITING

Save examples of your writing. Date them and collect them in a **portfolio**. Look through your portfolio from time to time to see how you are doing as a writer.

1 Organize Your Portfolio Try putting all your writing in order by date. Or, make special sections for works written for the same purpose or same audience. You might also group your writing by form—stories, research reports, or poems, for example.

2 Survey the Work in Your Portfolio Each time you add new work to your portfolio, ask yourself:

- How does this writing compare to other work I've done?
- Am I getting better in certain areas? What are they?
- Are there things that I didn't do as well this time? Why?

3 Think About How You Write As you look over your writing, think about the words you like to use, the kinds of sentences you write, and what you like to write about. All of those things together are your writing style. That is what makes you a super writer with a style all your own!

I write with **Style!**

he Writer's Craft

Good writers are always working on their writing. You can use the ideas in this section to make your writing the best it can be.

HOW TO WRITE FOR A SPECIFIC PURPOSE

Good writers change how and what they write to fit their main purpose.
The **purpose** is why you are writing.

PURPOSE	EXAMPLES	
To describe	You could write a description with lots of descriptive details to help your reader "see" what you are describing. My guitar is awesome. The body is a metallic black, and the new strings shine like silver.	For a poem, use colorful verbs to describe what something does. Sounds of A Guitar Strum, strum the silver strings, And sweet notes fill the air.
To inform or to explain	You might give directions to explain how to do something. To play the guitar, hold the neck with your left hand. Then curl your fingers over the frets. Use your right hand to strum or pick the strings over the sound hole.	Or, you could write a paragraph to give your readers important facts about a topic. An electric guitar has a solid body and six strings. The points under the strings change the vibrations into electronic signals. The signals are magnified by an amplifier and sent to loudspeakers where they are converted into sounds.
To persuade	In an advertisement, you can use persuasive words and phrases to convince someone to buy something. **Electric Guitars** **Is excellent sound quality what you want?** Then come on over to Guitar World. We've got the best brands at the best prices! **Guitar World** **101 Main Street** **555-8931**	In an editorial, give your opinion and use persuasive words to change the way things are. I think the school board should vote to keep our music program. I love music, and so do many of my friends. As a matter of fact, we try to finish our homework just so we can get to music class.

PURPOSE	EXAMPLES
To express your thoughts and feelings	Write a journal entry to tell about your personal thoughts and feelings. June 10, 2001 I just saw the Top Dogs in concert. I wish I could play like their lead guitarist!
To entertain	You could write a joke to make your readers laugh. What did the old guitar say to the new one? "Don't fret. I'll carry the tune for you!"
To learn	It helps to write things down when you are learning about a topic. That way you can see what you already know—and what you don't know. Listening to music can help you relax. Now I want to know how it affects your brain and your body.

HOW TO WRITE FOR A SPECIFIC AUDIENCE

Who will read what you write? Your **audience**. Knowing your audience will help you decide what words to use and what kinds of details to include.

AUDIENCE	EXAMPLES
Adults and people you don't know	Use formal language and details to help them understand what they might not know. I did very well at my guitar lesson today. I learned how to press the tips of my fingers on top of the strings to play different notes.
Your friends	Use informal language because they'll probably understand exactly what you mean. My guitar lesson was great. Now I can jam with any band!
People younger than you	Use simple language so they'll understand. My guitar lesson was fun. Now I can play a song.

The Writer's Craft, continued

HOW TO CHOOSE THE RIGHT WORDS

To help your readers really see what you are writing about, use just the right words.

❶ Use Specific Nouns Choose nouns that say exactly what you mean.

Just OK

> The boat went across the water.

Much Better

> The sailboat sped across the lake.

❷ Use Colorful Verbs Choose verbs that give the best picture of the action.

Just OK

> The wave came up on the beach.

Much Better

> The wave crashed on the beach.

❸ Add Sensory Words Use words that tell what you see, hear, smell, taste, and touch to help your readers imagine they are there!

Just OK

> Mark sat on the beach by the water. He pushed the sand around. The sun shone down on his skin.

Much Better

> Mark sat on the beach by the crashing waves. He sifted the soft, white sand through his fingers. The hot sun beat down on his parched skin, and he could almost taste the salty air.

❹ Use Words with Just the Right Meaning Some words seem similar in meaning but may give readers a different feeling.

Negative Connotation: skinny
Positive Connotation: slim, slender

❺ Use Figurative Language Figurative language can help your readers "see" ordinary things in new ways.

- Try using a **simile** with *like* or *as* to make comparisons.

> The man dove like a dolphin into the waves.

- Use a **metaphor** to tell what something is like, without using the words *like* or *as*:

> The man was a playful dolphin.

- Use **personification** to give human qualities to a non-human thing:

> Seagulls laughed overhead.

- You might want to use **hyperbole,** or an exaggeration, to add humor to your writing.

> The squawking gulls could be heard around the world.

HOW TO IMPROVE YOUR SENTENCES

1 Combine Sentences Try different ways to combine a lot of short sentences into one longer sentence.

Just OK

> I pushed off on my snowboard.
> I sped down the hill.
> I headed toward the clubhouse.

Much Better

> I pushed off on my snowboard and sped down the hill toward the clubhouse.

> I pushed off on my snowboard, sped down the hill, and headed toward the clubhouse.

2 Break Up Sentences If a sentence runs on too long, it becomes hard to follow. Break up run-on sentences to make your meaning clear.

Just OK

> The first time I went snowboarding, it was hard to get off the chairlift and I kept falling, but as I watched other snowboarders, I realized that most of them fell, too, then I didn't feel so bad.

Much Better

> The first time I went snowboarding, it was hard to get off the chairlift. I kept falling. As I watched other snowboarders, I realized that most of them fell, too. Then I didn't feel so bad.

3 Start Sentences in Different Ways Make your writing more interesting by varying the way your sentences begin. That way your readers won't get bored.

Just OK

> **Darcy** went snowboarding for the first time last winter. **Darcy** started out just fine. **Darcy** tried to make a turn, but lost her balance and fell into a snowbank. **Darcy** laughed at herself, brushed off the snow, and got right back on her feet. **Darcy** fell several more times, but finally made it down the hill!

Much Better

> **Last winter,** Darcy went snowboarding for the first time. **She** started out just fine. **When she tried to make a turn,** she lost her balance and fell into a snowbank. **Laughing at herself,** Darcy brushed off the snow and got right back on her feet. **After several more falls,** Darcy finally made it down the hill!

The Writer's Craft, continued

WHAT IS A PARAGRAPH?

A **paragraph** is a group of sentences that all tell about the same idea. The `topic sentence` tells the main idea of the paragraph. The other sentences give **supporting details**. The supporting details tell more about the main idea.

Sometimes a topic sentence that states the main idea comes at the beginning of a paragraph.

> **The Pike Place Market in Seattle is a great place to spend an afternoon.** At the market, you can shop for fresh fruits, vegetables, and flowers. You can watch the fishsellers toss fish across the aisles to one another. If you're hungry, you can find just about any kind of food in the many cafes and food stands.

Sometimes a topic sentence that states the main idea comes at the end of a paragraph.

> At the market, you can shop for fresh fruits, vegetables, and flowers. You can watch the fishsellers toss fish across the aisles to each other. If you're hungry, you can find just about any kind of food in the many cafes and food stands. **The Pike Place Market in Seattle is a great place to spend an afternoon.**

HOW TO ORGANIZE PARAGRAPHS

There are many ways to organize your paragraphs.

1. **Sequence Paragraphs** Some paragraphs are organized by sequence. `Time order words` tell when things happen.

> One day I went fishing with Dad. **First** we rowed to the middle of the lake. **After** we put slimy worms on our hooks, we tossed our lines overboard. **Then** we waited forever for the fish to bite! We **finally** caught one fish. When Dad goes fishing again, I'm staying home!

2. **Comparison Paragraphs** Some paragraphs tell how things are alike and different. `Comparison words` signal the similarities and differences.

> **Like** human beings, whales are mammals. **Both** produce milk and give birth to live young. **Unlike** most mammals, **however,** whales store oxygen longer. This allows them to take fewer breaths and stay underwater longer.

3. **Paragraphs in Space Order** For a description, try using **space order** to tell what you see in order—left to right, near to far, or top to bottom. `Direction words and phrases` tell where things are.

> An octopus looks strange. Its head and body look like one big bulb. **Radiating from** the bulb are eight tentacles. Each tentacle has two rows of suckers **along the underside.** It uses the suckers to grip rocks and find food.

4 **Cause-and-Effect Paragraphs** In this kind of paragraph, the topic sentence tells the **cause**, or why something happens. Detail sentences tell the **effects**, or what happens as a result.

> Ricky was floating on his surfboard. Suddenly, he spotted a large, dark object swimming toward him. "Could it be a shark?" he thought. His heart pounded. He paddled frantically toward the beach. Looking back, he saw a huge log bobbing among the waves!

5 **Paragraphs in Logical Order** The order in which you present your ideas can vary with your topic. You may want to present ideas in order from general to specific or from most important to least important.

> If we over-fish the ocean, there will not be enough fish left to reproduce. Although there would be food at first, there would not be enough to feed people later. Several important fish species could go extinct. Other fish that depend on those fish for food would also suffer.

6 **Opinion Paragraphs** In an opinion paragraph, give your opinion about something. State your opinion in the **topic sentence.** Give the reasons for your opinion in the detail sentences.

> **I think the octopus is a fascinating sea creature.** It defends itself so well! An octopus turns colors to match its surroundings so predators can't see it. It ejects an inky cloud when it senses danger. It also has a soft body that fits into small hiding places. Don't you think the octopus is fascinating, too?

7 **Persuasive Paragraphs** A persuasive paragraph, begins with a **thesis statement** that gives your opinion or tells the main idea. Facts, reasons, and statistics that support your opinion are the **supporting arguments**.

> **The Eastern North Pacific gray whale should be put back on the endangered species list.** It was removed from the list in 1994 because its population stabilized. However, of the three large populations of gray whales, one is extinct and another is endangered. Gray whales stay close to the shore, and can become entangled in fishing nets. Their breeding grounds in Baja, California, are threatened by the expansion of salt-extraction plants. We should act now to save the Eastern North Pacific gray whale.

The Writer's Craft, continued

HOW TO PUT PARAGRAPHS TOGETHER

If you write more than two paragraphs, organize your writing into three parts: the **introduction**, the **body**, and the **conclusion**.

1 **Write a Strong Introduction** Name the topic and grab your readers' interest.

- **Ask a question.**

  > What's so hot about smoking?

- **Express an emotion or an opinion.**

  > Smoking isn't just bad—it can kill you!

- **Describe an action or event.**

  > Smoking is one of the biggest killers in the U.S.

- **Make a startling statement, or give an interesting or unusual fact.**

  > Cigarettes contain more than fifteen harmful chemicals.

2 **Develop the Topic in the Body** Present your supporting details. Organize the paragraphs so they work together in the best order to support your main idea or thesis statement.

3 **Write a Conclusion** Express an emotion or include a thoughtful idea.

> The easiest way to break a bad habit like smoking is never to start it in the first place!

HOW TO MAKE YOUR WRITING FLOW

1 **Use Transition Words** Words or phrases that help connect paragraphs are transition words. They will help your readers follow your ideas.

Examples:

As a result	Also	Even though
As soon as	In addition	However
Finally	Like	On the other hand
Then	Plus	Yet

2 **Use the Same Point of View** If you are expressing how you feel about something, tell about *your* feelings, not someone else's. If you are writing about a character or another person, use details that show how that person thinks or feels.

> I think that smoking is an awful habit. If someone offers
> ~~my friend~~ me a cigarette, ~~he~~ I always says I, "No way."

3 **Use the Same Verb Tenses** Keep your verbs all in the same tense so your readers won't get confused about when things happen.

> When someone offers me a cigarette, though, I always
> say, "No way." That's because I ~~knew~~ know how bad it ~~was~~ is
> for my lungs.

Smoking: A Bad Habit to Start

What's so hot about smoking? Nothing! I think that some kids start smoking because it makes them feel like they are grown up. Other kids just want to be part of the "in" crowd. When someone offers me a cigarette, though, I always say "No way." That's because I know how bad it is for my **lungs**.

Did you know that your **lungs** take nearly 26,000 breaths a day? They need clean air and oxygen to expand and contract the way they should. All the chemicals in cigarette smoke cause emphysema. This disease destroys the tiny air sacs in your lungs where oxygen and carbon dioxide are exchanged.

As soon as emphysema starts, it damages your **lungs**. Eventually every breath becomes a struggle. Wouldn't it be smart, then, to protect your lungs like you do other parts of your body?

Plus, if you decide to smoke, you are affecting other people's lungs as well as your own. About 3,000 non-smokers die every year from second-hand smoke. Young children are especially at risk because their lungs are just developing. Do you really want to harm someone else just to be "cool"?

Sooner or later someone is going to offer you a cigarette. Before you decide, take a deep breath of clean, fresh air. Think about how good you feel now. Then play it safe. Don't smoke!

INTRODUCTION
The introduction grabs the readers' interest and states the writer's opinion.

BODY
The body includes details, facts, and arguments to support the writer's opinion.

This writer connected paragraphs by **repeating a word or phrase** and by using **transition words**.

All the sentences go together to show this writer's point of view about the topic. The verbs the writer uses are all in the present tense.

CONCLUSION
In the last paragraph, the writer tries to convince the readers to take action.

The Writer's Craft, continued

HOW TO MAKE YOUR WRITING BETTER

The words that you choose, the way that you put them together, and the ideas that you present make your writing unique. Try these techniques.

❶ Show, Don't Tell You can just tell your readers about an event or a person. To give your readers the best picture, though, show them exactly what you mean!

This tells:

> Kevin hated eating in the cafeteria. He was new at school and didn't know anyone. So he sat in a corner by himself. Then one day, a girl in his math class asked him to sit at her table. After that, Kevin felt much more comfortable.

This shows:

> "I can't wait to finish my lunch and get out of here," thought Kevin. "I don't know anyone, anyway."
>
> Then one day, Kevin heard a cheery voice from behind him. "Hey, do you want to sit with us?" the girl asked. It was Roberta from his math class.
>
> "Sure," said Kevin, grinning. "How's it going?" he asked Roberta.

❷ Elaborate *Elaborate* means "Tell me more!" Try these ways to add information to your writing.

- **Tell what came before or after.**

  Without Elaboration

  > The ball dropped into the basket.

  With Elaboration

  > After rolling around on the rim, the ball finally dropped into the basket.

- **Add sensory details to clearly show what something is like.**

  Without Details

  > Their player made an attempt for the basket. The entire crowd watched as the ball arched across the court and sank into the net without touching the rim.

  With Details

  > Their tallest player made an attempt for the basket. The entire crowd watched silently as the orange ball arched high across the court and sank into the net without touching the skinny metal rim.

- **Add examples, facts, and other details.**

  Without Details

  > The fans cheered.

  With Details

  > The excited fans jumped up out of their seats, clapped their hands, and stomped their feet.

- **Add quotations or dialogue.**

  Without Dialogue

  > The fans shouted.

  With Dialogue

  > "Go, Rangers, go! You can do it!" the fans shouted.

❸ **Develop Your Own Writing Style and Voice**

As a writer, you have your own voice, or personality. That's because your writing will show the kinds of words you like, what ideas are important to you, and how you feel about things. To keep your writing interesting and exciting, let your readers "see" who you are.

Just OK

> I dribbled the ball through the zone. I made a shot for the basket. The ball rolled for a while on the basket rim, then fell in. I made the final shot to win the game.

Much Better

> My heart was pounding. I dribbled the ball through the zone and took my best shot. I just stood there with my arms still raised up in the air. Would the ball ever stop rolling on the rim? When it finally dropped into the basket, I couldn't believe it! It was awesome! That basket put us ahead to win the game by one point!

Sentences

A sentence is a group of words that expresses a complete thought.
Every sentence has a subject and a predicate.
Every sentence begins with a capital letter.

SENTENCE TYPES	EXAMPLES
A **declarative sentence** tells something. It ends with a period.	The football game was on Friday. The coach made an important announcement.
An **interrogative sentence** asks a question. It ends with a question mark.	Can you tell me the news?

Kinds of Questions

Questions That Ask for a "Yes" or "No" Answer	Answers
Is it about the team?	Yes.
Did the team win the game?	Yes.
Has the coach ever made an announcement like this before?	No.
Are the players sad?	No.
Were the fans surprised?	Yes.

Tag Questions	
You will tell me the news, **won't you**?	Yes, I will. OR No, I won't.
You didn't forget it, **did you**?	Yes, I did. OR No, I didn't.

Questions That Ask for Specific Information	
Who heard the announcement?	The team and the fans heard the announcement.
What did the coach say?	He said the team will play in a special game.
Where will the team play this game?	In Hawaii.
When did the coach find out?	Right before the game.
Why was our team chosen?	Our team was chosen because we won a lot of games.
How many games has the team won this year?	All ten of them.
Which coach made the announcement?	The tall one.

SENTENCE TYPES, continued	EXAMPLES
An **exclamatory sentence** shows surprise or strong emotion. It ends with an exclamation mark.	That's fantastic news! I can't believe it!
An **imperative sentence** gives a command. It usually begins with a verb. It often ends with a period. If an imperative sentence shows strong emotion, it ends with an exclamation mark.	Give the team my congratulations. Don't keep any more secrets from me ever again!

NEGATIVE SENTENCES	EXAMPLES
A **negative sentence** uses a **negative word** to say "no."	The game in Hawaii was **not** boring! **Nobody** in our town missed it on TV. Our team **never** played better.

Negative Words

never	no one
no	not
nobody	nothing
none	nowhere

Use only one negative word in a sentence.

> anything
> The other team could not do ~~nothing~~ right.

> any
> They never scored ~~no~~ points.

CONDITIONAL SENTENCES	EXAMPLES
Some sentences tell how one thing depends on another. These sentences often use verbs like can, will, could, would, or might.	**If** our team returns on Saturday, **then** we will have a party. **Unless** it rains, we can have the party on the football field. Or, we could have a dance in the gym **if** the coach lets us.

Sentences, continued

COMPLETE SENTENCES	EXAMPLES
A **complete sentence** has a **subject** and a **predicate**. A complete sentence expresses a complete thought.	**Many people** **visit our National Parks**. Grand Canyon National Park, Arizona

A **fragment** is not a sentence. It is not a complete thought. You can add information to a fragment to turn it into a complete sentence.	**Fragment:** **Complete sentences:**
	a fun vacation You can have a fun vacation.
	                 Will we have a fun vacation at the park?
	                 Go to a national park and have a fun vacation.

SUBJECTS	EXAMPLES
	To find the subject in a sentence, ask yourself: **Whom or what is the sentence about?**
The **complete subject** includes all the words that tell about the subject.	**My favorite parks** are in the West. **People from all over the world** visit them.
The **simple subject** is the most important word in the complete subject.	My favorite **parks** are in the West. **People** from all over the world visit them.
A **compound subject** has two or more simple subjects joined by **and** or **or**.	**Yosemite** and **Yellowstone** are the most interesting to me. Either **spring or fall** is a good time to visit these parks.
Sometimes the subject is a **pronoun**. Be sure to include the pronoun in the sentence. ***But:*** When you give a command, you do not have to include the subject. The subject **you** is understood in an imperative sentence.	The map shows the campsites. **They** are by the river. Follow the rules of the park. Don't disturb the animals. Never throw trash in the streams.

Subject Pronouns

Singular	Plural
I	we
you	you
he, she, it	they

PREDICATES	EXAMPLES

The predicate of a sentence tells what the subject is, has, or does.

The **complete predicate** includes all the words in the predicate.	Yosemite **is a beautiful park**. It **has huge waterfalls**. People **hike to the waterfalls**.
The **simple predicate** is the **verb**. It is the most important word in the predicate.	Yosemite **is** a beautiful park. It **has** huge waterfalls. People **hike** to the waterfalls. Waterfall in Yosemite National Park
A **compound predicate** has two or more verbs joined by **and** or **or**.	At Yosemite, some people **fish and swim**. My family **hiked** to the river **or stayed** in the cabin. I **have gone** to Yosemite often **and have enjoyed** every visit.

SUBJECT-VERB AGREEMENT	EXAMPLES

The verb must always agree with the subject of the sentence.

A **singular subject** names one person or thing. Use a **singular verb** with a singular subject. A **plural subject** tells about more than one person or thing. Use a **plural verb** with a plural subject.	Another popular **park is** the Grand Canyon. **It has** a powerful river. The **cliffs are** beautiful. **We were amazed** by their colors.

Singular and Plural Verbs

Singular	Plural
The park **is** big.	The parks **are** big.
The park **was** beautiful.	The parks **were** beautiful.
The park **has** campsites.	The parks **have** campsites.
The park **does** not **open** until spring.	The parks **do** not **open** until spring.

Sentences, continued

SUBJECT-VERB AGREEMENT, continued	EXAMPLES
Study the chart to see how **action verbs** agree with their subjects. When you tell about one other person or thing, use an action verb that ends in **s**.	**More Singular and Plural Verbs** Singular I **hike** in the park. You **hike** in the park. He **hike**s in the park. She **hike**s in the park. The dog **hike**s in the park. Plural We **hike** in the park. You **hike** in the park. They **hike** in the park. The dogs **hike** in the park.
The **subject** and **verb** must agree, even when other words come between them.	The **hikers** in the park **are looking** for animals. A **snake** with lots of stripes **lives** in this area.
If the simple subjects in a **compound subject** are connected by **and**, use a plural verb.	A **mule and** a **guide are** available for a trip down the canyon.
Sometimes the simple subjects in a **compound subject** are connected by **or**. Look at the last simple subject. If it is singular, use a **singular verb**. If it is plural, use a **plural verb**.	These **rafts or** this **boat is** the best way to go down the river. This **raft or** these **boats are** the best way to go down the river. Mule riders in the Grand Canyon
The **subject** and **verb** must agree even if the subject comes after the verb.	There **are** other amazing **parks** in Arizona. Here **is** a **list** of them.
In some questions, look for the **subject** between the **helping and main verbs**. The helping verb must agree with the subject.	**Has** your **friend visited** the parks? **Have** your **friends visited** the parks?

PHRASES	EXAMPLES
A **phrase** is a group of related words that does not have a subject and a predicate.	**during the gold rush** **before the discovery of gold**
A **phrase** can be part of a complete sentence.	Many people came to California **during the gold rush**. **Before the discovery of gold**, about 15,000 people lived there.

CLAUSES	EXAMPLES
A **clause** is a group of words that has a **subject** and a **verb**. Some clauses are complete sentences. Some clauses are not.	The **population** of California **increased** to about 100,000 by 1849. because **miners came** to California
An **independent clause** expresses a complete thought and can stand alone as a sentence. A **dependent clause** does not express a complete thought. It is not a sentence.	The miners were called "forty-niners." because so many arrived in 1849

Prospectors panned for gold in rivers and streams.

Words That Can Signal a Dependent Clause

Cause Words	Time Words		Words that Express Conditions	Relative Pronouns	
because	after	whenever	although	that	who
since	as	while	as long as	which	whom
	before	until	if		whose
	when		unless		

A **dependent clause** can be combined with an **independent clause** to form a sentence.	The miners were called "forty-niners" because so many arrived in 1849. <u>independent clause</u> <u>dependent clause</u> When they found gold, the miners got rich. <u>dependent clause</u> <u>independent clause</u>

Sentences, continued

SIMPLE SENTENCES	EXAMPLES
A **simple sentence** is one independent clause. It has a **subject** and a **predicate**.	**The miners** **needed goods and services**.

COMPOUND SENTENCES	EXAMPLES
When you join two independent clauses, you make a **compound sentence**. Use a **coordinating conjunction** to join the clauses.	Some people opened food markets. The miners bought food. ▼ **Some people opened food markets, and the miners bought food.** Other people opened stores. It was still hard to get supplies. ▼ **Other people opened stores, but it was still hard to get supplies.** **Coordinating Conjunctions** and nor but or for yet
Put a **comma** before the conjunction or use a **semi-colon** and no conjunction.	The miners used gold to buy things, and the shopkeepers ended up with the gold. The miners used gold to buy things; the shopkeepers ended up with the gold.

COMPLEX SENTENCES	EXAMPLES

To make a **complex sentence**, join an independent clause with one or more dependent clauses.
 	
If the dependent clause comes first, put a **comma** after it.
	Many writers visited the camps where the miners worked.
	   independent clause dependent clause
	
	While they were there, the writers wrote stories about the miners.
	   dependent clause independent clause

COMPOUND-COMPLEX SENTENCES	EXAMPLES

You can make a **compound-complex sentence** by joining two or more independent clauses and a dependent clause.	Many miners never became rich, but they decided to settle in the West
	   independent clause independent clause
	
	because they found other jobs in California.
	      dependent clause

Parts of Speech

All the words in the English language can be categorized into eight groups. These groups are the eight parts of speech. Words are grouped into the parts of speech by the way they are used in a sentence.

THE EIGHT PARTS OF SPEECH	EXAMPLES
A **noun** names a person, place, thing, or idea.	**Samantha** lives in **Minnesota**. She skates on the **ice** every **day** to build her **skill**.
A **pronoun** takes the place of a noun.	**She** practices a dance routine for a show.
An **adjective** describes a noun or a pronoun.	She is a **powerful** skater. She is **graceful**, too.
A **verb** can tell what the subject of a sentence does or has. A **verb** can also link a word in the predicate to the subject.	Samantha **twists**, **turns**, and **jumps**. She **has** talent! Like many skaters, Samantha **is** a competitor. But, unlike most skaters, Samantha **is** deaf.
An **adverb** describes a verb, an adjective, or another adverb.	The music plays **loudly**, but she cannot hear it. Still, Samantha has become a **very** good skater. How can she perform **so** well?
A **preposition** shows how two things or ideas are related. It introduces a prepositional phrase.	A skating coach helps Samantha skate **on** the ice. He gives her signals as she moves **around** the rink. **During** the show, the people **in** the stands cheer **for** the skater.
A **conjunction** connects words or groups of words.	Samantha can't hear the people cheer, **but** she sees their smiles. Samantha smiles **and** waves back to the crowd.
An **interjection** expresses strong feeling.	Some people shout, "**Hooray!**" Others say, "**Wow!** What a talented skater!"

Nouns

A noun names a person, place, thing, or idea.
There are many different kinds of nouns.

COMMON AND PROPER NOUNS	EXAMPLES
A **common noun** names any person, place, thing, or idea.	A **teenager** sat by the **ocean** and read a **book**. It was about **ecology**.
A **proper noun** names one particular person, place, thing, or idea. The important words in a proper noun start with a <u>capital letter</u>.	**Daniel** sat by the **Atlantic Ocean** and read *Save the Manatee.*

COMPOUND NOUNS	EXAMPLES
A **compound noun** is two or more words that express one idea. A compound noun can be: • two words • two words joined into one word • a hyphenated word	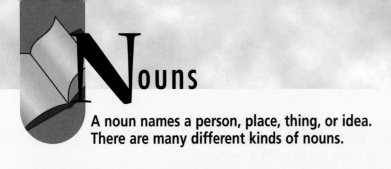 A manatee Some people call manatees **sea cows**. Manatees live in shallow waters where there is plenty of **sunlight**. In his book, Daniel saw a picture of a manatee baby and a **grown-up**.

COLLECTIVE NOUNS	EXAMPLES
A **collective noun** names a group of people, animals, places, or things.	Daniel took pictures of manatees on a trip to Florida with his **family**.

Some Collective Nouns

Groups of People	Groups of Animals	Groups of Places	Groups of Things
band	flock	Hawaiian Islands	mail
class	herd		money
family	litter	United States	set
team	pack		trash

A collective noun can be the **subject** of a sentence. It usually needs a **singular verb** because the group is seen as one unit.	Our **class** **hopes** to see the pictures Daniel took. His **club** **has** already **seen** them.

SINGULAR AND PLURAL NOUNS	EXAMPLES

> **The singular form of a count noun names one thing.
> The plural form names more than one thing.**

Count nouns are nouns that you can count. Follow these rules to make a count noun plural:

- Add **-s** to most count nouns.

desk	book	teacher	apple	line
desk**s**	book**s**	teacher**s**	apple**s**	line**s**

- If the noun ends in **x**, **ch**, **sh**, **s**, or **z**, add **-es**.

box	lunch	dish	glass	waltz
box**es**	lunch**es**	dish**es**	glass**es**	waltz**es**

- For nouns that end in a consonant plus **y**, change the **y** to **i** and add **-es**.

story	sky	city	penny	army
stor**ies**	sk**ies**	cit**ies**	penn**ies**	arm**ies**

- For nouns that end in a vowel plus **y**, just add **-s**.

boy	toy	day	monkey	valley
boy**s**	toy**s**	day**s**	monkey**s**	valley**s**

- For most nouns that end in **f** or **fe**, change the **f** to **v** and add **-es**. For some nouns that end in **f**, just add **-s**.

leaf	knife	half	roof	chief
lea**ves**	kni**ves**	hal**ves**	roof**s**	chief**s**

- If the noun ends in a vowel plus **o**, add **-s**. For some nouns that end in a consonant plus **o**, add **-s**. For others, add **-es**.

radio	kangaroo	banjo	potato	tomato
radio**s**	kangaroo**s**	banjo**s**	potato**es**	tomato**es**

- A few count nouns have irregular plural forms.

child	foot	person	man	woman
children	**feet**	**people**	**men**	**women**

- For a few count nouns, the singular and plural forms are the same.

deer	fish	salmon	sheep	trout
deer	**fish**	**salmon**	**sheep**	**trout**

Nouns, continued

SINGULAR AND PLURAL NOUNS	EXAMPLES
Noncount nouns are nouns that you cannot count. A noncount noun does not have a plural form.	My favorite museum has **furniture** and **art**. Sometimes I wonder how much **money** each item is worth.

Types of Noncount Nouns

Activities and Sports

				Examples
baseball	camping	dancing	fishing	I love to play **soccer**.
golf	singing	soccer	swimming	

Category Nouns

clothing	equipment	furniture	hardware	jewelry	My **equipment** is in the car.
machinery	mail	money	time	weather	

Food

bread	cereal	cheese	corn	flour	I'll drink some **water** on my way
lettuce	meat	milk	rice	salt	to the game.
soup	sugar	tea	water		

You can count some food items by using a measurement word like **cup**, **slice**, **glass**, or **head** plus the word **of**. To show the plural form, just make the measurement word plural.

I'll drink **two glasses of water** on my way to the game.

Ideas and Feelings

democracy	enthusiasm	freedom	fun	health	I'll also listen to the radio for
honesty	information	knowledge	luck	work	**information** about the weather.

Materials

air	fuel	gasoline	gold	The radio says the **air** is heavy.
metal	paper	water	wood	What does that mean?

Weather

fog	hail	heat	ice	lightning	Uh-oh! First came the **lightning**
rain	smog	snow	sunshine	thunder	and the **thunder**. I want
					sunshine for my next
					soccer game!

Some words have more than one meaning. Add **-s** for the plural only if the noun means something you can count.	Throw me those **baseballs**. I want to learn to play **baseball**.

ARTICLES	EXAMPLES
An **article** is a word that helps identify a noun. An article often comes before a count noun.	After **the** game, we found **a** coat and **an** umbrella on **the** field.
Use **a** or **an** before **nouns** that are not specific. Use **the** before **nouns** that are specific.	**A boy** walked around the field. **The coach's son** walked around the field.
Use **a** before a word that starts with a consonant sound. Use **an** before a word that starts with a vowel sound.	a **b**all a **g**ate a **p**layer a **o**ne-way street (o is pronounced like w) a **c**ap a **k**ick a **n**et a **u**niform (u is pronounced like y) **a** **e** **i** **o** **u** **silent h** an **a**nt an **e**lbow an **i**nch an **o**live an **u**mbrella an **h**our an **a**pron an **e**el an **i**dea an **o**cean an **a**mount an **e**lection an **o**wl an **ar**tist an **or**ange
Do not use **a** or **an** before a noncount noun.	The soccer ball was made of ~~a~~ leather.
Do not use **the** before the name of: • a city or state • most countries • a language • a day, a month, or most holidays • a sport or activity • most businesses • a person.	Our next game will be in **Dallas**. Games in **Texas** are always exciting. We will play a team from **Mexico**. People will be cheering in **Spanish** and **English**. The game will take place on **Monday**. Is that in **February**? Yes, on **President's Day**. That will be a good day to play **soccer**. The fans will have hot dogs to eat from **Sal's Market**. You may even see **Sal** himself.

Nouns, continued

POSSESSIVE NOUNS	EXAMPLES
A **possessive noun** is the name of an owner. All possessive nouns include an **apostrophe**.	Several bands performed in our **town's** parade. Everyone liked the **musicians'** costumes.
Follow these rules to make a noun possessive:	
• If there is one owner, add **'s** to the owner's name.	Some kids played the trumpet. One **boy's** trumpet was very loud. **Marsha's** baton went high in the air.
But: If the owner's name ends in **s**, you can add **'s** or just the apostrophe. Either is correct.	**Louis's** hat fell off. **Louis'** hat fell off.
• A noun that names two or more owners is plural and often ends in **s**. If so, just add **'**.	The **girls'** section sang loud songs. I could barely hear my **brothers'** tubas.
But: If the plural noun that names the owners does not end in **s**, add **'s**.	The **men's** cooking club marched with the band. The **children's** band rode on tricycles.

CONCRETE AND ABSTRACT NOUNS	EXAMPLES
A **concrete noun** names something you can see, touch, hear, smell, or taste.	The **band** will be in the **parade** that goes down **Main Street**.
An **abstract noun** names something you can think about but cannot see, touch, hear, smell, or taste.	The parade will add to the **spirit** of the **day**.

A parade

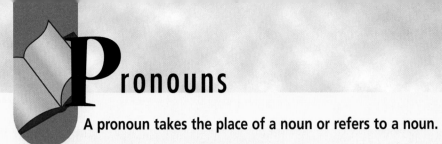

Pronouns

A pronoun takes the place of a noun or refers to a noun.

NOUN AND PRONOUN AGREEMENT	EXAMPLES
	When nouns and pronouns agree, they both tell about the same person, place, or thing.
The noun is the **antecedent**, and the **pronoun** refers to it.	**Janet and Scott** talk to a counselor. **They** learn about careers. antecedent pronoun
A **pronoun** must agree in number with the noun it refers to. **Singular pronouns** refer to one person. **Plural pronouns** refer to more than one person.	The counselor has an office at school. ~~They~~ ^{He} meets there with students. **Some Singular and Plural Pronouns** Singular Pronouns Plural Pronouns I, me, my, mine we, us, our, ours you, your, yours you, your, yours he, him, his she, her, hers ——— they, them, their, theirs it, its
Use **she, her,** and **hers** to tell about females. Use **he, him**, and **his** to tell about males.	Janet is interested in animals. ~~He~~ ^{She} wants to know what veterinarians do. Scott wants the counselor to tell ~~her~~ ^{him} about careers in photography.

Pronouns, continued

PERSON OF PRONOUNS	EXAMPLES
Use a **first-person pronoun** to talk about yourself.	**I** may want to be a photographer some day. At **our** house **we** take pictures of **my** family all the time.
Use a **second-person pronoun** to identify the person you are talking to.	Scott, do **you** have a photograph of **your** grandparents? Did **you** use this camera to take the picture?
Use a **third-person pronoun** to identify the person or thing you are talking about.	Scott got a new video camera for **his** birthday. Mother gave **it** to Scott. **She** thinks **he** will be a movie director someday.

USES OF PRONOUNS	EXAMPLES
Use a **subject pronoun** as the **subject** of a sentence.	**Janet** likes animals. **She** works at a pet shop.

Subject Pronouns

Singular	Plural
I	we
you	you
he, she, it	they

The pronoun **it** can be used as a **subject** to refer to a noun.	Janet lives near the **shop**. **It** is on First Street.
But: The pronoun **it** can be the **subject** without referring to a specific noun.	**It** is interesting to work in the shop. **It** is fun to play with the animals. **It** is important to take care of them, too.
Sometimes you talk about a person twice in a sentence. Use a **reflexive pronoun** to refer to the **subject**.	**Janet** taught **herself** about the life cycle of parrots. The **shop owners themselves** learned some things from Janet.

Subject and Reflexive Pronouns

Singular		Plural	
I	myself	we	ourselves
you	yourself	you	yourselves
he	himself		
she	herself	they	themselves
it	itself		

USES OF PRONOUNS, continued	EXAMPLES
You can use an **object pronoun** after an **action verb**. You can also use an **object pronoun** after a **preposition**.	The parrots get hungry at 5 o'clock. Janet **feeds** **them** every day. The parrots squawk **at her** to say "thank you." **Object Pronouns** <table><tr><td>Singular</td><td>Plural</td></tr><tr><td>me</td><td>us</td></tr><tr><td>you</td><td>you</td></tr><tr><td>him, her, it</td><td>them</td></tr></table>
A **possessive pronoun** tells who or what owns something. A **possessive pronoun** can refer to the name of an owner. It is sometimes called a **possessive adjective**. A **possessive pronoun** can take the place of a **person's name and what the person owns**.	Janet's posters are about pet care. **Her** posters show what dogs need. Which one is **Janet's poster**? The big one is **hers**.

Possessive Pronouns

Use these pronouns to refer to the name of an owner. These pronouns always come before a noun and act as adjectives.		Use these pronouns to replace a person's name and what the person owns. These pronouns are always used alone.	
Singular	Plural	Singular	Plural
my	our	mine	ours
your	your	yours	yours
his, her, its	their	his, hers, its	theirs

DEMONSTRATIVE PRONOUNS	EXAMPLES
A **demonstrative pronoun** points out a specific noun without naming it.	Look at the puppies. **That** is a cute puppy. **Those** are sleeping. **Demonstrative Pronouns** <table><tr><td></td><td>Singular</td><td>Plural</td></tr><tr><td>Nearby</td><td>this</td><td>these</td></tr><tr><td>Far Away</td><td>that</td><td>those</td></tr></table>

Pronouns, continued

INDEFINITE PRONOUNS	EXAMPLES
When you are not talking about a specific person or thing, use an **indefinite pronoun**.	**Everybody** loves to visit the pet shop. **Something** is happening in the pet shop today.

Some Indefinite Pronouns

These **indefinite pronouns** are always singular and need a **singular verb**.

another	each	everything	nothing
anybody	either	neither	somebody
anyone	everybody	nobody	someone
anything	everyone	no one	something

Examples

Someone is photographing the dogs.
Nobody knows why.

These **indefinite pronouns** are always plural and need a **plural verb**.

both	few	many	several

Several of the dogs **are eating**.
Both of the puppies **have** bones.

These **indefinite pronouns** can be either singular or plural.

all	any	most	none	some

Look at the phrase that follows the pronoun. If the noun in the phrase is plural, use a **plural verb**. If not, use a **singular verb**.

All of the dogs **are barking**.
All of their food **is gone**.

RELATIVE PRONOUNS	EXAMPLES
A **relative pronoun** introduces a **relative clause**. It connects, or relates, the clause to a word in the sentence.	**Some Relative Pronouns** who whose that whom which
Use **who**, **whom**, or **whose** for people.	The man **who photographed the dogs** is a writer.
Use **which** for things.	His book, **which** I have read, shows all kinds of dogs.
Use **that** for people or things.	The writer **that** created the book is famous. The photo **that** I like best in his book was taken in the pet shop.

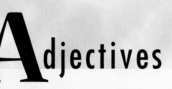djectives

An adjective describes, or modifies, a noun or pronoun.
It can tell what kind, which one, how many, or how much.

DESCRIPTIVE ADJECTIVES	EXAMPLES
An **adjective** can tell what something is like. It can tell the color, size, or shape. It can describe a feeling. An adjective can tell how something sounds, feels, looks, tastes, or smells. An egret	Where can you find **brown** rabbits and **white** egrets? A swamp has **large** and **small** animals like these. The egret has **round** eyes and a **pointed** beak. I feel **happy** when I spend a day in the swamp. I like the **noisy** birds. The egrets are **beautiful**. **Adjectives That Appeal to the Senses** | Hearing	Touch	Sight	Taste	Smell
---	---	---	---	---
crunchy	hard	beautiful	bitter	fishy
noisy	rough	dark	salty	fragrant
quiet	smooth	huge	sour	fresh
soft	wet	shiny	sweet	rotten	
Usually, an **adjective** comes before the noun it describes. *But:* A **predicate adjective** appears in the predicate and still describes the noun or pronoun in the **subject**.	An **old alligator** hides in the **dark mud**. The **alligator** is **powerful**. **It** is **dangerous**, too. An alligator
Sometimes two or more **adjectives** come before a **noun**. Use a comma (**,**) between the adjectives if they both describe the noun.	Alligators walk on **short, strong** legs.
An **adjective** is never plural, even if the **noun** it describes is plural.	Many **hungry birds** look for food near the water. Their **eyes** are **good**, but they don't see the alligator. Soon the **tasty birds** are the alligator's dinner!

Adjectives, continued

DEMONSTRATIVE ADJECTIVES	EXAMPLES
A **demonstrative adjective** points out the noun that follows it. It answers the question "Which one?"	**These** otters are by my boat. **That** otter over there belongs to one of them. **Demonstrative Adjectives** |	Singular	Plural
---	---	---
Nearby	this	these
Far Away	that	those	

NUMBER WORDS	EXAMPLES
Number words are often used as **adjectives**. Sometimes the number word tells the **order** that things are in.	Today in the swamp I saw **one** snake, **two** alligators, and **six** turtles. The **first** day I saw many kinds of birds. The **second** day I saw a lot of alligators. What will I see on the **third** day?

INDEFINITE ADJECTIVES	EXAMPLES
Use an **indefinite adjective** when you are not sure of the exact number. Some indefinite adjectives tell **how many** things there are. Use these adjectives before nouns you can count. Some indefinite adjectives tell **how much** there is of something. Use these adjectives before nouns you cannot count.	I didn't see **much** wildlife on the third day. All I saw were **a few** frogs. **Some Indefinite Adjectives** | To Tell How Many	To Tell How Much
many insects	**much** sunshine
a few insects	**a little** sunshine
some insects	**some** sunshine
several insects	**not much** sunshine
no insects	**no** sunshine	
In a negative sentence, use **any** instead of **some**.	I saw some turtles, too. However, I didn't see ~~some~~ any insects.

PROPER ADJECTIVES	EXAMPLES
A **proper adjective** is formed from a proper noun. It always begins with a <u>capital letter</u>.	There are many swamps in America. The **American** alligator is found in the southeastern United States.

ADJECTIVES THAT COMPARE	EXAMPLES

Adjectives can help you show how things are alike or different.

Use a **comparative adjective** to show how **two** things are alike or different. Add **-er** to most adjectives. Also use **than**. Use **more. . .than** if the adjective has three or more syllables.	Deserts may be small or large. The Sechura Desert in South America is **smaller than** the Sahara Desert in Africa.  Sahara Desert Is the Sechura Desert **more interesting than** the Sahara Desert?
You can use either **-er** or **more** to make a comparison with some two-syllable adjectives. **Be sure not to use both**.	Most desert animals are ~~more~~ livelier at night than during the day. Desert flowers are ~~more~~ prettier than swamp grasses.
Use a **superlative adjective** to compare **three or more** things. Add **-est** to most adjectives. Use **the** before the adjective. Use **the most** with the adjective if it has three or more syllables.	The Sahara Desert is **the largest** desert in the world. The Libyan Desert has **the** world's **highest** record temperature. Both habitats have some of **the most interesting** animals in the world.
Some **adjectives** have **special forms** for comparing things: good bad some little better worse more less best worst most least	Today's weather in the desert is **bad**. Tomorrow's weather will be **worse**. Next week's weather is expected to be **the worst** of the summer.
Use **less** or **the least** to compare things you cannot count. Use **fewer** or **the fewest** to compare things you can count.	Deserts have **less** rainfall than swamps. Deserts have **the least** rainfall of any habitat. Some deserts have **fewer** days of rain than others. Which desert had **the fewest** number of visitors last year?

Verbs

Every sentence is divided into two parts: a subject and a predicate. The verb is the key word in the predicate. A verb tells what a subject does or links words in a sentence.

ACTION VERBS	EXAMPLES
An **action verb** tells what the subject does. Most verbs are action verbs.	The dancers **leap** across the stage. The spotlight **shines** on the lead dancers. Each dancer **twirls** around and around.
Some **action verbs** tell about an action that you cannot see.	The audience **enjoys** the lively music.

Ballet dancer

LINKING VERBS	EXAMPLES
A **linking verb** connects, or links, the subject of a sentence to a word in the predicate.	The dancers **look** powerful.
The word in the predicate can describe the subject.	Their costumes **are** colorful.
Or, the word in the predicate can be another way to name the subject.	These dancers **are** ballerinas.

Linking Verbs

Forms of the Verb *be*
am	was
is	were
are	

Other Linking Verbs
appear	seem	become
feel	smell	taste
look		

HELPING VERBS	EXAMPLES
Some verbs are made up of more than one word. The last word is called the **main verb**. It shows the action. The verb that comes before is the **helping verb**.	Ballet dancers **are regarded** as athletes and storytellers. They **can jump** high into the air. They **might leap** several feet across the stage. They **are building** up muscle strength.

HELPING VERBS, continued	EXAMPLES
The **helping verb** agrees with the subject.	The dancers **have** **practiced** for hours. The exercise **has** **made** them strong.
The word <u>not</u> always comes between the **helping verb** and the main verb.	The dancers **do** <u>not</u> **tell** a story in the usual way.
Other <u>adverbs</u> can come between a **helping verb** and the **main verb,** or appear in other places in the sentence.	They **will** <u>never</u> **use** their voices to tell a story. The story **is** <u>always</u> **told** through their graceful movements. <u>Often</u> slow movements **will** **show** an emotion like sadness. Happiness **is** **shown** <u>best</u> by quick, springy movements.
In questions, the <u>subject</u> comes between the **helping verb** and the **main verb**.	**Have** <u>you</u> **seen** a performance? **Does** <u>your family</u> **enjoy** ballet?

Helping Verbs

Forms of the Verb *be*

am	was
is	were
are	

Forms of the Verb *do*

do	did
does	

Forms of the Verb *have*

have	had
has	

Other Helping Verbs

To express ability:
> I **can** dance.
> I **could** do the jump.

To express possibility:
> I **may** dance tonight.
> I **might** dance tonight.
> Perhaps I **could** do the dance.

To express a need or want:
> I **must** dance more often.
> I **would** like to dance more often.

To express an intent:
> I **will** dance more often.

To express something you ought to do:
> I **should** practice more often.
> I **ought** to practice more often.

Verbs, continued

TRANSITIVE VERBS	EXAMPLES	
Action verbs can be transitive or intransitive. A **transitive verb** needs an **object** to complete its meaning. The object receives the action of the verb.	**Not complete:** Many cities **use**	**Complete:** Many cities **use fireworks**.
	Not complete: Fireworks **make**	**Complete:** Fireworks **make noise**.
	Not complete: They also **provide**	**Complete:** They also **provide** a good **celebration**.
The object can be a **direct object**. A direct object answers one of these questions: • Whom? • What?	The noise **surprises** the **audience**. The people in the audience **cover** their **ears**.	

INTRANSITIVE VERBS	EXAMPLES
An **intransitive verb** does not need an object to complete its meaning.	**Complete:** The people in our neighborhood **cheer**. They **shout**. They **laugh**.
An **intransitive verb** may end the sentence, or it may be followed by other words that tell how, where, or when. These additional words are not objects since they do not receive the action of the verb.	The fireworks **glow** brightly. Then slowly, they **disappear** in the sky. The show **ends** by midnight.

Fireworks

PRESENT TENSE VERBS	EXAMPLES
The tense of a verb shows when an action happens.	
The **present tense** of a verb tells about an action that is happening now.	My mom **looks** at her charts. She **checks** her computer screen.
The **present tense** of a verb can also tell about an action that happens regularly or all the time.	My mom **works** for the local TV station. She **is** a weather forecaster. She **reports** the weather every night at 5 p.m.
The **present progressive** form of a verb tells about an action as it is happening. It uses the helping verb **am**, **is**, or **are** and a main verb. The main verb ends in **-ing**.	Right now, she **is getting** ready for the show. "I can't believe it!" she says. "I **am looking** at the biggest storm of the century!" "**Are** those high winds **traveling** toward the coast?" asks her boss.

PAST TENSE VERBS	EXAMPLES
The **past tense** of a verb tells about an action that happened earlier, or in the past.	Yesterday, my mom **warned** everyone about the hurricane. The storm **moved** over the ocean toward land. We **did** not **know** exactly when it would hit.
The past tense form of a **regular verb** ends with **-ed**. See page 469 for spelling rules.	The shop owners in our town **covered** their windows with wood. We **closed** our shutters and **stayed** inside.
Irregular verbs have **special forms** to show the past tense. See the chart on pages 450–451.	The storm **hit** land. The sky **grew** very dark. It **began** to rain.

Some Irregular Verbs

Present Tense	Past Tense
begin	began
do	did
grow	grew
hit	hit

Verbs, continued

PAST TENSE VERBS, continued	EXAMPLES
The **past progressive** form of a verb tells about an action that was happening over a period of time in the past. It uses the helping verb **was** or **were** and a main verb. The main verb ends in **-ing**.	The wind **was blowing** at high speeds. Our shutters **were** really **shaking** during the storm. **Were** the trees **falling** down?

FUTURE TENSE VERBS	EXAMPLES
The **future tense** of a verb tells about an action that will happen later, or in the future. To show future tense, use: • the helping verb **will** plus a main verb. • the phrase **am going to**, **is going to**, or **are going to** plus a verb.	After the storm, everyone **will come** out of their houses. They **will inspect** the damage. I **am going to take** the tree branches out of my yard. The city **is** not **going to clean** every street. We **are** all **going to help** each other. **Are** you **going to help**?
The **future progressive** form of a verb tells about an action that will be happening during a period of time in the future. It uses the helping verbs **will be** plus a main verb. The main verb ends in **-ing**.	The weather forecasters **will be checking** radar screens for other storms. I **will be living** away from the shore as soon as possible! Wind damage from Hurricane Floyd, 1999

PERFECT TENSE VERBS	EXAMPLES

Verbs in the perfect tenses use the helping verbs *has*, *have*, or *had* and a form of the main verb that is called the *past participle*.

For **regular verbs**, the past tense and the past participle end in **-ed**.

Regular Verb	like	I like the Internet.
Past Tense	liked	I liked the Internet.
Past Participle	liked	I have always liked the Internet.

Irregular verbs have special forms for the past tense and past participle. See pages 450–451.

Irregular Verb	know	I know a lot about the Internet.
Past Tense	knew	I knew very little about the Internet last year.
Past Participle	known	I have known about the Internet for a long time.

Use the **present perfect tense** when you want to tell about: • an action that began in the past and may still be going on. • an action that happened in the past, but you aren't sure of the exact time.	The public **has used** the Internet since the mid-1980s. This year, we **have gone** to many different Web sites. The information on the Internet **has** not **been** hard to find. **Have** you **found** some interesting Web sites?
The **past perfect tense** tells about an action that was completed before some other action in the past.	Before the Web was developed, people **had done** their research in the library. Librarians **had helped** people find information long before the invention of computers.
The **future perfect tense** tells about an action that will be completed at a specific time in the future.	By 2010, researchers **will have started** using a new Internet. By the end of next year, 100,000 people **will have visited** our Web site.
Verbs in the **perfect tenses** can describe ongoing action.	Our school librarian **has been using** the Internet for a long time. She **had been helping** us learn the Internet until last year. By graduation, we **will have been using** the Internet a lot.

Verbs, continued

FORMS OF IRREGULAR VERBS

Irregular Verb	Past Tense	Past Participle	Irregular Verb	Past Tense	Past Participle
be: am, is	was	been	eat	ate	eaten
are	were	been	fall	fell	fallen
beat	beat	beaten	feed	fed	fed
become	became	become	feel	felt	felt
begin	began	begun	fight	fought	fought
bend	bent	bent	find	found	found
bind	bound	bound	fly	flew	flown
bite	bit	bitten	forget	forgot	forgotten
blow	blew	blown	freeze	froze	frozen
break	broke	broken	get	got	got, gotten
bring	brought	brought			
build	built	built	give	gave	given
burst	burst	burst	go	went	gone
buy	bought	bought	grow	grew	grown
catch	caught	caught	have	had	had
choose	chose	chosen	hear	heard	heard
come	came	come	hide	hid	hidden
cost	cost	cost	hit	hit	hit
creep	crept	crept	hold	held	held
cut	cut	cut	hurt	hurt	hurt
dig	dug	dug	keep	kept	kept
do	did	done	know	knew	known
draw	drew	drawn	lay	laid	laid
dream	dreamed, dreamt	dreamed, dreamt	lead	led	led
			leave	left	left
drink	drank	drunk	lend	lent	lent
drive	drove	driven	let	let	let

FORMS OF IRREGULAR VERBS, continued

Irregular Verb	Past Tense	Past Participle	Irregular Verb	Past Tense	Past Participle
lie	lay	lain	sink	sank	sunk
light	lit	lit	sit	sat	sat
lose	lost	lost	sleep	slept	slept
make	made	made	slide	slid	slid
mean	meant	meant	speak	spoke	spoken
meet	met	met	spend	spent	spent
pay	paid	paid	stand	stood	stood
prove	proved	proved, proven	steal	stole	stolen
			stick	stuck	stuck
put	put	put	sting	stung	stung
quit	quit	quit	strike	struck	struck
read	read	read	swear	swore	sworn
ride	rode	ridden	swim	swam	swum
ring	rang	rung	swing	swung	swung
rise	rose	risen	take	took	taken
run	ran	run	teach	taught	taught
say	said	said	tear	tore	torn
see	saw	seen	tell	told	told
seek	sought	sought	think	thought	thought
sell	sold	sold	throw	threw	thrown
send	sent	sent	understand	understood	understood
set	set	set	wake	woke, waked	woken, waked
shake	shook	shaken			
show	showed	shown	wear	wore	worn
shrink	shrank	shrunk	weep	wept	wept
shut	shut	shut	win	won	won
sing	sang	sung	write	wrote	written

Verbs, continued

TWO-WORD VERBS	EXAMPLES
A **two-word verb** is a verb followed by a preposition.	I like to **call** you, but you never answer me.
	The coach **calls off** the game because of the rain.
The meaning of the two-word verb is different from the meaning of the verb by itself.	The workers **call for** higher pay.

Some Two-Word Verbs

Verb	Meaning	Example
break	to split into pieces	I didn't **break** the window with the ball.
break down	to stop working	Did the car **break down** again?
break up	to end	The party will **break up** before midnight.
	to come apart	The ice on the lake will **break up** in the spring.
bring	to carry something with you	**Bring** your book to class.
bring up	to suggest	She **brings up** good ideas at every meeting.
	to raise children	**Bring up** your children to be good citizens.
check	to make sure you are right	We can **check** our answers at the back of the book.
check in	to stay in touch with someone	I **check in** with my mom at work.
check up	to see if everything is okay	The nurse **checks up** on the patient every hour.
check off	to mark off a list	Look at your list and **check off** the girls' names.
check out	to look at something carefully	Hey, Marisa, **check out** my new bike!
fill	to put as much as possible into a container or space	**Fill** the pail with water.
fill in	to color or shade in a space	Please **fill in** the circle.
fill out	to complete	Marcos **fills out** a form to order a book.
get	to go after something	I'll **get** some milk at the store.
	to receive	I often **get** letters from my pen pal.
get ahead	to go beyond what is expected of you	She worked hard to **get ahead** in math class.
get along	to be on good terms with	Do you **get along** with your sister?
get out	to leave	Let's **get out** of the kitchen.
get over	to feel better	I hope you'll **get over** the flu soon.
get through	to finish	I can **get through** this book tonight.

Some Two-Word Verbs

Verb	Meaning	Example
give	to hand something to someone	We **give** presents to the new baby.
give out	to stop working	If she runs ten miles, her energy will **give out**.
give up	to quit	I'm going to **give up** eating candy.
go	to move from place to place	Did you **go** to the mall on Saturday?
go on	to continue	Why do the boys **go on** playing after the bell rings?
go out	to go someplace special	Let's **go out** to lunch on Saturday.
look	to see or watch	Don't **look** directly at the sun.
look forward	to be excited about something that will happen	My brothers **look forward** to summer vacation.
look over	to review	She always **looks over** her answers before she gives the teacher her test.
look up	to hunt for and find	We **look up** information on the Internet.
pick	to choose	I'd **pick** Lin for class president.
pick on	to bother or tease	My older brothers always **pick on** me.
pick up	to go faster	Business **picks up** in the summer.
	to gather or collect	**Pick up** your clothes!
run	to move quickly on foot	Juan will **run** in a marathon.
run into	to see someone you know unexpectedly	Did you **run into** Chris at the store?
run out	to suddenly have nothing left	The cafeteria always **runs out** of nachos.
stand	to be in a straight up-and-down position	I have to **stand** in line to buy tickets.
stand for	to represent	A heart **stands for** love.
stand out	to be easier to see	You'll really **stand out** with that orange cap.
turn	to change direction	We **turn** right at the next corner.
turn up	to appear	Clean your closet and your belt will **turn up**.
	to raise the volume	Please **turn up** the radio.
turn in	to go to bed	On school nights I **turn in** at 9:30.
	to give back	You didn't **turn in** the homework yesterday.
turn off	to make something stop	Please **turn off** the radio.

Verbs, continued

ACTIVE AND PASSIVE VERBS	EXAMPLES
A verb is **active** if the **subject** is doing the action.	In this sentence, the subject—Mr. Ingram—does the selling: **Mr. Ingram** **sold** hamburgers for a nickel in 1921.
A verb is **passive** if the **subject** is not doing the action.	In this sentence, Mr. Ingram still does the selling, but he is not the subject. He is named after the word **by**. **Hamburgers** **were sold** by Mr. Ingram for a nickel in 1921. Sometimes the person or thing doing the action may not be named. **Hamburgers** **were sold** for a nickel in 1921.

VERBALS	EXAMPLES
	A verbal is a word made from a verb but used as another part of speech.
An **infinitive** is a verb form that begins with **to**. It can be used as a noun, an adjective, or an adverb.	Mr. Ingram liked **to cook**. *noun* When you go to the hamburger stand, Mr. Ingram is the man **to see**. *adjective* Mr. Ingram cooks **to have** fun. *adverb*
A **gerund** is a verb form that ends in **-ing**. It is used as a noun. It can be the subject of a sentence, the object of a verb, or the object of a preposition.	**Cooking** was Mr. Ingram's best talent. *subject* Mr. Ingram enjoys **cooking**. *object of the verb* Mr. Ingram was very talented at **cooking**. *object of the preposition*
A **participle** is a verb form that is used as an adjective. It ends in **-ing** or **-ed**.	His **sizzling** hamburgers smelled good. He made them from **flattened** meatballs.
A **participle** can start a **phrase**. Be sure to place the phrase next to the noun it describes.	**Standing** by the grill, Mr. Ingram cooked the hamburgers. ***Not:*** Mr. Ingram cooked the hamburgers, **standing** by the grill.

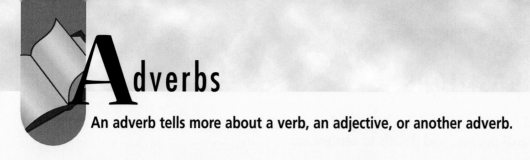

Adverbs

An adverb tells more about a verb, an adjective, or another adverb.

USE OF ADVERBS	EXAMPLES
An **adverb** can tell about a **verb**. It can come before or after the verb.	Our team **always wins** our basketball games. The whole team **plays well**.
An **adverb** can make an **adjective** or another **adverb** stronger.	Gina is **really good** at basketball. She plays **extremely well**.

TYPES OF ADVERBS	EXAMPLES
Adverbs answer one of the following questions: • How? • Where? • When? • How much? or How often?	Gina **carefully** aims the ball. She tosses the ball **high**, but it misses the basket. She will try again **later**. She **usually** scores.

ADVERBS THAT COMPARE	EXAMPLES
Some **adverbs** compare actions. Add **-er** to compare two actions. Add **-est** to compare three or more actions.	Gina runs **fast**. Gina runs **faster** than her guard. Gina runs **the fastest** of all the players.
If the **adverb** ends in **-ly**, use **more** or **less** to compare two actions. Use **the most** or **the least** to compare three or more actions.	Gina aims **more carefully** than Jen. Jen aims **less carefully** than Gina. Gina aims **the most carefully** of all the players on her team. Jen aims **the least carefully** of all.
Be careful not to use an adjective when you need an adverb. Never use an adverb after a **linking verb**.	Everyone plays ~~fair~~ *fairly*. My teacher is ~~fairly~~.

Prepositions

A preposition comes at the beginning of a prepositional phrase.
Prepositional phrases add details to sentences.

USES OF PREPOSITIONS	EXAMPLES
Some **prepositions** show location.	The Chávez Community Center is **by my house**. The pool is **behind the building**.
Some **prepositions** show time.	The Youth Club's party will start **after lunch**.
Some **prepositions** show direction.	Go **through the building** and **around the fountain** to get to the pool. The snack bar is **down the hall**.
Some **prepositions** have multiple uses.	We'll make new friends **at the party**. Meet me **at my house**. Come **at noon**.

PREPOSITIONAL PHRASES	EXAMPLES
A **prepositional phrase** starts with a **preposition** and ends with a noun or a pronoun. It includes all the words in between. The noun or pronoun is the **object of the preposition**.	I made a new friend **at the party**. Next week I'm going to the movies **with her**.

Some Prepositions

Location		Time	Direction	Other Prepositions	
above	near	after	across	about	for
behind	next to	before	around	against	from
below	off	during	down	along	of
beside	on	till	into	among	to
between	out	until	out of	as	with
by	outside		through	at	without
in	over		toward	except	
inside	under		up		

Conjunctions and Interjections

A conjunction connects words or groups of words.
An interjection expresses strong feeling.

CONJUNCTIONS	EXAMPLES
A **coordinating conjunction** connects words, phrases, or clauses.	The zoos in San Diego **and** Atlanta have giant pandas. In China, giant pandas can be found in the wild **or** in panda reserves. Pandas will eat other animals, **but** mostly they eat bamboo. **Coordinating Conjunctions** Conjunctions — Uses **and** — To connect two ideas that are alike **but, yet** — To show a difference between two ideas **nor** — To put two negative ideas together **or** — To show a choice between two ideas **so, for** — To show how one idea follows another
Correlative conjunctions are used in pairs. The pair connects phrases or words.	In the past, pandas lived **not only** in central China **but also** in southern China and Vietnam. Now **both** the giant panda **and** the red panda are rare. **Either** a survey of wild pandas **or** protection of their habitat could help save the pandas. **Some Correlative Conjunctions** both . . . and either . . . or neither . . . nor not only . . . but also whether . . . or

Conjunctions and Interjections, continued

CONJUNCTIONS, continued	EXAMPLES
A **subordinating conjunction** introduces a **dependent clause** in a complex sentence. It connects the **dependent clause** to the main clause.	Pandas can't find enough bamboo to eat **because their habitat is being destroyed**. **If all the bamboo is wiped out**, the pandas will die. **Some Subordinating Conjunctions** after before till although if until as in order that when as if since where as long as so that while because though
A **conjunctive adverb** joins two independent clauses. Use a semicolon before the conjunction and a comma after it.	Pandas do not easily digest plants; **therefore,** they need to eat large amounts of bamboo. China has set aside bamboo-rich reserves for pandas; **however,** these reserves have not always supplied enough food for the pandas. **Some Conjunctive Adverbs** besides meanwhile then consequently moreover therefore however nevertheless thus

INTERJECTIONS	EXAMPLES
An **interjection** is a word or phrase that shows strong feeling. An exclamation mark follows an interjection that stands alone.	**Help!** **Ouch!** **Oops!** **Oh boy!** **Oh my!** **Wow!**
An interjection used in a sentence can be followed by a comma or an exclamation mark.	**Oh**, it's a baby panda! **Hooray!** The baby panda has survived!

Capital Letters

A reader can tell that a word is special in some way if it begins with a capital letter.

PROPER NOUNS	EXAMPLES

A common noun names any person, place, thing, or idea.
A proper noun names one particular person, place, thing, or idea.

All the important words in a **proper noun** start with a capital letter.

	Common Noun	Proper Noun
Person	captain	**C**aptain **M**eriwether **L**ewis
Place	land	**L**ouisiana **T**erritory
Thing	team	**C**orps of **D**iscovery
Idea	destiny	**M**anifest **D**estiny

Proper nouns include:

- names of people and their titles

Laura Roberts
Captain Meriwether Lewis

But: *Do not capitalize a title if it is used without a name:*

The captain's co-leader on the expedition was William Clark.

- abbreviations of titles

Mr. Ramos
Mrs. Ramos
Dr. Schuyler
Ms. Nguyen

Abbreviations of Titles

Capt. for the captain of a boat or in the armed forces
Pres. for the president of a country, a company, a club, or an organization
Sen. for a member of the U.S. Senate
Rep. for a member of the U.S. House of Representatives

- words like **Mom** and **Dad** when they are used as names

"**Mom**, can you tell me more about the expedition?" said Laura.

But: *Do not capitalize names if they follow a word like* my.

I ask my **mom** lots of questions.

- organizations

United Nations   Science Club   Wildlife Society   Lodi City Council

- names of languages, subject areas, and religions

Spanish   Mathematics   Buddhism
Vietnamese   Social Studies   Christianity

Capital Letters, continued

PROPER NOUNS, continued	EXAMPLES

- names of geographic places

Cities and States
Dallas, Texas
Miami, Florida
St. Louis, Missouri

Countries
Iran
Ecuador
Cambodia

Continents
Asia
South America
Africa

Streets and Roads
King Boulevard
Main Avenue
First Street

Landforms
Rocky Mountains
Sahara Desert
Grand Canyon

Public Spaces
Hemisfair Plaza
Central Park
Muir Camp

Bodies of Water
Yellowstone River
Pacific Ocean
Great Salt Lake
Gulf of Mexico

Buildings, Ships, and Monuments
Empire State Building
Titanic
Statue of Liberty

Planets and Heavenly Bodies
Earth
Jupiter
Milky Way

- abbreviations of geographic places

Words Used in Addresses

Avenue	Ave.	Highway	Hwy.	South	S.
Boulevard	Blvd.	Lane	Ln.	Square	Sq.
Court	Ct.	North	N.	Street	St.
Drive	Dr.	Place	Pl.	West	W.
East	E.	Road	Rd.		

Abbreviations for State Names in Mailing Addresses

Alabama	AL	Hawaii	HI	Massachusetts	MA	New Mexico	NM	South Dakota	SD
Alaska	AK	Idaho	ID	Michigan	MI	New York	NY	Tennessee	TN
Arizona	AZ	Illinois	IL	Minnesota	MN	North Carolina	NC	Texas	TX
Arkansas	AR	Indiana	IN	Mississippi	MS	North Dakota	ND	Utah	UT
California	CA	Iowa	IA	Missouri	MO	Ohio	OH	Vermont	VT
Colorado	CO	Kansas	KS	Montana	MT	Oklahoma	OK	Virginia	VA
Connecticut	CT	Kentucky	KY	Nebraska	NE	Oregon	OR	Washington	WA
Delaware	DE	Louisiana	LA	Nevada	NV	Pennsylvania	PA	West Virginia	WV
Florida	FL	Maine	ME	New Hampshire	NH	Rhode Island	RI	Wisconsin	WI
Georgia	GA	Maryland	MD	New Jersey	NJ	South Carolina	SC	Wyoming	WY

- months, days, special days and holidays

January	July	Sunday	New Year's Day
February	August	Monday	Mother's Day
March	September	Tuesday	Thanksgiving
April	October	Wednesday	Hanukkah
May	November	Thursday	Kwanzaa
June	December	Friday	
		Saturday	

PROPER ADJECTIVES	EXAMPLES
A **proper adjective** is formed from a **proper noun**. Capitalize proper adjectives.	Napoleon Bonaparte was from **Europe**. He was a **European** leader in the 1800s. Napoleon ruled the country of **France**. He was the **French** emperor.

IN LETTERS	EXAMPLES

Capitalize the first word used in the **greeting** or in the **closing** of a letter.
 	
Street, city, and state names in the address, as well as their abbreviations, are also capitalized.
	Dear Kim,
	    I wish you could explore the Academy of Natural Sciences with me. I've learned so much about the flora and fauna that Lewis and Clark found. The museum even has some of the original samples! I'll tell you about it when I get home. See you soon.
	
	                Your friend,
	                Jamal
	
	Kim Messina
	10250 W. Fourth St.
	Las Vegas, NV 89015

IN TITLES AND QUOTATIONS	EXAMPLES
Capitalize the **first word** in a **direct quotation**.	Clark said, "**There is great joy in camp.**" "**We are in view of the ocean**," he said "**It's the Pacific Ocean**," he added. "**We are finally here.**"
All important words in a **title** begin with a capital letter. Short words like *a, an, the, in, at, of,* and *for* are not capitalized unless they are the first or last word in the title.	**book:** *The Longest Journey* **poem:** "Leaves of Grass" **magazine:** *Flora and Fauna of Arizona* **newspaper:** *The Denver Post* **song:** "The Star-Spangled Banner" **game:** Exploration! **TV series:** "Bonanza" **movie:** *The Lion King*

Punctuation Marks

Punctuation marks make words and sentences easier to understand.

PERIOD	EXAMPLES
Use a **period**:	
• at the end of a statement or a polite command	Georgia read the paper to her mom.
	Tell me if there are any interesting articles.
• after an abbreviation	There's a new restaurant on Stone St. near our house.
	It opens at 10 a.m. today.
	But: *Do not use a period in an acronym:*
	National Aeronautics and Space Administration **NASA**
	Do not use a period in the abbreviation of a state name written in a mailing address:
	Massachusetts **MA** Illinois **IL** Texas **TX** California **CA** Florida **FL** Virginia **VA**
• after an initial	The owner is J.J. Malone.
• to separate dollars and cents. The period is the decimal point.	The article says lunch today costs only $1.50.
• in an Internet address. The period is called a dot.	The restaurant has a Web site at www.jjmalone.org.

QUESTION MARK	EXAMPLES
Use a **question mark**:	
• at the end of a question	What kind of food do they serve**?**
• after a question that comes at the end of a statement	The food is good, isn't it**?**
	But: *Use a period after an indirect question. In an indirect question, you tell about a question you asked.*
	I asked how good the food could be for only $1.50.

EXCLAMATION MARK	EXAMPLES
Use an **exclamation mark**: • after an interjection • at the end of a sentence to show that you feel strongly about something	Wow**!** One-fifty is a really good price**!**

COMMA	EXAMPLES
Use a **comma**: • to separate three or more items in a series	Articles about the school**,** a big sale**,** and a new movie were also in the newspaper. The school will buy a new bus**,** 10 computers**,** and books for the library.
• when you write a number with four or more digits	There was $500**,**000 in the school budget.
• before the **coordinating conjunction** in a compound sentence. See page 457 for a list of coordinating conjunctions.	The school could buy books**, or** it could buy a sound system. All the teachers discussed it**, and** they decided books were more important.
• to set off a short word or phrase at the beginning of a sentence	Good**,** we really need some new books.
• to set off words that interrupt a sentence	Books about geography**,** for example**,** would be great additions to the library.
• before a question at the end of a statement	We need books on that topic**,** don't we?
• to set off the name of a person someone is talking to	Georgia**,** does the article say why the school is buying a new bus? Just a minute, Mom**,** let me look.
• between two or more adjectives that tell about the same noun	The old**,** rusty school bus is broken.

Punctuation Marks, continued

COMMA, continued	EXAMPLES
Use a **comma**:	
• before and after an appositive phrase. An **appositive phrase** renames the noun or pronoun before it.	Mr. Ivanovich, **the bus driver,** says the bus will cost too much to fix.
• after a long **introductory phrase**	**In the last few months,** the bus had to be fixed six times.
• after an **introductory clause**	**Because the bus is old,** it keeps breaking down.
• before someone's exact words	Mr. Ivanovich said, "It is time for a new bus!"
• after someone's exact words if the sentence continues	"I agree," said the principal.
• before and after a **clause** if the clause is not necessary for understanding the sentence	At the end of the article, **where computers are discussed,** there is a letter by a student.
Use a **comma** in these places in a letter: • between the city and the state • between the date and the year • after the greeting • after the closing	144 North Ave. Milpas, AK July 3, 2002 Dear Mr. Okada, I really like computers and am glad that we have them at school, but ours are out-of-date. As principal, can you ask the school board to buy us new ones for next year? Sincerely, Patrick Green

SEMICOLON	EXAMPLES
Use a **semicolon**:	
• to separate two simple sentences used together without a conjunction	Some movies advertised in this paper look interesting; others don't.
• before a conjunctive adverb that joins two simple sentences. Use a **comma** after the adverb. See page 458 for a list of conjunctive adverbs.	I'd like to go to the movies today; however, my favorite store is having a sale.
• to separate a group of words in a series if the words in the series already have commas	It is selling warm, fluffy coats; green, red, and orange mittens; and summer shorts!

APOSTROPHE	EXAMPLES
Use an **apostrophe** when you write a **possessive noun**.	

• If there is one owner, add **'s** to the owner's name.	The **newspaper's** ads for yard sales are interesting, too.
	But: *If the owner's name ends in* s, *you can add* **'s** *or just the apostrophe. Either is correct.*
	    Mrs. **Ramos's** chair is for sale.
	    Mrs. **Ramos'** chair is for sale.

• If there is more than one owner, add **'** after the **s**.	The **Martins'** dog had puppies, and I want to buy one. ***But:*** *If the plural noun that names the owners does not end in* s, *add* **'s**. The **Children's** Choir is holding a yard sale.

	EXAMPLES	
Use an **apostrophe** to replace the letters left out in a **contraction**.		***Exceptions:***
• In contractions with a verb and **not**, the word **not** is usually shortened to **n't**.	could not I **couldn't** go to the yard sale. couldn't	cannot can't will not won't I am not I'm not
• In many other contractions, the verb is shortened.	I would **I'd** like to see the vase you bought. I'd	

Punctuation Marks, continued

QUOTATION MARKS	EXAMPLES
Use **quotation marks** to show:	
• a speaker's exact words	**"**Listen to this!**"** Georgia said.
• the exact words quoted from a book or other printed material	The announcement in the paper was **"**The world-famous writer Josie Ramón will be at Milpas Library Friday night.**"**
• the title of a song, poem, or short story	Her poem **"**Speaking**"** is famous.
• the title of a magazine article or newspaper article	It appeared in the magazine article **"**How to Talk to Your Teen.**"**
• the title of a chapter from a book	On Friday night she'll be reading **"**Getting Along,**"** a chapter from her new book.
• words used in a special way	We will be **"**all ears**"** at the reading.
Always put **periods** and **commas** inside quotation marks.	"She is such a great writer**,"** Georgia said. " I'd love to meet her**."**

COLON	EXAMPLES
Use a **colon**:	
• after the greeting in a business letter	
• to separate hours and minutes	
• to start a list	

356 Oak St.
Milpas, AK
Sept. 24, 2002

Features Editor
Milpas Post
78 Main St.
Milpas, AK

Dear Sir or Madam**:**

Please place this announcement in the calendar section of your paper. Friday at 7**:**15 p.m., the writer Josie Ramón will be speaking at Milpas Library. When people come, they should bring**:**

1. Questions for Ms. Ramón.
2. Money to purchase her new book.
3. A cushion to sit on!

Thank you.

Sincerely,

Hector Quintana

DASH	EXAMPLES
Use a **dash** to: • show a break in an idea or the tone in a sentence • emphasize a word, a series of words, a phrase, or a clause	It's so helpful to read the paper—I really like the ads—to find out what is happening in town. There's so much information here—restaurant openings, store sales, news stories about people in our town.

PARENTHESES	EXAMPLES
Use **parentheses** around extra information in a sentence.	This news story (written by my mom) is very interesting!

HYPHEN	EXAMPLES
Use a **hyphen** to: • connect words in a number and in a fraction • join some words to make a compound word • connect a letter to a word • divide words at the end of a line. Always divide the word between two syllables.	The news story reported on a survey of **seventy-five** people. **One-third** of them wasted water everyday. A **15-year-old** boy and his **great-grandmother** have started an awareness campaign. They have sent **e-mail** messages to everyone they know. They also designed a **T-shirt** for their campaign. Please join us in our aware-ness campaign.

ITALICS AND UNDERLINES	EXAMPLES
When you are using a computer, use **italics** for the names of: • magazines and newspapers • books • plays, movies, musicals, music albums, and TV series When you write by hand, use an **underline** to indicate italics.	I just read an article about a good book in the *Milpas Post*. The name of the book is *My Hopes and Dreams*. The article said the new movie *All About Jack* is based on this book. The Milpas Post gave that new movie, All About Jack, a great review.

Spelling

Follow these rules and your spelling will get better and better.

HOW TO BE A BETTER SPELLER

Spelling Tips

1. To learn a new word:
- Study the word and look up its meaning.
- Say the word out loud. Listen as you repeat it again.
- Picture how the word looks.
- Spell the word out loud several times.
- Write the word five or ten times for practice. Try to use the word often in a sentence until you are sure you know its spelling.

2. Learn the following spelling rules.

3. Use a dictionary to check your spelling.

4. Keep a notebook of words that are hard for you to spell.

Q + U	EXAMPLES
Always put a **u** after a **q**.	The **qu**ick but **qu**iet **qu**arterback asked **qu**antities of **qu**estions. ***Exceptions:*** Iraq Iraqi

IE, EI	EXAMPLES
Use **i** before **e** except after **c**.	The f**ie**rce rec**ei**ver was always ready to catch the ball. ***Exceptions:*** • **ei**ther, h**ei**ght, th**ei**r, w**ei**rd, s**ei**ze • w**ei**gh, n**ei**ghbor (and other words where **ei** has the long **a** sound)

PLURALS	EXAMPLES
To form the plural of a noun that ends in **x**, **ch**, **sh**, **s**, or **z**, add **-es**. For most other nouns, just add **-s**.	Their team was called the Fox**es**. Their players made great catch**es** in the end zone.

Y TO I	EXAMPLES
If a word ends in a consonant plus **y**, change the **y** to **i** before you add **-es**, **-ed**, **-er**, or **-est**.	The coach was the happ**iest** when his players tr**ied** their best.
For words that end in a **vowel** plus **y**, just add **-s** or **-ed**.	For five day**s** before the game, the team stay**ed** at practice an extra 30 minutes.
If you add **-ing** to a verb that ends in **-y**, do not change the **y** to **i**.	The players learned a lot from study**ing** videos of their games.

-ED, -ING, -ER, -EST	EXAMPLES
When a word ends in silent **e**, drop the **e** before you add **-ed**, **-ing**, **-er**, or **-est**.	The players notic**ed** what they did wrong. Lat**er**, they talked about their mistakes.
When a one-syllable word ends in one vowel and one consonant, double the final consonant before you add an ending.	Then they pla**nn**ed some new plays for the game. They got set for their **big**g**est** challenge.

PREFIXES AND SUFFIXES	EXAMPLES	
Add a **prefix** to the beginning of a root word. Do not change the spelling of the **root word**.	They **re**played the video often. The team never got **dis**couraged.	**Some Prefixes and Suffixes**
When you add a consonant **suffix**, do not change the spelling of the **root word**.	We had a **love**ly day for the game. *Exception:* happy happiness	Prefixes anti- in- pre- bi- im- re- dis- inter- sub- extra- mis- un- Suffixes Beginning with a Consonant -ful -ly -ness -less -ment -tion
For most **root words** that end in silent **e**, drop the **e** before adding a vowel **suffix**.	Our quarterback won the Most **Valu**able Player award for the game.	Suffixes Beginning with a Vowel -able -ent -ish -al -er -ive -ant -ible -ous

Glossary of Literary Terms

Action/Reaction Action/reaction is the connection between one action or event and another that occurs as a result.

> *See also* **Characterization**

Advertisement An advertisement is a public notice of something that is for sale. It generally uses persuasive techniques.

> *See also* **Persuasion**

Alliteration Alliteration is the repetition of the same or similar consonant sounds at the beginning of words. An example from "Human Family" is

> I've <u>s</u>ailed upon the <u>s</u>even <u>s</u>eas
> and <u>s</u>topped in every land

> *See also* **Assonance; Consonance**

Article An article is a short piece of nonfiction writing on a specific topic. Articles usually appear in newspapers and magazines.

> Examples: **"Twins," "Saving the Peregrine Falcon"**

Assonance Assonance is the repetition of the same or similar vowel sounds between different consonants in words that are close together. An example is the recurring long *e* sound in this line from "Old Man Mangrove":

> All year long he
> Drops gr<u>ee</u>n l<u>ea</u>ves

> *See also* **Alliteration; Consonance**

Autobiography An autobiography is the story of a person's life written by that person.

> Example: **"The Circuit"**

Biographical Fiction Biographical fiction is a story that tells the facts of a real person's life and includes fictional details as well. It may be written from the point of view of a real or an imaginary character; the conversations are usually invented.

Biography A biography is the story of a person's life written by another person.

> Example: **"Anne Frank," "Teammates"**

Cause and Effect Cause and effect is the relationship between two events. The one that happens first, the cause, brings about the effect that follows. This sentence from "The Great Migration" is an example of cause and effect:

> Many northern workers were angry because they had to compete with migrants for housing and jobs.

Chant A chant is a type of poetry that is meant to be read aloud. It has a strong beat and musical language.

Character A person, animal, or imaginary creature in a story is called a character.

> *See also* **Characterization; Character Traits**

Characterization Characterization is the way a writer creates and develops a character. Writers use a variety of ways to bring a character to life: through descriptions of the character's appearance, thoughts, feelings, and actions; through the character's words; through the words or thoughts of other characters.

> *See also* **Character Traits; Motive; Point of View**

Character Sketch A character sketch is a short, vivid description of a person.

> *See also* **Characterization; Character Traits**

Character Traits Character traits are the special qualities of personality that writers give their characters.

> *See also* **Character; Characterization**

Climax The climax of a story or play is the turning point or most important event. At the climax, the resolution of the story is in sight. For example, in "The Mother Who Lost Her Daughter," the climax occurs when Zeus tells Hades that he must return Persephone to her mother for part of the year.

> *See also* **Plot**

Complication Complication is part of the plot. It includes the events in a story that make it difficult for characters to solve problems.

> *See also* **Conflict and Resolution; Plot;**
> **Rising Action and Falling Action**

Compressed Language Compressed language is the use of only a few words to convey a great deal of meaning. Poets often use compressed language.

Conflict and Resolution Conflict and resolution are parts of the plot of a story. Conflict describes the problem a character has, and resolution tells how or if the problem is solved.

> *See also* **Plot**

Consonance Consonance is the repetition of the final consonant sound preceded by different vowels. An example of consonance is *clip clop*.

> *See also* **Alliteration; Assonance**

Description A description is writing that tells about a person, place, or thing. It often uses images that appeal to the five senses: sight, sound, touch, smell, and taste. An example from "Amir" is

> When I saw the garden for the first time, so green among the dark brick buildings, I thought back to my parents' Persian rug. It showed climbing vines, rivers and waterfalls, grapes, flower beds, singing birds, everything a desert dweller might want. The garden's green was as soothing to the eye as the deep blue of that rug.

Dialogue Dialogue is what characters say to one another. Writers use dialogue to develop characters, move the plot forward, and add interest. In most writing, dialogue is set off by quotation marks; in play scripts, however, dialogue appears without quotation marks.

Diary A diary is a book written by a person about his or her own life as it is happening. It is made up of entries that are written shortly after the events occur. The writer of a diary often expresses feelings and opinions about what has happened.

> Example: **"The Diary of a Young Girl"**

Essay An essay is a short piece of nonfiction writing that deals with a single subject. Its purpose may be to inform, to entertain, or to persuade.

> Example: **"Talking Walls"**

Exaggeration Exaggeration is saying that something is bigger or more important than it actually is.

> *See also* **Hyperbole**

Glossary of Literary Terms, continued

Fable A fable is a short story that teaches a lesson about life. Many fables have animals instead of humans as characters. Fables often state the lesson they are teaching at the end.

Family History A family history is a record that includes important information about your ancestors and the people now in your family. It tells how family members are related and describes important events such as births, weddings, and deaths.

Example: **"The Keeping Quilt"**

Fantasy Fantasy is writing that includes unreal or magical characters and events. Fairy tales, science fiction, and fables are examples of fantasy.

See also **Science Fiction**

Fiction Fiction is writing that is made up by the writer. The events and characters may be based in part on reality, as in biographical, historical, or realistic fiction; or they may be made up entirely. Fiction includes novels and short stories.

Examples: **"Amir," "A House of My Own"**

Figurative Language Figurative language is the use of words or phrases to express something different than their usual meanings. Writers use figurative language to say things in vivid and imaginative ways, but what they say is not really true. Hyperbole, imagery, metaphor, personification, and simile are examples of figurative language.

See also **Hyperbole; Imagery; Metaphor; Personification; Simile**

Flashback A flashback is an interruption in the action of a story to tell about something that happened earlier. It is often used to give the reader background information about a character or situation.

Folk Tale A folk tale is a very old and simple story that has been passed down through the years. Most folk tales were told for generations before they were written down.

Example: **"The Clever Wife"**

Foreshadowing Foreshadowing is a hint that an author gives about an event that will happen later in a story.

Free Verse Free verse is poetry with lines that do not have regular rhyme and regular rhythm. Free verse often sounds like ordinary speech.

Examples: **"Chrysalis Diary," "Mother to Son"**

See also **Poetry; Rhyme; Rhythm**

Genre Genre is a kind or type of literature. The four main genres are fiction, nonfiction, poetry, and drama.

Goal and Outcome Goal and outcome are the parts of the plot that tell what a character's ambition is and whether he or she attains it.

See also **Plot**

Historical Fiction Historical fiction is a story based on events that actually happened or people who actually lived. It may be written from the point of view of a real or an imaginary character, and it usually includes invented dialogue.

Example: **"Ginger for the Heart"**

How-to Article A how-to article is a short piece of writing that gives step-by-step directions for making or doing something.

Example: **"Starting a Community Garden"**

Hyperbole Hyperbole is extreme exaggeration for the purpose of emphasis or humor. The line "Check out this twenty-foot trout" from "Big Eaters" is an example of hyperbole.

See also **Exaggeration**

Imagery Imagery is the use of words and phrases that create mental pictures in readers' minds. It helps readers imagine how things look, sound, taste, smell, and feel. Because it appeals to the five senses, it is sometimes called sensory language.

See also **Figurative Language**

Interview An interview is a meeting between two people in which one person asks questions of the other one.

Example: **"An Interview with Poet Gary Soto,"** from **"The Power of Poetry"**

Journal A journal is a personal record. It may include accounts of events, stories, poems, sketches, thoughts, essays, interesting information one has collected, or just about anything the journal writer wishes to include. It is similar to a diary.

Legend A legend is a traditional story about a famous person or event. The subject of a legend can be a real or a make-believe person. Legends often contain elements of fantasy and usually exaggerate the subject's personal qualities or accomplishments.

Letter A letter is a message written and sent from one person to another. Letters can be personal and private, or public, as a letter to the editor of a newspaper is.

Metaphor A metaphor is a kind of figurative language that compares two unlike things by saying that one thing is the other thing. An example from "The Clever Wife" is

. . . the magistrate's eyebrows . . .
became flying birds of astonishment.

See also **Figurative Language; Simile**

Meter Meter is a pattern of stressed and unstressed syllables in poetry.

See also **Rhythm**

Mood and Tone Mood is the overall feeling that a piece of writing gives to the reader. For example, the mood in the poem "Big Eaters" is playful. Tone is the author's attitude toward what he or she wrote. The tone of "Big Eaters" is mildly annoyed.

Motive A motive is the reason a character has for his or her thoughts, feelings, actions, or words. For example, in "The Clever Goatherd," Manuel tells his story because he wants to marry the king's daughter.

See also **Characterization**

Myth A myth is a very old story that explains something about the world. Myths often involve gods, goddesses, and other superhuman characters.

Example: **"The Mother Who Lost Her Daughter"**

Narrative Poetry Narrative poetry is poetry that tells a story. It has characters, a setting, and a plot; it may include elements of poetry such as rhythm and rhyme.

See also **Poetry**

Glossary of Literary Terms, continued

Nonfiction Nonfiction is writing that tells about real people, real places, and real events.

> Examples: **"Teammates," "The Great Migration," "The Big Blast"**

Onomatopoeia Onomatopoeia is the use of words that imitate the sounds associated with the things they describe. *Buzz*, for the sound of a bee; *hiss*, for the sound of a snake; and *gurgle*, for the sound of a stream are examples of onomatopoeia.

Pantomime Pantomime is communication through the use of gestures, body movements, and facial expressions, rather than through speech.

Personification In personification, animals, things, or ideas are described as having human characteristics. An example from "The Circuit" is

> Finally the mountains around the valley reached out and swallowed the sun.

Persuasion Persuasion is an attempt to affect the feelings, beliefs, and actions of others. Persuasion is used in advertisements, editorials, sermons, and political speeches. In "The Mother Who Lost Her Daughter," Demeter persuades Zeus to help her get back Persephone.

Photo-Essay A photo-essay is a short nonfiction piece that includes photographs and captions. The photographs are as important as the words in giving information to the reader.

Play A play is a story written to be performed by actors on a stage. In most plays, a story is told through the words and actions of actors in the roles of different characters.

> Example: **"The Mother Who Lost Her Daughter"**

Plot Plot is the series of events that makes up a story, play, or narrative poem. Plot is usually divided into four parts: problem or conflict, complication, climax, and resolution.

> *See also* **Climax; Complication; Conflict and Resolution; Problem and Solution; Rising Action and Falling Action**

Poetry Poetry is a kind of writing that expresses ideas in few words. Poets often choose words and phrases that appeal to our senses. Many poems are arranged in sections called stanzas and use rhythm and rhyme.

> Examples: **"Some Rivers,"** from **"A Celebration of the Everglades," "We're All in the Telephone Book"**

> *See also* **Imagery; Rhyme; Rhythm; Stanza**

Point of View Point of view is the particular view from which a story is told. In a story told from the first-person point of view, the narrator is a character in the story who uses words such as *I*, *me*, and *we*. A story told from the third-person point of view is told by a narrator outside the story who uses words such as *he*, *she*, and *they*.

> Example of first-person point of view: **"The Diary of a Young Girl"**

> Example of third-person point of view: **"Anne Frank"**

Problem and Solution Problems and solutions are parts of the plot of a story. Problems are described at the beginning of a story. Solutions are described at the end.

See also **Plot**

Realistic Fiction Realistic fiction is literature about imaginary characters who really could exist and imaginary events that could actually happen.

Example: **"Amir"**

Repetition Repetition is the repeating of words or phrases to create an effect. An example from the poem "Two Baby Snail Kites" is

> Apple snails for dinner.
> Apple snails for lunch.
> And every Sunday morning,
> apple snails for brunch.

See also **Rhythm**

Report A report is a short piece of nonfiction writing on a particular topic. It is different from an essay in that it usually includes only facts and does not express opinions.

Rhyme Rhyme is the repetition of sounds at the ends of words. Rhyme helps create rhythm and adds a musical quality to the poetry.

Examples in **"Old Man Mangrove"** and **"Two Baby Snail Kites,"** from **"A Celebration of the Everglades"**

Rhyme Scheme Rhyme scheme is the pattern of rhyme in a poem.

See also **Rhyme**

Rhythm Rhythm is a musical quality resulting from the repetition of stressed and unstressed syllables in poetry. Rhythm is also created by the repetition of words, phrases, and sentences.

Rising Action and Falling Action Rising action and falling action are parts of the plot. Actions or events that lead to the climax are the rising action. The actions or events that follow the climax are the falling action.

See also **Climax; Complication; Conflict and Resolution; Plot**

Science Fiction Science fiction is a story based on real or imaginary scientific discoveries. It often takes place in the future.

Example: **"Fat Men from Space"**

See also **Historical Fiction; Realistic Fiction**

Self-portrait A self-portrait is a description that a person writes or tells about himself or herself.

Examples in **"Beyond the Color Lines"**

Sensory Language *See* **Imagery**

Setting The setting is the time and the place in which the events of a story occur. The setting of "Amir," for example, is Cleveland, Ohio, in the present day.

Short Story A short story is a short fiction piece that has a single problem and a simple plot.

Simile A simile is a comparison between two unlike things that uses the words *like*, *as*, or *than*. Similes are one kind of figurative language. An example from "The Circuit" is

> The dirt floor...looked like a road map.

Stanza A stanza is a group of lines that form a unit in a poem. A stanza in a poem is similar to a paragraph in prose writing. Stanzas are separated by spaces.

Examples in **"Old Man Mangrove,"** from **"A Celebration of the Everglades"**

Glossary of Literary Terms, continued

Story A story is a piece of fiction writing that has characters, a setting, and a plot.

Style Style is a particular way of writing. It is developed through choice of words, tone, sentence length, and use of imagery and dialogue.

See also **Word Choice**

Suspense Suspense is a feeling of curiosity, tension, or excitement in the reader. Suspense makes the reader want to find out what is going to happen next. In "Fat Men From Space," for example, there is a feeling of suspense when William gets the news bulletins of the invasion by the spacemen.

Theme A theme is the main idea in a work of literature. It is often a message that can be expressed very simply. The theme of "Human Family," for example, is that no matter how much people differ, they are basically alike.

Tone *See* **Mood and Tone**

Word Choice Word choice is the kind of language an author uses. Word choice is one of the elements that contribute to style.

See also **Style**

Glossary of Key Vocabulary

Many words have more than one meaning. The definitions in this glossary are for the words as they are introduced in the selections in this book.

Pronunciation Key

Symbols for Consonant Sounds

b	box		p	pan	
ch	chick		r	ring	
d	dog		s	bus	
f	fish		sh	fish	
g	girl		t	hat	
h	hat		th	Earth	
j	jar		th	father	
k	cake		v	vase	
ks	box		w	window	
kw	queen		wh	whale	
l	bell		y	yarn	
m	mouse		z	zipper	
n	pan		zh	treasure	
ng	ring				

Symbols for Short Vowel Sounds

a	hat	
e	bell	
i	chick	
o	box	
u	bus	

Symbols for Long Vowel Sounds

ā	cake	
ē	key	
ī	bike	
ō	goat	
yū	mule	

Symbols for R-controlled Sounds

ar	barn	
air	chair	
ear	ear	
īr	fire	
or	corn	
ur	girl	

Symbols for Variant Vowel Sounds

ah	father	
aw	ball	
oi	boy	
ow	mouse	
oo	book	
ü	fruit	

Miscellaneous Symbols

shun	fraction	$\frac{1}{2}$
chun	question	?
zhun	division	$2\overline{)100}^{50}$

Parts of an Entry

The **pronunciation** shows you how to say the word.

part of speech
n. for noun
v. for verb
adj. for adjective
adv. for adverb

The **entry** shows how the word is spelled and how it is broken into syllables.

be·gin (bi-gin) *v.* to start or do the first part *When will we **begin** to practice the play?* Past tense: **began** *I **began** to learn my part last week.*

The **definition** gives the meaning of the word.

The **sample sentence** uses the word in a way that shows its meaning.

Sometimes there is additional information about the word.

A

a·buse (u-**byūs**) *n.* mean words or treatment *Many people work to prevent **abuse** of animals.*

ad·just (u-**just**) *v.* to get used to *It takes time to **adjust** to living in a new place.*

ad·vanced (ad-**vanst**) *adj.* up-to-date; the most recent *We are lucky to have the most **advanced** computers at our school.*

ad·ver·si·ty (ad-**vur**-su-tē) *n.* hard times; difficult situation *Facing and overcoming **adversity** made her a stronger person.*

ag·i·tat·ed (**aj**-u-tā-tid) *adj.* nervous; upset; worried *We became **agitated** by the news that a storm was coming.*

a·like (u-**līk**) *adj.* like one another *My sister and I look **alike**.*

an·nex (**an**-eks) *n.* a part added to a building *We are building an **annex** to our garage.*

appalling arrogance strong and shocking pride *He had few friends because of his **appalling arrogance**.*

a·pron (**ā**-prun) *n.* piece of clothing worn over a person's other clothes to protect them *When Mom cooks, she always wears an **apron**.*

at·ten·tion (u-**ten**-shun) *n.* care and thoughtfulness *The teacher asked us to give our full **attention** to the speaker.*

av·a·lanche (**av**-u-lanch) *n.* a sudden falling of snow or rock down a mountain *The hikers ran from the path of the **avalanche**.*

B

ba·bush·ka (bu-**būsh**-ku) *n.* a scarf worn over the head and tied under the chin *Her grandmother often wore a colorful **babushka**.*

bear fruit to produce ripe fruit in time for harvest *We hope our new apple tree will **bear fruit** this fall.*

be·long·ing (bi-**long**-ing) *n.* a comfortable feeling of being in the right place *She had no sense of **belonging** when she visited the country for the first time.*

ben·e·fit (**ben**-u-fit) *n.* a good result or reward for doing something *An enjoyable trip is a **benefit** of careful planning.*

board (bord) *n.* a flat piece of wood *He used a **board** to fix the fence.*

boast·ful (**bōst**-ful) *adj.* speaking with too much pride; bragging *She was **boastful** in talking about how many contests she had won.*

both·er (**both**-ur) *v.* to make an effort *I didn't **bother** to find out if Inez was home before I went to her house.*

bou·quet (bō-**kā**) *n.* a bunch of flowers *The child gave the princess a beautiful **bouquet**.*

brag·gart (**brag**-urt) *n.* a person who brags or praises himself or herself too much *No one wants to be around a **braggart** for very long.*

bouquet

bride (brīd) *n.* a woman about to be married or just married *The **bride** wore a beautiful long white dress.*

C

call-up notice a message from the Nazi police that ordered a person to be at a certain place at a certain time *They were frightened when they received the **call-up notice**.*

camp foreman the person in charge of workers in a camp *The **camp foreman** hires the workers.*

ca·nal (ku-**nal**) *n.* a waterway built by people *The **canal** carries water from the river to the fields of growing crops.*

ca·pa·bil·i·ty (kā-pu-**bil**-u-tē) *n.* the ability to do something well *He has the **capability** to become a good teacher.*

cap·ture (**kap**-chur) *v.* to take or catch by force *They used a trap to **capture** the skunk.*

cat·er·pil·lar (**kat**-ur-pil-ur) *n.* the worm-like stage in the life cycle of a butterfly or moth *A **caterpillar** is sometimes furry and colorful.*

cav·i·ty (**kav**-u-tē) *n.* a hole in a tooth *The dentist filled the* **cavity** *with a special hard material.*

cease (sēs) *v.* to stop *She asked me to* **cease** *the noise so she could talk on the phone.*

cel·e·brate (**sel**-u-brāt) *v.* to have special activities in honor of an event *We will* **celebrate** *my birthday with a visit to the zoo.*

cer·e·mo·ny (**sair**-u-mō-nē) *n.* a formal event *They wore their best clothes for the wedding* **ceremony**.

chal·lenge (**chal**-unj) *v.* to disagree with; take a stand against *He decided to* **challenge** *the rule about who could enter the contest.*

change (chānj) *n.* something different *Sunshine is a nice* **change** *after the rain.*

chron·i·cle (**kron**-u-kul) *n.* a record of events in the order in which they happened; history *He kept a* **chronicle** *of his trip across Africa.*

chrys·a·lis (**kris**-u-lis) *n.* the stage in the life of some insects when they are enclosed in a hard shell *A caterpillar changes into a* **chrysalis**, *and a* **chrysalis** *changes into a butterfly.*

chrysalis

clev·er·ness (**klev**-ur-nis) *n.* intelligence *Her parents and teachers were amazed at the child's* **cleverness**.

col·o·niz·er (**kol**-u-nīz-ur) *n.* a plant or animal that moves to a new place to live *The tiny plant was a* **colonizer** *that did well in its new surroundings.*

com·bat (kom-**bat**) *v.* to fight against *Combat waste—recycle newspapers, cans, and glass!*

com·mon (**kom**-un) *adj.* ordinary *Our dog is not a special kind, he's just a* **common** *dog.*

com·mu·ni·ca·tion (ku-myū-nu-**kā**-shun) *n.* the sending and receiving of messages *Sign language is a means of* **communication** *for deaf people.*

com·mu·ni·ty (ku-**myū**-nu-tē) *n.* a group of people who live in the same neighborhood *We got to know everyone in our little* **community** *very quickly.*

com·pete (kum-**pēt**) *v.* to try to win a contest or game *My sister will* **compete** *in the spelling bee contest.*

con·ceit·ed (kun-**sē**-tid) *adj.* too proud of oneself *After she won the speech contest, she became very* **conceited**.

con·cen·trate (**kon**-sun-trāt) *v.* to focus on or think about only one thing *It's hard to* **concentrate** *on homework when the TV is on.*

concentration camp a place where prisoners of war are held *She lived to tell the story of her years in the* **concentration camp**.

con·di·tion (kun-**dish**-un) *n.* health or physical state *People who play sports must keep in good* **condition**.

con·duc·tor (kun-**duk**-tur) *n.* a leader or guide on a trip *The* **conductor** *led the group through the unfamiliar city.*

con·fi·dent (**kon**-fu-dunt) *adj.* feeling sure of yourself; believing in yourself *George was* **confident** *that he would pass the test.*

con·ti·nu·i·ty (kon-tu-**nü**-u-tē) *n.* going on or continuing in the same way *The* **continuity** *of their lives was interrupted by the war.*

con·ver·sa·tion (kon-vur-**sā**-shun) *n.* a friendly talk between two or more people *We had a long* **conversation** *on the telephone.*

crafts·man·ship (**krafts**-mun-ship) *n.* the skill or ability to do special work *The beautiful chair he made is an example of fine* **craftsmanship**.

crate (krāt) *n.* a box; container *Each* **crate** *was packed with oranges.*

cra·ter (**krā**-tur) *n.* a bowl-shaped hole at the top of a volcano *The scientists looked down into the volcano's* **crater**.

cre·a·tiv·i·ty (krē-ā-**ti**-vu-tē) *n.* the ability to think of new ideas and to express them *Her art showed great* **creativity**.

cru·el (**krü**-ul) *adj.* mean *It was* **cruel** *to tease Carla about her funny old shoes.*

crys·tal (**kris**-tul) *n.* very high quality glass that people value for its beauty *She has a collection of beautiful pieces of old* **crystal**.

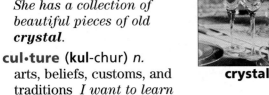
crystal

cul·ture (**kul**-chur) *n.* arts, beliefs, customs, and traditions *I want to learn more about Japanese* **culture**.

cus·tom (**kus**-tum) *n.* a way of acting that is special to a nation or culture *In some countries it is the* **custom** *to bow when you meet someone.*

D

damp (damp) *adj.* slightly wet; moist *The house was cold and* **damp** *in winter.*

dan·gle (**dang**-gul) *v.* to hang down loosely *We watched the spider* **dangle** *from its thread.*

debt (det) *n.* money that is owed to another person *He saved his money to pay his* **debt**.

de·ci·sion (di-**sizh**-un) *n.* a choice *She could not make a* **decision** *about which job to take.*

declare war on to tell a country of plans to fight against it *Many people did not think the U.S. would* **declare war on** *Germany in 1941.*

de·light (di-**līt**) *v.* to make very happy *The trip to the zoo will* **delight** *the children.*

den·tist (**den**-tist) *n.* a doctor who cleans and repairs teeth *Your* **dentist** *will teach you how to take care of your teeth.*

de·ter·mined (di-**tur**-mund) *adj.* having one's mind set on doing something *Robert was* **determined** *to finish his work before dark.*

di·ar·y (**dī**-ur-ē) *n.* a notebook in which private thoughts are written *She wrote in her* **diary** *each night and kept it in a secret place.*

dike (dīk) *n.* a wall of stone or earth that holds back water *The* **dike** *protected the town from flooding.*

discriminate against to harm or treat differently from others because of color, race, age, or religion *When we* **discriminate against** *others, we are being unfair to them.*

dis·solve (di-**zolv**) *v.* to disappear; vanish *Mountains* **dissolve** *in the distance when we drive away from them.*

dome (dōm) *n.* a large round top *The building was covered by a* **dome**.

dream (drēm) *n.* a strong hope; an important goal *Her* **dream** *was to become a great actress.*

dull (dul) *adj.* not shiny *Coins become* **dull** *very quickly when many people handle them.*

E

earth·quake (**urth**-kwāk) *n.* a sudden movement of the earth *The* **earthquake** *damaged houses and bridges throughout a large area.*

ef·fect (u-**fekt**) *n.* result *The* **effect** *of the heavy rains was a dangerous flood.*

el·der (**el**-dur) *n.* an older person or leader *The village* **elder** *told the children stories and taught them old songs and dances.*

en·dan·gered (en-**dān**-jurd) *adj.* in danger of dying out or disappearing forever *For many years, the list of* **endangered** *animals grew very quickly.*

en·gaged (en-**gājd**) *adj.* promised in marriage *The* **engaged** *woman wore a large diamond ring.*

en·roll (en-**rōl**) *v.* to sign up *She will* **enroll** *at the middle school this year.*

en·vi·ron·ment (en-**vī**-run-munt) *n.* the air, land, and water that people, plants, and animals need to live *Each of us can do things to protect the* **environment**.

ep·i·dem·ic (ep-i-**dem**-ik) *n.* a sickness or disease that affects most of the people in a place *Our school was closed during the flu* **epidemic**.

e·rup·tion (i-**rup**-shun) *n.* a sudden, violent release of something *An eruption of ashes and lava poured out of the volcano.*

es·cape (e-**skāp**) *v.* to break loose or get free *They planned to escape by climbing over the high fence.*

ex·cel (ek-**sel**) *v.* to do something extremely well and better than others *The children in his family all excel in music.*

ex·cuse (ek-**skyūs**) *n.* a reason given for doing something *He used the hot day as an excuse for taking a nap.*

ex·haust·ed (eg-**zaw**-stid) *adj.* very tired *Sonia was exhausted after working all day in the garden.*

ex·o·dus (**ek**-su-dus) *n.* the move of a very large number of people from an area *There has been a recent exodus from the farm to the city.*

ex·pe·ri·ence (ek-**spear**-ē-uns) *n.* something that happens to a person *Meeting a bear in the woods is a frightening experience.*

ex·tinct (ek-**stingkt**) *adj.* not living anymore; gone forever *Dinosaurs are extinct.*

ex·tinc·tion (ek-**stingk**-shun) *n.* the end of life for a whole category of plants or animals *The blue whale was once hunted nearly to extinction.*

ex·traor·di·nar·y (ek-**stror**-du-nair-ē) *adj.* very unusual; special *He had an extraordinary ability to speak and write three languages well.*

F

fas·ten (**fas**-un) *v.* to attach; join; connect *When you get into a car, you should fasten your seat belt.*

feast (fēst) *n.* a large meal served for a special event *Mother spent hours preparing the Thanksgiving feast.*

fee (fē) *n.* money paid to do something *There was no fee for using the library.*

fill·ing (**fil**-ing) *n.* metal or other material used to fill a cavity *The new filling made my tooth feel much better.*

flat (flat) *n.* an apartment *Our flat has six rooms.*

flow (flō) *n.* a stream; steady movement *The flow of water ran across the sidewalk for hours.*

force (fors) **1.** *n.* power; energy *The force of the wind blew down trees.* **2.** *v.* to make something move *He tried to force open the door.*

free·dom (**frē**-dum) *n.* the state of not being under the control of another person *The American colonists won freedom from England.*

G

gar·ment (**gar**-munt) *n.* a piece of clothing *His favorite garment was an old jacket.*

ginger root the part of ginger, a spice plant, that grows underground *Ginger root adds an interesting flavor to foods.*

gloom·y (**glü**-mē) *adj.* sad; not cheerful *The rainy day made Kim feel gloomy.*

gold field a place where gold is found *People rushed to the gold field in hopes of becoming rich.*

grain (grān) *n.* the seed of wheat or other cereal grasses *The grain was used to make flour.*

gran·ar·y (**gran**-ur-ē) *n.* a place where grain is stored *After a good harvest, the granary will be full.*

granary

grape season the time of year when grapes are picked *Many workers are needed during grape season.*

H

har·vest (**har**-vist) *v.* to gather crops when they are ripe *Farmers use special machines to harvest their crops.*

harvest

harvest festival a celebration that takes place when harvest is over *Farmers and their families eat, dance, and play games at a harvest festival.*

hearing-impaired unable to hear or hear well *Teachers for hearing-impaired people learn special ways to help their students.*

his·tor·y (**his**-tur-ē) *n.* the story of a country and its people *We are studying the history of the United States.*

hos·til·i·ty (ho-**stil**-u-tē) *n.* hateful actions; mean thoughts *Their hostility toward us was plain to see by looking at their faces.*

hu·mil·i·a·tion (hyū-mil-ē-ā-shun) *n.* a feeling of shame or embarrassment *Her humiliation at being rudely scolded caused her to cry.*

hus·band (**huz**-bund) *n.* a man who is married *They have been husband and wife for ten years.*

I

ig·no·rance (**ig**-nur-uns) *n.* not having education or knowledge about something *He was not able to answer the question because of his ignorance on the subject.*

i·mag·ine (i-**maj**-un) *v.* to see something in your mind *Although I have never seen the place, I can imagine what it looks like.*

im·pres·sion (im-**presh**-un) *n.* idea *The painting gave me an impression of the sea.*

incomparable wisdom knowledge without equal or beyond compare *With her incomparable wisdom, she made the best decision possible.*

in·de·pen·dent (in-di-**pen**-dunt) *adj.* able to do things alone or without help *Learning to be independent is an important part of growing up.*

in·for·ma·tion (in-fur-**mā**-shun) *n.* facts *He collected all the information he could about teeth.*

in·spired (in-**spīrd**) *adj.* filled with ideas; encouraged to create *The inspired musicians wrote several new songs.*

in·ter·est·ed (**in**-tris-tid) *adj.* caring *An interested listener pays attention to the person who is speaking.*

in·ter·fere (in-tur-**fear**) *v.* to get in the way; block *It makes me angry when you interfere with the way I do things.*

in·tim·i·date (in-**tim**-u-dāt) *v.* to frighten *She tried to intimidate him by saying she would hit him if he didn't do what she wanted.*

in·vad·er (in-**vā**-dur) *n.* a person who enters a country by force to attack it or to steal *He watched a movie about an invader from space.*

in·va·sion (in-**vā**-zhun) *n.* the act of entering a country by force *The invasion of Poland by German troops began without warning.*

in·ven·tive (in-**ven**-tiv) *adj.* able to think of new ideas; creative *His inventive mind was full of plans for decorating his room.*

J

jour·ney (**jur**-nē) *n.* a trip *The journey across the ocean took almost a week by boat.*

K

ker·nel (**kur**-nul) *n.* a seed of corn or wheat *A kernel of corn was caught between his teeth.*

king·dom (**king**-dum) *n.* a country controlled by a king or queen *Children's stories often take place in a make-believe kingdom.*

L

labor camp a place where workers live *The employer cleaned up the labor camp before the workers arrived.*

land·ing (**lan**-ding) *n.* a flat area at the top of a number of steps *While climbing the stairs, she stopped to rest at the landing.*

land·lord (**land**-lord) *n.* a person who owns a building and takes money from others who live in it *Our **landlord** keeps our building in good repair.*

launch (lonch) *v.* to send into the air by force *The United States will **launch** a rocket into space this week.*

laun·dro·mat (**lawn**-dru-mat) *n.* a place of business with self-service washing machines and dryers *We take our dirty clothes to the **laundromat** every Saturday.*

la·va (**lah**-vu) *n.* hot melted rock that comes out of a volcano *The **lava** covered everything in its path as it flowed down the mountain.*

law (law) *n.* a rule made by the government that controls what people can and cannot do *Our town has a **law** to stop people from making a lot of noise.*

leg·a·cy (**leg**-u-sē) *n.* a thing or idea handed down from the past *His **legacy** to future generations was his belief in the importance of education.*

lev·ee (**lev**-ē) *n.* a wall of earth built along a river to prevent floods *They sat on the **levee** and watched the boats on the river.*

levee

lo·cal (**lō**-kul) *adj.* close to where you live, work, or go to school *We shop at the **local** markets and stores because they are convenient.*

lot (lot) *n.* a small piece of land *The empty **lot** was used as a playground by the neighborhood children.*

M

mag·ma (**mag**-mu) *n.* hot melted rock below the earth's surface *When **magma** reaches the earth's surface, it becomes lava.*

marsh (marsh) *n.* an area of low, wet land with grasses *A **marsh** may have fresh water or it may have salt water.*

matchless wit a clever and powerful mind that has no equal *Her **matchless wit** made everyone eager to talk with her.*

mat·ter (**mat**-ur) *v.* to be important *Nothing seems to **matter** when you are feeling bad.*

me·men·to (mu-**men**-tō) *n.* a reminder of the past; souvenir *The photograph was a **memento** of her vacation at the beach.*

me·mo·ri·al (mu-**mor**-ē-ul) *n.* something that keeps alive the memory of a person or event *The statue was a **memorial** to the great poet.*

mem·or·y (**mem**-ur-ē) **1.** *n.* the ability to remember *His **memory** is very good.* **2.** *n.* something remembered from the past *My **memory** of my fifth birthday is still very clear.*

mer·chant (**mur**-chunt) *n.* a person who sells things to make money *The **merchant** sold clothing for men, women, and children.*

migrant worker a person who moves from place to place to find work *The **migrant worker** stayed only a few weeks at each job.*

mi·gra·tion (mī-**grā**-shun) *n.* the move from one place to another by a group of people *The opening of new factories caused a **migration** of workers to the city.*

min·er (**mī**-nur) *n.* a worker who digs in the earth for minerals *The **miner** found gold in the mountain and became very rich.*

mon·u·ment (**mon**-yu-munt) *n.* something built to last a long time that honors a person or an event *The statue is a **monument** to the soldiers who fought in the war.*

mo·tive (**mō**-tiv) *n.* a reason for doing something *Her **motive** for phoning was to let her family know that she was all right.*

mur·al (**myur**-ul) *n.* a large picture painted on a wall or other large surface *Many people helped paint the **mural** on the bank building.*

N

net·work (**net**-wurk) *n.* a group of people or things that work together as one *He belongs to a **network** that helps deliver supplies in times of disaster.*

new·com·er (**nü**-kum-ur) *n.* a person who has recently come to an area *The class made the **newcomer** feel welcome.*

night·dress (**nīt**-dres) *n.* a loose garment worn in bed *Her old **nightdress** was soft and comfortable.*

O

ob·vi·ous (**ob**-vē-us) *adj.* clear *The thunder and lightning were **obvious** signs that a storm was coming.*

op·por·tu·ni·ty (op-ur-**tü**-nu-tē) *n.* a chance to do something *She was happy for the **opportunity** to earn some money of her own.*

or·di·nar·y (**ord**-un-air-ē) *adj.* not special; regular *We live in an **ordinary** neighborhood with ordinary neighbors.*

own (ōn) *v.* to have; possess *We do not **own** any pets but our friends let us play with the dog they **own**.*

own·er (**ō**-nur) *n.* the person to whom something belongs *Keith is the proud **owner** of a brand-new skateboard.*

P

pal·ace (**pal**-is) *n.* the home of a king or queen *The **palace** was built of beautiful stone and had more than 100 rooms.*

per·e·grine (**pair**-u-grin) *n.* a falcon; a hunting bird with a dark head, gray and white feathers, and a hooked bill *Peregrine falcons hunt and kill other birds for food.*

peregrine

per·mis·sion (pur-**mish**-un) *n.* approval to do something *We had **permission** from the farmer to walk across his land.*

pe·ti·tion (pu-**tish**-un) *n.* a form asking for change *Many people signed the **petition** for a new city park.*

plan·ta·tion (plan-**tā**-shun) *n.* a large farm with many workers *Crops from the **plantation** could feed many families.*

pol·lu·tion (pu-**lü**-shun) *n.* chemicals, dirt, smoke, and garbage that make the air, water, and soil unclean and unsafe *Pollution can harm or kill many living things.*

population shift a change in the number of people living in a certain area *The **population shift** lowered the number of farm families and increased the number of city families.*

por·tray (por-**trā**) *v.* to make a picture of *The pictures **portray** life as it was long ago.*

pow·er (**pow**-ur) *n.* the ability to make people do what you want *People can use their **power** to help others or hurt others.*

pre·oc·cu·pied (prē-**ok**-yu-pīd) *adj.* thinking about something else; lost in thought *She was so **preoccupied** that she didn't hear the knock on the door.*

pre·serve (pri-**zurv**) *v.* to keep safe; protect; keep the same from year to year *It will take a lot of work and money to **preserve** the old house.*

pres·sure (**presh**-ur) *n.* the energy used to press one thing against another *The **pressure** of the water caused the dam to break.*

pris·on·er (**priz**-u-nur) *n.* a person who is held in a place and not allowed to leave *The **prisoner** was kept in jail for three days.*

priv·i·lege (**priv**-u-lij) *n.* something special you get to do *It was a **privilege** for me to take dancing lessons.*

pro·vide (pru-**vīd**) *v.* to give or supply *My parents **provide** the money for my music lessons.*

Q

quilt (kwilt) *n.* a cover for a bed made of small pieces of cloth sewn together *Each piece of cloth in the **quilt** brought back a different memory.*

quilt

R

racial prejudice a dislike of people because of their race *Racial prejudice divides communities.*

re·al (rē-ul) *adj.* true; not imagined *Real stories are often more exciting than ones that are made up.*

re·ceive (ri-sēv) *v.* to get *I expect to **receive** a letter from my sister today.*

rec·og·nize (rek-ug-nīz) *v.* to know someone when you see him or her again *I will easily **recognize** her when I see her again.*

remarkably proud unusually pleased or satisfied *He was **remarkably proud** of himself for winning first place in the contest.*

rent (rent) *n.* money paid to live in an apartment or house that another person owns *We pay the **rent** for our house on the first day of every month.*

re·pair (ri-pair) *v.* to fix *She tried to **repair** the broken bowl so she could use it again.*

re·place (ri-plās) *v.* to put one thing in place of another *Mother couldn't find a new plate to **replace** the broken one.*

rep·re·sent (rep-ri-zent) *v.* to be an example or model of something *Some people think that cowboys **represent** the real West.*

re·shape (rē-shāp) *v.* to change into a new form *Can you **reshape** this ring so that it will fit my finger?*

re·spect (ri-spekt) *v.* to feel or show a high opinion of *We have great **respect** for our grandparents.*

re·ward (ri-word) *n.* money or a prize given for something a person does *He received a **reward** for finding and returning the bracelet.*

right (rīt) *n.* something that is allowed by law *Every adult citizen has the **right** to vote.*

rou·tine (rü-tēn) *n.* something that is done the same way all of the time *Part of my daily **routine** is to eat a good breakfast.*

runaway slave a person who tries to get away from someone who owns him or her *The **runaway slave** found freedom in the North.*

run·off (run-awf) *n.* rainfall that does not go into the ground, but runs from higher to lower ground *The **runoff** collected in the pools.*

S

se·cure (si-kyur) *adj.* safe; without worry or fear *She feels **secure** in the house when the doors are locked.*

seg·re·ga·tion (seg-ru-gā-shun) *n.* the separation of one group of people from another *Most people today believe that **segregation** is wrong.*

ser·i·ous (sear-ē-us) *adj.* thoughtful *He is a **serious** person and doesn't laugh very much.*

shack (shak) *n.* a small, poorly built house; hut *They hoped to move out of the **shack** into a better house.*

shed (shed) *v.* to lose by natural process *Some snakes **shed** their skins six times a year.* Past tense: **shed** *All the trees **shed** their leaves last month.*

shiv·er (shiv-ur) *v.* to shake with cold, fear, or excitement *The thought of walking home alone in the dark made him **shiver**.*

shock (shok) *n.* a great and sudden surprise *It was a **shock** to hear about his accident.*

short·age (shor-tij) *n.* too small a number or amount *There was a **shortage** of food and water after the flood.*

shrivel up to become dry and smaller in size *The crops began to **shrivel up** because there had been no rain for weeks.*

slav·er·y (**slā**-vur-ē) *n.* the custom or practice of owning slaves *In the United States, **slavery** ended more than one hundred years ago.*

space·man (**spās**-man) *n.* a man who comes from another planet *The **spaceman** arrived on Earth from Mars.* Plural: **spacemen** *The **spacemen** wore silver helmets.*

space·men (**spās**-men) the plural of **spaceman**

splin·ter (**splin**-tur) *n.* a small, thin, sharp piece of wood *A **splinter** in your finger can be quite painful.*

sprout (sprowt) *v.* to begin to grow *Certain seeds **sprout** very quickly.*

stair (stair) *n.* a set of steps that goes from one level or floor to the next *The **stair** went from the basement to the roof.*

sta·tion (**stā**-shun) *n.* a place that sends out radio signals *The **station** gives weather and traffic reports every hour.*

stay tuned stay on the same radio station *The announcer said, "**Stay tuned** for more news after these messages."*

steer (stear) *v.* to direct; guide *Can you **steer** me toward the library?*

sto·ry·tell·er (**stor**-ē-tel-ur) *n.* a person who tells stories *My little sister thinks grandma is the best **storyteller** at the library.*

stunned (stund) *adj.* greatly surprised *She was **stunned** to find the house on fire.*

sur·vive (sur-**vīv**) *v.* to live through a dangerous time or event *They were lucky to **survive** the terrible flood.*

sur·vi·vor (sur-**vī**-vur) *n.* an animal or plant that lives through a dangerous event *The pilot was the only **survivor** of the plane crash.*

swollen head a feeling of being better than others *He went around with a **swollen head** because he was the only student who got an A on the test.*

T

ta·ble·cloth (**tā**-bul-klawth) *n.* a cloth for covering a table, used especially at meals *Grandma always uses a special **tablecloth** for holiday meals.*

tack (tak) *n.* a small, sharp nail *He used a **tack** to hold the photo on the bulletin board.*

tai·lor (**tā**-lur) *n.* a person who makes and mends clothes to earn money *The **tailor** could easily fix the tear in her dress.*

temperate zone the area between the Tropic of Cancer and the Arctic Circle or between the Tropic of Capricorn and the Antarctic Circle *There are four distinct seasons in the countries of each **temperate zone**.*

tem·po·rar·y (**tem**-pu-rair-ē) *adj.* not permanent; for a limited time *My **temporary** summer job will end when school begins.*

threat (thret) *n.* words that tell of future harm *They made a **threat** to punish me if I didn't do my work.*

thrive (thrīv) *v.* to grow; do well *Plants **thrive** when they have water and light.*

tow·er (**tow**-ur) *n.* a tall and narrow structure or building *They could see for miles from the top of the **tower**.*

tower

trade (trād) *v.* to give one thing and take another in its place *Will you **trade** your apple for my orange?*

tra·di·tion (tru-**dish**-un) *n.* a way of acting that is passed from one generation to the next *Spending all our holidays together is a **tradition** in my family.*

trib·ute (**trib**-yūt) *n.* something given to show thanks or respect *The many flowers she received were a **tribute** to her wonderful performance.*

tri·umph (**trī**-umf) *n.* success; victory *We held a parade in honor of our team's **triumph**.*

trop·ics (**trop**-iks) *n.* the part of the earth's surface lying between the Tropic of Cancer and the Tropic of Capricorn *It is quite warm all year long in the **tropics**.*

U

un·a·like (un-u-līk) *adj.* different *He and his brother are **unalike** in most ways.*

un·der·world (**un**-dur-wurld) *n.* to ancient Greeks, the underground home for the dead *The hero of the mythical story traveled to the **underworld** to find his dead father.*

unusually clever more intelligent and creative than most people *He is **unusually clever** in the way he writes and says things.*

V

van·ish (**van**-ish) *v.* to disappear; fade *Clouds **vanish** quickly after a storm.*

va·ri·e·ty (vu-rī-u-tē) *n.* a number of different kinds *The **variety** in meals makes eating more interesting.*

vil·lage (**vil**-ij) *n.* a community that is smaller than a town *Anna knows everyone in her **village**.*

vil·lag·er (**vil**-i-jur) *n.* a person who lives in a village *The **villager** had a small garden and kept chickens.*

vine·yard (**vin**-yurd) *n.* a field where grapes are grown *Almost a hundred workers harvested grapes in the large **vineyard**.*

W

wash·room (**wosh**-rüm) *n.* a bathroom or a small room with a sink *We always like to know where the **washroom** is when we visit new places.*

wedding huppa a cloth supported on poles that a couple stands under when being married *The bride and groom said their vows under the **wedding huppa**.*

wetland wilderness low, wet land where people do not live *The **wetland wilderness** is now a national park.*

wetland wilderness

with·er (**with**-ur) *v.* to become dry *Plants **wither** when they don't get enough water.*

Y

year-round job a permanent job *He found a **year-round job** in his favorite city.*

Index of Skills

Reading and Learning Strategies, Critical Thinking, and Comprehension

Language and Vocabulary

Index of Skills, continued

Literary Concepts

Writing

Index of Skills, continued

Grammar, Mechanics, Usage, and Spelling

Listening, Speaking, Viewing, and Representing

Technology and Media

Research Skills

Index of Titles and Authors

Acknowledgments continued

Reprinted by permission of Susan Bergholz Literary Services, New York. All rights reserved.

The Bodley Head: (non-U.S. rights) "The Clever Wife" from *Sweet and Sour: Tales From China* by Carol Kendall and Yao-wen Li. Published by The Bodley Head.

Carolrhoda Books, Inc.: Excerpt from *Saving the Peregrine Falcon* by Caroline Arnold. Photos by Richard R. Hewett. Copyright © 1985 by Caroline Arnold. Published by Carolrhoda Books, Inc., Minneapolis, MN. Used by permission of the publisher. All rights reserved.

Chappell & Co., Inc.: "The House I Live In." Words and music by Lewis Allan and Earl Robinson. Copyright © 1942 (renewed) Chappell & Co., Inc. (ASCAP). All rights reserved. Used by permission.

Jewell Reinhart Coburn: "Legendary Origin of Vietnam" and "Rooster and the Jewel" from *Beyond the East Wind*, an award winning collection of Vietnamese folktales by Jewell Reinhart Coburn, Ph.D.

Dell Publishing, a division of Random House, Inc.: "Neshmayda and Suzette Aguayo" from *The Book of Twins* by Debra and Lisa Ganz, with Alex Tresniowsky. Photographs by Bill Ballenberg. Copyright © 1998 by Byron Preiss Visual Publications, Inc. and Dreammaker, Inc. Photographs copyright © 1998 by Bill Ballenberg. Used by permission of Dell Publishing, a division of Random House, Inc.

Doubleday, a division of Random House, Inc.: "Diary entry for July 8, 1942" from *The Diary Of A Young Girl—The Definitive Edition* by Anne Frank. Otto H. Frank & Mirjam Pressler, editors. Translated by Susan Massotty, translation copyright © 1995 by Doubleday, a division of Bantam Doubleday Dell Publishing Group, Inc. Used by permission of Doubleday, a division of Random House, Inc.

Florida Trend: "An Ominous Cloud Over The Everglades" by Marjory Stoneman Douglas. Copyright © 1988 *Florida Trend Magazine.*

Victoria Forrester: "In Music Meeting" from *Song and Dance* by Victoria Forrester.

Groundwood Books/Douglas & McIntyre: "Ginger for the Heart" from *Tales from Gold Mountain.* Text copyright © 1989 by Paul Yee. Illustrations copyright © 1989 by Simon Ng. First published in Canada by Groundwood Books/Douglas & McIntyre. Reprinted by permission of the publisher.

Harcourt, Inc.: Selected excerpts from *Teammates* by Peter Golenbock. Text copyright © 1990 by Golenbock Communications, Inc. Illustrations copyright © 1990 by Paul Bacon. Selections from *Sawgrass Poems: A View Of The Everglades* by Frank Asch. Text copyright © 1996 by Frank Asch, Introduction and Notes copyright © 1996 by Ted Levin, photographs copyright © 1996. Reprinted by permission of Harcourt, Inc.

HarperCollins Publishers: *Amir* by Paul Fleischman. Text copyright © 1997 by Paul Fleischman. "Starting a Community Garden" from *City Green* by DyAnne DiSalvo-Ryan. *The Great Migration* by Jacob Lawrence. Copyright © 1993 by The Museum of Modern Art, New York, and The Phillips Collection. "Chrysalis Diary" from *Joyful Noise: Poems for Two Voices* by Paul Fleischman. Text copyright © 1988 by Paul Fleischman. "The Mother Who Lost Her Daughter" from *The Robber Baby: Stories from the Greek Myths* by Anne Rockwell. Copyright © 1994 by Anne Rockwell. All used by permission of HarperCollins Publishers.

HarperCollins Publishers, Inc. William Morrow: "Open Letter to a Young Negro" by Jesse Owens, from *Blackthink* by Jesse Owens and Paul G. Neimark. Copyright © 1970 by Jesse Owens and Paul G. Neimark. Reprinted by permission of HarperCollins Publishers, Inc. William Morrow.

Holiday House, Inc.: "Janell" and "Jenny" from *Under Our Skin: Kids Talk About Race* by Debbie Holsclaw Birdseye. Text copyright © 1997 by Debbie Holsclaw Birdseye and Tom Birdseye. Photographs copyright © 1997 by Robert Crum. All rights reserved. Used by permission of Holiday House, Inc.

Henry Holt and Company, LLC: *Anne Frank* by Yona Zeldis McDonough. Text copyright © 1991, 1997 by Yona Zeldis McDonough. Reprinted by permission of Henry Holt and Company, LLC.

Houghton Mifflin Co.: (U.S. rights) "The Clever Wife" from *Sweet and Sour: Tales From China* by Carol Kendall and Yao-wen Li. Copyright © 1978 by Carol Kendall and Yao-wen Li. Reprinted by permission of Clarion Books/Houghton Mifflin Co. All rights reserved.

Alfred A. Knopf, a division of Random House, Inc.: "We're All in the Telephone Book" and "Mother to Son" from *Collected Poems* by Langston Hughes. Copyright © 1994 by the Estate of Langston Hughes. Excerpt from *Follow the Drinking Gourd* by Jeanette Winter. Copyright © 1988 by Jeanette Winter. All reprinted by permission of Alfred A. Knopf, a division of Random House, Inc.

David Krieger: From "Captain Cousteau's Legacy: Rising to Our Full Stature as Human Beings" by David Krieger, at Nuclear Age Peace Foundation website: www.wagepeace.org.

John Malone: "Bath" from *Poetry Playground* Course Materials by John Malone. Copyright © 1999 by John Malone. All rights reserved. Used by permission.

NASA/JPL/Caltech: "Mars Network." Courtesy of NASA/JPL/Caltech.

New Moon Publishing: "The Storyteller" by Dawn Lippert. Reprinted, with permission, from *New Moon ®: The Magazine For Girls And Their Dreams*, copyright New Moon Publishing, Duluth, MN.

Daniel Pinkwater: *Fat Men From Space* by Daniel Pinkwater.

Random House: "Human Family" from *I Shall Not Be Moved* by Maya Angelou. Copyright © 1990 by Maya Angelou. Reprinted by permission of Random House, Inc.

Scholastic: "Questions and Answers About Poetry" adapted from *A Fire in My Hands, a Book of Poems* by Gary Soto. Copyright © 1990 by Scholastic Inc. Reprinted by permission.

Simon & Schuster: "Christian Tico" from *Quilted Landscape: Conversations With Young Immigrants* by Yale Strom. Copyright © 1996 Yale Strom. *The Keeping Quilt* by Patricia Polacco. Copyright © 1988 Patricia Polacco. *Volcano: The Eruption and Healing of Mount St. Helens* by Patricia Lauber. Copyright © 1986 Patricia Lauber. Selected excerpts from *Hatchet* by Gary Paulsen. Copyright © 1987 Gary Paulsen. All reprinted with the permission of Simon & Schuster Books for Young Readers, an imprint of Simon & Schuster Children's Publishing Division.

Gary Soto: "Big Eaters," "Letter to a Father Working in Tulare, California," and "What They Don't Tell You About Cereal." Text copyright © 1999 by Gary Soto. Used with permission of the Author and BookStop Literary Agency.

Tilbury House Publishers: Untitled segment from "Diego Rivera" and "Vietnam Veterans Memorial" from *Talking Walls* by Margy Burns Knight. Copyright © 1992, Tilbury House, Publishers. Untitled segment from "Pablo Neruda" from *Talking Walls: The Stories Continue* by Margy Burns Knight © 1996, Tilbury House, Publishers.

University of New Mexico Press: Selected excerpts from *The Circuit* by Francisco Jiménez. Copyright © 1997 by Francisco Jiménez. Reprinted with permission from University of New Mexico Press.

World Almanac Group: "Looking for Life Elsewhere in the Universe" from *World Almanac for Kids.* Reprinted with permission from *The World Almanac for Kids 1998.* Copyright © 1997 World Almanac Education Group. All rights reserved.

Photographs:

AFF/AFS/Amsterdam: pp273, 274, 277 (Auguste van Pels, Peter van Pels, Hermann van Pels, Otto Frank, James Kleiman, © AFF/AFS/Amsterdam), pp273, 274, 277 (script from diary, Anne with neighbor, Miep Gies, © AFF/AFS/Amsterdam).

Angie Aguayo: pp161-163 (twins photos, © Angie Aguayo).

AP/Wide World Photos: pp104, 113 (detail), p105 (baseball players, © AP/Wide World Photos), p106 (Ted Williams, © AP/Wide World Photos), p107 (Robinson, © AP/Wide World Photos), p112 (Major League, © AP/Wide World Photos), p326 (Jesse Owens, © AP/Wide World Photos), p273 (Anne with Hannah Goslar, © AP/ Wide World Photos).

Archive Photos: p105 (stadium, © Henry Hammond/Archive Photos), p109 (Pee Wee Reese, © Archive Photos), p111 (Jackie Robinson, © New York Times Co./Archive Photos), p111 (Crosley Field, © APA/Archive Photos), p111 (Pee Wee Reese, © Sporting News/Archive Photos), p259 (German soldier with warning sign, © Popperfoto/Archive Photos), pp 258, 259, 260, 265, 266, 270, 275, 276 (Anne Frank family photos, © Anne Frank Fonds, Basel/Anne Frank House Amsterdam/Archive Photos), pp256, 257 (arrested Jews, Jews enroute to camps, © Archive Photos), p345, © Janet Sommer/Archive Photos).

Art Resource, NY: pp292, 293 (*Endangered Species*, Andy Warhol silk-screen, frog inset, © 2000 Andy Warhol Foundation for the Visual Arts, ARS, New York/Art Resource, NY).

Banco de México Diego Rivera & Frida Kahlo Museums Trust: p26 (The Mechanization of the Country, © 2000 Banco de México Diego Rivera & Frida Kahlo Museums Trust and Schalkwijk/Art Resource, NY).

Cascada Expediciones: p31 (fence, © Luis Hernan Herreros Infante/Cascada Expediciones).

CMCD: p36 (books, gramophone, telephone, television, telephone cords, power cords, clock and computer: CMCD, type block: Glenn Mitsui, Chinese text and English text: Steve Cole), p37 (power cords and type block: CMCD).

CORBIS: (All © CORBIS) p27 (Rivera), p28 (Lin), p29 (Vietnam Memorial), p30 (Neruda), p106 (Paige), p110 (Reese/Robinson), p137 (family), p290 (mountain background), p291 (Mt. Everest), pp250-251 (flag), pp250, 251 (soldiers at Normandy), p213 (crescent moon), pp254, 258, 271, 278 (inset), p256 (German aircraft, German at Pearl Harbor), p257 (soldiers on coast of Normandy), p261 (movable bookcase), p277 (Miep Gies), p282 (earthquake), p287 (Toussaint), p311 (Kissimmee River), p327 (race), p342 (harvesters), pp344-345 (stairs), p386 (giving a speech), p429 (gold miner), p448 (storm damage), p478 (astronaut), p480 (disabled athlete), p485 (satellite).

Cordon Art B.V.-Baarn-Holland: p214 "Sky and Water I" by M.C. Escher © 2000. All rights reserved.

Corel: (All © Corel) p216 (column), p313 (crane), p313 (Everglades at sunset), p432 (manatee), p441 (alligator), p441 (egret), p443 (Sahara Desert), p444 (ballet dancer), p446 (fireworks).

Digital Stock: p36 (Earth), p482 (launch).

Digital Vision Ltd.: (All © Digital Vision) p24, 32 (detail), p25 (Talking Walls), p394 (galaxy).

Janjaap Dekker: pp14, 15, 17, 19, 22 (detail, © Janjaap Dekker).

M.C. Escher: pp214-215 (*Sky and Water 1*, M.C. Escher, woodcut, 1938).

FPG International, LLC: pp168-169 (graduates: VCG).

Feldman & Associates, Inc.: pp142-143 (Family Group by Henry Moore).

Francine Seders Gallery: p174 (Jacob with family, © Courtesy of Jacob Lawrence and Francine Seders Gallery).

Henry Holt: p72 ("Libery" by Robert Silvers, reprinted with permission of the publisher, © Robert Silvers), pp261, 271, 278 (hiding place, close-up of apartment, full view of apartment).

Holiday House, Inc.: p91 (girls), pp92-95 ("Beyond the Color Lines," © 1997 by Robert Crum. All rights reserved. Used from *Under Our Skin: Kids Talk About Race* by permission of Holiday House, Inc.).

Houghton Mifflin Co.: p140 (inset, illustration from *The Mysteries of Harris Burdick* © 1984 by Chris Van Allsburg. Reprinted by permission of Houghton Mifflin Co. All rights reserved.).

The Image Works, Inc.: pp261, 271, 278 (hiding place, close-up of apartment, full view of apartment).

Jim Jennings: p305 (peregrine falcon, © Jim Jennings).

Kirkendahl Spring Photography: p246 (bicyclists at Mount St. Helens Volcanic Monument, © Kirkendahl Spring/Kirkendahl Spring Photography).

Liaison Agency Inc.: p7, p290, p363 (ice climbers: Gamma Liaison, Wald Beth), p255 (Hitler, © Hulton Getty/Liaison Agency), p257 (release of surviving Jews, © Hulton Getty/Liaison Agency).

Ted Levin: pp315, 316, 318, 319, 320, 321, 322 (alligator with turtle, corn crop, mangrove forest, young snail kites, manatees, Everglades at sunset, Frank Asch, detail, © Ted Levin).

Paul McDonough: p265 (Anne Frank at public hall, © Paul McDonough).

Miami Herald Publishing Co.: p313 (Marjory Stoneham Douglas, © Courtesy of Miami Herald Publishing Co.).

Lee Missbach: pp190-201 (Esperanza, © Leah Missbach).

Henry Moore Foundation: pp142-143 (detail) Reproduced by permission.

Museum of Jewish Heritage, New York: p255 (Star of David, © Gift of Sidi Herzberg, Museum of Jewish Heritage, New York).

The Museum of Modern Art, New York, and the Phillips Collection: p12 (The Studio. Paris [winter 1927-28; dated 1928]. Oil on canvas, 59" x 7' 7" [149.9 x 231.2 cm] © The Museum of Modern Art, New York. Gift of Walter P. Chrysler, Jr. Photograph © 2000 The Museum of Modern Art, New York. ARS, New York), pp172, 181 (detail), p173 (cover), p176 (busy train), p177 (damaged crops, walking), p178 (transportation, segregation), p179 (steel mills, landscape), p180 (schools) (All photos copyright © 1993 by The Museum of Modern Art, New York, and the Phillips Collection. Used by permission of HarperCollins Publishers.).

NASA: p212 (moon: NASA).

National Baseball Hall of Fame Library & Archive: p108 (Brooklyn Dodgers, © National Baseball Hall of Fame Library & Archive, Cooperstown, N.Y.).

National Museum of American Art: p170 (Pioneers of the West, © National Museum of American Art, Washington DC/Art Resource, NY).

Nova Development Corporation: (All © Nova Development Corporation) p268 (posters), p309 (whale).

Odyssey: p27 (Wall Painting, © Robert Frerck/Odyssey/Chicago).

PhotoDisc: p141 (pocketwatch), p168 (clouds), pp271, 274, 277 (frame), p294 (environmentalist), pp296, 297, 306 (falcon detail, Peregrine Falcon, © PhotoDisc), p376 (calculator, © PhotoDisc), p376 (cassette), p376 (fax), p376 (microphone), p377 (cell phone), p377 (video tape), p377 (camcorder), p378 (printer), p378 (computer), p378 (microphone), p379 (TV), p379 (keyboard), p383 (teacher & student), p390 (ram, tiger, koala), p390 (TV), p402 (student report), p405 (panda), p410 (writing), p427 (waterfall in Yosemite), p487 (wilderness).

PhotoEdit: pp6, 212, 289 (moon), p66 (student discussion, © Michael Newman), p68 (Luca Benini, © Michael Newman), p97 (soccer, © David Young Wolff), p100 (nuts background, © PhotoLink), p128 (kids planting tree, © Rhoda Sidney) p129 (people with wheelbarrow: Skjold, kids digging holes, © Deborah Davis), p210 (Cousin Hector, © PhotoDisc), p286 (peer conference, © Michael Newman), p360 (students in classroom, © Michael Newman), p423 (boy holding basketball, © Michael Newman).

Photo Link: p331 (soil background: Kent Knudson/PhotoLink).

PictureQuest: p137 (cricket, © David Simson/Stock, Boston/Picture Quest), p362 (students, © Nubar Alexanian/Stock, Boston Inc./PictureQuest), p431 (skater, Caroline Wood/Allstock/Picture Quest), p436 (town parade, Tim Ribar/Stock South/PictureQuest), p479 (coach, © Picture Quest), p484 (prisoner, © Sovfoto/Eastfoto/Picture Quest).

Rain City Productions: p240 (volcano, © Gary Rosenquist/Rain City Productions), p282 (volcano opens, side of mountain, rock shatters, © GaryRosenquist/Rain City Productions).

Richard R. Hewitt Photography: pp299, 300, 301, 302, 303 (rock climber, gluing peregrine egg, first crack in egg, full ring of egg broken, shell pops open, new chick, chick with puppet, © Richard R. Hewitt/Richard R. Hewitt Photography).

Scholastic Press, a division of Scholastic Inc.: p8 "Joy" from *Voices of the Heart* by Ed Young. Copyright © 1997 by Ed Young. Reprinted by permission.

Siede Preis: p73 (flag, Siede Preis).

Simon & Schuster Children's Publishing Division: p10 (Israeli Stamp reprinted with the permission of Simon & Schuster Books for Young Readers, an imprint of Simon & Schuster Children's Publishing Division from *The Space Between Our Footsteps* by Naomi Shihab Nye. Copyright © 1998 by Naomi Shihab Nye.), pp76, 84 (detail), p77-83, p132 ("The Keeping Quilt," Reprinted with permission.), p90, 98 (detail), p91 (boy), p96 (boy on subway, Reprinted with permission of Simon & Schuster Children's Publishing Division from *Quilted Landscape* by Yale Strom, © 1996 Yale Strom.).

Sony: (All courtesy of Sony Electronics) p376 (boombox), p376 (Discman), p376 (headphones/Walkman), p377 (DVD player).

The Stock Market: pp100-101 (the Golden Gate Bridge, © 98 Richard Berenholtz).

Stone: p38 (Native American drawings, © David Hiser), p87 (detail), pp88-89 (© Jon Bradley), p216 (tourists, © Rich Frishman), pp236, 238, 241, 243, 245 (detail, volcano blast, © Ralph Perry), p294 (sea turtle, seal inset, © Schrichte), p310 (Everglades detail, © David Job), p311 (tricolor heron, © Art Wolfe), pp311, 314 (Everglade aerial view, © David Job), pp344-345 (mother/son, © Kevin Horan), pp354-355 (kid with basketball, © Jon Riley), p428 (tourists on mules, © Tom Bean).

Tom Stack & Associates: p312 (Florida panther, © Victoria Hurst/Tom Stack & Associates).

U.S. Geological Survey: p242 (volcano, © Tom Casadevall/U.S. Geological Survey), pp241, 243 (mudflow, © Lyn Topinka/U.S. Geological Survey), pp244, 245 (Mount St. Helens before eruption/after eruptions, © Harry Glicken/U.S. Geological Survey).

USDA Forest Service: p243 (boulders, © Jim Hughes/USDA Forest Service).

USHMM Photo Archives: p264, (Entrance gate to Auschwitz concentration camp, © Instytut Pamieci, Narodoweij/Institute of National Memory).

Author Photos:

p21 (Gary Soto, © Janjaap Dekker); p31 (Margy Burns Knight); p46 (Dawn and Margaret Lippert); p58 (Daniel Manus Pinkwater, © 1999 Kathy McLaughlin); p83 (Patricia Polacco); p89B (Maya Angelou, Courtesy of Lordly & Dame, Inc.); p112 (Peter Golenbock); pp123, 234 (Paul Fleischman, © Becky Mojica); p154 (Paul Yee); p164 (Debbie and Lisa Ganz, © 1998 by Bill Ballenberg); p180 (Jacob Lawrence, © Spike Mafford); p200 (Sandra Cisneros, copyright © Diana Solis); p227 (Anne Rockwell, © Lizzy Rockwell); p246 (Patricia Lauber); p265 (Yona Zeldis McDonough); p304 (Caroline Arnold); p321 (Ted Levin, © Ted Levin); p321 (Frank Asch, © Ted Levin); p339 (Francisco Jiménez, © University of New Mexico Press); p353 (Carol Kendall, © Ruth Berman).

Illustrations:

Michelle Angers: pp15-19 (The Power of Poetry, © Michelle Angers); **Jean Cassels:** p298 (The Peregrine Falcon, © Jean Cassels/Portfolio Solutions LLC); **Centre Georges Pompidou:** pp70-71 (detail), p139 (Sense of Place, © L & M SERVICES B.V. Amsterdam 200315/Photo Phillippe Migeat/Centre Georges Pompidou); **Chi Chung:** p149 (Gold Rush Map); **David Diaz:** pp330-338, 340 (detail); **Leonid Gore:** p328 (painting; story of Brian, © Leonid Gore/HK Portfolio); **Merilee Heyer:** pp146, 155 (detail), pp147-154 (Ginger for the Heart), p204 (Character Map drawings); **Mary King/Sheryl Beranbaum:** p102 (In Music Meeting, © Mary King/Sheryl Beranbaum Rep.); **Kathleen Kinkopf:** pp116, 124 (detail), p117-123 (Amir) pp127, 130 (detail), pp128-129 (Community Garden); **The Mapping Specialist Limited:** pp27, 29, 31, 311 (Map, map inset, © The Mapping Specialists Limited), p237 (globe/map, © The Mapping Specialist Ltd.); **Sandra McMahon Medical Art:** pp237, 242 (diagram/mudflow, © Sandra McMahon/Sandra McMahon Medical Art), pp312, 313 (Everglades/water for life, © Sandra McMahon/Sandra McMahon Medical Art); **Mike Reed:** p144 (rooster art, © Mike Reed/HK Portfolio); **Bill Scott:** pp231, 235 (details), pp232-234 (Chrysalis Diary, © Bill Scott/Nachreiner Boie Art Factory Ltd.); **Francine Seders Gallery:** p175 (self portrait, © Courtesy Jacob Lawrence and Francine Seders Gallery); **Kat Thacker:** pp40-47 (Tales Across Time, © Kat Thacker/Iremli Holmberg Rep.), p219 (The Origin of Myths), pp218, 228 (details), pp220-227 (The Mother Who Lost Her Daughter); **Jean and Mou-sien Tseng:** pp346, 354 (details), pp347-353 (The Clever Wife, © Jean and Mou-sien Tseng); **Martin Walz:** p188 (Underground RR Map, © Martin Walz).

The High Point Development Team

Hampton-Brown extends special thanks to the following individuals and companies who contributed so much to the creation of this series.

Editorial: Susan Blackaby, Janine Boylan, Bonnie Brook, Shirleyann Costigan, Mary Cutler, Phyllis Edwards, Ramiro Ferrey, Cris Phillips-Georg, Fredrick Ignacio, Barbara Linde, Dawn Liseth, Daphne Liu, Sherry Long, Jacalyn Mahler, Marlyn Mangus, S. Michele McFadden, Debbi Neel, Wilma Ramírez, Michael Ryall, Sarita Chávez Silverman, Sharon Ursino, Andreya Valabek, Alison Wells, Virginia Yeater, Lynn Yokoe, Brown Publishing Network, Ink, Inc., and Learning Design Associates, Inc.

Design and Production: Lisa Baehr, Marcia Bateman Walker, Andrea Carter, Darius Detweiler, Jeri Gibson, Lauren Grace, Debbie Saxton, Curtis Spitler, Alicia Sternberg, Jennifer Summers, Debbie Wright Swisher, Margaret Tisdale, Andrea Erin Thompson, Donna Turner, Alex von Dallwitz, JR Walker, Teri Wilson, Adpartner, Bill Smith Studios, Chaos Factory & Associates, Ray Godfrey, Hooten Design, Proof Positive/Farrowlyne Associates, and Art Stopper.

Permissions: Barbara Mathewson